taste of home
COOKING
THROUGH THE
Seasons

taste of home

Editor in Chief: **Catherine Cassidy**
Vice President, Executive Editor/Books: **Heidi Reuter Lloyd**
Creative Director: **Ardyth Cope**
Food Director: **Diane Werner RD**
Senior Editor/Books: **Mark Hagen**
Editor: **Krista Lanphier**
Art Director: **Gretchen Trautman**
Content Production Supervisor: **Julie Wagner**
Layout Designers: **Kathy Crawford, Kathleen Bump, Catherine Fletcher, Heather Meinen**
Proofreader: **Beth Kong**
Recipe Asset Management System: **Coleen Martin, Sue A. Jurack**
Premedia Supervisor: **Scott Berger**
Recipe Testing & Editing: **Taste of Home Test Kitchen**
Food Photography: **Taste of Home Photo Studio**
Administrative Assistant: **Barb Czysz**

Chief Marketing Officer: **Lisa Karpinski**
Creative Director/Creative Marketing: **Jim Palmen**
Vice President/Book Marketing: **Dan Fink**

THE READER'S DIGEST ASSOCIATION, INC.
President and Chief Executive Officer: **Mary G. Berner**
President, U.S. Affinities: **Suzanne M. Grimes**
Senior Vice President, Chief Marketing Officer: **Amy J. Radin**
President, Global Consumer Marketing: **Dawn M. Zier**

©2009 Reiman Media Group, Inc.
5400 S. 60th Street
Greendale, WI 53129

International Standard Book Number (10):
0-89821-548-X
International Standard Book Number (13):
978-0-89821-548-9
Library of Congress Control Number:
2009936923

"Timeless Recipes from Trusted Home Cooks"
is a registered trademark of
Reiman Media Group, Inc.

PICTURED ON FRONT COVER:
Ozark Mountain Berry Pie
(p. 148), Roasted Chicken
with Rosemary (p. 53),
Gourmet Garden Tomato
Salad (p. 113), Hearty Hunter
Stew (p. 181) and Cranberry-
Topped Cake (p. 311).

PICTURED ON BACK COVER:
Smooth Strawberry Soup
(p. 27), Country-Style Vanilla
Ice Cream (p. 145) and Buttercup Yeast Bread (p. 193).

COVER PHOTOGRAPHY:
Rob Hagen, Dan Roberts (Photographers)
Stephanie Marchese, Grace Natoli Sheldon (Set Stylists)
Julie Herzfeldt, Sue Draheim (Food Stylists)

TABLE OF CONTENTS

A Change of *Seasons* Brings New Ideas to the Table

As one season rolls into the next, the passing months bring weather changes and a chance to update your cooking repertoire. The changing seasons also bring new ingredients to experiment with in the kitchen, and, for the cost-conscious cook, it makes sense to cook with seasonal produce when it's most flavorful and affordable. From summer's flame-broiled fare to winter's comforting casseroles, with *Taste of Home Cooking Through the Seasons*, the perfect dish is always at your fingertips. In fact, there are 597 delicious recipes from which to choose.

DISHES CHOCK-FULL OF NATURE'S GOODNESS

This beautiful cookbook is a perfect way to use up the luscious bounty from your own garden. Or, if you're a frequent visitor to farmers markets or you simply like to use produce when it's most available and at its ripest, it's a breeze to create a menu that's in tune with the weather. For instance, in the Autumn Harvest section, there are slow-cooked favorites and comforting soups, such as Apple Cider Beef Stew (p. 176) and Sweet Potato and Pear Soup (p. 180). Similarly, refreshing salads, such as Papaya-Avocado Tossed Salad (p. 34), and other veggie-packed dishes await you in Spring Bounty. There's truly an endless variety of recipes for the creative cook to choose from!

SEARCHING FOR RECIPES IS EASY!

This colorful book is divided into four sections, Spring Bounty, Summer Splash, Autumn Harvest and Winter Comforts, to make searching for recipes easy. Each section has six chapters that include appetizers, beverages, soups, sandwiches, side dishes, salads, breads, entrees, desserts and dishes for holidays or special gatherings. It's a breeze to create a menu, whether there's snow or green grass on the ground. Simply flip to a seasonal section and browse the chapters for recipes. Or, turn to the General Index in the back and search for recipes according to a particular ingredient, such as asparagus, blueberries, sausage or zucchini. You can also search the index for the type of recipe you would like to make, such as a side dish, slow cooker recipe, appetizer or beverage. We've organized the book so that it's easy to plan the menu of your dreams.

TANTALIZING MENUS FOR THE HOLIDAYS

Meal planning during the holidays can be hectic, so we created a Special Occasions chapter at the end of each section. This chapter features menus for a variety of celebrations. For instance, the Special Occasions chapter in the Spring Bounty section has menus for St. Patrick's Day, Mardi Gras, Easter, Cinco de Mayo and Mother's Day, and the Special Occasions chapter in the Winter Comforts section has menus for Hanukkah, Christmas, New Year's and Valentine's Day. This is the place to turn to for mouthwatering dishes when celebrating holidays and other special occasions any time of the year.

HUNDREDS OF DELICIOUS RECIPES & HANDY TIPS

Throughout the book, you'll find plenty of helpful hints, culinary information and kitchen shortcuts for the busy home cook. Plus, there are so many amazing recipes to choose from in this big collector's edition book that you can make a different one every day well past a year-and-a-half! From elegant entrees to showstopping desserts, the endless variety of easy-to-make dishes will ensure your family is satisfied any day of the week during any time of the year! And like all of our recipes, rest assured, each has been thoroughly tested and approved by our experienced Test Kitchen staff.

This beautiful, all-encompassing cookbook will help turn your dinner table into a heartwarming spot where memories are made...the whole year through. From our home to yours, we wish you a treasure trove of scrumptious kitchen adventures!

Spring is the season of beginnings.
It's time to put away warm sweaters
and stockings, start cleaning out the
closets and open the windows to let
in the sweet aroma of spring air.
Food cravings gradually change from
slow-cooked meats and stews to
delectable dishes chock-full of the
season's colorful bounty. Now is the
opportunity to whip up scrumptious
recipes filled with fresh spring fruits
and vegetables, such as rhubarb,
asparagus, ruby-red strawberries,
chives, apricots and more.

Spring Bounty

11   14   17   18

APPETIZERS & BEVERAGES

10

CHIVE CRAB CAKES

CINDY WORTH, LAPWAI, IDAHO
These tasty crab cakes are perfect for appetizers, or try them with a salad for a light meal.

PREP: 20 min. + chilling **COOK:** 10 min./batch

  4 egg whites
  1 egg
  6 tablespoons minced chives
  3 tablespoons all-purpose flour
  1 to 2 teaspoons hot pepper sauce
  1 teaspoon baking powder
1/2 teaspoon salt
1/4 teaspoon pepper
  4 cans (6 ounces each) crabmeat, drained, flaked and cartilage removed
  2 cups panko (Japanese) bread crumbs
  2 tablespoons canola oil

1 In a large bowl, lightly beat the egg whites and egg. Add the chives, flour, pepper sauce, baking powder, salt and pepper; mix well. Fold in the crab. Cover and refrigerate for at least 2 hours.

2 Place the bread crumbs in a shallow bowl. Drop the crab mixture by 1/4 cupfuls into the crumbs. Gently coat with crumbs and shape into 3/4-in.-thick patties.

3 In a large nonstick skillet, cook the crab cakes in the oil in batches over medium-high heat for 3-4 minutes on each side or until golden brown.

YIELD: 6 servings.

SMOKED SALMON NEW POTATOES

TASTE OF HOME TEST KITCHEN
This recipe is what today's nutritious eating is all about—fresh ingredients, healthy fish and low-fat dairy products. Plus, you're bound to get rave reviews when guests uncover these baby stuffed potatoes.

PREP: 20 min. **COOK:** 25 min.

 36 small red potatoes (about 1-1/2 pounds)
  1 package (8 ounces) reduced-fat cream cheese, cubed
  2 packages (3 ounces each) smoked salmon or lox
  2 tablespoons chopped green onion
  2 teaspoons dill weed
  2 teaspoons lemon juice
1/8 teaspoon salt
1/8 teaspoon pepper
Fresh dill sprigs

1 Place the potatoes in a large saucepan and cover with water. Bring to a boil. Reduce heat; simmer, uncovered, for 20-22 minutes or until tender.

2 Meanwhile, in a food processor, combine the cream cheese, salmon, onion, dill, lemon juice, salt and pepper. Cover and process until smooth; set aside.

3 Drain potatoes and immediately place in ice water. Drain and pat dry with paper towels. Cut a thin slice off the bottom of each potato to allow it to sit flat. With a melon baller, scoop out a small amount of potato (discard or save for another use).

4 Pipe or spoon the salmon mixture into the potatoes. Garnish with dill sprigs.

YIELD: 3 dozen.

CREAMY MANDARIN COOLER

RENEE RICHARDSON, POUNDING MILL, VIRGINIA
This frothy and flavorful concoction is as fast to fix as it is refreshing. It makes a delicious, cool splash at breakfast or any other time of day, such as an excellent after-dinner treat. I think it tastes like an old-fashioned Dreamsicle.

PREP/TOTAL TIME: 5 min.
- 3/4 cup 2% milk
- 1/4 cup orange juice
- 1 can (11 ounces) mandarin oranges, undrained
- 1 carton (6 ounces) fat-free orange creme yogurt
- 1 package (1 ounce) instant vanilla pudding mix
- 12 to 15 ice cubes

Orange wedges and green grapes, optional

1 In a blender, combine the milk, orange juice, undrained mandarin oranges, yogurt, pudding mix and ice cubes; cover and process for 20 seconds or until smooth. Stir if necessary. Pour into chilled glasses and garnish with orange wedges and grapes if desired. Serve immediately.

YIELD: 5 servings.

A RAINBOW OF FLAVORS
There are a variety of creamy coolers you can create by using the recipe above. You can substitute the orange juice with pineapple juice and the canned mandarin oranges with pineapples for a tropical flair. Or use apple juice instead of orange, canned pears instead of mandarin oranges, and vanilla yogurt instead of orange creme for a fall-flavored cooler.

DIPLOMA APPETIZERS

JOANNE SHEW CHUK, ST. BENEDICT, SASKATCHEWAN
We use these appetizers for all sorts of occasions. In fact, I regularly freeze them so I'm always prepared...even if unexpected guests drop in. For graduation parties, just tie them with strips of green onion.

PREP: 20 min. + freezing BAKE: 15 min.
- 16 to 20 green onions
- 2-1/2 cups chopped fresh mushrooms
- 1/4 cup butter, cubed
- 1 package (8 ounces) cream cheese, cubed
- 1/2 teaspoon Worcestershire sauce
- 1/4 teaspoon salt
- 1/4 teaspoon pepper
- 1/8 teaspoon garlic salt
- 32 slices white or wheat bread, crusts removed

Melted butter
- 1 cup boiling water

1 Cut green tops off onions; set aside. Chop enough of the remaining onions to measure 1/2 cup.

2 In a large skillet, saute onions and mushrooms in butter until onions are tender. Add cream cheese and seasonings; stir over low heat until cheese is melted, about 2 minutes. Remove from the heat; cool slightly.

3 Flatten the bread with a rolling pin. Spread 1 tablespoon of mushroom mixture on each slice and roll up. Place in a single layer on greased baking sheets. Freeze for 30 minutes. Frozen unbaked roll-ups may be stored in airtight containers in the freezer for up to 1 month.

4 Brush with melted butter. Bake at 375° for 15-20 minutes or until lightly browned. Cut reserved onion tops in half lengthwise. Place in boiling water for 1 minute; drain and cool. Tie a strip around each roll-up.

YIELD: 32 servings.

HERBED LEEK TART

JEAN ECOS, HARTLAND, WISCONSIN
This savory, non-traditional tart is a favorite among family and friends!

PREP: 25 min. **BAKE:** 20 min. + cooling

- 3 cups thinly sliced leeks (about 4 medium)
- 1/2 cup chopped sweet red pepper
- 4 garlic cloves, minced
- 2 tablespoons olive oil
- 1-1/2 cups (6 ounces) shredded Swiss cheese
- 2 tablespoons Dijon mustard
- 1 teaspoon herbes de Provence
- 1 package (15 ounces) refrigerated pie pastry
- 1 teaspoon milk
- 2 tablespoons chopped almonds or walnuts, optional

1 In a large skillet, saute the leeks, red pepper and garlic in oil until tender. Remove from the heat; cool for 5 minutes. Stir in the cheese, mustard and herbs; set aside.

2 On a lightly floured surface, roll each sheet of pastry into a 12-in. circle. Transfer to parchment paper-lined baking sheets. Spoon leek mixture over pastry to within 2 in. of edges. Fold edges of pastry over filling, leaving center uncovered. Brush folded pastry with milk; sprinkle with nuts if desired.

3 Bake at 375° for 20-25 minutes or until the crust is golden and filling is bubbly. Using the parchment paper, slide tarts onto wire racks. Cool for 10 minutes before cutting. Serve warm. Refrigerate leftovers.

YIELD: 2 tarts (8 servings each).

EDITOR'S NOTE: Look for herbes de Provence in the spice aisle. It is also available from Penzeys Spices. Call 1-800/741-7787 or visit www.penzeys.com.

TANGY PARTY PUNCH

JENNIFER BANGERTER, NIXA, MISSOURI
As social chair one year during college, I tried to come up with a more interesting beverage than the usual one. This pastel punch was always a hit at receptions and parties. It has a bubbly, citrusy flavor that is refreshing.

PREP/TOTAL TIME: 10 min.

- 1 can (46 ounces) pineapple juice, chilled
- 1 can (46 ounces) orange juice, chilled
- 1 can (12 ounces) frozen limeade concentrate, thawed
- 1 can (12 ounces) frozen lemonade concentrate, thawed
- 3 liters ginger ale, chilled
- 1 pint each orange, lemon and lime sherbet

1 In a large punch bowl, combine the pineapple juice, orange juice, limeade and lemonade concentrate. Stir in the ginger ale. Add medium-sized scoops of the sherbet to the punch. Serve immediately.

YIELD: 8 quarts.

CLASSIC SPINACH DIP

JOYCE FOGLEMAN, STAFFORD, TEXAS
Everywhere I take this cool dip, I'm asked for the recipe. I don't make it at home because I'm afraid that's all I'd eat the entire day. Best of all, it comes together in no time.

PREP: 10 min. + chilling

- 4 cups fresh baby spinach, chopped
- 2 tablespoons water
- 2/3 cup sliced water chestnuts, chopped
- 1/3 cup sour cream
- 1/3 cup mayonnaise
- 4 teaspoons vegetable soup mix
- 1 green onion, chopped

Assorted crackers

1 In a microwave-safe bowl, combine spinach and water. Cover and microwave on high for 45-60 seconds or until wilted; drain. Cool slightly and squeeze dry.

2 In a small bowl, combine the water chestnuts, sour cream, mayonnaise, soup mix, onion and spinach. Chill for at least 1 hour. Serve with crackers.

YIELD: 1-1/2 cups.

SENIOR STRAWBERRY SLUSH

THELMA RUSH, MT. PLEASANT, TENNESSEE

Here's fruity refreshment that can flavor a gathering without a fuss! Simply stir up the berries, juices, water and sugar, then freeze. Add soda before serving and you're all set. Keep one thing in mind, though: You may want to make extra, because people are always coming back for seconds!

PREP: 10 min. + freezing

- 6 cups boiling water
- 2 cups sugar
- 2 packages (10 ounces each) frozen sweetened sliced strawberries
- 4 cups pineapple juice
- 2-1/2 cups orange juice
- 1/2 cup lemon juice
- 1 liter lemon-lime soda, chilled

1 In a large bowl, stir the water and sugar together until the sugar is dissolved. Add the strawberries and juices; stir until combined. Pour into two 12-cup fluted tube pans or a large freezer container.

2 Remove from the freezer 1-1/2 hours before serving. Place fruit mixture in a punch bowl; stir in soda.

YIELD: 5 quarts.

DEVILED EGGS WITH DILL

MARY PRIOR, RUSH CITY, MINNESOTA

Deviled eggs are a great side dish for Easter, but they also are a fantastic snack. This easy-to-make version of the classic appetizers has a hint of Worcestershire and a slight tang of mustard. Try using Dijon for an extra layer of flavor.

PREP/TOTAL TIME: 20 min.

- 6 hard-cooked eggs
- 2 tablespoons reduced-fat mayonnaise
- 1-1/2 teaspoons cider vinegar
- 3/4 teaspoon prepared mustard
- 1/4 teaspoon Worcestershire sauce
- 1/4 teaspoon salt
- Dash pepper
- 12 fresh dill sprigs

1 Cut eggs in half lengthwise. Remove the yolks; set aside egg whites and four yolks (discard remaining yolks or save for another use).

2 In a large bowl, mash reserved yolks. Stir in the mayonnaise, vinegar, mustard, Worcestershire sauce, salt and pepper. Stuff or pipe into egg whites. Garnish with dill. Refrigerate until serving.

YIELD: 1 dozen.

MANGO TANGO SMOOTHIES

TASTE OF HOME TEST KITCHEN

With a cup of milk and a half cup of yogurt, this smoothie is rich in calcium and makes an excellent choice for breakfast on the run. For added convenience, you can buy mango chunks that are already peeled and chopped.

PREP/TOTAL TIME: 10 min.

- 1 cup chopped peeled mango
- 1 medium ripe banana, frozen, peeled and sliced
- 1 cup fat-free milk
- 1/2 cup reduced-fat plain yogurt
- 1/2 cup unsweetened pineapple juice

1 In a blender, combine all ingredients; cover and process until smooth. Pour into chilled glasses; serve immediately.

YIELD: 2 servings.

ASPARAGUS HAM TARTLETS

ELAINE ANDERSON, NEW GALILEE, PENNSYLVANIA
We have our own asparagus patch, and each spring I look forward to making treats like these tartlets. I enjoy them as a mini meal or as appetizers. They freeze well and are very popular at parties.

PREP: 20 min. + chilling **BAKE:** 25 min.

   1 package (3 ounces) cream cheese, softened
1/4 cup butter, softened
3/4 cup plus 1 tablespoon all-purpose flour, divided
1/4 cup cornmeal
   1 egg
1/3 cup heavy whipping cream
3/4 cup shredded Swiss cheese
1/2 cup diced fully cooked ham
  18 fresh asparagus tips (cut into 1-inch pieces)

1 Beat cream cheese and butter until smooth. Beat in 3/4 cup flour and cornmeal. Cover and refrigerate for 1 hour.

2 Shape dough into 18 balls. Press onto the bottom and up the sides of greased miniature muffin cups.

3 In a large bowl, whisk egg and cream. Stir in remaining flour until smooth. Add cheese and ham.

4 Spoon about 1 tablespoon into each cup. Bake at 425° for 7 minutes. Reduce heat to 325°. Top each tart with an asparagus tip. Cover loosely with foil. Bake 17-20 minutes longer or until a knife inserted near the center comes out clean.

YIELD: 1-1/2 dozen.

LEMON-BERRY PITCHER PUNCH

MARGARET O'BRYON, BEL AIR, MARYLAND
If you need to satisfy a large group of people, you can double or triple the recipe for this refreshing beverage to accommodate them. The tangy combination of lemonade and cranberry juice is a real thirst-quencher on a warm day.

PREP/TOTAL TIME: 10 min.

1/2 cup sweetened lemonade drink mix
   4 cups cold water
2/3 cup cranberry juice, chilled
1-1/2 cups lemon-lime soda, chilled

1 In a pitcher, combine the drink mix, water and cranberry juice. Stir in soda. Serve immediately.

YIELD: about 6 cups.

MUSHROOM-STUFFED SHRIMP

KAROLEE PLOCK, BURWELL, NEBRASKA
Hosting a party? These fancy bites will be a hit. The stuffing adds a delicious dimension to already tasty shrimp. Plus, it's an easy appetizer to make. They can also be used as a delicious main course if served with rice or pasta.

PREP/TOTAL TIME: 25 min.

  12 uncooked shell-on jumbo shrimp (about 1 pound)
1/2 teaspoon chicken bouillon granules
   1 tablespoon hot water
3/4 cup soft bread crumbs
   2 tablespoons finely chopped fresh mushrooms
   2 tablespoons finely chopped celery
   1 teaspoon reduced-fat butter
1/4 teaspoon garlic powder
   4 drops hot pepper sauce

1 Peel and devein the shrimp, leaving the tails on. Butterfly each shrimp along the outside curve. Open the shrimp flat, then place with the tails up in an 8-in. square baking dish coated with cooking spray.

2 Dissolve the bouillon in hot water. Stir in the remaining ingredients. Spoon about 1 teaspoon onto each shrimp. Bake at 375° for 5-8 minutes or until shrimp turn pink. Serve warm.

YIELD: 1 dozen.

EDITOR'S NOTE: This recipe was tested with Land O'Lakes light stick butter.

> **HOW TO BUTTERFLY SHRIMP**
> After the shrimp is deveined, use the tip of a paring knife to cut a slit along the back side of the shrimp, but not all the way through. Leave the shrimp attached near the tail.

RADISH DIP

DONNA SMITH, FAIRPORT, NEW YORK
This creamy dip is easy to throw together and makes a zippy appetizer when served with cauliflower and broccoli florets or even rye bread cubes.

PREP/TOTAL TIME: 15 min.

    1 cup (8 ounces) fat-free plain yogurt
    1 cup chopped radishes (about 13)
  1/3 cup reduced-fat mayonnaise
  1/4 teaspoon hot pepper sauce
  1/8 teaspoon pepper
Assorted fresh vegetables

1 In a large bowl, combine the first five ingredients. Cover and refrigerate until serving. Serve with vegetables.

YIELD: about 1-1/3 cups.

FRUITY MINT COOLER

LINNEA REIN, TOPEKA, KANSAS
This sweet, refreshing drink uses tea as its base. The mint is mild but lingers on the tongue.

PREP/TOTAL TIME: 15 min.

    8 individual tea bags
 1/2 to 3/4 cup minced fresh mint
    4 cups boiling water
1-1/2 cups sugar
    6 ounces frozen lemonade concentrate, thawed
    6 ounces frozen limeade concentrate, thawed
  3/4 cup orange juice
    3 quarts cold water

1 Place tea bags and mint in a heat-resistant pitcher or bowl; add boiling water. Let stand for 5 minutes; strain. Stir in sugar,

concentrates and orange juice; refrigerate. Just before serving, place mint mixture in a large punch bowl; stir in cold water.

YIELD: 4-1/2 quarts.

MOJITO

TASTE OF HOME TEST KITCHEN
The traditional Mojito is made with rum, which is both pleasant and mildly sweet. The version made with tequila is tart and has a more distinctive alcohol taste, but it is still refreshing.

PREP/TOTAL TIME: 5 min.

    1 to 2 lime wedges
    2 mint sprigs
    2 teaspoons confectioners' sugar
 3/4 to 1 cup ice cubes
    2 ounces light rum
 1/2 cup club soda, chilled

GARNISH:
Mint sprig and lime slice

1 Squeeze lime wedge into a highball glass; drop lime into the glass. Add mint and confectioners' sugar; muddle. Add ice. Pour rum and club soda into glass; stir. Garnish as desired.

YIELD: 1 serving.

EDITOR'S NOTE: For a tequila mojito, substitute silver tequila (such as Jose Cuervo Clasico) for the rum.

SPRINGTIME STRAWBERRY MALTS

TASTE OF HOME TEST KITCHEN

Why limit yourself to having a malt only when you go out? This refreshing treat is a great way to indulge without using up gas in the tank. It makes mealtime fun for the whole family.

PREP/TOTAL TIME: 10 min.

- 1/4 cup milk
- 2 tablespoons strawberry syrup
- 1/2 cup malted milk powder
- 6 fresh or frozen strawberries
- 1 quart vanilla ice cream, softened

1 Place the milk, strawberry syrup, malted milk powder, strawberries and ice cream in a blender; cover and process until smooth. Pour into chilled glasses. Serve immediately.

YIELD: 4 servings.

WHAT IS MALTED MILK POWDER?

This simple powder makes ice cream mixed with syrup so much tastier. Made from a mixture of malted barley, wheat flour, and whole milk, the concoction is evaporated until it forms a powder. It may also contain additional ingredients, such as flavorings (like chocolate or vanilla), preservatives and vitamins.

CRAB-STUFFED ARTICHOKES

SUZANNE STROCSHER, BOTHELL, WASHINGTON

Looking for an impressive luncheon presentation? Rely on this delicious recipe for stuffed artichokes that my mother passed on to me. They're surprisingly easy to make.

PREP: 50 min. **BAKE:** 20 min.

- 4 medium artichokes
- 2 tablespoons plus 2 teaspoons lemon juice, divided
- 4 pouches (3.53 ounces each) premium crabmeat, drained
- 1/2 cup shredded reduced-fat Swiss cheese
- 1/2 cup soft bread crumbs
- 1/3 cup reduced-fat mayonnaise
- 1/3 cup chopped green pepper
- 1/4 cup finely chopped onion
- 1/2 teaspoon salt

1 Using a sharp knife, level the bottom of each artichoke and cut 3/4 in. from the top. Using kitchen scissors, snip off tips of outer leaves; brush cut edges with 2 tablespoons lemon juice.

2 Stand artichokes in a Dutch oven; add 2 in. of water. Bring to a boil. Reduce heat; cover and simmer for 25-30 minutes or until leaves near the center almost pull out easily.

3 Invert artichokes to drain. With a spoon, carefully scrape out the fuzzy center portion of artichokes and discard.

4 In a large bowl, combine the crab, cheese, bread crumbs, mayonnaise, green pepper, onion, salt and remaining lemon juice. Gently spread artichoke leaves apart; fill with stuffing.

5 Place in an ungreased 8-in. square baking dish; add 1/2 in. of warm water. Cover and bake at 350° for 20-25 minutes or until heated through and leaves near the outer edge pull out easily.

YIELD: 4 servings.

ASPARAGUS STRUDEL

DONA ERHART, STOCKBRIDGE, MICHIGAN
Celebrate the arrival of spring by serving this strudel for Easter brunch. Watch the savory slices disappear from the table!

PREP: 25 min. **BAKE:** 40 min. + cooling

- 2 cups water
- 3/4 pound fresh asparagus, trimmed and cut into 1-inch pieces
- 2 medium leeks (white portion only), thinly sliced
- 1-1/4 cups butter, divided
- 2 cups (8 ounces) shredded Gruyere or Swiss cheese
- 3 eggs, lightly beaten
- 2 tablespoons lemon juice
- 2 tablespoons minced fresh parsley
- 1 tablespoon minced fresh mint
- 1 tablespoon minced fresh dill
- 1/3 cup sliced almonds, toasted
- Dash cayenne pepper
- 32 sheets phyllo dough, (14 inches x 9 inches)

1 In a large skillet, bring water to a boil. Add asparagus; cover and boil for 3 minutes. Drain and immediately place asparagus in ice water. Drain and pat dry. In the same skillet, saute leeks in 1/4 cup butter for 5 minutes or until tender.

2 In a large bowl, combine the asparagus, leeks, cheese, eggs, lemon juice, parsley, mint, dill, almonds and cayenne.

3 Melt remaining butter. Place one sheet of phyllo dough on a work surface (keep remaining dough covered with plastic wrap and a damp towel to avoid drying out). Brush with the butter. Repeat layers seven times. Spoon a fourth of vegetable mixture along the short end of dough to within 1 in. of edges. Fold long sides 1 in. over filling. Roll up jelly-roll style, starting with a short side. Place seam side down on a greased baking sheet.

4 Repeat, making three more strudels. Brush the tops with remaining butter. Bake at 350° for 40-45 minutes or until golden brown. Cool for 10 minutes before slicing.

YIELD: 4 strudels, 8 slices each.

SPICY MINT TEA

IONE BANKS, JEFFERSON, OREGON
In the old days, a steaming cup of mint tea was said to dispel headaches, heartburn and indigestion. I don't know about that, but I do know that this tea refreshes me every time.

PREP/TOTAL TIME: 15 min.

- 6 cups water
- 2 cinnamon sticks
- 4 whole cloves
- 4 whole allspice
- 2 cups fresh mint leaves
- Honey, optional

1 Bring the water, cinnamon, cloves and allspice to a boil. Boil for 1 minute. Stir in mint leaves. Remove from heat and steep for 5 minutes. Strain into cups. Sweeten with honey if desired.

YIELD: 4 servings.

CREAM-FILLED STRAWBERRIES

KARIN POROSLAY, WESLEY CHAPEL, FLORIDA
These plump berries filled with a creamy pudding mixture are so elegant-looking and luscious-tasting that they're perfect for parties or special gatherings.

PREP: 30 min. + chilling

- 18 large fresh strawberries
- 1 cup cold fat-free milk
- 1 package (1 ounce) instant vanilla pudding mix
- 2 cups whipped topping
- 1/4 teaspoon almond extract

1 Remove stems from strawberries; cut a deep X in the top of each berry. Spread berries apart.

2 In a bowl, whisk milk and pudding mix for 2 minutes. Fold in whipped topping and almond extract. Pipe or spoon about 5 teaspoons into each berry. Chill until serving.

YIELD: 18 strawberries.

SPINACH CHEESE SWIRLS

MARY NICHOLS, DOVER, NEW HAMPSHIRE
These super-easy sandwiches are brimming with spinach and onion flavor. Using refrigerated pizza dough shaves minutes off prep time and creates a golden brown crust. You can enjoy them warm or cold.

PREP: 10 min. BAKE: 25 min.

   1 tube (13.8 ounces) refrigerated pizza crust
   1 package (10 ounces) frozen chopped spinach,
      thawed and drained
   2 cups (8 ounces) shredded part-skim mozzarella cheese
   1 cup finely chopped onion
   1 garlic clove, minced

1 On a lightly floured surface, roll pizza dough into a 14-in. x 10-in. rectangle. In a large bowl, combine the spinach, cheese, onion and garlic; spoon over dough to within 1 in. of edges. Roll up jelly-roll style, starting with a long side; tuck ends under and pinch seam to seal.

2 Place seam side down on a baking sheet coated with cooking spray. Bake at 400° for 25-27 minutes or until golden brown. Cut into slices.

YIELD: 4 servings.

BUNNY PINEAPPLE SMOOTHIES

TASTE OF HOME TEST KITCHEN
After trying these bunny-topped smoothies from our Test Kitchen, you'll want to hop back to the buffet for extra servings. Flavored with orange juice, pineapple sherbet and pina colada yogurt, they add a tropical taste to morning meals.

PREP/TOTAL TIME: 15 min.

   2 cups orange juice
   2 pints pineapple sherbet
   4 cartons (8 ounces each) pina colada yogurt
   4 medium bananas, quartered
   1 cup milk
   1 teaspoon vanilla extract
   2 cups whipped topping, divided
   1 drop red food coloring

1 In a blender, combine half of the orange juice, sherbet, yogurt, bananas, milk and vanilla; cover and process until smooth. Pour into chilled glasses. Repeat.

2 Place 1-1/2 cups whipped topping in a pastry or plastic bag; cut a medium hole in a corner of the bag. Pipe a bunny face on each smoothie.

3 Tint the remaining whipped topping with the food coloring; place in another bag. Cut a small hole in a corner of the bag. Pipe the eyes, nose and inside of ears on each bunny face. Beginning from the nose, gently pull a toothpick through the whipped topping toward the edge of the glass to form whiskers. Serve immediately.

YIELD: 10 servings.

AVOCADO DIP

KAY DUNHAM, AMITY, MISSOURI
I created this appetizer because I couldn't find a guacamole that I really liked. My husband doesn't usually like these kinds of dips, but he really likes this one!

PREP/TOTAL TIME: 15 min.

  2 medium ripe avocados, peeled and pitted
  1 package (8 ounces) fat-free cream cheese
1/3 cup plain yogurt
1/3 cup picante sauce
  1 tablespoon lime juice
1/2 teaspoon salt
1/4 teaspoon garlic powder
Tortilla chips

1 Mash avocados and cream cheese until smooth. Stir in the next five ingredients. Serve with chips. Refrigerate leftovers.

YIELD: 2-1/2 cups.

ABOUT AVOCADOS
The easiest avocados to peel and slice are those that are ripe yet firm. (Very ripe, soft avocados are best used for mashing.) To ripen, place the avocado in a paper bag with an apple. Poke holes in the bag, leave at room temperature from 1 to 3 days. To slice, cut the avocado in half lengthwise. Twist halves in opposite directions to separate. Carefully tap the seed with the blade of a sharp knife. Rotate the knife to loosen the seed and lift it out. Scoop out the flesh from each half with a large metal spoon and slice.

STRAWBERRY SALSA

ANGELA PACKHAM, OAKVILLE, MANITOBA
Guests often try to guess the secret ingredient in my salsa. None think of strawberries...but many ask for the recipe.

PREP: 10 min. + chilling

2-1/2 cups finely chopped fresh strawberries
  1 cup chopped green pepper
  2 tablespoons chopped green onions
  2 tablespoons minced fresh parsley
1/3 cup prepared Catalina salad dressing
Dash hot pepper sauce
Pepper to taste
Tortilla chips

1 In a large bowl, combine the strawberries, green pepper, onions and parsley. Stir in the salad dressing, hot pepper sauce and pepper. Cover and refrigerate for 2 hours. Serve with the tortilla chips.

YIELD: 3 cups.

CUCUMBER SHRIMP APPETIZERS

PATRICIA KILE, GREENTOWN, PENNSYLVANIA
When my friend's husband needed lower-fat snacks, she served him this fresh-tasting shrimp spread. Cucumber slices are a fun and healthy alternative to crackers.

PREP/TOTAL TIME: 10 min.

  1 can (8 ounces) unsweetened crushed pineapple, drained
  1 can (4 ounces) tiny shrimp, rinsed and drained
1/4 cup reduced-fat mayonnaise
  1 tablespoon finely chopped green onion
  2 teaspoons Dijon mustard
1-1/2 teaspoons minced fresh dill
  1 medium cucumber (8 inches), cut into 1/4-inch slices
Fresh dill sprigs, optional

1 In a bowl, combine the pineapple, shrimp, mayonnaise, onion, mustard and dill. Spoon onto cucumber slices. Garnish with dill sprigs if desired.

YIELD: 32 appetizers.

SOUPS & SANDWICHES

CHILLED CUCUMBER SOUP

SHIRLEY KIDD, NEW LONDON, MINNESOTA
This is a wonderful way to use up cucumbers. It's so refreshing during spring because it reminds us that summer is coming!

PREP: 10 min. + chilling

      2 medium cucumbers
      2 cups buttermilk
    1/2 cup reduced-fat sour cream
  1-1/2 teaspoons sugar
      1 teaspoon dill weed
    1/2 teaspoon salt
    1/8 teaspoon white pepper
      2 green onions, chopped
  Fresh dill, optional

1 Cut four thin slices of cucumber; set aside for garnish. Peel and finely chop remaining cucumbers. In a large bowl, combine the buttermilk, sour cream, sugar, dill, salt, pepper, green onions and chopped cucumbers.

2 Refrigerate for 4 hours or overnight. Garnish with the cucumber slices and fresh dill if desired.

YIELD: 4 servings.

COOL AS A CUKE
Cucumbers are vining plants that are part of the same family of plants as squash, pumpkins and gourds. If you prefer to have your cucumbers seedless, first, peel or score the cucumber. Cut lengthwise in half. Using a teaspoon or a melon baller, run the tip under the seeds to loosen and remove, then discard, the seeds.

HEAVENLY EARTH BURGERS

WENDY MCGOWAN, FONTANA, CALIFORNIA
Packed with nutrition, these rice-and-bean patties make a fun and filling hand-held entree. Fresh parsley and carrots lend flecks of color, and sunflower kernels a touch of crunchiness.

PREP: 25 min. **COOK:** 10 min.

  1-1/2 cups cooked brown rice
    1/2 cup finely chopped onion
    1/4 cup sunflower kernels
    1/4 cup seasoned bread crumbs
    1/2 cup shredded carrot
      3 tablespoons minced fresh parsley
      2 tablespoons reduced-sodium soy sauce
    1/2 teaspoon dried thyme
      1 egg
      1 egg white
      1 cup garbanzo beans or chickpeas, rinsed and drained
  1-1/2 teaspoons canola oil
      6 whole wheat hamburger buns, split
      6 lettuce leaves
      6 slices tomato
      6 slices onion

1 In a large bowl, combine the first eight ingredients. In a food processor, combine the egg, egg white and garbanzo beans; cover and process until smooth. Stir into rice mixture. Shape into six patties.

2 In a nonstick skillet coated with cooking spray, cook patties in oil for 5-6 minutes on each side or until lightly browned and crisp. Serve on buns with lettuce, tomato and onion.

YIELD: 6 servings.

WHITE BEAN FENNEL SOUP

DONNA QUINN, ROUND LAKE BEACH, ILLINOIS
This filling soup is often requested for company dinners. A hint of fennel accents the flavor of this quick-to-fix bean soup, and spinach and tomatoes offer a bit of color.

PREP: 10 min. **COOK:** 45 min.
- 1 large onion, chopped
- 1 small fennel bulb, thinly sliced
- 1 tablespoon olive oil
- 5 cups reduced-sodium chicken broth or vegetable broth
- 1 can (15 ounces) white kidney or cannellini beans, rinsed and drained
- 1 can (14-1/2 ounces) diced tomatoes, undrained
- 1 teaspoon dried thyme
- 1/4 teaspoon pepper
- 1 bay leaf
- 3 cups shredded fresh spinach

1 In a large saucepan, saute the onion and fennel in oil until tender. Add the broth, beans, tomatoes, thyme, pepper and bay leaf; bring to a boil. Reduce the heat; cover and simmer for 30 minutes or until fennel is tender.

2 Discard bay leaf. Add spinach; cook 3-4 minutes longer or until spinach is wilted.

YIELD: 5 servings.

SAVORY HAM WRAPS

RUTH PETERSON, JENISON, MICHIGAN
The great dressing is what makes the tender, savory wraps so special. They're so easy to make, and if you don't have tortilla wraps, the ingredients go nicely with good, homestyle bread, too.

PREP/TOTAL TIME: 20 min.
- 1/4 cup mayonnaise
- 1 tablespoon milk
- 3/4 teaspoon sugar
- 1/4 teaspoon prepared mustard
- 1/8 teaspoon celery seed
- Dash salt

- 2 flour tortillas (10 inches), room temperature
- 1/4 pound thinly sliced deli ham
- 1/3 cup shredded Swiss cheese
- 2/3 cup shredded lettuce
- 1 medium tomato, seeded and chopped
- 1 green onion, chopped

1 In a small bowl, whisk the first six ingredients; spread evenly over each tortilla. Layer with the ham and cheese. Top with the lettuce, tomato and onion. Roll up tightly; secure with toothpicks if desired.

YIELD: 2 servings.

REUBEN DELI SANDWICHES

GIGI LAFAVE RYAN, LONGMONT, COLORADO
Here's a new twist on the classic Reuben sandwich. The filling is easy to prepare and keeps well in the fridge. Add a salad and dessert, and you have a delicious lunch.

PREP/TOTAL TIME: 30 min.
- 3/4 cup mayonnaise
- 1 tablespoon chili sauce
- 1-1/2 teaspoons prepared mustard
- 1/4 teaspoon prepared horseradish
- 1 can (14 ounces) sauerkraut, rinsed and well drained
- 3/4 pound finely chopped corned beef (about 3 cups)
- 2 cups (8 ounces) shredded Swiss cheese
- 30 slices rye bread
- 1/2 cup butter, softened

1 In a large bowl, combine mayonnaise, chili sauce, mustard and horseradish. Stir in the sauerkraut, corned beef and the shredded Swiss.

2 Spread 1/3 cup mayonnaise mixture on 15 slices of bread; top with the remaining bread. Lightly butter the outsides of bread. Toast the sandwiches on a hot griddle for 4-5 minutes on each side or until golden brown.

YIELD: 15 servings.

DILLED POTATO-LEEK SOUP

AGNES WARD, STRATFORD, ONTARIO
It's your "leeky day," because this smooth, comforting soup is scrumptious and always gets rave reviews.

PREP/TOTAL TIME: 30 min.

- 1 cup sliced leeks (white portion only)
- 1 celery rib, chopped
- 1-1/2 teaspoons butter
- 2 cups chicken broth
- 1-1/2 cups cubed peeled Yukon Gold potatoes
- 1 large carrot, finely chopped
- 1/2 teaspoon dried thyme
- 1/4 teaspoon salt
- 1/8 teaspoon pepper
- 1/2 cup buttermilk
- 1-1/2 teaspoons snipped fresh dill or 1/2 teaspoon dill weed

Herb potato chips and finely shredded leeks, optional

1 In a large saucepan, saute leeks and celery in butter until tender. Stir in the broth, potatoes, carrot, thyme, salt and pepper. Bring to a boil. Reduce heat; cover and simmer for 10-15 minutes or until vegetables are tender. Cool slightly.

2 Transfer to a blender; cover and process until smooth. Return to the pan. Whisk a small amount of soup into buttermilk; return all to the pan, stirring constantly. Add dill; heat through (do not boil). Garnish if desired.

YIELD: 3-3/4 cups.

GUACAMOLE CHICKEN WRAPS

TASTE OF HOME TEST KITCHEN
Seasoned chicken, guacamole and salsa add finger-lickin' Southwest flavor and flair to these zesty wraps.

PREP/TOTAL TIME: 10 min.

- 1/2 cup guacamole
- 4 spinach tortillas (8 inches)
- 1/2 cup salsa
- 1 cup (4 ounces) shredded Mexican cheese blend
- 2 packages (6 ounces each) ready-to-use Southwestern chicken strips
- 4 lettuce leaves

1 Spread the guacamole over half of each tortilla. Layer with salsa, cheese, chicken and lettuce to within 2 in. of edges. Roll up tightly.

YIELD: 4 servings.

EDITOR'S NOTE: This recipe was prepared with Louis Rich cooked chicken breast.

VIDALIA ONION SOUP

RUBY JEAN BLAND, GLENNVILLE, GEORGIA
The onions are definitely the stars in this traditional favorite soup. Rich Swiss cheese delightfully tops off a heaping bowl of sweet, succulent Vidalia onions.

PREP: 50 min. **BAKE:** 10 min.

- 4 to 5 large Vidalia or sweet onions, chopped
- 3 tablespoons butter
- 1/4 teaspoon pepper
- 1 tablespoon all-purpose flour
- 4 cups beef broth
- 1-1/2 cups water
- 1 bay leaf
- 8 slices French bread, toasted
- 1/2 cup shredded Swiss cheese

1 In a Dutch oven or soup kettle, saute the onions in butter until lightly browned. Sprinkle with pepper and flour. Cook and stir for 1 minute. Add broth, water and bay leaf; simmer for 30-40 minutes, stirring occasionally.

2 Discard bay leaf. Ladle into ovenproof soup bowls; top with bread and cheese. Bake at 400° for 10 minutes or until cheese is golden brown.

YIELD: 8 servings (2 quarts).

APRICOT-PISTACHIO CHICKEN SALAD SANDWICHES

LESLEY PEW, LYNN, MASSACHUSETTS

I ordered an entree similar to this at the local museum cafe and liked it so much I decided to make something similar. At the museum it was served as a filling for a sandwich made with lettuce, tomato and thinly sliced red onion. I tend to serve it as a salad during spring. It's really good on a hot day.

PREP/TOTAL TIME: 20 min.

- 1-1/2 cups shredded rotisserie chicken
- 1/3 cup chopped dried apricots
- 2 tablespoons mayonnaise
- 2 tablespoons sour cream
- 4 teaspoons coarsely chopped pistachios
- 1 teaspoon prepared horseradish
- 1 teaspoon whole grain mustard
- 1 teaspoon honey
- Dash salt
- Dash white pepper
- Dash hot pepper sauce
- 4 slices sourdough bread
- 2 Bibb lettuce leaves
- 2 slices tomato
- 2 slices sweet onion

1 In a small bowl, combine the first 11 ingredients. Spread over two slices of bread; top with lettuce, tomato, onion and remaining bread.

YIELD: 2 servings.

HEARTY VEGGIE SANDWICHES

MICKI SANNAR, HIGHLAND, UTAH

This vegetarian delight is not only healthy, it tastes great, too. Any way you slice it, this is one refreshing, flavor-filled sandwich!

PREP/TOTAL TIME: 20 min.

- 2 teaspoons mayonnaise
- 2 teaspoons prepared mustard
- 4 slices whole wheat bread
- 4 slices cheddar cheese (3/4 ounce each)
- 2 slices red onion
- 1/4 cup sliced ripe olives, drained
- 1 small tomato, sliced
- 1 medium ripe avocado, peeled and sliced
- 1/8 teaspoon pepper
- 4 tablespoons Italian salad dressing
- 2 lettuce leaves

1 Spread the mayonnaise and mustard over two slices of bread; layer with the cheese, onion, olives, tomato and the avocado. Sprinkle with pepper.

2 Drizzle each sandwich with 1 tablespoon of dressing. Top with lettuce. Drizzle remaining dressing over remaining bread; place over sandwiches.

YIELD: 2 servings.

SUPER SANDWICHES

If you enjoy grilled sandwiches, you may want to invest in an electric or stovetop griddle, which will allow you to grill four to six sandwiches at a time. Enhance a sandwich with toppings such as guacamole, salsa, cheese spreads, mayonnaise, Swiss cheese, blue cheese, sauteed mushrooms or strips of crisp bacon.

MATZO BALL SOUP

TASTE OF HOME TEST KITCHEN
Although this soup is a tradition during the Jewish holiday of Passover, it's delicious any time of the year. You can make the soup a day ahead and reheat it just before serving.

PREP: 25 min. + chilling COOK: 2 hours
BROTH:
- 10 cups water
- 12 garlic cloves, peeled
- 3 medium carrots, cut into chunks
- 3 small turnips, peeled and cut into chunks
- 2 medium onions, cut into wedges
- 2 medium parsnips, peeled and cut into chunks
- 1 medium leek (white portion only), sliced
- 1/4 cup minced fresh parsley
- 2 tablespoons snipped fresh dill
- 1 teaspoon salt
- 1 teaspoon pepper
- 3/4 teaspoon ground turmeric

MATZO BALLS:
- 3 eggs, separated
- 3 tablespoons water or chicken broth
- 3 tablespoons rendered chicken fat
- 1-1/2 teaspoons salt, divided
- 3/4 cup matzo meal
- 8 cups water

1 Combine all ingredients for broth in a large soup kettle. Bring to a boil. Reduce heat; cover and simmer for 2 hours.

2 Meanwhile, for matzo balls, in a large bowl, beat the egg yolks on high speed for 2 minutes or until thick and lemon-colored.

Add the water, chicken fat and 1/2 teaspoon salt. In another bowl, beat egg whites on high until stiff peaks form; fold into yolk mixture. Fold in matzo meal. Cover and refrigerate for at least 1 hour or until thickened.

3 In another large soup kettle, bring the 8 cups of water to a boil; add the remaining salt. Drop eight rounded tablespoonfuls of the matzo ball dough into the boiling water. Reduce the heat; cover and simmer for 20-25 minutes or until a toothpick inserted into a matzo ball comes out clean (do not lift the cover while simmering).

4 Strain the broth, discarding the vegetables and seasonings. Carefully remove the matzo balls from water with a slotted spoon; place one matzo ball in each soup bowl. Add broth.

YIELD: 8 servings.

FIDDLEHEAD SOUP

KAREN GRASLEY, QUADEVILLE, ONTARIO
My family loves this delicious soup made with fiddlehead ferns. We have been hunting for and harvesting wild edible plants for a number of years now. Fiddleheads are one of the first plants to sprout in the spring, so we get them while we can. If you like, use asparagus for the soup.

PREP/TOTAL TIME: 30 min.
- 1 cup fiddleheads or sliced fresh asparagus
- 1 cup sliced fresh mushrooms
- 3/4 cup sliced leeks (white portion only)
- 1/4 cup sliced green onions
- 1/2 cup butter, cubed
- 1/4 cup all-purpose flour
- 1/2 teaspoon salt
- 1/8 teaspoon cayenne pepper
- 3 cups milk
- 1 cup chicken broth
- 1 teaspoon lemon juice

1 In a large saucepan, cook the fiddleheads, mushrooms, leeks and onions in butter until the onions are tender, about 4 minutes.

2 Remove from the heat; stir in the flour, salt and cayenne. Gradually add the milk and broth, stirring until blended. Bring to a gentle boil; cook and stir for 10 minutes. Reduce heat; simmer, uncovered, for 10 minutes or until heated through. Stir in lemon juice.

YIELD: 4 servings.

FIDDLEHEAD FERNS
The unfurled fronds of certain fern species have been used for dietary purposes over the centuries by people all over the world. Two species that are harvested in the spring in North America are ostrich and cinnamon ferns. To cook fiddleheads, first remove the brown skin that covers them. Experts suggest cooking fiddleheads thoroughly before consuming them. The recommendation is to boil or steam them for at least 20 minutes to avoid toxins and bitterness.

DELI MONTE CRISTOS

DARLENE VANWIE, CLAYTON, NEW YORK
Looking for a change of pace from the typical Reuben or grilled cheese? This was a famous sandwich in the islands years ago. We make it often, and I always get requests for more. Serve warm with your favorite pickles.

PREP/TOTAL TIME: 10 min.

- 4 slices rye bread
- 4 thin slices deli ham
- 2 thin slices deli turkey
- 2 tablespoons deli coleslaw
- 2 tablespoons Thousand Island salad dressing
- 2 slices Swiss cheese
- 2 eggs

1 On two slices of bread, layer a slice of ham and turkey, coleslaw, salad dressing and cheese. Top with remaining ham and bread. In a shallow bowl, whisk the eggs. Dip both sides of sandwiches in eggs.

2 In a nonstick skillet coated with cooking spray, toast the sandwiches over medium heat for 2-3 minutes on each side or until cheese is melted.

YIELD: 2 servings.

TUNA SALAD BISCUIT CUPS

SUSAN JAMES, COKATO, MINNESOTA
These easy biscuit "boats" are filled with a tasty tuna salad that gets a nice crunch from water chestnuts. They're great for buffets and fast meals on the go.

PREP/TOTAL TIME: 25 min.

- 1 tube (12 ounces) refrigerated buttermilk biscuits
- 1/2 cup mayonnaise
- 2 tablespoons sweet pickle relish
- 1 tablespoon soy sauce
- 1/4 teaspoon dill weed
- 1 can (12 ounces) tuna, drained and flaked
- 1 can (8 ounces) water chestnuts, drained and finely chopped

1 Flatten each biscuit into a 3-in. circle and press into a greased muffin cup. Bake at 400° for 10-12 minutes or until golden brown. Cool for 5 minutes on a wire rack.

2 Meanwhile, in a small bowl, combine the mayonnaise, relish, soy sauce and dill. Stir in tuna and water chestnuts. Spoon into biscuit cups. Serve immediately.

YIELD: 5 servings.

SMOOTH STRAWBERRY SOUP

JANICE MITCHELL, AURORA, COLORADO
Each year, we wait impatiently for the strawberries to start producing so we can make this great soup. The berry flavor is complemented by the cinnamon-sugar croutons.

PREP: 15 min. + chilling

- 1 quart strawberries, halved
- 2 cups apple juice
- 1 cup (8 ounces) sour cream
- 1/2 cup packed brown sugar
- 1/2 cup honey
- 2 tablespoons lemon juice
- 1-1/2 cups half-and-half cream
- 3 tablespoons orange juice, optional

CINNAMON-SUGAR CROUTONS:
- 3 slices white bread, crusts removed and cubed
- 2 tablespoons butter
- 1 teaspoon cinnamon-sugar

1 In a large bowl, combine first six ingredients. Place half of the mixture in a blender; cover and process until pureed. Transfer to a large bowl. Repeat with the remaining strawberry mixture.

2 Stir in cream and orange juice if desired. Cover and refrigerate for 2 hours.

3 Meanwhile, for croutons, in a small skillet over medium heat, saute the bread cubes in butter until golden brown. Remove from heat. Sprinkle with the cinnamon-sugar; toss to coat. Cool. Stir the soup before serving; garnish with cinnamon-sugar croutons.

YIELD: 6 servings.

MOM'S EGG SALAD SANDWICHES

TIRZAH LUJAN, WICHITA FALLS, TEXAS

This is the recipe for my mom's favorite sandwich. Green pepper and celery add crunch to the well-flavored and creamy classic sandwich, while fresh tomatoes and lettuce lend a splash of color.

PREP/TOTAL TIME: 15 min.

       1 package (3 ounces) cream cheese, softened
    1/4 cup mayonnaise
       1 tablespoon chili sauce
    1/2 teaspoon salt
    1/8 teaspoon pepper
       8 hard-cooked eggs, chopped
    1/4 cup chopped green pepper
    1/4 cup chopped celery
       2 tablespoons finely chopped onion
       2 tablespoons diced pimientos, drained
       1 tablespoon minced fresh parsley
      12 slices white bread
       6 lettuce leaves
       6 slices tomato

1 In a small bowl, beat the cream cheese, mayonnaise, chili sauce, salt and pepper. Stir in the eggs, green pepper, celery, onion, pimientos and parsley.

2 On six slices of bread, layer lettuce, tomato and 1/2 cup egg salad. Top with remaining bread.

YIELD: 6 servings.

CUCUMBER CHICKEN SALAD SANDWICHES

EVA WRIGHT, GRANT, ALABAMA

I dress up chicken salad with crunchy cucumber and dill for this refreshing sandwich, which is ready in just 10 minutes.

PREP/TOTAL TIME: 10 min.

       1 cup cubed cooked chicken breast
    1/3 cup chopped seeded peeled cucumber
    1/4 cup fat-free mayonnaise
    1/4 teaspoon salt
    1/8 teaspoon dill weed
       2 lettuce leaves
       4 slices tomato
       2 sandwich buns, split

1 In a small bowl, combine the first five ingredients. Place the lettuce and tomato on bun bottoms; top with the chicken salad. Replace bun tops.

YIELD: 2 servings.

CURRY CARROT-LEEK SOUP

VALERIE ENGEL, SAN JOSE, CALIFORNIA

This recipe comes from an old Yorkshire cookbook I picked up in England, where leeks are very popular. The curry powder lends just the right amount of zip. I like to serve the soup with French bread, followed by scones with lemon curd for dessert.

PREP: 15 min. **COOK:** 30 min.

       1 pound leeks (white portion only), thinly sliced
       1 pound carrots, coarsely chopped
       2 teaspoons butter
       1 medium potato, peeled and diced
    1/2 teaspoon curry powder
       4 cups reduced-sodium chicken broth
    1/4 teaspoon salt
    1/4 teaspoon pepper

1 In a large saucepan, saute leeks and carrots in butter until leeks are tender. Add potato and curry powder; cook and stir for 2 minutes. Add broth, salt and pepper; bring to a boil.

2 Reduce heat; cover and simmer for 15-20 minutes or until the vegetables are very tender. Cool slightly.

3 Process in batches in a food processor or blender until pureed. Return to the pan; heat through.

YIELD: 6 servings.

CREAMY SPRING SOUP

DORA HANDY, ALLIANCE, OHIO
At the end of a tiring cold day, I wanted something quick and warm to satisfy my hunger. So I created the recipe for this filling soup, which comes together in a flash.

PREP/TOTAL TIME: 25 min.

    1 can (14-1/2 ounces) reduced-sodium chicken broth
    4 fresh asparagus spears, trimmed and cut into 2-inch pieces
    4 baby carrots, julienned
1/2 celery rib, chopped
    1 green onion, chopped
Dash garlic powder
Dash pepper
3/4 cup cooked elbow macaroni
    1 can (5-1/2 ounces) evaporated milk
3/4 cup fresh baby spinach

1 In a large saucepan, combine first seven ingredients. Bring to a boil. Reduce heat; cover. Simmer for 5 minutes or until vegetables are tender. Stir in pasta, milk and spinach; heat through.

YIELD: 2 servings.

ASPARAGUS TIPS
The peak months for buying asparagus are April and May. When buying, look for firm, straight, uniform-size spears. The tips should be closed with crisp stalks. It's best to use asparagus within a few days of purchase. For longer storage, place bundled stalks upright in a bowl filled with 1 inch of water; refrigerate. Or wrap the cut ends in moist paper towels.

SPINACH GARLIC SOUP

MARILYN PARADIS, WOODBURN, OREGON
During the years I owned and operated a deli, and this was one of the most popular soups I served.

PREP: 25 min. **COOK:** 10 min.

    1 package (10 ounces) fresh spinach, trimmed
      and coarsely chopped
    4 cups chicken broth
1/2 cup shredded carrots
1/2 cup chopped onion
    8 garlic cloves, minced
1/3 cup butter, cubed
1/4 cup all-purpose flour
3/4 cup heavy whipping cream
1/4 cup milk
1/2 teaspoon pepper
1/8 teaspoon ground nutmeg

1 In a 5-qt. Dutch oven, bring spinach, broth and carrots to a boil. Reduce heat; simmer 5 minutes, stirring occasionally. Remove from heat; cool to lukewarm.

2 Meanwhile, in a large skillet, saute the onion and garlic in the butter until onion is soft, about 5-10 minutes. Add the flour; cook and stir over low heat for 3-5 minutes. Add to spinach mixture. Cool slightly.

3 Puree in small batches in a blender until finely chopped. Place in a large saucepan. Add the cream, milk, pepper and nutmeg; heat through but do not boil.

YIELD: 4-6 servings.

ARTICHOKE MELTS

JILL GROSS, ROSELLE, ILLINOIS
These open-faced egg and artichoke melts are a favorite at my home. The Dijon mustard adds a nice zip, making them more exciting than plain grilled cheese. When my husband can't make it home for dinner, I treat myself to this sandwich instead of making a whole meal.

PREP/TOTAL TIME: 20 min.

      1 can (14 ounces) water-packed artichoke hearts, rinsed,
        drained and chopped
1-1/2 cups (6 ounces) shredded cheddar cheese
      3 tablespoons mayonnaise
      1 tablespoon Dijon mustard
  1/2 teaspoon dried thyme
      6 slices rye or pumpernickel bread
      3 hard-cooked eggs, sliced

1 In a bowl, combine the artichokes, cheese, mayonnaise, mustard and thyme; set aside. Place bread on a baking sheet; broil 4 in. from the heat until toasted. Turn over. Place egg slices on untoasted side of bread; spread with artichoke mixture. Broil for 3-5 minutes or until cheese is melted and top is golden brown.

YIELD: 3-6 servings.

ASPARAGUS CRESS SOUP

TERESA LILLYCROP, PUSLINCH, ONTARIO

Here's a refreshing soup that combines two spring treats—asparagus and watercress. Serve it as the first course to a special meal with family or friends.

PREP/TOTAL TIME: 30 min.

  3/4 cup chopped green onions
  1/4 cup butter, cubed
    3 tablespoons all-purpose flour
2-1/2 cups chicken broth
1-1/2 pounds fresh asparagus, trimmed and
         cut into 1-inch pieces
  1/2 bunch watercress, stems removed
         (about 1 cup, lightly packed)
1-1/2 cups half-and-half cream
  3/4 teaspoon salt
  1/4 teaspoon white pepper
  1/8 teaspoon cayenne pepper
Sour cream

1 In a large saucepan, saute the onion in butter 3-4 minutes or until soft. Stir in the flour to form a smooth paste. Cook for 2 minutes. Gradually stir in broth and bring to a boil. Add the asparagus and watercress; cover and simmer 5-7 minutes or until vegetables are tender. Cool.

2 In a blender, process soup in batches until smooth. Return all to pan; stir in cream. Heat on low until cooked through (do not boil). Season with the salt, white pepper and cayenne. Serve with a dollop of sour cream.

YIELD: 6 servings.

FENNEL CARROT SOUP

MARLENE BURSEY, WAVERLY, NOVA SCOTIA

This pretty, orange soup is perfect as a first course for a special-occasion dinner. It gets delicious flavor from toasted fennel seeds and curry powder, which are a pleasant complement to the carrots, apple and sweet potato.

PREP: 10 min. COOK: 45 min.

  1/2 teaspoon fennel seed
    1 tablespoon butter
1-1/2 pounds carrots, sliced
    1 medium sweet potato, peeled and cubed
    1 medium apple, peeled and cubed
    3 cans (14-1/2 ounces each) vegetable broth
    2 tablespoons uncooked long grain rice
  1/4 teaspoon curry powder
    1 bay leaf
    1 tablespoon lemon juice
    1 teaspoon salt
  1/4 teaspoon white pepper
    2 tablespoons minced fresh parsley

1 In a large saucepan, saute the fennel seed in butter for 2-3 minutes or until lightly toasted. Add carrots, sweet potato and apple; saute for 5 minutes.

2 Stir in the broth, rice, curry powder and bay leaf; bring to a boil. Reduce heat; cover and simmer for 30 minutes or until rice and vegetables are very tender.

3 Remove from the heat and cool slightly. Discard bay leaf. In a blender, process soup in batches until pureed. Return to saucepan. Stir in lemon juice, salt and pepper. Cook for 5 minutes or until heated through. Sprinkle with parsley.

YIELD: 8 servings.

WATERCRESS

A member of the mustard family, watercress grows in water, and is cultivated as well as found wild near streams and brooks. Like mustard greens, watercress has a peppery and slightly bitter flavor. The leaves are small, a rich green color and crisp; the stems are hollow. When purchasing watercress, choose bunches with vibrantly-colored and crisp leaves, making sure they are not wilted or yellow. Watercress can be used in salads, soups or as a garnish.

SPINACH SAUSAGE SOUP

BONITA KRUGLER, ANDERSON, INDIANA
Chock-full of potatoes, Italian sausage and spinach, this hearty soup is sure to disappear fast. Not only is it delicious and easy to make, but it freezes well. Adjust the amount of chicken broth to suit your family's preference.

PREP/TOTAL TIME: 30 min.

- 1 pound bulk Italian sausage
- 4 cans (14-1/2 ounces each) chicken broth
- 8 small red potatoes, quartered and thinly sliced
- 1 envelope Italian salad dressing mix
- 2 cups fresh spinach or frozen chopped spinach

1 In a large skillet, brown sausage over medium heat until no longer pink. Meanwhile, in a Dutch oven, combine the broth, potatoes and salad dressing mix. Bring to a boil; cover and simmer for 10 minutes or until potatoes are tender.

2 Drain sausage. Add sausage and spinach to broth mixture; heat through.

YIELD: 10 servings (2-1/2 quarts).

GREEK BURGERS

MICHELLE CURTIS, BAKER CITY, OREGON
My stepdad's parents were born in Greece, so when I served these to him he really enjoyed the flavor.

PREP/TOTAL TIME: 25 min.

- 1 tablespoon Dijon mustard
- 1 tablespoon lemon juice
- 1 tablespoon finely chopped onion
- 1 garlic clove, minced
- 1/2 teaspoon dried rosemary, crushed
- 1/2 teaspoon salt
- 1/4 teaspoon pepper
- 1 pound ground lamb
- 4 hamburger buns or hard rolls, split
Sliced cucumbers and tomatoes, optional
Ranch salad dressing, optional

1 In a large bowl, combine the first seven ingredients. Crumble lamb over mixture and mix well. Shape into four patties.

2 Pan-fry, grill or broil until no longer pink. Serve on buns with cucumbers, tomatoes and ranch dressing if desired.

YIELD: 4 servings.

CLUB SANDWICHES

JANET MILLER, MIDLAND, TEXAS
I'm a busy wife, mother, grandmother and great-grandmother, who loves to cook and sew. One of my family's favorite sandwiches is what we call "hunka munka." It makes a satisfying and complete meal.

PREP/TOTAL TIME: 25 min.

- 1/2 cup mayonnaise
- 4 French rolls, split
- 1 cup shredded lettuce
- 8 slices tomato
- 1 medium ripe avocado, peeled and sliced
- 1/4 cup prepared Italian salad dressing
- 1/2 teaspoon coarsely ground pepper
- 12 cooked bacon strips
- 1/2 pound sliced deli turkey
- 1/2 pound sliced deli ham
- 4 slices Swiss cheese

1 Spread mayonnaise over cut sides of rolls. On roll bottoms, layer the lettuce, tomato and avocado. Drizzle with dressing; sprinkle with pepper. Layer with the bacon, turkey, ham and cheese. Replace roll tops.

YIELD: 4 servings.

SIDES, SALADS & BREADS

FEATHERLIGHT SCONES

STEPHANIE MOON-MARTIN, BREMERTON, WISCONSIN
Scones fit into just about every meal. This dough bakes up beautifully into fully golden wedges. We love the tender triangles with butter and cinnamon-sugar.

PREP/TOTAL TIME: 30 min.
- 3 cups all-purpose flour
- 3 teaspoons baking powder
- 1/2 teaspoon baking soda
- 1/2 teaspoon salt
- 1 cup cold butter, cubed
- 1 egg
- 1 cup vanilla yogurt
- 1/2 teaspoon vanilla extract
- 2 teaspoons milk
- Sugar

1 In a large bowl, combine the flour, baking powder, baking soda and salt; cut in butter until the mixture resembles coarse crumbs. Stir in the egg, yogurt and vanilla just until combined. Turn onto a floured surface; knead 6-8 times.

2 Roll into a 9-in. circle; cut into eight wedges. Place on an ungreased baking sheet. Brush the tops with milk; sprinkle with the sugar.

3 Bake the scones at 425° for 12-15 minutes or until golden brown. Serve warm.

YIELD: 8 servings.

PAPAYA-AVOCADO TOSSED SALAD

TASTE OF HOME TEST KITCHEN
Fruit is a terrific addition to green salads in summer. Papaya and avocado add tropical flavor to this refreshing side dish.

PREP/TOTAL TIME: 25 min.
- 4 cups torn red leaf lettuce
- 4 cups torn green leaf lettuce
- 1 medium papaya, peeled, seeded and sliced
- 1 large ripe avocado, peeled and sliced
- 1/2 cup sliced red onion

DRESSING:
- 1/4 cup olive oil
- 3 tablespoons lemon juice
- 1 tablespoon grated lemon peel
- 2 teaspoons white wine vinegar
- 1 teaspoon sugar
- 1/8 teaspoon salt

1 In a large salad bowl, gently toss lettuce, papaya, avocado and onion. In a jar with a tight-fitting lid, combine the dressing ingredients; shake well. Drizzle over salad; toss to coat.

YIELD: 8 servings.

STRAWBERRY-BACON SPINACH SALAD

RUTH HAYWARD, LAKE CHARLES, LOUISIANA
This colorful spinach salad is sweet and crunchy with a tangy dressing. I made it for our prayer group, and everyone enjoyed it.

PREP/TOTAL TIME: 15 min.
- 1 package (6 ounces) fresh baby spinach
- 1 pint fresh strawberries, sliced
- 8 bacon strips, cooked and crumbled
- 1/4 cup chopped red onion
- 1/4 cup chopped walnuts
- 1 cup mayonnaise
- 1/2 cup sugar
- 1/4 cup raspberry vinegar

1 In a salad bowl, combine the spinach, strawberries, bacon, onion and walnuts. In a small bowl or pitcher, combine the mayonnaise, sugar and vinegar. Serve with salad.

YIELD: 6-8 servings.

BACON-CHIVE POTATO SALAD

KAREN WHITE, LAWRENCEBURG, TENNESSEE
This creamy and colorful salad is always requested for all of our picnics. It's so quick to prepare, goes with almost anything and is really yummy while still warm, but just as delicious when chilled! For a potluck, simply double the recipe.

PREP: 30 min. + chilling

2-1/2 pounds small red potatoes
1/2 cup real bacon bits
1/4 cup minced chives
3/4 cup mayonnaise
3/4 teaspoon ground mustard
1/2 teaspoon salt
1/4 teaspoon pepper

1 Place potatoes in a large saucepan and cover with water. Bring to a boil. Reduce heat; cover and cook for 15-20 minutes or until tender. Drain and cool. Cut into wedges; place in a serving bowl. Add bacon and chives.

2 In a small bowl, combine the mayonnaise, mustard, salt and pepper. Spoon over salad; toss to coat. Refrigerate for at least 1 hour before serving.

YIELD: 8 servings.

ONE POTATO, TWO POTATO
When buying potatoes, look for those that are firm, well shaped and free of blemishes. Avoid potatoes that are wrinkled, cracked or sprouting. If kept in a cool, dark, well-ventilated place, most potatoes will keep for up to 2 weeks. However, new potatoes should be used within 4 days of purchase.

When boiling potatoes, drop a pea-size dab of margarine or butter into the water as it comes to a boil. It stops the foam that would otherwise boil over and make a mess.

GARLIC ONION FOCACCIA

CINDY CAMERON, OMAHA, NEBRASKA
I use my bread machine to prepare the dough for this savory Italian flat bread. It's a great addition to any meal. At times, I make it for myself as a main-dish "pizza."

PREP: 25 min. + rising **BAKE:** 15 min.

1 cup water (70° to 80°)
2 tablespoons olive oil
1 tablespoon sugar
1 teaspoon salt
3 cups bread flour
1-1/2 teaspoons active dry yeast
2 large onions, thinly sliced
2 garlic cloves, minced
3 tablespoons butter
1 cup (4 ounces) shredded part-skim mozzarella cheese
2 tablespoons grated Parmesan cheese

1 In a bread machine pan, place the first six ingredients in order suggested by manufacturer. Select dough setting (check dough after 5 minutes of mixing; add 1 to 2 tablespoons of the water or flour if needed).

2 When cycle is completed, turn dough onto floured surface. Roll into 12-in. circle. Transfer to a 14-in. pizza pan coated with cooking spray. Cover; let rise in a warm place until doubled, about 30 minutes.

3 In a large skillet, cook the onions and garlic in butter over medium heat for 15-20 minutes or until onions are golden brown, stirring frequently.

4 With the end of a wooden spoon handle, make indentations in dough at 1-in. intervals. Top with onion mixture and sprinkle with cheese. Bake at 400° for 15-20 minutes or until golden brown. Remove to a wire rack. Cut into wedges and serve warm.

YIELD: 12 servings.

DANDELION JELLY

DONNA BOHATY, ROCKFORD, ILLINOIS
This easy-to-make jelly is a great way to celebrate spring. Its old-fashioned flavor brings back memories of days gone by.

PREP: 30 min. **PROCESS:** 5 min.

- 2 cups dandelion blossoms
- 1 quart water
- 1 package (1-3/4 ounces) powdered fruit pectin
- 5-1/2 cups sugar
- 2 tablespoons orange or lemon extract
- 4 to 6 drops green food coloring, optional

1 In a large saucepan, bring dandelion blossoms and water to a boil; boil for 4 minutes. Strain through a damp jelly bag or cheesecloth, reserving 3 cups liquid. Discard blossoms.

2 In a Dutch oven, combine dandelion liquid and pectin. Bring to a full rolling boil, stirring constantly. Add sugar; return to a full rolling boil. Boil for 1 minute; stirring constantly.

3 Remove from the heat; add extract and food coloring if desired. Skim off foam. Ladle hot mixture into hot sterilized half-pint jars, leaving 1/4-in. headspace. Remove the air bubbles; wipe rims and adjust lids. Process for 5 minutes in a boiling-water canner.

YIELD: about 6 half-pints.

EDITOR'S NOTE: Verify that dandelions have not been treated with chemicals. The processing time listed is for altitudes of 1,000 feet or less. Add 1 minute to the processing time for each 1,000 feet of additional altitude.

BREAD AND BUTTER PICKLES

KAREN OWEN, RISING SUN, INDIANA
My mom always made these crisp pickles when we were kids, and she gave me the recipe. They are pleasantly tart and so good.

PREP: 30 min. **PROCESS:** 15 min. + standing

- 4 pounds cucumbers, sliced
- 8 small onions, sliced
- 1/2 cup canning salt

- 5 cups sugar
- 4 cups white vinegar
- 2 tablespoons mustard seed
- 2 teaspoons celery seed
- 1-1/2 teaspoons ground turmeric
- 1/2 teaspoon ground cloves

1 In a large container, combine the cucumbers, onions and salt. Cover with crushed ice and mix well. Let stand for 3 hours. Drain; rinse and drain again.

2 In a large kettle, combine the sugar, vinegar and seasonings; bring to a boil. Add cucumber mixture; return to a boil. Ladle hot mixture into hot jars, leaving 1/4-in. headspace. Adjust caps. Process for 15 minutes in a boiling-water bath. Remove jars to a wire rack to cool completely.

YIELD: 7 pints.

SPRING SALAD

MARI MALMQUIST, HAYWARD, WISCONSIN
Our family has been savoring this salad for over 75 years. It goes back to my Bavarian grandmother. With a large family to raise, she turned to the garden for inexpensive ingredients. The lightly dressed tomatoes, cucumbers and radishes are still a hit at meals and potlucks today.

PREP: 15 min. + chilling

- 2 medium tomatoes, seeded and chopped
- 2 cups thinly sliced radishes
- 1 large cucumber, quartered, seeded and chopped
- 1/2 cup white vinegar
- 1/2 cup water
- 1/2 cup sugar
- 1/2 teaspoon salt
- 1/4 teaspoon pepper

1 In a large bowl, combine tomatoes, radishes and cucumber. In a small bowl, whisk together the vinegar, water, sugar, salt and pepper until sugar is dissolved. Pour over vegetable mixture; toss to coat evenly. Cover and refrigerate for at least 1 hour. Serve with a slotted spoon.

YIELD: 6 servings.

GREEN GODDESS SALAD DRESSING

PAGE ALEXANDER, BALDWIN CITY, KANSAS

It's no trick to fix this time-honored dressing. Made with fresh ingredients, it's a real treat compared to store-bought dressing.

PREP/TOTAL TIME: 10 min.

- 1 cup mayonnaise
- 1/2 cup sour cream
- 1/4 cup chopped green pepper
- 1/4 cup packed fresh parsley sprigs
- 3 anchovy fillets
- 2 tablespoons lemon juice
- 2 green onion tops, coarsely chopped
- 1 garlic clove, peeled
- 1/4 teaspoon pepper
- 1/8 teaspoon Worcestershire sauce

1 Place all the ingredients in a blender; cover and process until smooth. Transfer to a bowl or jar; cover and store in the refrigerator.

YIELD: 2 cups.

SOUR CREAM 'N' CHIVE BISCUITS

LUCILE PROCTOR, PANGUITCH, UTAH

I grow chives in my front yard and like to use them in as many recipes as I can. These moist, tender biscuits are delectable as well as attractive. Serve them with butter or sliced ham and cheese.

PREP/TOTAL TIME: 30 min.

- 2 cups all-purpose flour
- 1 tablespoon baking powder
- 1/2 teaspoon salt
- 1/4 teaspoon baking soda
- 1/3 cup shortening
- 3/4 cup sour cream
- 1/4 cup milk
- 1/4 cup minced chives

1 In a large bowl, combine dry ingredients. Cut in shortening until the mixture resembles coarse crumbs. With a fork, stir in the sour cream, milk and chives until the mixture forms a ball.

2 On a lightly floured surface, knead five to six times. Roll to 3/4-in. thickness; cut with a 2-in. biscuit cutter. Place on an ungreased baking sheet.

3 Bake the biscuits at 350° for 12-15 minutes or until golden brown. Serve warm.

YIELD: 12-15 biscuits.

BISCUIT BASICS

Here are some rules of thumb when making biscuits. Stir the dry ingredients together with a fork to evenly distribute the baking powder or soda. Use cold butter or shortening, and cut in only until the mixture resembles coarse crumbs. For a more tender biscuit, do not overmix or overknead the dough. When reworking trimmings, handle the dough as little as possible and use as little additional flour as needed. Biscuits are done when they're golden brown on the top and bottom. The sides will always be a little light.

VIDALIA ONION SPINACH SALAD

LOIS FETTING, NELSON, WISCONSIN
Sweet onions and spinach make a delightful combination in this unique spring salad. Onions also star in the tangy Dijon dressing and in the homemade croutons.

PREP/TOTAL TIME: 30 min.

CROUTONS:
 4 cups soft bread crumbs
 1/3 cup finely chopped Vidalia or other sweet onion
 1 tablespoon dried parsley flakes
 6 tablespoons butter, melted
 1 egg, lightly beaten
Oil for frying

DRESSING:
 1/3 cup chopped Vidalia or other sweet onion
 1/3 cup cider vinegar
 1/3 cup honey
 1 teaspoon Dijon mustard
 1/2 cup plus 2 tablespoons olive oil
 1 teaspoon poppy seeds

SALAD:
 16 cups torn fresh spinach
 1/2 pound sliced bacon, cooked and crumbled
 1 medium Vidalia or other sweet onion, sliced and separated into rings

1 In a large bowl, combine bread crumbs, onion and parsley. Stir in butter and egg. Shape into 1/2-in. balls.

2 In an electric skillet, heat 1 in. of oil to 375°. Fry croutons for 10-15 seconds, turning to brown all sides. Drain on paper towels.

3 For the dressing, combine the onion, vinegar, honey and mustard in a blender; cover and process until smooth. While processing, gradually add the olive oil in a steady stream. Stir in the poppy seeds.

4 In a salad bowl, toss spinach, bacon, onion rings and croutons. Serve with dressing.

YIELD: 16 servings.

CARROT RAISIN SALAD

DENISE BAUMERT, DALHART, TEXAS
This traditional salad is one of my mother-in-law's favorites. It's fun to eat because of its crunchy texture, and the raisins give it a slightly sweet flavor. Plus, it's easy to prepare.

PREP/TOTAL TIME: 10 min.
 4 cups shredded carrots (about 4 large)
 3/4 to 1-1/2 cups raisins
 1/4 cup mayonnaise
 2 tablespoons sugar
 2 to 3 tablespoons milk

1 Place the carrots and raisins in a large bowl. In a small bowl, combine the mayonnaise, sugar and enough milk to achieve dressing consistency. Pour over carrot mixture; toss to coat.

YIELD: 8 servings.

STORING HOMEMADE SALAD DRESSINGS
The "shelf life" of homemade salad dressings varies somewhat. In general, vinaigrettes can be kept refrigerated for up to 2 weeks. Dairy-based dressings, like buttermilk, and dressings made with fresh ingredients, like chopped onion, fresh herbs, tomato sauce and chopped hard-cooked egg, will keep up to 1 week.

CREAMED SWEET PEAS

JEAN PATTEN, PINEVILLE, LOUISIANA
Mom's garden in the '40s provided us with many delicious vegetables, but her sweet peas were the best. She would pick them fresh, shell them and fix the best creamed sweet peas ever on her huge woodstove.

PREP/TOTAL TIME: 20 min.

- 1 tablespoon all-purpose flour
- 1/4 cup sugar
- 2/3 cup milk
- 2 cups fresh sweet peas or 1 package (10 ounces) frozen peas, thawed
- 1/4 teaspoon pepper

1 In a large saucepan, combine the flour, sugar and milk. Stir in peas and pepper; bring to a boil. Reduce heat; simmer for 10-12 minutes or until the peas are heated through and sauce has thickened.

YIELD: 4 servings.

SUNSHINE MUFFINS

JOYCE MINGE JOHNS, JACKSONVILLE, FLORIDA
These hearty muffins are packed with goodies like pineapple, coconut, raisins and pecans. We enjoy them with coffee in the morning.

PREP: 15 min. **BAKE:** 20 min. + cooling

- 1-1/2 cups all-purpose flour
- 2/3 cup sugar
- 1 teaspoon baking powder
- 1 teaspoon baking soda
- 1 teaspoon ground cinnamon
- 1/4 teaspoon salt
- 2 eggs
- 1 cup finely shredded carrots
- 2/3 cup vegetable oil
- 1/2 cup crushed pineapple, drained
- 1/2 cup flaked coconut
- 1/2 cup raisins
- 1/2 cup chopped pecans

1 In a bowl, combine flour, sugar, baking powder, baking soda, cinnamon and salt. In another bowl, beat eggs; add carrots, oil and pineapple. Stir into dry ingredients just until moistened. Fold in coconut, raisins and pecans. Fill greased or paper-lined muffin cups two-thirds full.

2 Bake at 350° for 20-25 minutes or until a toothpick inserted near centers comes out clean. Cool in pan 10 minutes; remove from pan and cool on wire rack.

YIELD: about 1 dozen.

LEMON POPPY SEED BREAD

KAREN DOUGHERTY, FREEPORT, ILLINOIS
If the days that you have time for baking are few and far between, try this extra-quick bread. You'll love the ease of preparation and the delicious flavor.

PREP: 10 min. **BAKE:** 35 min. + cooling

- 1 package (18-1/4 ounces) white cake mix
- 1 package (3.4 ounces) instant lemon pudding mix
- 1 cup warm water
- 4 eggs
- 1/2 cup canola oil
- 4 teaspoons poppy seeds

1 In a large bowl, combine the cake mix, pudding mix, water, eggs and oil; beat on low speed for 30 seconds. Beat on medium for 2 minutes. Fold in poppy seeds.

2 Pour into two greased 9-in. x 5-in. loaf pans. Bake at 350° for 35-40 minutes or until a toothpick inserted near the center comes out clean. Cool in pans for 10 minutes before removing to a wire rack.

YIELD: 2 loaves (16 slices each).

GOLDEN BAKED ONIONS

CHRIS GASKILL, KNOXVILLE, TENNESSEE
I love to invent new dishes, but I also enjoy making tried-and-true recipes, like my mom's baked onions. The onions are a rich and satisfying side dish with poultry and beef, but they can also be a meal all by themselves.

PREP: 20 min. **BAKE:** 25 min.

- 6 large sweet onions, thinly sliced
- 1/4 cup butter, cubed
- 1 can (10-3/4 ounces) condensed cream of chicken soup, undiluted
- 1/2 cup milk
- 1/8 teaspoon pepper
- 3 cups (12 ounces) shredded Swiss cheese, divided
- 6 slices French bread (3/4 inch thick)
- 2 tablespoons butter, melted

1 In a large skillet, saute onions in butter until tender. In a large bowl, combine the soup, milk, pepper and 2 cups cheese. Stir in onions.

2 Transfer to a greased 2-qt. baking dish. Sprinkle with the remaining cheese. Brush bread slices with melted butter on one side. Arrange buttered side up over cheese.

3 Bake, uncovered, at 350° for 25-30 minutes or until bubbly. If desired, broil 4-6 in. from heat until bread is golden brown. Let stand for 5 minutes before serving.

YIELD: 6-8 servings.

SWEET ON SWEET ONIONS

Vidalia and other sweet onions are mild-flavored onions that are high in sugar and water content and low in tear-inducing sulfur compounds. Because of these properties, they are not suited for long-term storage, so you should use them within several weeks of purchase. Vidalias are in season during spring, but a variety of other sweet onions are available almost all year long.

SOUR CREAM CUCUMBERS

PAMELA EATON, LAMBERTVILLE, MICHIGAN
My mom always served this sweet-tart cucumber recipe with her Hungarian chicken paprika. The sauce is creamy and the cucumbers have a nice crunch.

PREP: 15 min. + chilling

- 1/2 cup sour cream
- 3 tablespoons white vinegar
- 1 tablespoon sugar
- Pepper to taste
- 4 medium cucumbers, thinly sliced
- 1 small sweet onion, thinly sliced and separated into rings

1 In a serving bowl, combine the sour cream, vinegar, sugar and pepper. Stir in cucumbers and onion. Cover and refrigerate for at least 4 hours. Serve with a slotted spoon.

YIELD: 8 servings.

RISOTTO WITH ASPARAGUS

STEPHANIE MARCHESE, WHITEFISH BAY, WISCONSIN
This is a rich-tasting, elegant dish! It gets great flavor from the onion and wine combination.

PREP: 10 min. **COOK:** 30 min.

- 1 pound asparagus, trimmed and cut into 2-inch pieces
- 7-1/2 cups chicken broth
- 1/2 cup finely chopped onion
- 1/4 cup olive oil
- 3 cups uncooked arborio rice
- 1 cup dry white wine
- 1 tablespoon butter
- 1/4 cup grated Parmesan cheese
- Salt and pepper to taste

1 Place asparagus in a large saucepan; add 1/2 in. of water. Bring to a boil. Reduce heat; cover and simmer for 3 minutes or until crisp-tender. Drain and set aside.

2 In a large saucepan, bring broth to a boil. Reduce the heat; cover and maintain at a simmer. In a large heavy skillet, cook onion in oil over medium heat until tender. Add rice and stir to coat well; cook 3 minutes longer. Add wine and cook until absorbed.

3 Stir in 1 cup simmering broth. Cook until broth is almost completely absorbed, stirring frequently, then add another cup of simmering broth. Repeat until only about 1/4 cup of broth remains (discard remaining broth); the process should take about 20 minutes. Rice should be slightly firm in center and look creamy.

4 Add asparagus; heat through. Remove from the heat; add the butter, Parmesan cheese, salt and pepper. Serve immediately.

YIELD: 12 servings.

MINT DRESSING FOR FRUIT

DIANE THOMPSON, NUTRIOSO, ARIZONA
This mild minty dressing nicely complements fresh fruits such as melon, strawberries, blueberries and peaches.

PREP/TOTAL TIME: 10 min.
- 1/2 cup sour cream
- 2 tablespoons minced fresh mint
- 2 tablespoons minced fresh cilantro
- 2 tablespoons olive oil
- 2 tablespoons cider vinegar
- 1 teaspoon sugar
- 1 teaspoon lemon juice
- 1/2 teaspoon ground cumin
- Assorted fresh fruit

1 In a small bowl, combine the sour cream, mint, cilantro, oil, vinegar, sugar, lemon juice and cumin. Serve with fruit.

YIELD: about 1 cup.

SPRINGTIME SALAD

MOLLY PAYNE, BUFFALO, MINNESOTA
Tender green asparagus and juicy red strawberries star in this colorful salad, which I often make for spring luncheons and showers. It tastes as terrific as it looks!

PREP: 20 min. + chilling
- 1 cup water
- 1 pound fresh asparagus, trimmed
- 1/4 cup sugar
- 1/4 cup canola oil
- 2 tablespoons cider vinegar
- 1-1/2 teaspoons sesame seeds
- 1 teaspoon poppy seeds
- 1 teaspoon grated onion
- 1/4 teaspoon salt
- 1/8 teaspoon paprika
- 1/8 teaspoon Worcestershire sauce
- 2 cups sliced fresh strawberries
- 1/4 cup crumbled blue cheese, optional

1 In a large skillet, bring water to a boil. Add asparagus; cover and boil for 3 minutes. Drain and immediately place asparagus in ice water. Drain and pat dry; set aside.

2 In a jar with a tight-fitting lid, combine the sugar, oil, vinegar, sesame seeds, poppy seeds, onion, salt, paprika and Worcestershire sauce; shake well. Cover and refrigerate for 1 hour.

3 In a large bowl, combine the asparagus and strawberries. Drizzle with dressing and toss to coat. Sprinkle with crumbled blue cheese if desired.

YIELD: 6 servings.

FESTIVE PEA SALAD

J. O'NEALL, WESTMINSTER, COLORADO
If you have little time and big appetites to satisfy, try this cold pea salad. It's an easy way to get bacon lovers to eat their veggies.

PREP: 15 min. + chilling

    1 package (16 ounces) frozen petite peas, thawed
1-1/2 cups fresh snow peas, trimmed and halved
    1 cup halved thinly sliced red onion
    1 jar (2 ounces) diced pimientos, drained
1/3 cup mayonnaise
1/3 cup sour cream
    1 teaspoon minced fresh mint
1/4 teaspoon salt
1/8 teaspoon white pepper
Dash to 1/8 teaspoon ground nutmeg
    5 bacon strips, cooked and crumbled

1 In a large bowl, combine the peas, onions and pimientos. In a small bowl, combine the mayonnaise, sour cream, mint, salt, pepper and nutmeg.

2 Pour over pea mixture; toss to coat. Cover and refrigerate for at least 1 hour. Just before serving, stir in the bacon.

YIELD: 8 servings.

RHUBARB-RIBBON BRUNCH CAKE

MARY BLENK, CUMBERLAND, MAINE
My dad has always had a flourishing rhubarb patch. So, I knew I should try to create a recipe with his endless supply. This cake can be served at breakfast or as an elegant finish to a special meal.

PREP: 30 min. **BAKE:** 1 hour + cooling

3/4 cup sugar
    3 tablespoons cornstarch
1/4 teaspoon ground cinnamon
1/8 teaspoon ground nutmeg
1/3 cup cold water
2-1/2 cups sliced fresh or frozen rhubarb
    3 to 4 drops food coloring, optional

BATTER:
2-1/4 cups all-purpose flour
 3/4 cup sugar
 3/4 cup cold butter, cubed
 1/2 teaspoon baking powder
 1/2 teaspoon baking soda
 1/2 teaspoon salt
   1 egg, lightly beaten
   1 carton (6 ounces) vanilla yogurt
   1 teaspoon vanilla extract

TOPPING:
   1 egg, beaten
   8 ounces Mascarpone cheese
 1/4 cup sugar
 1/2 cup chopped pecans
 1/4 cup flaked coconut

1 In a large saucepan, combine the sugar, cornstarch, cinnamon, nutmeg and water until smooth. Add rhubarb. Bring to a boil; cook and stir for 2 minutes or until thickened. Add food coloring if desired. Set aside.

2 For batter, in a large bowl, combine flour and sugar; cut in butter until mixture resembles coarse crumbs. Set aside 1 cup for topping. Add the baking powder, baking soda and salt to the remaining crumb mixture. In a small bowl, combine egg, yogurt and vanilla; stir into batter until smooth. Spread into a greased 9-in. springform pan.

3 For topping, combine the egg, Mascarpone cheese and sugar; spoon over the batter. Top with the rhubarb mixture. Add pecans and coconut to reserved crumb mixture; sprinkle over the top.

4 Bake at 350° for 60-65 minutes or until a toothpick inserted near the center comes out clean. Cool on a wire rack for 20 minutes; remove sides of pan. Cool completely.

YIELD: 12 servings.

EDITOR'S NOTE: If using frozen rhubarb, measure rhubarb while still frozen, then thaw completely. Drain in a colander, but do not press liquid out.

SPRING GREENS WITH BERRIES

VIKKI PECK, POLAND, OHIO
My sister-in-law gave me this salad recipe years ago, and it quickly became a family favorite. It's crisp, colorful, goes together in a snap and complements a variety of entrees.

PREP/TOTAL TIME: 15 min.

    2 packages (5 ounces each) spring mix salad greens
    1 can (11 ounces) mandarin oranges, drained
  3/4 cup sliced fresh strawberries
  3/4 cup fresh raspberries
  1/2 cup slivered almonds, toasted

ORANGE VINAIGRETTE:

  1/4 cup canola oil
    1 tablespoon red wine vinegar
    1 tablespoon orange juice
    1 tablespoon honey
    1 teaspoon grated orange peel
    1 teaspoon Dijon mustard
  1/4 teaspoon salt
  1/8 teaspoon pepper

1 In a large bowl, combine the greens, oranges, berries and almonds. In a jar with a tight-fitting lid, combine the vinaigrette ingredients; shake well. Drizzle over salad and toss to coat.

YIELD: 7 servings.

TOUCH OF SPRING MUFFINS

GAIL SYKORA, MENOMONEE FALLS, WISCONSIN
Strawberries and rhubarb are a winning combination, and their sweet-tart pairing makes these lovely muffins delightful as part of a meal or as a snack. Remember this recipe when your backyard rhubarb is ready to cut or you see fresh stalks at the store.

PREP: 10 min. BAKE: 25 min.

    2 cups all-purpose flour
  1/2 cup sugar
    1 tablespoon baking powder
  1/2 teaspoon salt
    1 egg
  3/4 cup milk
  1/3 cup canola oil
  1/2 cup sliced fresh strawberries
  1/2 cup sliced fresh rhubarb

TOPPING:

    6 small fresh strawberries, halved
    2 teaspoons sugar

1 In a large bowl, combine the flour, sugar, baking powder and salt. In a small bowl, beat the egg, milk and oil until smooth. Stir into dry ingredients just until moistened. Fold in strawberries and rhubarb.

2 Fill greased or paper-lined muffin cups three-fourths full with the batter. Place a strawberry half, cut side down, on each. Sprinkle with the sugar.

3 Bake at 375° for 22-25 minutes or until a toothpick inserted near the center comes out clean. Cool for 5 minutes before removing from pan to a wire rack. Serve warm.

YIELD: 1 dozen.

LET'S TALK RHUBARB
Although the leaves of the rhubarb plant are poisonous, the stalks make delicious sauces and baked goods. When using fresh rhubarb, look for stalks that are crisp and brightly colored. Tightly wrap them in a plastic bag and store in the refrigerator for up to 3 days. To use, wash the stalks and remove the poisonous leaves before using. One pound of rhubarb yields about 3 cups chopped.

    To freeze, wash and dry the stalks, chop into 1/2-inch pieces, store in releasable plastic bags and freeze.

55   51   47   52

ENTREES

53

CARAMELIZED ONION BROCCOLI QUICHE

KIM PETTIPAS, OROMOCTO, NEW BRUNSWICK
This is a wonderful recipe for brunch or for supper, paired with a green salad. The combination of broccoli, sweet onions and feta cheese is truly delicious.

PREP: 55 min. + rising **BAKE:** 50 min. + standing

   3 cups sliced sweet onions
   1 teaspoon sugar
1/2 teaspoon salt
   2 teaspoons olive oil
   2 cups frozen shredded hash brown potatoes, thawed
   1 tube (11 ounces) refrigerated breadsticks
   3 cups frozen chopped broccoli, thawed and drained
   1 cup (4 ounces) crumbled feta cheese
   2 eggs
   2 egg whites
3/4 cup fat-free milk

1 In a large nonstick skillet, cook the onions, sugar and salt in oil over low heat for 40 minutes or until onions are softened and liquid has evaporated. Reduce heat to medium-low; add hash browns. Cook 8-10 minutes longer or until potatoes are golden brown. Remove from the heat and set aside.

2 To make the crust, unroll breadstick dough onto a lightly floured surface and separate into strips. Pinch several bread-sticks together, end to end, forming a rope. Holding one end of rope, loosely coil dough to form a circle. Add remaining breadsticks to coil, one at a time, pinching ends together. Tuck end under; pinch to seal. Cover and let rest for 10 minutes.

3 Roll into a 10-1/2-in. to 11-in. circle. Transfer to an ungreased 9-in. pie plate. Spoon onion mixture into crust. Top with the broccoli and cheese.

4 In a large bowl, whisk the eggs, egg whites and milk; pour over cheese (pie plate will be full). Bake 350° for 40 minutes. Cover edges with foil. Bake 10-12 minutes longer or until a knife inserted near the center comes out clean. Let stand for 10 minutes before cutting.

YIELD: 6 servings.

EDITOR'S NOTE: This recipe was tested with Pillsbury refrigerated breadsticks.

PAN-FRIED TROUT

FELICIA CUMMINGS, RAYMOND, MAINE
One summer when my husband and I were enjoying our first "getaway" in years, we found ourselves stranded in our cabin cruiser with a dead battery. When hunger set in, my husband rigged up a fishing line, and soon there were two trout sizzling on the portable grill. We eventually returned home all right...and kept the recipe we'd devised while stranded in the water.

PREP/TOTAL TIME: 20 min.

   4 lake trout fillets (about 8 ounces each)
1/2 cup grated Parmesan cheese
1/2 cup bacon-flavored crackers, crushed
1/2 cup cornmeal
1/4 to 1/2 teaspoon garlic salt
Pinch pepper
   2 eggs
1/2 cup milk
1/2 cup canola oil
Lemon wedges and/or minced chives or parsley, optional

1 Rinse fish in cold water; pat dry. In a shallow bowl, combine the cheese, cracker crumbs, cornmeal, garlic salt and pepper. In another bowl, beat eggs and milk. Dip fish in the egg mixture, then gently roll in the crumb mixture.

2 In a large skillet, fry fish in oil for 3-4 minutes on each side or until it flakes easily with a fork. Garnish with lemon, chives and/or parsley if desired.

YIELD: 4 servings.

TARRAGON CHICKEN KIEV

ANN HARRIS, FRESNO, CALIFORNIA
I like to make this dish when I have company. It's delicious and rich, especially when I use fresh tarragon from my garden.

PREP: 1-1/2 hour + freezing **BAKE:** 20 min.

 6 tablespoons butter, softened, divided
1-1/2 teaspoons minced fresh tarragon or
 1/2 teaspoon dried tarragon
 4 boneless skinless chicken breast halves
Salt, pepper and ground nutmeg to taste
 1 egg
 2 tablespoons water
 1/2 cup all-purpose flour
 1/2 cup dry bread crumbs

LEMON TARRAGON SAUCE:

 3 tablespoons butter
4-1/2 teaspoons all-purpose flour
 1/2 teaspoon ground mustard
1-1/4 cups chicken broth
1-1/2 teaspoons minced fresh tarragon or
 1/2 teaspoon dried tarragon
 2 egg yolks
 1 tablespoon lemon juice

1 In a small bowl, combine 3 tablespoons butter and tarragon; chill. Shape tarragon butter into four 2-in. logs; freeze until firm. Flatten chicken to 1/8-in. thickness; season with salt, pepper and nutmeg. Center a butter log on each chicken breast. Roll up and tuck in ends; secure with a toothpick. In a shallow bowl, beat egg and water. Coat chicken with flour, then dip in egg mixture and roll in bread crumbs. In a skillet, cook chicken in remaining butter until golden brown. Transfer to a greased 8-in. square baking pan. Bake, uncovered, at 350° for 20 minutes or until chicken juices run clear.

2 Meanwhile, for sauce, melt butter in a saucepan over low heat. Stir in flour and mustard until smooth. Gradually stir in broth and tarragon. Bring to a boil; cook and stir for 2 minutes or until thickened. Reduce heat. In a bowl, combine egg yolks and lemon juice. Gradually whisk a small amount of hot mixture into yolks. Return all to the pan, stirring constantly. Cook and stir until sauce reaches 160°, about 1 minute. Discard toothpicks from chicken; serve with sauce.

YIELD: 4 servings.

GREEK SPINACH PIZZA

KAY YOUNG, PORT CLINTON, OHIO
Round out this pizza with a salad or fresh vegetable relish tray. Sometimes, I serve a side of low-fat ranch dressing to dip the veggies and pizza crust.

PREP/TOTAL TIME: 20 min.

 2 cups fresh baby spinach
 3 tablespoons olive oil
 3 teaspoons Italian seasoning
 1 prebaked thin Italian bread shell crust (10 ounces)
 2 plum tomatoes, thinly sliced
 1 cup (4 ounces) crumbled feta cheese
 1/4 cup shredded part-skim mozzarella cheese
 1/4 cup chopped pitted Greek olives
 2 tablespoons chopped sweet onion

1 In a small bowl, toss the spinach, oil and Italian seasoning. Place crust on an ungreased 12-in. pizza pan. Arrange spinach mixture over crust to within 1/2 in. of edge. Place tomatoes on top; sprinkle with the cheeses, olives and onion.

2 Bake at 450° for 10-15 minutes or until cheese is melted and edges are lightly browned.

YIELD: 6-8 slices.

KALAMATA OLIVES
Kalamata olives, also called Greek olives, are purple-black, almond-shaped olives native to Greece. They're usually packed in either olive oil or vinegar, giving them a stronger flavor than most other olives. Kalamata olives can be found in larger supermarkets as well as smaller ethnic grocery stores.

JAPANESE STEAK SALAD

DIANE HALFERTY, CORPUS CHRISTI, TEXAS
We enjoy all kinds of ethnic foods. This beef recipe is easy to make and very tasty. With a sweet soy marinade and fresh veggies, there's lots to love in this main-dish salad.

PREP: 25 min. + marinating **COOK:** 20 min.

3 tablespoons sherry or reduced-sodium chicken broth
3 tablespoons rice vinegar
3 tablespoons reduced-sodium soy sauce
2 tablespoons hoisin sauce
1/2 teaspoon minced fresh gingerroot
1 boneless beef sirloin steak (1 inch thick and 1-1/4 pounds)
2 green onions, chopped
1 tablespoon sugar
1 tablespoon sesame oil
1/3 cup fresh snow peas
3 cups sliced Chinese or napa cabbage
3 cups torn romaine
1/3 cup uncooked instant rice
1/2 cup julienned carrot
1/2 cup thinly sliced cucumber
1/2 cup sliced radishes

1 In a small bowl, combine the first five ingredients. Pour 1/3 cup into a large resealable plastic bag; add beef. Seal bag and turn to coat; refrigerate for at least 2 hours. For dressing, add the onions, sugar and sesame oil to the remaining marinade. Cover and refrigerate until serving.

2 In a small saucepan, bring 1 in. of water to a boil. Add the peas. Reduce heat; cover and simmer for 2-3 minutes or until crisp-tender. Drain and immediately place peas in ice water. Drain and pat dry. Combine the cabbage, romaine and peas; place on a serving platter.

3 Drain and discard marinade. Broil beef 4-6 in. from the heat for 8-10 minutes on each side or until meat reaches desired doneness (for medium-rare, a meat thermometer should read 145°; medium, 160°; well-done, 170°). Let stand for 5 minutes before slicing.

4 Meanwhile, cook rice according to package directions. Arrange the carrot, cucumber and radishes on cabbage mixture. Top with rice and beef; drizzle with dressing.

YIELD: 4 servings.

ANGEL HAIR PASTA WITH GARDEN VEGETABLES

JUNE BARRUS, SPRINGVILLE, UTAH
Boy, this recipe is good! It tastes like a million bucks, but it's done in only a half hour.

PREP/TOTAL TIME: 30 min.

8 ounces uncooked angel hair pasta
1 cup sliced fresh mushrooms
1 cup thinly sliced fresh carrots
1 cup fresh snow peas
1 cup chopped sweet yellow, red or green pepper
1/3 cup chopped fresh basil
2 garlic cloves, minced
2 tablespoons olive oil
2 teaspoons cornstarch
1 cup vegetable broth or chicken broth
1/4 teaspoon salt
3 medium tomatoes, peeled and chopped
1/4 cup grated Parmesan cheese

1 Cook the pasta according to package directions. Meanwhile, in large nonstick skillet, saute the mushrooms, carrots, snow peas, yellow pepper, basil and garlic in oil for 2-3 minutes or until crisp-tender.

2 In a small bowl, combine the cornstarch, broth and salt until smooth; gradually stir into the vegetable mixture. Bring to a boil. Cook and stir for 1-2 minutes or until the vegetables are crisp-tender and sauce is thickened.

3 Remove from heat; stir in tomatoes. Drain pasta; divide among four plates. Top with vegetables; sprinkle with cheese.

YIELD: 4 servings.

SNOW PEA PRIMER
Also called Chinese snow peas, snow peas are a legume similar to beans, lentils, peas and soybeans. However, snow pea pods are entirely edible, not just the seeds. To use, rinse with cold water, remove the strings and cut off the stem ends. Do not shell. If you want to use them raw, blanch before using.

DEEP-DISH CHICKEN POTPIE

BONNIE JEAN LINTICK, KATHRYN, ALBERTA
I adapted this recipe from a cookbook that I have had for many years. It's an excellent way to use up leftover chicken. Even though it takes a bit of time to prepare, everyone agrees it's well worth it. Sometimes I make small individual pies and freeze them to have on hand.

PREP: 25 min. **BAKE:** 50 min.

 2 cups all-purpose flour
1/4 teaspoon salt
2/3 cup cold butter, cubed
1/4 cup cold water

FILLING:
2-1/2 cups cubed cooked chicken
 2 cups fresh or frozen peas
 2 medium potatoes, peeled and cubed
 3 medium carrots, thinly sliced
 2 celery ribs, finely chopped
1/4 cup finely chopped onion
 3 tablespoons butter
 3 tablespoons all-purpose flour
 1 to 2 tablespoons chicken bouillon granules
1-1/2 teaspoons dried tarragon
Pepper to taste
 1 cup milk
1/2 cup chicken broth
Additional milk

1 In a large bowl, combine flour and salt; cut in butter until crumbly. Gradually add water, tossing with a fork until dough forms a ball. Set aside a third of the dough. Roll out remaining dough to fit a 2-1/2-qt. baking dish. Transfer pastry to baking dish; trim even with edge; set aside.

2 For the filling, in a large bowl, combine the chicken, peas, potatoes, carrots, celery and onion; set aside. In a large saucepan, melt butter. Stir in the flour, bouillon, tarragon and pepper until smooth. Gradually stir in the milk and broth. Bring to a boil; cook and stir for 2 minutes or until thickened. Stir into chicken mixture; spoon into crust.

3 Roll out the reserved dough to fit top of pie. Make cutouts in pastry. Place over filling; trim, seal and flute edges. Brush the additional milk over pastry.

4 Bake at 375° for 50-60 minutes or until crust is golden brown and filling is bubbly.

YIELD: 6 servings.

RICE-STUFFED CORNISH HENS

DOROTHY ANDERSON, OTTAWA, KANSAS
These moist golden hens are a tradition at our house on special occasions. We think the spiced rice stuffing with cinnamon, sweet raisins and honey goes so well with the birds and makes the meal a special one.

PREP: 20 min. **BAKE:** 1 hour

3/4 cup chopped onion
3/4 cup chopped celery
1/2 cup butter, softened, divided
 3 cups cooked rice
3/4 cup raisins
1/3 cup chopped walnuts
 3 tablespoons honey
 2 tablespoons lemon juice
3/4 teaspoon ground cinnamon
1/2 teaspoon salt
1/8 teaspoon pepper
 6 Cornish game hens (about 20 ounces each)

1 In a large skillet, saute onion and celery in 3 tablespoons butter until tender; remove from heat. Stir in rice, raisins, walnuts, honey, lemon juice, cinnamon, salt and pepper. Stuff hens.

2 Place on a rack in a large shallow baking pan. Rub remaining butter over skin. Bake, uncovered, at 375° for 1 hour or until a meat thermometer reads 180°.

YIELD: 6 servings.

WILD ASPARAGUS QUICHE

MARY WEAVER, GLENWOOD SPRINGS, COLORADO
I enjoy hunting for wild asparagus, and once I decided to use it to make a quiche. The wild variety tastes best, but store-bought will work, too!

PREP: 45 min. **BAKE:** 25 min.

CRUST:
- 1 cup all-purpose flour
- 1 teaspoon salt
- 1/2 cup shortening
- 1/4 cup cold water

FILLING:
- 1-1/2 cups (12 ounces) 1% cottage cheese
- 4 eggs
- 2 cups 1% milk
- 2 tablespoons all-purpose flour
- 1 teaspoon Dijon mustard
- Dash hot pepper sauce
- 2 cups fresh wild asparagus, cut in 1/2-inch pieces
- 2/3 cup shredded Swiss cheese
- Paprika

1 For crust, in a small bowl, combine the flour and salt. Cut in shortening until mixture forms fine crumbs. Add water; toss with a fork until the mixture forms a ball.

2 On a floured surface, roll out dough to fit 10-in. quiche pan. Transfer pastry to the quiche pan. Trim pastry to 1/2 in. beyond edge of plate; flute edges. Line unpricked pastry shell with a double thickness of heavy-duty foil. Bake at 400° for 5 minutes. Remove foil; bake 5 minutes longer.

3 For filling, in a blender, combine the cottage cheese, eggs, milk, flour, mustard and pepper sauce; cover and process until smooth. Pour into crust.

4 Arrange asparagus evenly over filling. Sprinkle with Swiss cheese and paprika. Bake at 375° for 25-30 minutes or until a knife inserted near the center comes out clean.

YIELD: 6 servings.

ARTICHOKE STEAK SALAD

TASTE OF HOME TEST KITCHEN
Loaded with veggies and laced with a tasty herb dressing, this satisfying, grilled-steak salad from our Test Kitchen boasts an easygoing elegance. Pair it with a crusty loaf of bread and red wine or iced tea for a patio dinner or picnic.

PREP/TOTAL TIME: 25 min.
- 2 pounds boneless beef sirloin steaks
- 12 cherry tomatoes
- 1 medium red onion, sliced
- 1 jar (7-1/2 ounces) marinated artichoke hearts, drained and sliced
- 1 cup sliced fresh mushrooms
- 1/4 cup red wine vinegar
- 1/4 cup olive oil
- 1 teaspoon sugar
- 1 teaspoon salt
- 1/2 teaspoon dried oregano
- 1/2 teaspoon dried rosemary, crushed
- 1/2 teaspoon pepper
- 1/2 teaspoon minced garlic
- 6 cups torn fresh spinach

1 Grill steaks, covered, over medium heat or broil 4 in. from the heat for 5-7 minutes on each side or until meat reaches desired doneness (for medium-rare, a meat thermometer should read 145°; medium, 160°; well-done, 170°).

2 Meanwhile, in a large bowl, combine the tomatoes, onion, artichokes and mushrooms. In a small bowl, whisk the vinegar, oil, sugar, salt, oregano, rosemary, pepper and garlic. Pour over vegetable mixture; toss to coat.

3 Thinly slice steaks across the grain. Add beef and spinach to vegetable mixture; toss to coat.

YIELD: 6 servings.

CHIVE-HAM BRUNCH BAKE

EDIE DESPAIN, LOGAN, UTAH
Canned ham and biscuit mix get this brunch dish ready quickly. To lighten up the casserole a bit, try using fat-free milk and a reduced-fat biscuit/baking mix.

PREP: 15 min. **BAKE:** 25 min.

 1/2 cup chopped onion
   1 tablespoon butter
   1 can (5 ounces) chunk ham, drained
   1 medium tomato, chopped
   2 cups biscuit/baking mix
 1/2 cup water
   1 cup (4 ounces) shredded Swiss or cheddar cheese
   2 eggs
 1/4 cup milk
 1/4 teaspoon dill weed
 1/4 teaspoon salt
 1/8 teaspoon pepper
   3 tablespoons minced chives

1 In a small skillet, saute onion in butter until tender. Stir in ham and tomato; set aside.

2 In a small bowl, combine biscuit mix and water. Press onto the bottom and 1/2 in. up the sides of a greased 13-in. x 9-in. baking dish. Spread ham mixture over the crust; sprinkle with cheese. In a bowl, beat the eggs, milk, dill, salt and pepper; pour over cheese. Sprinkle with chives.

3 Bake, uncovered, at 350° for 25-30 minutes or until a knife inserted near center comes out clean. Let stand for 5 minutes before cutting.

YIELD: 8 servings.

CHIVES APLENTY
As the smallest species of the onion family, chives are referred to in the plural form because they grow in clumps. Often planted to repel certain types of insects, the leaves are chopped and used to add a light onion flavor to omelettes, soups, salads and more. Chives can be stored in the refrigerator for a few days. Or, mince them and store in a plastic container in the freezer.

RACK OF LAMB WITH FIGS

SYLVIA CASTANON, LONG BEACH, CALIFORNIA
Your Easter dinner guests are sure to enjoy this special preparation of roasted lamb that is served with a full-bodied sauce made with port wine and figs. I got the recipe from my grandmother and get lots of requests for it. My butcher prepares the French-cut rack of lamb for me.

PREP: 30 min. **BAKE:** 25 min.

   2 racks of lamb (2 pounds each)
   1 teaspoon salt, divided
   1 cup water
   1 small onion, finely chopped
   1 garlic clove, minced
   1 tablespoon canola oil
   2 tablespoons cornstarch
   1 cup port wine or 1/2 cup grape juice plus 1/2 cup reduced-sodium beef broth
  10 dried figs, halved
 1/4 teaspoon pepper
 1/2 cup coarsely chopped walnuts, toasted

1 Rub the lamb with 1/2 teaspoon salt. Place meat side up on a rack in a greased roasting pan. Bake, uncovered, at 375° for 25-30 minutes or until meat reaches desired doneness (for medium-rare, a meat thermometer should read 145°; medium, 160°; well-done, 170°).

2 Remove to a serving platter; cover loosely with foil. Add 1 cup water to roasting pan; stir to loosen browned bits from pan. Using a fine sieve, strain mixture; set drippings aside.

3 In a small saucepan, saute the onion and garlic in oil until tender. Stir in the cornstarch until blended; gradually add the wine, drippings, figs, pepper and the remaining salt. Bring to a boil. Reduce the heat to medium-low; cook, uncovered, until the figs are tender and sauce is thickened, about 10 minutes, stirring occasionally.

4 Sprinkle walnuts over lamb; serve with fig sauce.

YIELD: 6-8 servings.

TORTELLINI PRIMAVERA

SUSIE PIETROWSKI, BELTON, TEXAS

This decadent tortellini with spinach, mushrooms and tomatoes always brings compliments. Dressed up with fresh Parmesan cheese, no one even notices it's meatless!

PREP/TOTAL TIME: 30 min.

- 1 package (19 ounces) frozen cheese tortellini
- 1/2 pound sliced fresh mushrooms
- 1 small onion, chopped
- 2 garlic cloves, minced
- 2 teaspoons butter
- 2/3 cup fat-free milk
- 1 package (8 ounces) fat-free cream cheese, cubed
- 1 package (10 ounces) frozen chopped spinach, thawed and squeezed dry
- 1 teaspoon Italian seasoning
- 1 large tomato, chopped
- 1/4 cup shredded Parmesan cheese

1 Cook tortellini according to package directions. Meanwhile, in a large nonstick skillet coated with cooking spray, saute the mushrooms, onion and garlic in butter until tender. Stir in milk; heat through. Stir in cream cheese until blended. Add spinach and Italian seasoning; heat through.

2 Drain tortellini; toss with sauce and tomato. Sprinkle with Parmesan cheese.

YIELD: 5 servings.

REFRESHING SIDE SALAD

A light, crispy side salad is a tasty accompaniment to the Tortellini Primavera. In a jar with a tight-fitting lid, combine 1/4 cup each lemon juice and olive oil, 2 tablespoons balsamic vinegar, 2 minced garlic cloves, 1 teaspoon each salt, lemon peel and Dijon mustard, and 1/2 teaspoon pepper; shake. Simply toss with 5 cups of your favorite greens, such as Boston lettuce or Romaine.

SAVORY OMELET CUPS

JOAN CHURCHILL, DOVER, NEW HAMPSHIRE

I replaced the pastry portion of this recipe with a light crepe-like cup. Baked in tiny oven-proof dishes, they're filled with cheese, leeks, scallions, olives and sun-dried tomatoes. My son, a vegetarian, always asks for them.

PREP: 40 min. BAKE: 10 min.

- 1/4 cup sun-dried tomatoes (not packed in oil)
- 1/2 cup water, divided
- 3 eggs
- 6 egg whites
- 2 tablespoons minced fresh cilantro
- 4 teaspoons butter, melted
- 1/2 teaspoon salt
- 1/4 teaspoon pepper
- 1/3 cup shredded provolone cheese
- 1 cup chopped leeks (white portion only)
- 2 green onions, chopped
- 1 tablespoon olive oil
- 2 tablespoons chopped Greek olives
- 2 teaspoons minced fresh oregano or 1/2 teaspoon dried oregano
- 1/4 cup grated Parmesan cheese
- 1 tablespoon honey

1 Place tomatoes in a small bowl. Cover with 1/4 cup water; let stand for 30 minutes. Meanwhile, in a large bowl, whisk the eggs, egg whites, cilantro, butter, salt, pepper and remaining water.

2 Heat an 8-in. nonstick skillet coated with cooking spray; pour about 1/2 cup egg mixture into center of skillet. Lift and tilt pan to evenly coat the bottom. Cook for 1-1/2 to 2 minutes or until top appears dry; turn and cook 30-45 seconds longer or until set. Remove from pan and press into a 1-cup baking dish or ramekin coated with cooking spray. Repeat with remaining egg mixture, making three more omelet cups (coat skillet with cooking spray as needed). Sprinkle provolone cheese into cups.

3 Drain the tomatoes; chop and set aside. In a large nonstick skillet, saute leeks and onions in oil until tender. Stir in tomatoes, olives and oregano; cook over medium heat for 2-3 minutes. Spoon into omelet cups. Sprinkle with the Parmesan cheese; drizzle with honey.

4 Bake at 350° for 10-12 minutes or until heated through.

YIELD: 4 servings.

SALMON WITH CREAMY DILL SAUCE

SUSAN EMERY, EVERETT, WASHINGTON
There's nothing like fresh salmon, and my mom bakes it just right so it nearly melts in your mouth. The sour cream sauce is subtly seasoned with dill and horseradish so that it doesn't overpower the delicate salmon flavor.

PREP/TOTAL TIME: 30 min.

- 1 salmon fillet (about 2 pounds)
- 1 to 1-1/2 teaspoons lemon-pepper seasoning
- 1 teaspoon onion salt
- 1 small onion, sliced and separated into rings
- 6 lemon slices
- 1/4 cup butter

DILL SAUCE:
- 1/3 cup sour cream
- 1/3 cup mayonnaise
- 1 tablespoon finely chopped onion
- 1 teaspoon lemon juice
- 1 teaspoon prepared horseradish
- 3/4 teaspoon dill weed
- 1/4 teaspoon garlic salt

Pepper to taste

1 Line a 15-in. x 10-in. x 1-in. baking pan with heavy-duty foil; grease lightly. Place salmon skin side down on foil. Sprinkle with lemon-pepper and onion salt. Top with onion and lemon. Dot with butter. Fold foil around salmon; seal tightly,

2 Bake at 350° for 20 minutes. Open foil. Broil 4-6 in. from the heat for 8-12 minutes or until the fish flakes easily with a fork.

3 Combine the sauce ingredients until smooth. Serve with the salmon.

YIELD: 6 servings.

ROASTED CHICKEN WITH ROSEMARY

ISABEL ZIENKOSKY, SALT LAKE CITY, UTAH
This is a lot like pot roast, only it uses chicken instead of beef. The rosemary gives it a sweet taste and blends well with the garlic, butter and parsley.

PREP: 20 min. BAKE: 2 hours + standing

- 1/2 cup butter, cubed
- 4 tablespoons minced fresh rosemary or 2 tablespoons dried rosemary, crushed
- 2 tablespoons minced fresh parsley
- 3 garlic cloves, minced
- 1 teaspoon salt
- 1/2 teaspoon pepper
- 1 whole roasting chicken (5 to 6 pounds)
- 6 small red potatoes, halved
- 6 medium carrots, halved lengthwise and cut into 2-inch pieces
- 2 medium onions, quartered

1 In a small saucepan, melt butter; stir in the seasonings. Place chicken breast side up on a rack in a roasting pan; tie drumsticks together with kitchen string. Spoon half of the butter mixture over chicken. Place the potatoes, carrots and onions around chicken. Drizzle remaining butter mixture over vegetables.

2 Cover and bake at 350° for 1-1/2 hours, basting every 30 minutes. Uncover; bake 30-60 minutes longer or until a meat thermometer reaches 180° and the vegetables are tender, basting occasionally.

3 Cover with foil and let stand for 10-15 minutes before carving. Serve with vegetables.

YIELD: 9 servings.

BATTER-FRIED FISH

NANCY JOHNSON, CONNERSVILLE, INDIANA
Whether I'm fixing cod fillets or my husband's catch of the day, this batter makes the fish fry up golden and crispy. Club soda gives it a different twist...and the sweet and zippy sauce complements the fish nicely.

PREP/TOTAL TIME: 15 min.
- 1/2 pound cod
- 2 tablespoons all-purpose flour
- 2 to 3 tablespoons cornstarch
- 1/4 teaspoon each garlic powder, onion powder, salt, cayenne pepper and paprika
- 1/8 teaspoon dried oregano
- 1/8 teaspoon dried thyme
- 1/3 cup club soda
- Oil for frying
- 1/4 cup orange marmalade
- 1 to 2 tablespoons prepared horseradish

1 Rinse fillets in cold water; pat dry. Place the flour in a large resealable plastic bag; add fish one piece at a time. Seal bag; toss to coat. In a shallow bowl, combine the cornstarch, seasonings and soda.

2 In a heavy skillet, heat 1 in. of oil. Dip floured fillets into the batter; fry over medium heat for 2-3 minutes on each side or until the fish flakes easily with a fork. Combine marmalade and horseradish; spoon over fish.

YIELD: 2 servings.

SLOW-COOKED BEEF BRISKET

ANNA STODOLAK, VOLANT, PENNSYLVANIA
When my husband and I were both working full-time, we loved this recipe's 10-hour cook time. The beef brisket tastes so good after simmering all day in the crockpot, and the cinnamon and chili sauce add a unique touch to the gravy.

PREP: 10 min. COOK: 8-1/2 hours
- 1 large onion, sliced
- 1 fresh beef brisket (3 to 4 pounds), cut in half
- 1/4 teaspoon pepper
- 1 jar (4-1/2 ounces) sliced mushrooms, drained
- 3/4 cup beef broth
- 1/2 cup chili sauce
- 1/4 cup packed brown sugar
- 2 garlic cloves, minced
- 1/4 cup all-purpose flour
- 1/4 cup cold water

1 Place onion in a 5-qt. slow cooker. Rub brisket with pepper; place over onion. Top with mushrooms. In a bowl, combine the broth, chili sauce, brown sugar and garlic; pour over brisket. Cover and cook on low for 8-9 hours or until meat is tender.

2 Remove brisket and keep warm. In a small bowl, combine flour and water until smooth; stir into cooking juices. Cover and cook on high for 30 minutes or until thickened. Slice brisket; serve with gravy.

YIELD: 6-8 servings.

EDITOR'S NOTE: This is a fresh beef brisket, not corned beef.

SELECTING BEEF BRISKET
Most cuts of fresh beef brisket you'll find at the grocery store are trimmed first cut, which weigh 3 to 4 pounds (this is what you want to use for the recipe above). A whole brisket is actually made of two cuts, the first cut and a smaller, triangular second cut, which is attached to the first cut. A butcher will usually have the two separated. When at the grocery store, be sure the beef brisket is labeled according to what kind you need.

CHICKEN TOSTADAS WITH MANGO SALSA

ERIN RENOUF MYLROIE, SANTA CLARA, UTAH
The ginger adds a pleasant zing to this twist on a traditional tostada. It's so easy to eat healthful foods when good fresh salsa is around.

PREP: 30 min. + marinating **COOK:** 20 min.

- 1/3 cup orange juice
- 5 tablespoons lime juice, divided
- 1 teaspoon garlic powder
- 1 teaspoon ground cumin
- 1 pound boneless skinless chicken breast halves
- 2 medium mangoes, peeled and diced
- 1 small red onion, chopped
- 1/2 cup minced fresh cilantro
- 1 serrano pepper, seeded and minced
- 2 tablespoons finely chopped candied ginger
- 1 tablespoon brown sugar
- 1/4 teaspoon salt
- 6 corn tortillas (6 inches)
- 3 cups coleslaw mix
- 6 tablespoons sour cream

1 In a large resealable plastic bag, combine the orange juice, 3 tablespoons lime juice, garlic powder and cumin; add chicken. Seal bag and turn to coat; refrigerate for at least 20 minutes.

2 For salsa, in a small bowl, combine the mangoes, onion, cilantro, serrano pepper, ginger, brown sugar, salt and remaining lime juice. Cover and chill until serving.

3 Drain and discard marinade. Place chicken on a broiler pan coated with cooking spray. Broil 4-6 in. from heat for 5-7 minutes on each side or until a meat thermometer reads 170°. Cut into thin strips.

4 In a nonstick skillet, cook the tortillas over medium heat for 1-2 minutes on each side or until lightly browned. Top each with coleslaw mix, chicken, mango salsa and sour cream.

YIELD: 6 servings.

EDITOR'S NOTE: When cutting hot peppers, disposable gloves are recommended. Avoid touching your face.

COQ AU VIN

LINDA CLARK, STONEY CREEK, ONTARIO
Don't let the name fool you, this upscale classic is deliciously home-style. The dish with potatoes, chicken, carrots has a ton of flavor in every bite.

PREP: 20 min. **BAKE:** 50 min.

- 6 medium red potatoes, quartered
- 1/2 cup water
- 2 medium carrots, sliced
- 1 can (10-3/4 ounces) condensed cream of mushroom soup, undiluted
- 1/2 cup white wine or chicken broth
- 1-1/2 teaspoons chicken bouillon granules
- 1 teaspoon minced garlic
- 1/2 teaspoon dried parsley flakes
- 1/4 teaspoon dried thyme
- 1/4 teaspoon pepper
- 4 boneless skinless chicken breast halves (6 ounces each)
- 1/2 pound sliced fresh mushrooms
- 4 bacon strips, cooked and crumbled
- 1/3 cup chopped green onions

1 Place potatoes and water in a microwave-safe dish; cover and microwave on high for 3 minutes. Add carrots; cook 4 minutes longer or until vegetables are tender. Drain.

2 In a large bowl, combine the soup, wine or broth, bouillon, garlic, parsley, thyme and pepper. Cut each chicken breast half into three pieces. Add the chicken, potato mixture, mushrooms, bacon and onions to soup mixture; stir to coat.

3 Transfer to a greased 13-in. x 9-in. baking dish. Cover and bake at 350° for 50-55 minutes or until chicken juices run clear.

YIELD: 6 servings.

 58

 68

 68

 70

DESSERTS

 60

STRAWBERRY CUSTARD TORTE

BRENDA BODNAR, EUCLID, OHIO

This elegant dessert is as beautiful as it is delicious. Not only is it ultra-easy to prepare, but it's a make-ahead recipe, so there's no last-minute fussing when company is coming.

PREP: 30 min. + chilling **BAKE:** 30 min. + cooling

   1 package (18-1/4 ounces) yellow cake mix
1/3 cup sugar
   1 tablespoon cornstarch
1/8 teaspoon salt
   1 cup milk
   2 egg yolks, lightly beaten
   1 tablespoon butter
   1 teaspoon vanilla extract
   1 carton (8 ounces) frozen whipped topping, thawed
   1 package (12 ounces) frozen sweetened sliced strawberries, thawed and drained
Sliced fresh strawberries and mint leaves, optional

1 Prepare and bake the cake according to package directions, using two greased and floured 9-in. round baking pans. Cool for 10 minutes; remove from pans to wire racks to cool completely.

2 In a saucepan, combine sugar, cornstarch and salt; gradually stir in milk until smooth. Bring to a boil over medium heat; cook and stir for 2 minutes or until thickened. Remove from the heat. Stir a small amount of the hot filling into egg yolks; return all to pan, stirring constantly. Bring to a gentle boil; cook and stir for 2 minutes. Remove from the heat. Stir in butter and vanilla. Cover and refrigerate until chilled.

3 Place half of the whipped topping in a large bowl; add the strawberries. Cut each cake horizontally into two layers. Place bottom layer on a serving plate; spread with half of strawberry mixture. Top with a second cake layer; spread with custard. Top with a third cake layer; spread with remaining strawberry mixture. Top with remaining cake layer and whipped topping. Refrigerate overnight. Garnish with strawberries and mint if desired.

YIELD: 12 servings.

POPPY SEED CHIFFON CAKE

BARBARA SONSTEBY, MESA, ARIZONA
This terrific cake recipe was given to me by my grandchild. I hope you enjoy it as much as we do.

PREP: 35 min. **BAKE:** 50 min. + cooling

   7 eggs, separated
1/2 cup poppy seeds
   1 cup hot water
   2 cups all-purpose flour
1-1/2 cups sugar
   3 teaspoons baking powder
   1 teaspoon salt
1/4 teaspoon baking soda
   1 cup canola oil
   2 teaspoons vanilla extract
1/2 teaspoon cream of tartar

1 Let eggs stand at room temperature for 30 minutes. In a small bowl, soak poppy seeds in hot water for 15 minutes.

2 In a large bowl, combine the flour, sugar, baking powder, salt and baking soda. In a bowl, whisk the egg yolks, oil, vanilla and poppy seeds with water. Add to dry ingredients; beat until well blended. In another large bowl, beat egg whites and cream of tartar until stiff peaks form. Fold into batter.

3 Pour into an ungreased 10-in. tube pan. Cut through the batter with a knife to remove the air pockets. Bake at 350° for 50-55 minutes or until cake springs back when lightly touched.

4 Immediately invert pan; cool completely, about 1 hour. Run a knife around side and center tube of pan. Remove cake to a serving plate.

YIELD: 12-16 servings.

BERRY CREAM PIE

SUE YAEGER, BOONE, IOWA

I found this recipe in an old cookbook and made it for a family gathering. The pie was gone in no time. It's a perfect springtime treat.

PREP: 15 min. COOK: 15 min. + chilling

FILLING:
- 1/2 cup sugar
- 3 tablespoons cornstarch
- 3 tablespoons all-purpose flour
- 1/2 teaspoon salt
- 2 cups milk
- 1 egg, lightly beaten
- 1/2 teaspoon vanilla extract
- 1/2 teaspoon almond extract, optional
- 1/2 cup heavy whipping cream
- 1 pastry shell (9 inches), baked

GLAZE:
- 1/2 cup crushed strawberries
- 1/2 cup water
- 1/4 cup sugar
- 2 teaspoons cornstarch
- 1-1/2 cups quartered strawberries
- 1-1/2 cups fresh raspberries

1 In a large saucepan, combine the sugar, cornstarch, flour and salt; gradually stir in milk until smooth. Cook and stir over medium-high heat until thickened and bubbly. Reduce heat; cook and stir 2 minutes more.

2 Remove from heat and stir a small amount of the hot filling into egg; return all to saucepan, stirring constantly. Bring to a gentle boil; cook and stir for 2 minutes. Remove from the heat; gently stir in vanilla and almond extract if desired. Cool to room temperature.

3 In a small bowl, beat the cream until stiff peaks form; fold into filling. Pour into pastry shell. Chill for at least 2 hours.

4 Prepare glaze 2 hours before serving. In a large saucepan, combine crushed strawberries and water; cook for 2 minutes.

Combine sugar and cornstarch; gradually add to the pan. Cook and stir until thickened and clear; strain. Cool for 20 minutes.

5 Meanwhile, arrange quartered strawberries and raspberries over filling; pour glaze evenly over berries. Refrigerate for 1 hour.

YIELD: 6-8 servings.

LEMON CAKE CUSTARD

BRENDA SANDERS, HAMPSTEAD, NORTH CAROLINA

This old-time dessert is still a wonderful finale to a meal. It's light and rich at the same time, with a wonderful lemon flavor. I hope you enjoy it.

PREP: 20 min. + standing BAKE: 25 min.

- 3 eggs
- 1 cup sugar, divided
- 1/4 cup all-purpose flour
- 1/4 teaspoon salt
- 1-1/4 cups milk
- 1/3 cup lemon juice
- 2 tablespoons butter, melted
- 1 tablespoon grated lemon peel

1 Separate the eggs and let stand at room temperature for 30 minutes. In a large bowl, combine 1/2 cup sugar, flour and salt. Stir in the milk, lemon juice, butter and lemon peel. Beat egg yolks; add to lemon mixture.

2 In a small bowl, beat egg whites on medium speed until soft peaks form. Gradually add remaining sugar, 2 tablespoons at a time, beating on high until stiff peaks form and the sugar is dissolved. Fold into lemon mixture.

3 Spoon into six greased 8-oz. ramekins or baking dishes. Place in a 13-in. x 9-in. baking pan. Add 1 in. of hot water to pan.

4 Bake custard, uncovered, at 350° for 25-30 minutes or until a toothpick inserted near center comes out clean. Serve immediately or chill.

YIELD: 6 servings.

STRAWBERRY RHUBARB TORTE

KATHLEEN KOWSKI, TRINITY, NORTH CAROLINA
This pretty, airy cake will delight your tastebuds! My children, especially my son, really enjoyed this dessert while they were growing up.

PREP: 40 min. + chilling

- 2 cups sliced fresh or frozen rhubarb
- 1/3 cup water
- 2 tablespoons plus 4-1/2 teaspoons sugar, divided
- 3 tablespoons plus 1 teaspoon strawberry gelatin
- 2/3 cup heavy whipping cream
- 1/4 teaspoon vanilla extract
- 14 ladyfingers, split
- 1 teaspoon cornstarch
- 1 teaspoon cold water
- 1/2 cup sliced fresh strawberries

1 In a small saucepan, bring rhubarb, water and 2 tablespoons sugar to a boil. Reduce the heat; simmer, uncovered, for 6-8 minutes or until rhubarb is tender. Cool slightly. Cover and refrigerate 1/3 cup rhubarb liquid for glaze.

2 Place rhubarb and remaining liquid in a blender; cover and process until pureed. Return to saucepan. Bring to a boil; stir in gelatin until dissolved. Refrigerate for at least 15 minutes or until slightly thickened.

3 Meanwhile, in a large bowl, beat the cream until it begins to thicken. Add vanilla; beat until stiff peaks form. Fold whipped cream into rhubarb mixture.

4 Arrange half of the ladyfingers on bottom of an ungreased 6-in. springform pan. Spread half of the rhubarb mixture into pan. Arrange the remaining ladyfingers over rhubarb mixture;

carefully spread with remaining rhubarb mixture. Refrigerate for 8 hours or overnight.

5 Transfer reserved rhubarb liquid to a small saucepan; stir in remaining sugar. Bring to a boil. Combine the cornstarch and water until smooth. Gradually stir into pan. Bring to a boil; cook and stir for 2 minutes or until thickened. Spread over rhubarb layer. Arrange strawberry slices over glaze. Remove sides of pan.

YIELD: 4 servings.

BERRY SHORTBREAD DREAMS

MILDRED SHERRER, FORT WORTH, TEXAS
Raspberry jam adds fruity sweetness to these rich-tasting cookies. They will absolutely melt in your mouth!

PREP: 20 min. + chilling **BAKE:** 15 min.

- 1 cup butter, softened
- 2/3 cup sugar
- 1/2 teaspoon almond extract
- 2 cups all-purpose flour
- 1/3 to 1/2 cup seedless raspberry jam

GLAZE:

- 1 cup confectioners' sugar
- 1/2 teaspoon almond extract
- 2 to 3 teaspoons water

1 In a large bowl, cream butter and sugar until light and fluffy. Beat in extract; gradually add the flour until dough forms a ball. Cover and refrigerate for 1 hour or until dough is easy to handle.

2 Roll into 1-in. balls. Place 1 in. apart on ungreased baking sheets. Using the end of a wooden spoon handle, make an indentation in the center. Fill with jam.

3 Bake at 350° for 14-18 minutes or until edges are lightly browned. Remove to wire racks to cool. Spoon additional jam into cookies if desired. Combine confectioners' sugar, extract and enough water to achieve drizzling consistency; drizzle over cookies.

YIELD: about 3-1/2 dozen.

SIX-LAYER COCONUT CAKE

ANGELA LEINENBACH, MECHANICSVILLE, VIRGINIA

I found this recipe when going through my grandmother's old files. There's nothing quite like a slice of this traditional Southern cake. The creamy filling has a wonderful orange flavor, and the frosting is chock-full of coconut. It is simply the best.

PREP: 70 min. + chilling **BAKE:** 25 min.

- 1 cup butter, softened
- 3 cups sugar
- 3 teaspoons vanilla extract
- 4 cups cake flour
- 1 teaspoon baking soda
- 1/2 teaspoon each baking powder and salt
- 2 cups buttermilk
- 6 egg whites

FILLING:
- 1/2 cup sugar
- 2 tablespoons cornstarch
- 1 cup orange juice
- 4 eggs, lightly beaten
- 1/4 cup butter
- 2 tablespoons grated orange peel
- 1 teaspoon orange extract

FROSTING:
- 1 cup sugar
- 2 egg whites
- 1/2 cup water
- 1/4 teaspoon salt
- 1/8 teaspoon cream of tartar
- 1/4 teaspoon vanilla extract
- 2 cups flaked coconut

1 In a large bowl, cream butter and sugar until light and fluffy. Add vanilla. Combine the flour, baking soda, baking powder and salt; add to creamed mixture alternately with buttermilk. In another large bowl and with clean beaters, beat egg whites on high speed until stiff peaks form; gently fold into batter.

2 Pour the cake batter into three greased and floured 9-in. round baking pans. Bake at 350° for 25-30 minutes or until a toothpick inserted near the center of each cake comes out clean. Cool for 10 minutes; Remove cakes from pans to wire racks to cool completely.

3 For the filling, in a saucepan, combine sugar and cornstarch. Gradually stir in the orange juice until smooth. Cook and stir over medium-high heat until thickened and bubbly. Reduce heat; cook and stir 2 minutes longer. Remove from the heat. Stir a small amount of the hot filling into eggs; return all to pan, stirring constantly. Bring to a gentle boil; cook and stir 2 minutes longer. Remove from the heat. Gently stir in butter, orange peel and extract. Cool to room temperature without stirring. Cover and refrigerate.

4 For the frosting, in a large heavy saucepan, combine sugar, egg whites, water, salt and the cream of tartar over low heat or combine the ingredients in a double boiler over simmering water. With a portable mixer, beat on low speed for 1 minute. Continue beating on low over low heat until the frosting reaches 160°, about 12 minutes. Pour into the bowl of a heavy-duty stand mixer; add vanilla. Beat on high until frosting forms stiff peaks, about 7 minutes.

5 Using the blade of a long, serrated knife, split each cake into two horizontal layers. Place the bottom layer on a serving plate; top with 1/3 cup filling and spread over the cake layer. Repeat four more times. Top with remaining cake layer. Spread frosting over top and sides of cake. Sprinkle with coconut. Store the frosted cake in the refrigerator until serving.

YIELD: 12-14 servings.

YOGURT LEMON PIE

ELSIE CULVER, BIG ARM, MONTANA

This tasty recipe came about by experimenting in my kitchen. I'm a grandmother and great-grandmother, and when I'm not baking for relatives or friends, I'm busy tending my cherry orchard or skiing, bowling or dancing! The beauty of this dessert is that it takes only 5 ingredients to put together.

PREP/TOTAL TIME: 15 min.

- 1 package (8 ounces) cream cheese, softened
- 2 cups plain yogurt
- 1/3 cup milk
- 1 package (3.4 ounces) instant lemon pudding mix
- 1 pastry shell or graham cracker crust (9 inches), baked and cooled

Whipped topping, optional

Lemon peel, cut into thin strips, optional

1 In a large bowl, beat cream cheese, yogurt and milk until smooth. Beat in pudding mix until thickened.

2 Spoon into the crust. Serve immediately or refrigerate until serving time. Garnish with whipped topping and lemon peel strips if desired.

YIELD: 8-10 servings.

DAFFODIL CAKE

GRACE SCOWEN, KELOWNA, BRITISH COLUMBIA

I've made this cake for my children, grandchildren and great-grandchildren. It is their favorite birthday cake...it's light and tasty, and lends itself beautifully to decorating. I often place a small arrangement of fresh flowers in the center.

PREP: 45 min. **BAKE:** 35 min. + cooling

    6 egg whites
1/2 teaspoon cream of tartar
1/2 teaspoon vanilla extract
2/3 cup sugar
1/2 cup cake flour
1/2 teaspoon baking powder
1/2 teaspoon salt

YELLOW CAKE:

    6 egg yolks
    2 tablespoons warm water
1/2 cup cake flour
1/2 cup sugar
    1 teaspoon baking powder
1/8 teaspoon salt
1/2 teaspoon vanilla extract

FROSTING:

1/2 cup sugar
    4 teaspoons all-purpose flour
Pinch salt
    1 cup pineapple juice
    1 carton (8 ounces) frozen whipped topping, thawed

1 Place the egg whites in a large bowl; let stand at room temperature for 30 minutes. Add cream of tartar and vanilla; beat on medium speed until foamy. Gradually beat in sugar, 1 tablespoon at a time, until soft peaks form. Combine the flour, baking powder and salt; fold into egg white mixture. Set aside.

2 For cake, in another large bowl, beat the egg yolks and water until thick and lemon-colored. Combine flour, sugar, baking powder and salt; gradually beat into egg yolk mixture. Beat in the vanilla.

3 Alternately spoon yellow batter and white batter into an ungreased 10-in. tube pan. Bake at 350° for 35-40 minutes or until a toothpick inserted near the center comes out clean. Immediately invert pan; cool completely.

4 For frosting, combine the sugar, flour and salt in a small saucepan. Stir in pineapple juice until blended. Bring to a boil; cook and stir for 2 minutes or until thickened. Cool. Fold in whipped topping.

5 Remove cake from pan to a serving plate. Spread frosting over top and sides of cake. Store in the refrigerator.

YIELD: 12 servings.

LEMON CRUMB BARS

ANNA MILLER, QUAKER CITY, OHIO

I'm always looking for a great new cookie or bar to try, but I often return to this tried-and-true recipe. My husband loves the combination of sweet and salty!

PREP: 15 min. **BAKE:** 40 min. + cooling

    1 package (18-1/4 ounces) lemon cake mix
1/2 cup cold butter
    1 egg
    2 cups crushed saltines (about 60 crackers)
    3 egg yolks
    1 can (14 ounces) sweetened condensed milk
1/2 cup lemon juice

1 In a large bowl, beat cake mix, butter and egg until crumbly. Stir in cracker crumbs; set aside 2 cups for topping.

2 Press remaining crumb mixture into a 13-in. x 9-in. baking dish coated with cooking spray. Bake at 350° for 18-20 minutes or until edges are lightly browned.

3 In a small bowl, beat the egg yolks, milk and lemon juice. Pour over crust; sprinkle with the reserved crumb mixture. Bake 20-25 minutes longer or until edges are lightly browned. Cool on a wire rack. Cut into bars. Store in the refrigerator.

YIELD: 2 dozen.

SPRING BREEZE CHEESECAKE PIE

DEANNA TAYLOR, AINSWORTH, NEBRASKA

I combined two of my favorites (cheesecake and rhubarb) to come up with this mouthwatering dessert. It's so creamy and colorful. Everyone who tries it likes it.

PREP: 30 min. + chilling **COOK:** 15 min. + cooling

- 1 package (8 ounces) cream cheese, softened
- 1/3 cup sugar
- 1 cup (8 ounces) sour cream
- 2 teaspoons vanilla extract
- 1 carton (8 ounces) frozen whipped topping, thawed
- 1 graham cracker crust (9 inches)

TOPPING:

- 3 cups chopped fresh or frozen rhubarb
- 1/3 cup sugar
- 1/8 teaspoon ground cinnamon
- 1 tablespoon cornstarch
- 2 tablespoons cold water

1 In a small bowl, beat cream cheese until smooth. Gradually beat in sugar. Beat in sour cream and vanilla. Set aside 1/2 cup whipped topping for garnish; cover and refrigerate. Beat 1/2 cup whipped topping into cream cheese mixture; fold in remaining whipped topping. Spoon into the crust. Cover and refrigerate for at least 2 hours.

2 For topping, in a large saucepan, bring the rhubarb, sugar and cinnamon to a boil. Reduce heat; simmer, uncovered, for 5-8 minutes or until rhubarb is tender. In a small bowl, combine the cornstarch and cold water until smooth. Gradually stir into rhubarb mixture. Return to a boil; cook and stir for 1-2 minutes or until thickened. Cool to room temperature.

3 Cut pie into slices; top with rhubarb sauce and reserved whipped topping.

YIELD: 6-8 servings.

BERRY-FILLED PHYLLO FLOWERS

MARJORIE HENNIG, GREEN VALLEY, ARIZONA

This makes a beautiful finale for holiday meals. You can use any type of fresh fruit you'd like. Sometimes I use fresh apricots or peaches in addition to the berries.

PREP: 25 min. **BAKE:** 10 min. + cooling

- 4 sheets phyllo dough (14 inches x 9 inches)
- 1 teaspoon butter, melted
- 1 tablespoon confectioners' sugar

FILLING:

- 1/2 cup heavy whipping cream
- 2 tablespoons confectioners' sugar
- 1 tablespoon orange juice
- 1/4 teaspoon vanilla extract
- 1 cup sliced fresh strawberries
- 1/4 cup fresh raspberries
- 1/4 cup fresh blueberries

Additional fresh berries

1 Coat two 10-oz. custard cups with cooking spray. Place on a baking sheet.

2 Place sheets of phyllo dough in a single layer on a work surface; coat with cooking spray. Cut in half widthwise. Layer four pieces in each custard cup, alternating corner points (allow ends to hang over edge). Brush phyllo cups with butter. Sprinkle with confectioners' sugar.

3 Bake at 375° for 7-12 minutes or until golden brown. Cool for 10 minutes before carefully removing phyllo cups to a wire rack to cool completely.

4 For filling, in a small bowl, beat cream until it begins to thicken. Add confectioners' sugar, orange juice and vanilla; beat until stiff peaks form. Fold in the strawberries, raspberries and blueberries. Spoon into flower cups. Top with additional berries. Serve immediately.

YIELD: 2 servings.

MINI COCONUT MERINGUE PIE

LOIS BAYLIFF, FINDLAY, OHIO
This cute coconut pie has a fluffy meringue filling that bakes to beautiful, tall peaks and is sprinkled with toasted coconut flakes.

PREP: 45 min. **BAKE:** 10 min. + chilling

- 1/2 cup all-purpose flour
- 1/8 teaspoon salt
- 2 tablespoons shortening
- 2 tablespoons cold water

FILLING:

- 3 tablespoons sugar
- 4-1/2 teaspoons cornstarch
- 1 cup 2% milk
- 2 egg yolks
- 3 tablespoons flaked coconut
- 1 tablespoon butter

MERINGUE:

- 1 egg white
- 1/8 teaspoon cream of tartar
- 2 tablespoons sugar

Flaked coconut, toasted, optional

1 In a small bowl, combine flour and salt; cut in shortening until crumbly. Gradually add water, tossing with a fork until dough forms a ball. Cover and refrigerate for 15 minutes or until easy to handle.

2 On a lightly floured surface, roll out pastry to fit a 5-in. pie plate. Transfer to pie plate. Trim to 1/2 in. beyond edge of plate; flute edges. Line unpricked pastry shell with a double thickness of heavy-duty foil.

3 Bake at 450° for 5 minutes. Remove foil; bake 5 minutes longer. Cool on a wire rack.

4 For filling, in a small saucepan, combine the sugar, cornstarch, milk and egg yolks. Cook and stir over medium heat until mixture

reaches 160° or is thick enough to coat the back of a metal spoon. Remove from the heat. Gently stir in the coconut and butter. Pour into crust.

5 For meringue, in a small bowl, beat egg white and cream of tartar on medium speed until soft peaks form. Gradually beat in sugar, 1 tablespoon at a time, on high until stiff glossy peaks form and sugar is dissolved. Spread evenly over hot filling, sealing edges to crust.

6 Bake at 350° for 10-15 minutes or until meringue is golden brown. Cool on a wire rack for 30 minutes. Refrigerate for at least 3 hours before serving.

YIELD: 2 servings.

LEMON-STRAWBERRY ICEBOX DESSERT

GAIL MARSHALL, FT. LAUDERDALE, FLORIDA
This fun frosty treat came from a very dear elderly friend who was a great cook. I think of her whenever I make it. It's simple, cool and refreshing. You can also add fresh blueberries for a beautiful red-white-and-blue patriotic showstopper!

PREP: 15 min. + freezing

- 1 quart fresh strawberries, hulled
- 1/2 gallon vanilla ice cream, softened
- 1 can (12 ounces) frozen lemonade concentrate, thawed
- 2 teaspoons grated lemon peel

1 Place the strawberries in a food processor; cover and process until pureed. Transfer to a large bowl; add ice cream, lemonade concentrate and lemon peel. Beat until blended.

2 Pour into an ungreased 13-in. x 9-in. dish. Cover and freeze overnight. Remove from freezer 15 minutes before serving.

YIELD: 12 servings.

BROWNIE BAKED ALASKA

CAROL TWARDZIK, SPY HILL, SASKATCHEWAN

The name Baked Alaska originated at Delmonico's Restaurant in New York City in 1876 and was created in honor of the newly acquired territory of Alaska.

PREP: 50 min. + freezing BAKE: 5 min.

- 2 squares (1 ounce each) unsweetened chocolate
- 1/2 cup shortening
- 1 cup sugar
- 1 teaspoon vanilla extract
- 2 eggs
- 3/4 cup all-purpose flour
- 1/2 teaspoon baking powder
- 1/2 teaspoon salt
- 1 cup chopped walnuts, optional
- 1 quart strawberry ice cream, slightly softened
- 1 quart vanilla ice cream, slightly softened

MERINGUE:
- 5 egg whites
- 2/3 cup sugar
- 1/2 teaspoon cream of tartar

1 In a large saucepan, melt chocolate and shortening; remove from the heat. Stir in sugar and vanilla. Add eggs, one at a time, beating well after each addition. Combine the flour, baking powder and salt; stir into chocolate mixture. Add nuts if desired.

2 Spread into a greased 9-in. round baking pan. Bake at 350° for 20-25 minutes or until a toothpick inserted near the center comes out with moist crumbs (do not overbake). Cool for 10 minutes before removing from pan to a wire rack to cool completely.

3 Meanwhile, line an 8-in. or 9-in. round bowl (1-1/2-qts.) with foil. Quickly spread strawberry ice cream over bottom and up sides of bowl, leaving the center hollow; cover and freeze for 30 minutes. Pack vanilla ice cream into center; cover and freeze.

4 To assemble, place the brownie base on a 10-in. ovenproof serving plate. Unmold ice cream onto brownie. Return to the freezer while preparing meringue.

5 In a heavy saucepan or double boiler over simmering water, combine the egg whites, sugar and cream of tartar. Heat over low heat while beating egg white mixture with a portable mixer on low speed for 1 minute, scraping down sides of bowl. Continue beating until mixture reaches 160°. Remove from the heat. Beat on high speed until stiff peaks form.

6 Quickly spread over ice cream and brownie. Bake at 500° for 2-5 minutes or until meringue is lightly browned. (Or return to the freezer until ready to bake.) Transfer to a serving plate; serve immediately.

YIELD: 12 servings.

MANGO DELIGHT

CANDY MCMENAMIN, LEXINGTON, SOUTH CAROLINA

My son and I found this South American recipe while doing some research for a school project about Colombia. We made the dish as a visual aid for his project, and it was a hit! It's cool, refreshing and contains plenty of fresh, delicious mangoes.

PREP: 35 min. + chilling

- 5 medium ripe mangoes, peeled and pitted
- 1 cup evaporated milk
- 3/4 cup sugar
- 1 cup orange juice
- 3 envelopes unflavored gelatin
- 2 cups whipped topping

1 Cut the mangoes into large chunks; place in a food processor. Cover and process until smooth; transfer to a large bowl. Stir in milk and sugar; set aside.

2 Place orange juice in a small saucepan; sprinkle gelatin over juice. Let stand for 2 minutes. Heat over low heat, stirring until gelatin is completely dissolved. Stir into mango mixture. Fold in whipped topping.

3 Transfer to an 8-cup mold coated with cooking spray. Cover and refrigerate for 2 hours or until firm. Just before serving, unmold onto a serving platter.

YIELD: 10 servings.

UNMOLDING GELATIN

First, loosen the gelatin from the top edge of the mold by gently pulling the gelatin away from the edge with a moistened finger. Then dip the mold up to its rim in a sink or large pan of warm water for a few seconds or until the edges begin to release from the side of the mold. Place a plate over the mold and invert. Carefully lift the mold from the gelatin dessert.

APRICOT PASTRY BARS

NANCY FOUST, STONEBORO, PENNSYLVANIA
Perfect for a casual gathering or fancier event, this recipe is a crowd-pleaser. These special bars were among 40 kinds of cookies and bars I made for my niece's wedding reception.

PREP: 45 min. **BAKE:** 35 min. + cooling

- 4 cups all-purpose flour
- 1 cup plus 2 tablespoons sugar, divided
- 3 teaspoons baking powder
- 1/2 teaspoon salt
- 1/4 teaspoon baking soda
- 1 cup shortening
- 3 eggs, separated
- 1/4 cup milk
- 1-1/2 teaspoons vanilla extract
- 4 cans (12 ounces each) apricot filling
- 1 cup chopped walnuts

1 In a large bowl, combine the flour, 1 cup sugar, baking powder, salt and baking soda. Cut in shortening until mixture resembles coarse crumbs.

2 In a small bowl, whisk egg yolks, 2 egg whites, milk and vanilla; gradually add to crumb mixture, tossing with a fork until dough forms a ball. Divide in half, making one portion slightly larger.

3 Roll out larger portion of dough between two large sheets of waxed paper into a 17-in. x 12-in. rectangle. Transfer to an ungreased 15-in. x 10-in. x 1-in. baking pan. Press pastry onto the bottom and up the sides of pan; trim pastry even with top edges. Spread apricot filling over dough; sprinkle with walnuts.

4 Roll out remaining pastry to fit top of pan; place over filling. Trim, seal and flute edges. Cut slits in top. Whisk remaining egg white; brush over pastry. Sprinkle with remaining sugar.

5 Bake at 350° for 35-40 minutes or until golden brown. Cool on a wire rack.

YIELD: about 4 dozen.

GRANNY'S RHUBARB PIE

BLANCHE BANINSKI, MINTO, NORTH DAKOTA
This recipe originated with my grandmother, who baked many different rhubarb desserts. This was always a favorite of mine.

PREP: 20 min. **BAKE:** 1-1/4 hours

- 3 cups all-purpose flour
- 1-1/2 teaspoons salt
- 1 cup shortening
- 1 egg
- 5 tablespoons cold water
- 1 teaspoon white vinegar

FILLING:

- 3 cups sliced fresh or frozen rhubarb (1/2-inch pieces)
- 2 cups sliced peeled tart apples
- 1 can (8 ounces) crushed pineapple, drained
- 1/4 cup honey
- 1 tablespoon lemon juice
- 1 cup sugar
- 3 tablespoons all-purpose flour
- 1 tablespoon butter

1 In a large bowl, combine flour and salt. Cut in shortening until mixture resembles coarse crumbs. Combine egg, water and vinegar; stir into flour mixture until a ball forms.

2 Divide the dough in half. On a lightly floured surface, roll out one portion; transfer to a 9-in. pie plate. Trim the pastry even with the edge of the pie plate.

3 For filling, in a large bowl, combine the rhubarb, apples, pineapple, honey and lemon juice. Combine sugar and flour; add to rhubarb mixture. Pour into crust. Dot with butter.

4 Roll out remaining pastry to fit top of pie. Place over filling. Trim, seal and flute edges. Cut slits in pastry. Bake at 350° for 1-1/4 hours or until the pastry is golden brown and the apples are tender.

YIELD: 6-8 servings.

SHAPING A FLUTED EDGE PIE CRUST

To "flute" a pie crust means to make a V-shape or scalloped edge on the pie crust using the thumb and fingers. A fluted edge is suitable for a single- or double-crust pie. The pastry should be trimmed to 1/2 in. beyond the rim of the pie plate for a single-crust pie and 1 in. for a double-crust pie.

This overhang is then turned under to form the built-up edge. Position your index finger on the edge of the crust, pointing out. Place the thumb and index finger of your other hand on the outside edge and pinch dough around the index finger to form a V shape. Continue around the edge.

ALMOND-BUTTER COOKIE BOUQUET

KRISSY FOSSMEYER, HUNTLEY, ILLINOIS
I make these cookie pops often during the year. You can cover the foam with tissue paper or cellophane. Add a bow if you like. They make a great centerpiece or hostess gift. Not only do the cookies look pretty, they taste good, too.

PREP: 2 hours + chilling **BAKE:** 10 min./batch + cooling

1-1/4 cups butter, softened
1-3/4 cups confectioners' sugar
   2 ounces almond paste
   1 egg
1/4 cup milk
   1 teaspoon vanilla extract
   4 cups all-purpose flour
1/2 teaspoon salt
Wooden skewers or lollipop sticks

ICING:
   1 cup confectioners' sugar
   4 teaspoons evaporated milk
Food coloring of your choice

1 In a large bowl, cream butter and confectioners' sugar until light and fluffy; add almond paste. Beat in the egg, milk and vanilla. Combine flour and salt; gradually add to the creamed mixture and mix well. Cover and refrigerate for 1 hour.

2 On a lightly floured surface, roll out dough to 1/4-in. thickness. Cut out with floured 3-in. cookie cutters. Place 1 in. apart on ungreased baking sheets. Insert skewers or sticks. Bake at 375° for 7-8 minutes or until firm. Let stand for 2 minutes before emoving to wire racks to cool.

3 In a bowl, whisk confectioners' sugar and milk. Divide into small bowls; tint with food coloring. Gently spread icing over cooled cookies. Decorate with other colors of icing if desired.

YIELD: about 2-1/2 dozen.

TROPICAL MERINGUE TARTS

TASTE OF HOME TEST KITCHEN
What a special treat! As pretty as an Easter basket, these tender meringue shells are filled with creamy pudding, then topped with fresh fruit and coconut. The perfect showstopper dessert for company.

PREP: 30 min. + standing **BAKE:** 50 min. + cooling

   4 egg whites
   1 teaspoon white vinegar
   1 teaspoon vanilla extract
   1 teaspoon cornstarch
   1 cup sugar
1-1/4 cups cold fat-free milk
   1 package (1 ounce) sugar-free instant vanilla pudding mix
   1 cup reduced-fat whipped topping
   1 cup cubed fresh pineapple
   2 medium kiwifruit, peeled and sliced
   2 tablespoons flaked coconut, toasted

1 Place egg whites in a large bowl; let stand at room temperature for 30 minutes. Meanwhile, line a baking sheet with parchment paper or foil. Draw ten 3-in. circles on paper; set aside.

2 Add vinegar and vanilla to egg whites; beat on medium speed until soft peaks form. Beat in cornstarch. Gradually beat in sugar, 2 tablespoons at a time, on high until stiff glossy peaks form and sugar is dissolved.

3 Cut a small hole in the corner of pastry or plastic bag; insert a large star pastry tip (#6B). Fill the bag with meringue. Pipe the meringue in a spiral fashion to fill in circles on prepared pan. Pipe twice around the base of each shell in a spiral fashion to make the sides.

4 Bake at 275° for 50-60 minutes or until set and dry. Turn oven off and leave door closed; leave meringues in oven for 1 hour.

5 For filling, in a large bowl, whisk the milk and pudding mix for 2 minutes. Let stand for 2 minutes or until soft-set. Fold in whipped topping. Spoon into meringue shells. Top with the pineapple, kiwi and coconut.

YIELD: 10 servings.

STRAWBERRY BANANA CREPES

SHELLY SOULE, LAS VEGAS, NEVADA

My family often has company over for breakfast or brunch, and these light fruit-topped crepes are our favorite. The sweet sensations are as fast to make as they are fabulous. You can cook the crepes the night before, refrigerate them with waxed paper in between, then fill and top them in the morning.

PREP: 20 min. + chilling **COOK:** 10 min.

      1 cup all-purpose flour
      1 tablespoon sugar
  1/2 teaspoon ground cinnamon
1-1/2 cups milk
      2 eggs
      1 to 2 tablespoons butter, divided

FILLING:

      1 package (8 ounces) cream cheese, softened
      1 carton (8 ounces) frozen whipped topping, thawed
  1/2 cup confectioners' sugar

TOPPING:

      2 cups sliced fresh strawberries
      2 medium firm bananas, sliced
  1/4 cup sugar, optional

1 In a large bowl, combine the flour, sugar, cinnamon, milk and eggs. Cover and refrigerate for 1 hour.

2 In an 8-in. nonstick skillet, melt 1 teaspoon butter. Stir batter; pour about 2 tablespoons into the center of skillet. Lift and tilt pan to evenly coat bottom. Cook until top appears dry; turn and cook 15-20 seconds longer. Remove to a wire rack.

3 Repeat with remaining batter, add butter to a skillet as needed. When cool, stack crepes with waxed paper on paper towels in between.

4 In a large bowl, beat the filling ingredients until smooth. Spread 2 rounded tablespoonfuls on each crepe; roll up. In a large bowl, combine topping ingredients; spoon over crepes.

YIELD: 18 crepes.

RHUBARB MERINGUE PIE

ELAINE SAMPSON, COLESBURG, IOWA

My husband's grandmother was a great cook and didn't always share her secrets, so we are fortunate to have her recipe for rhubarb cream pie. I added one of my favorite crusts and a never-fail meringue.

PREP: 50 min. + chilling **BAKE:** 65 min. + cooling

  3/4 cup all-purpose flour
  1/4 teaspoon salt
  1/4 teaspoon sugar
  1/4 cup shortening
      1 tablespoon beaten egg
  1/4 teaspoon white vinegar
      3 to 4-1/2 teaspoons cold water

FILLING:

      3 cups chopped fresh or frozen rhubarb
      1 cup sugar
      2 tablespoons all-purpose flour
Dash salt
      3 egg yolks
      1 cup heavy whipping cream

MERINGUE:

      4 teaspoons plus 1/3 cup sugar, divided
      2 teaspoons cornstarch
  1/3 cup water
      3 egg whites
  1/8 teaspoon cream of tartar

1 In a small bowl, combine the flour, salt and sugar; cut in the shortening until crumbly. Combine the egg and vinegar, then sprinkle over the crumb mixture. Gradually add water, tossing with a fork until a ball forms. Cover and chill for 1 hour or until easy to handle.

2 On a lightly floured surface, roll out pastry to fit a 9-in. pie plate. Trim to 1/2 in. beyond edge of plate; flute edges.

3 For filling, place rhubarb in crust. Whisk the sugar, flour, salt, egg yolks and cream; pour over rhubarb. Bake at 350° for 50-60 minutes or until a knife comes out clean.

4 For meringue, in a small saucepan, combine 4 teaspoons sugar and cornstarch. Gradually stir in the water. Bring to a boil, stirring constantly; cook for 1-2 minutes or until thickened. Cool to room temperature.

5 In a small bowl, beat egg whites and cream of tartar until frothy. Add cornstarch mixture; beat on high until soft peaks form. Gradually beat in remaining sugar, 1 tablespoon at a time, on high until stiff glossy peaks form and sugar is dissolved.

6 Spread evenly over hot filling, sealing edges to crust. Bake for 15 minutes or until meringue is golden brown. Cool on a wire rack for 1 hour. Store in the refrigerator.

YIELD: 6-8 servings.

EDITOR'S NOTE: If using frozen rhubarb, measure rhubarb while still frozen, then thaw completely. Drain in a colander, but do not press liquid out.

PINEAPPLE UPSIDE-DOWN CAKE

KAREN ANN BLAND, GOVE, KANSAS
Here's a traditional spring dessert that's been updated with packaged items for convenience.

PREP: 10 min. BAKE: 45 min.
- 1/4 cup butter, melted
- 1 can (20 ounces) sliced pineapple
- 10 pecan halves
- 1 jar (12 ounces) apricot preserves
- 1 package (18-1/4 ounces) yellow cake mix

1 Pour butter into a well-greased 13-in. x 9-in. baking dish. Drain pineapple, reserving 1/4 cup juice. Arrange pineapple slices in prepared pan; place a pecan half in the center of each slice. Combine the apricot preserves and reserved pineapple juice; spoon over pineapple slices.

2 Prepare cake batter according to package directions; pour over pineapple.

3 Bake at 350° for 45-50 minutes or until a toothpick inserted near the center comes out clean. Immediately invert onto a large serving platter. Cool sightly; serve warm.

YIELD: 12-15 servings.

COCONUT PECAN CUPCAKES

TINA HARRISON, PRAIRIEVILLE, LOUISIANA
Pecan lovers have lots to cheer about with these flavorful cupcakes. I created the recipe for my best friend, Ann, who said she loved Italian cream cake but didn't want a whole cake. They have a wonderful aroma and fabulous flavor.

PREP: 50 min. BAKE: 20 min. + cooling
- 5 eggs, separated
- 1/2 cup shortening
- 1/2 cup butter, softened
- 2 cups sugar
- 3/4 teaspoon vanilla extract
- 1/4 teaspoon almond extract
- 1-1/2 cups all-purpose flour
- 1/4 cup cornstarch
- 1/2 teaspoon baking soda
- 1/2 teaspoon salt
- 1 cup buttermilk
- 2 cups flaked coconut
- 1 cup finely chopped pecans

FROSTING:
- 1 package (8 ounces) cream cheese, softened
- 1/4 cup butter, softened
- 1/2 teaspoon vanilla extract
- 1/4 teaspoon almond extract
- 3-3/4 cups confectioners' sugar
- 3/4 cup chopped pecans

1 Let eggs stand at room temperature for 30 minutes. In a large bowl, cream the shortening, butter and sugar until light and fluffy. Add egg yolks, one at a time, beating well after each addition. Stir in extracts. Combine the flour, cornstarch, baking soda and salt; add to the creamed mixture alternately with buttermilk, beating well after each addition.

2 In a small bowl, beat egg whites on high speed until stiff peaks form. Fold into batter. Stir in coconut and pecans.

3 Fill paper-lined muffin cups three-fourths full. Bake at 350° for 20-25 minutes or until a toothpick comes out clean. Cool 10 minutes; remove from pans to wire racks to cool completely.

4 In a large bowl, combine frosting ingredients until smooth; frost cupcakes. Store in the refrigerator.

YIELD: 2 dozen.

DUTCH APRICOT PIE

JOANNE HUTMACHER, LEMOORE, CALIFORNIA
I freeze several bagfuls of apricots when they are in season, thinking of this pie all the while. At holiday time, there's nothing like a luscious taste of summer. The crunchy pecans in the topping make this dessert extra special.

PREP: 15 min. + standing **BAKE:** 45 min.

- 3/4 cup sugar
- 2 tablespoons quick-cooking tapioca
- 4 cups sliced fresh apricots (about 16)
- 1 tablespoon lemon juice
- Pastry for single-crust pie (9 inches)

TOPPING:
- 2/3 cup all-purpose flour
- 1/2 cup sugar
- 1/2 cup chopped pecans, toasted
- 1/4 cup butter, melted

1 In a small bowl, combine sugar and tapioca. Add apricots and lemon juice; toss to coat. Let stand for 15 minutes. Line a 9-in. pie plate with pastry. Trim pastry to 1/2 in. beyond edge of plate; flute edges. Pour filling into crust.

2 For topping, in a small bowl, combine the flour, sugar and pecans. Stir in the butter. Sprinkle over filling. Cover edges loosely with foil.

3 Bake at 350° for 15 minutes. Remove foil; bake 25-30 minutes longer or until crust is golden brown and filling is bubbly. Cool on a wire rack. Store in the refrigerator.

YIELD: 8 servings.

BUTTERMILK CAKE WITH CARAMEL ICING

ANNA JEAN ALLEN, WEST LIBERTY, KENTUCKY
This cake is so moist and tender, it melts in your mouth! It's been a favorite cake recipe of my family since the 1970s and goes over really well at church potluck meals.

PREP: 35 min. **BAKE:** 45 min. + cooling

- 1 cup butter, softened
- 2-1/3 cups sugar
- 3 eggs
- 1-1/2 teaspoons vanilla extract
- 3 cups all-purpose flour
- 1 teaspoon baking soda
- 1 cup buttermilk

ICING:
- 1/4 cup butter, cubed
- 1/2 cup packed brown sugar
- 1/3 cup heavy whipping cream
- 1 cup confectioners' sugar

1 In a large bowl, cream butter and sugar until light and fluffy. Add eggs, one at a time, beating well after each addition. Beat in vanilla. Combine flour and baking soda; add to creamed mixture alternately with buttermilk, beating well after each addition (batter will be thick).

2 Pour into a greased and floured 10-in. fluted tube pan. Bake at 350° for 45-50 minutes or until a toothpick inserted near the center comes out clean. Cool for 10 minutes before removing from pan to a wire rack to cool completely.

3 For icing, in a small saucepan, combine the butter, brown sugar and cream. Bring to a boil over medium heat, stirring constantly. Remove from the heat; cool for 5-10 minutes. Whisk in confectioners' sugar. Drizzle over cake.

YIELD: 12-16 servings.

APRICOT SESAME COOKIES

JEANNE ALLEN, WEBSTER, NEW YORK

This recipe is great to make for special occasions. The cookies freeze beautifully, so they can conveniently be made ahead of time. Substitute peach, strawberry or raspberry jam if you like. They never last long on a buffet table.

PREP: 25 min. **BAKE:** 10 min./batch

   1 cup butter, softened
1/2 cup sugar
   1 teaspoon almond extract
   2 cups all-purpose flour
1/2 teaspoon salt
1/4 cup plus 3 tablespoons sesame seeds
   6 tablespoons apricot jam

1 In a large bowl, cream butter and sugar until light and fluffy. Beat in extract. Combine flour and salt; gradually add to the creamed mixture and mix well.

2 Roll into 1-in. balls; roll in sesame seeds. Place 2 in. apart on ungreased baking sheets.

3 Using the end of a wooden spoon handle, make an 3/8-in. deep indentation in the center of each ball. Fill with jam. Bake at 400° for 10-12 minutes or until lightly browned. Remove to wire racks to cool.

YIELD: 4 dozen.

SOFTENING BUTTER
When creaming butter, it should be soft enough so a table knife can glide through it. To soften the butter quickly, microwave the sticks at 70 percent power in 10-second intervals about three times.

TROPICAL MACADAMIA CUSTARD DESSERT

BRENDA MELANCON, GONZALES, LOUISIANA

My husband's co-workers always love my desserts, especially the cookies and bars. They enjoyed these bars for their unique flavor...and everyone asked for the recipe! Believe it or not, most of them are men.

PREP: 15 min. **BAKE:** 40 min. + cooling

   1 package (16 ounces) ready-to-bake refrigerated white chip macadamia nut cookie dough, divided
   3 eggs
   1 can (20 ounces) unsweetened crushed pineapple, well drained
   1 can (12 ounces) evaporated milk
   1 package (7 ounces) dried tropical fruit bits
1/3 cup packed brown sugar
   2 tablespoons all-purpose flour
1-1/2 teaspoons rum extract
Whipped topping and maraschino cherries

1 Let dough stand at room temperature for 5-10 minutes to soften. Press nine portions of dough into a greased 9-in. square baking pan. Bake at 350° for 10 minutes or until set. Let stand for 2 minutes.

2 Meanwhile, in a bowl, combine the eggs, pineapple, milk, dried fruit, brown sugar, flour and extract. Pour over crust. Crumble the remaining dough over filling.

3 Bake for 30-35 minutes or until top is golden brown. Cool on a wire rack. Cut into squares; garnish with whipped topping and cherries. Refrigerate leftovers.

YIELD: 12 servings.

83   79   74   83

SPECIAL OCCASIONS

75

CORNED BEEF AND CABBAGE

EVELYN KENNEY, TRENTON, NEW JERSEY
This is my standby for classic corned beef, whether celebrating St. Paddy's day or even for an autumn meal.

PREP: 10 min. **COOK:** 2-3/4 hours

- 1 corned beef brisket (4 to 6 pounds)
- 2 tablespoons brown sugar
- 2 to 3 bay leaves
- 16 to 24 small potatoes, peeled
- 8 to 12 carrots, halved
- 1 large head cabbage, cut into wedges

Minced fresh parsley, optional

HORSERADISH SAUCE:
- 3 tablespoons butter
- 2 tablespoons all-purpose flour
- 1 to 1-1/2 cups cooking liquid (from brisket)
- 1 tablespoon vinegar
- 1 tablespoon sugar
- 1/4 cup horseradish

1 Place brisket in a large Dutch oven; cover with water. Add brown sugar and bay leaves. (If spice packet is enclosed with brisket, add it also.) Bring to a boil. Reduce heat; cover and simmer for 2 hours.

2 Add potatoes and carrots. Return to boiling. Reduce heat; cover and simmer 30-40 minutes or until meat and vegetables are just tender. If your Dutch oven is not large enough for cabbage to fit, remove potatoes and carrots and keep warm (they can be returned to cooking liquid and heated through before serving).

3 Add cabbage; cover and cook about 15 minutes or until tender. Discard bay leaves. Remove cabbage and meat.

4 Strain and remove about 1-1/2 cups cooking liquid. Let meat stand a few minutes. Slice meat across the grain. Serve with the Horseradish Sauce. Garnish with fresh minced parsley if desired.

5 For horseradish sauce, in a small saucepan, melt butter. Blend in flour. Add 1 cup cooking liquid; stir until smooth. Add the vinegar, sugar and horseradish. Cook and stir over medium heat until thickened and bubbly. Adjust seasoning with additional vinegar, sugar or horseradish if needed. Thin sauce, if necessary, with remaining cooking liquid.

YIELD: 8-12 servings and about 1-1/2 cups horseradish sauce.

COLCANNON POTATOES

MARILOU ROBINSON, PORTLAND, OREGON
Every Irish family has its own version of this classic dish...my recipe comes from my father's family in Ireland. It's part of my St. Patrick's Day menu, along with lamb chops, carrots and soda bread. It's the pot of gold at the end of the rainbow.

PREP: 10 min. **COOK:** 35 min.

- 2 pounds cabbage, shredded
- 2 cups water
- 4 pounds potatoes, peeled and quartered
- 2 cups milk
- 1 cup chopped green onions

Salt and coarsely ground pepper to taste
- 1/4 cup butter, melted

Crumbled cooked bacon and minced fresh parsley

1 In a large saucepan, bring cabbage and water to a boil. Reduce heat; cover and simmer for 10-12 minutes or until tender. Drain, reserving cooking liquid. Keep cabbage warm.

2 Place cooking liquid and potatoes in a large saucepan; add enough additional water to cover the potatoes. Bring to a boil. Reduce heat; cover and cook for 15-17 minutes or until tender. Drain and keep warm.

3 In a small saucepan, bring milk and onions to a boil; remove from the heat. In a large bowl, mash potatoes. Add the milk mixture; beat until blended. Beat in the cabbage, salt and pepper. Drizzle with the melted butter, bacon and parsley.

YIELD: 12-16 servings.

GRASSHOPPER PIE

MELISSA SOKASITS, WARRENVILLE, ILLINOIS
This pie has become a classic dinner finale in our family. We make it for special occasions, but because it's so delicious, now I make it any time throughout the year!

PREP: 15 min. + chilling

- 1-1/2 cups cold milk
- 1 package (3.9 ounces) instant chocolate pudding mix
- 2-3/4 cups whipped topping, divided
- 1 package (4.67 ounces) mint Andes candies, chopped, divided
- 1 chocolate crumb crust (9 inches)
- 1/4 teaspoon mint extract
- 2 drops green food coloring, optional

1 In a small bowl, whisk milk and pudding mix for 2 minutes. Let stand for 2 minutes or until soft-set. Fold in 3/4 cup whipped topping. Fold in 3/4 cup candies. Spoon into crust.

2 In another bowl, combine extract and remaining whipped topping; add food coloring if desired. Spread over pudding layer; sprinkle with remaining candies. Cover and refrigerate for 4 hours or until set.

YIELD: 8 servings.

SEEING GREEN ON ST. PATRICK'S DAY
Chicago's St. Patrick's day celebration is one of the largest in the country, and has one of the most unusual traditions—dyeing the Chicago river green. Although the formula for the dye is a closely guarded secret, it doesn't harm the environment. The dyeing of the river begins at 10:45 a.m. every year on St. Pat's.

IRISH SODA BREAD

EVELYN KENNEY, TRENTON, NEW JERSEY
Some people consider bread to be the most important part of a meal...and this bread just might satisfy such folks! It comes from an old recipe and is by far the best soda bread I've ever tried. With the addition of raisins, it is moist and delicious!

PREP: 20 min. BAKE: 1 hour

- 4 cups all-purpose flour
- 1/4 cup sugar
- 1 teaspoon salt
- 1 teaspoon baking powder
- 1 teaspoon baking soda
- 1/4 cup cold butter, cubed
- 1-1/3 cups buttermilk
- 1 egg, lightly beaten
- 2 cups raisins
- 3 to 4 tablespoons caraway seeds

Milk

1 In a large bowl, combine the flour, sugar, salt, baking powder and baking soda. Cut in butter until mixture resembles coarse meal. Combine buttermilk and egg; stir into dry ingredients just until moistened. Stir in raisins and caraway seeds.

2 Turn out onto a floured surface and knead lightly until smooth. Shape the dough into a ball and place on a greased baking pan. Pat into a 7-in. round loaf. Cut a 4-in. cross about 1/4 in. deep on top to allow for expansion. Brush top with milk.

3 Bake at 375° for 1 hour or until golden brown.

YIELD: 1 loaf.

CHICKEN AND OKRA GUMBO

CATHERINE BOUIS, PALM HARBOR, FLORIDA
We used to live in New Orleans, but our stomachs don't know we moved to Florida yet. I still make many Creole dishes, and gumbo is one of our favorites.

PREP: 40 min. **COOK:** 2 hours

- 1 broiler/fryer chicken (2-1/2 to 3 pounds), cut up
- 2 quarts water
- 1/4 cup canola oil or bacon drippings
- 2 tablespoons all-purpose flour
- 2 medium onions, chopped
- 2 celery ribs, chopped
- 1 medium green pepper, chopped
- 3 garlic cloves, minced
- 1 can (28 ounces) tomatoes, drained
- 2 cups fresh or frozen sliced okra
- 2 bay leaves
- 1 teaspoon dried basil
- 1 teaspoon salt
- 1/2 teaspoon pepper
- 1 to 2 teaspoons hot pepper sauce
- 2 tablespoons sliced green onions

Minced fresh parsley
Hot cooked rice

1 Place chicken and water in a large kettle. Cover and bring to a boil. Reduce heat; cover and simmer for 30-45 minutes or until chicken is tender.

2 Remove chicken; reserve broth. Set chicken aside until cool enough to handle. Remove chicken from bones; discard bones and cut meat into cubes; set aside.

3 In a soup kettle, combine oil or drippings and flour until smooth. Cook over medium-high heat for 5 minutes, stirring constantly. Reduce the heat to medium. Cook and stir about 5 minutes more or until mixture is reddish-brown (the color of a penny). Turn the heat to high. Stir in 2 cups reserved broth. Bring to a boil; cook and stir for 2 minutes or until thickened.

4 Add the chopped onions, celery, green pepper and garlic; cook and stir for 5 minutes. Add the tomatoes, okra, bay leaves, basil, salt, pepper and pepper sauce. Cover and simmer for 1-1/2 to 2 hours.

5 Discard bay leaves. Garnish with green onions and parsley. Serve with rice.

YIELD: 8-10 servings.

NEW ORLEANS BEIGNETS

BETH DAWSON, JACKSON, LOUISIANA
These sweet French doughnuts are square instead of the traditional round shape and have no hole in the middle. They're a regular part of breakfast in New Orleans.

PREP: 15 min. **COOK:** 35 min.

- 1 package (1/4 ounce) active dry yeast
- 1/4 cup warm water (110° to 115°)
- 1 cup evaporated milk
- 1/2 cup canola oil
- 1/4 cup sugar
- 1 egg
- 4-1/2 cups self-rising flour

Oil for deep-fat frying
Confectioners' sugar

1 In a large bowl, dissolve yeast in warm water. Add the milk, oil, sugar and egg and 2 cups flour. Beat until smooth. Stir in enough remaining flour to form a soft dough (dough will be sticky). Do not knead. Cover and refrigerate overnight.

2 Punch dough down. Turn onto a floured surface; roll into a 16-in. x 12-in. rectangle. Cut into 2-in. squares.

3 In an electric skillet or deep-fat fryer, heat oil to 375°. Fry squares, a few at a time, until golden brown on both sides. Drain on paper towels. Roll warm beignets in confectioners' sugar.

YIELD: 4 dozen.

EDITOR'S NOTE: As a substitute for each cup of self-rising flour, place 1-1/2 teaspoons baking powder and 1/2 teaspoon salt in a measuring cup. Add all-purpose flour to measure 1 cup.

SEAFOOD JAMBALAYA

KRISTIN ARNETT, ELKHORN, WISCONSIN

Jambalaya has quite a history in New Orleans, and uses a variety of ingredients, like tomatoes, onion, green pepper, sausage, and some kind of seafood. This recipe is wonderful when celebrating Mardi Gras. I use andouille, but kielbasa works well, too.

PREP: 25 min. BAKE: 45 min.

- 1/2 pound whole fresh mushrooms, sliced
- 3 medium onions, chopped
- 2 medium green peppers, chopped
- 3 celery ribs
- 3 garlic cloves, minced
- 2 tablespoons olive oil
- 1 package (16 ounces) smoked sausage, cubed
- 1 pound cooked large shrimp, peeled and deveined
- 1 pound frozen cooked crawfish tail meat, thawed
- 1 can (14-1/2 ounces) chicken broth
- 1 can (14-1/2 ounces) diced tomatoes
- 2 tablespoons Worcestershire sauce
- 2 tablespoons Cajun seasoning
- 1 to 3 teaspoons hot pepper sauce
- 1/4 teaspoon white pepper
- 4 cups cooked long grain white rice

1 In a large Dutch oven, saute the mushrooms, onions, pepper, celery and garlic in oil. Add the sausage, shrimp, crawfish, broth, tomatoes, seasonings and rice.

2 Bake, uncovered, at 325° for 45 minutes or until heated through, stirring after 20 minutes.

YIELD: 8-10 servings.

EDITOR'S NOTE: You can use cooked chicken, crab and ham in place of the crawfish and shrimp.

MARDI GRAS KING CAKE

LISA MOUTON, ORLANDO, FLORIDA

This frosted yeast bread is the highlight of our annual Mardi Gras party. If you want to hide a token inside, do so by cutting a small slit in the bottom of the baked cake...and remember to warn your guests!

PREP: 40 min. + rising BAKE: 20 min. + cooling

- 1 package (1/4 ounce) active dry yeast
- 1/2 cup warm water (110° to 115°)
- 1/2 cup warm milk (110° to 115°)
- 1/3 cup shortening
- 1/3 cup sugar
- 1 teaspoon salt
- 1 egg
- 4 to 4-1/2 cups all-purpose flour
- 2 cans (12-1/2 ounces each) almond cake and pastry filling

GLAZE:

- 3 cups confectioners' sugar
- 1/2 teaspoon vanilla extract
- 3 to 4 tablespoons water
  Purple, green and gold colored sugar

1 In a large bowl, dissolve yeast in warm water. Add the milk, shortening, sugar, salt, egg and 2 cups flour. Beat on medium speed for 3 minutes. Beat until smooth. Stir in enough of the remaining flour to form a soft dough (dough will be sticky).

2 Turn onto a floured surface; knead until smooth and elastic, about 6-8 minutes. Place in a greased bowl, turning once to grease top. Cover and let rise in a warm place until doubled, about 1 hour.

3 Punch the dough down. Turn onto a lightly floured surface; divide in half. Roll one portion into a 16-in. x 10-in. rectangle. Spread the almond filling to within 1/2 in. of edges. Roll up jelly-roll style, starting with a long side; pinch seam to seal. Place seam side down on a greased baking sheet; pinch the ends together to form a ring. Repeat with the remaining dough and filling. Cover and let rise until doubled, about 1 hour.

4 Bake at 375° for 20-25 minutes or until golden brown. Cool on a wire rack. For glaze, combine the confectioners' sugar, vanilla and enough water to achieve desired consistency. Spread over cooled cakes. Sprinkle with colored sugars.

YIELD: 2 cakes (12 servings each).

EDITOR'S NOTE: This recipe was tested with Solo brand cake and pastry filling. Look for it in the baking aisle.

PROOFING YEAST

To test or "proof" yeast to verify whether it's still active, dissolve 1 teaspoon sugar in 1/2 cup warm water (110°-115°). Sprinkle with 1 packet or 2-1/4 teaspoons active dry yeast. Stir and let stand for 10 minutes. After 10 minutes, the mixture should be foamy and can be used immediately. Remember to deduct 1/2 cup liquid from the recipe to adjust for the water used in the test.

APRICOT-GLAZED HAM

GALELAH DOWELL, FAIRLAND, OKLAHOMA

Glazing a bone-in ham with apricot jam gives it an attractive look and delicious flavor. It's the star of many of our Sunday suppers.

PREP: 15 min. **BAKE:** 1-1/4 hours
- 1/2 fully cooked bone-in ham (6 to 8 pounds)
- 1/2 cup packed brown sugar
- 2 to 3 tablespoons ground mustard
- Whole cloves
- 1/2 cup apricot preserves

1 Place ham on a rack in a shallow roasting pan. Score the surface of the ham, making diamond shapes 1/2 in. deep. Combine brown sugar and mustard; rub over surface of ham. Insert a clove in the center of each diamond.

2 Place the ham on a rack in a shallow roasting pan. Bake, uncovered, at 325° for 1 hour. Spoon preserves over ham. Bake 15-30 minutes longer or until a meat thermometer reads 140° and ham is heated through.

3 Remove leftover ham from bone and cube. Refrigerate or freeze remaining ham (may be frozen for up to 2 months).

YIELD: 18-20 servings.

MOIST CARROT CAKE

GERI FRAHM, GRETNA, NEBRASKA

One sweet bite of this heavenly cake and you'll be on cloud nine. Not only is the cake moist and flavorful, the icing is truly to-die-for.

PREP: 35 min. **BAKE:** 45 min. + cooling
- 1-1/3 cups sugar
- 1/2 cup packed brown sugar

- 1 cup unsweetened applesauce
- 1/2 cup canola oil
- 2 eggs
- 2 egg whites
- 2 teaspoons vanilla extract
- 2-1/2 cups all-purpose flour
- 2 teaspoons baking powder
- 2 teaspoons ground cinnamon
- 1/2 teaspoon salt
- 1/2 teaspoon baking soda
- 2 cups shredded carrots
- 1 can (8 ounces) unsweetened crushed pineapple, drained
- 1/2 cup golden raisins
- 1/2 cup finely chopped walnuts

FROSTING:
- 5 ounces reduced-fat cream cheese
- 1 package (3 ounces) cream cheese, softened
- 1 teaspoon vanilla extract
- 2 cups confectioners' sugar
- 1/4 cup finely chopped walnuts, toasted

1 In a large bowl, beat the sugars, applesauce, oil, eggs, egg whites and vanilla until well blended. Combine flour, baking powder, cinnamon, salt and baking soda; gradually beat into sugar mixture until blended. Stir in the carrots, pineapple, raisins and walnuts.

2 Transfer to a 10-in. fluted tube pan coated with cooking spray. Bake at 350° for 45-55 minutes or until a toothpick inserted near the center comes out clean. Cool for 10 minutes before removing from pan to wire rack to cool completely.

3 For frosting, in a large bowl, beat cream cheeses and vanilla until fluffy. Beat in confectioners' sugar until smooth. Frost cake. Sprinkle with walnuts. Store in the refrigerator.

YIELD: 16 servings.

ARTICHOKES AU GRATIN

MARJORIE BOWEN, COLORADO SPRINGS, COLORADO
This makes a great side dish for any spring dinner. My niece served this at a family gathering and was kind enough to share the recipe.

PREP: 20 min. BAKE: 20 min.

- 2 cans (14 ounces each) water-packed artichoke hearts, rinsed, drained and quartered
- 1 garlic clove, minced
- 1/4 cup butter, divided
- 2 tablespoons all-purpose flour
- 1/2 teaspoon salt
- 1/4 teaspoon pepper
- 1-1/2 cups milk
- 1 egg, lightly beaten
- 1/2 cup shredded Swiss cheese, divided
- 1 tablespoon dry bread crumbs
- 1/8 teaspoon paprika

1 In a small skillet, saute artichokes and garlic in 2 tablespoons butter until tender. Transfer to a greased 1-qt. baking dish.

2 In a small saucepan, melt remaining butter. Stir in flour, salt and pepper until smooth. Gradually add milk. Bring to a boil; cook and stir for 2 minutes or until thickened. Remove from heat. Stir a small amount of hot mixture into egg; return all to pan, stirring constantly. Stir in 1/4 cup cheese until melted.

3 Pour over the artichokes; sprinkle with remaining cheese. Combine the crumbs and paprika; sprinkle over top. Bake, uncovered, at 400° for 20-25 minutes or until heated through.

YIELD: 4-6 servings.

TRADITIONAL HOT CROSS BUNS

BARBARA JEAN LULL, FULLERTON, CALIFORNIA
These yummy yeast rolls dotted with raisins and currants are traditionally topped with a white glaze in the shape of a cross and served at Easter. The cinnamon and allspice give this recipe just the right hint of spice.

PREP: 20 min. + rising BAKE: 15 min. + cooling

- 2 packages (1/4 ounce each) active dry yeast
- 2 cups warm milk (110° to 115°)
- 1/3 cup butter, softened
- 2 eggs, lightly beaten
- 1/4 cup sugar
- 1-1/2 teaspoons salt
- 6 to 7 cups all-purpose flour
- 1/2 cup raisins
- 1/2 cup dried currants
- 1 teaspoon ground cinnamon
- 1/4 teaspoon ground allspice
- 2 tablespoons water
- 1 egg yolk

Confectioners' sugar icing

1 In a large bowl, dissolve yeast in milk. Stir in the butter, eggs, sugar and salt. Combine 3 cups flour, raisins, currants, cinnamon and allspice; add to yeast mixture and mix well. Stir in enough remaining flour to form a soft dough.

2 Turn onto a floured surface and knead until smooth and elastic, about 6-8 minutes. Place in a greased bowl, turning once to grease top. Cover and let rise in a warm place until doubled, about 1 hour.

3 Punch dough down; shape into 1-1/2- to 2-in. balls. Place 2 in. apart on greased baking sheets. Using a sharp knife, cut a cross on top of each roll. Cover and let rise until doubled, about 30 minutes. Beat water and egg yolk; brush over rolls.

4 Bake at 375° for 15-20 minutes or until golden brown. Cool on wire racks. Pipe icing over rolls.

YIELD: 2-1/2 dozen.

BEEF-STUFFED SOPAIPILLAS

LARA PENNELL, IRVING, TEXAS

When we were kids, after my brothers' football game, we would all descend on a local restaurant for wonderful Southwestern stuffed sopaipillas. This recipe takes me back to that delicious childhood memory. Even my Canadian husband raves about these!

PREP/TOTAL TIME: 30 min.

 2 cups all-purpose flour
 1 teaspoon salt
 1 teaspoon baking powder
 1/2 cup water
 1/4 cup evaporated milk
 1-1/2 teaspoons canola oil
Additional oil for frying

FILLING:

 1 pound ground beef
 3/4 cup chopped onion
 1/2 teaspoon salt
 1/2 teaspoon garlic powder
 1/4 teaspoon pepper

SAUCE:

 1 can (10-3/4 ounces) condensed cream of chicken soup, undiluted
 1/2 cup chicken broth
 1 can (4 ounces) chopped green chilies
 1/2 teaspoon onion powder
 2 cups (8 ounces) shredded cheddar cheese

1 In a large bowl, combine the flour, salt and baking powder. Stir in water, milk and oil with a fork until a ball forms. On a lightly floured surface, knead dough gently for 2-3 minutes. Cover and let stand for 15 minutes. Divide into four portions; roll each into a 6-1/2-in. circle.

2 In an electric skillet or deep-fat fryer, heat oil to 375°. Fry circles, one at a time, for 2-3 minutes on each side or until golden brown. Drain on paper towels.

3 In a large skillet, cook beef and onion until meat is no longer pink; drain. Stir in the salt, garlic powder and pepper. In a large saucepan, combine the soup, broth, chilies and onion powder; cook for 10 minutes or until heated through.

4 Cut a slit on one side of each sopaipilla; fill with 1/2 cup of meat mixture. Top with cheese. Serve with sauce.

YIELD: 4 servings.

BEER MARGARITAS

TASTE OF HOME TEST KITCHEN

There's nothing more refreshing than this cool combination of two popular drinks, beer and lime margaritas.

PREP/TOTAL TIME: 10 min.

 3/4 cup limeade concentrate
 1 bottle (12 ounces) beer
 6 ounces vodka
 6 ounces water
Ice cubes, optional
Lime slices

1 In a pitcher, combine the limeade concentrate, beer, vodka and water. Serve over ice if desired in pilsner or highball glasses. Garnish with lime slices.

YIELD: 4 servings.

EDITOR'S NOTE: This recipe was tested with Corona beer.

TRES LECHES CAKE

TASTE OF HOME TEST KITCHEN

"Tres leches" means "three milks" in Spanish. This traditional cake is great for celebrating Cinco de Mayo or bringing to potlucks.

PREP: 45 min. **BAKE:** 20 min. + chilling

- 4 eggs, separated
- 2/3 cup sugar, divided
- 2/3 cup cake flour
- Dash salt
- 3/4 cup heavy whipping cream
- 3/4 cup evaporated milk
- 3/4 cup sweetened condensed milk
- 2 teaspoons vanilla extract
- 1/4 teaspoon rum extract

TOPPING:
- 1-1/4 cups heavy whipping cream
- 3 tablespoons sugar
- Sliced fresh strawberries, optional

1 Let eggs stand at room temperature for 30 minutes. Line a 9-in. springform pan with waxed paper; grease and flour the paper. Set aside. In a large bowl, beat egg yolks for 2 minutes. Add 1/3 cup sugar; beat for 3 minutes or until mixture is thick and lemon-colored. Fold in flour, a third at a time.

2 In another large bowl and with clean beaters, beat egg whites and salt on medium speed until soft peaks form. Gradually add remaining sugar, 1 tablespoon at a time, beating on high until stiff peaks form. Stir a third of the whites into the yolk mixture. Fold in remaining whites.

3 Spread the batter into prepared pan. Bake at 350° for 20-25 minutes or until top springs back when lightly touched. Cool for 10 minutes before removing from pan to a wire rack to cool completely.

4 In a small bowl, combine cream, evaporated milk, condensed milk and extracts. Transfer cake to a serving plate. Poke holes in top of cake with a skewer. Gradually spoon milk mixture over top. Cover and refrigerate for 2 hours.

5 For topping, in a small bowl, beat cream until it begins to thicken. Add sugar; beat until stiff peaks form. Spread over cake. Garnish with strawberries if desired.

YIELD: 8-10 servings.

CHICKEN TORTILLA SOUP

LAURA JOHNSON, LARGO, FLORIDA

This soup is as good as (if not better than) any kind I've had in a restaurant. I get so many compliments...I know you will, too!

PREP/TOTAL TIME: 25 min.

- 1 large onion, chopped
- 2 tablespoons olive oil
- 1 can (4 ounces) chopped green chilies
- 2 garlic cloves, minced
- 1 jalapeno pepper, seeded and chopped
- 1 teaspoon ground cumin
- 5 cups chicken broth
- 1 can (15 ounces) tomato sauce
- 1 can (14-1/2 ounces) diced tomatoes with garlic and onion, undrained
- 3 cans (5 ounces each) white chicken, drained
- 1/4 cup minced fresh cilantro
- 2 teaspoons lime juice
- Salt and pepper to taste
- Crushed tortilla chips
- Shredded Monterey Jack cheese or cheddar cheese

1 In a large saucepan, saute the onion in oil; add the chilies, garlic, jalapeno and cumin. Stir in the broth, tomato sauce and tomatoes. Bring to a boil. Reduce heat; stir in chicken. Simmer, uncovered, for 10 minutes. Add the cilantro, lime juice, salt and pepper. Top with chips and cheese.

YIELD: 7 servings.

EDITOR'S NOTE: When cutting hot peppers, disposable gloves are recommended. Avoid touching your face.

CINCO DE MAYO

May 5th celebrates and commemorates The Battle of Puebla, where on May 5, 1862, an outnumbered Mexican army fought from early daybreak to evening to defeat French troops at Puebla de Los Angeles, a small town in east-central Mexico. Although this battle is not considered a major victory in the battle between Mexico and France, it unified Mexico's resistance against the French, and six years later, the French withdrew. Cinco de Mayo is a national holiday in Mexico, but is celebrated vigorously in the U.S.

CHEESE SOUFFLES

LYNN MCALLISTER, MT. ULLA, NORTH CAROLINA
Great for brunch, light late-night supper for two or as a versatile side dish, these melt-in-your-mouth souffles are flavorful, fluffy and fun.

PREP: 15 min. **BAKE:** 20 min.

4-1/2 teaspoons butter
4-1/2 teaspoons all-purpose flour
1/2 cup 2% milk
1/2 cup shredded cheddar cheese
2 eggs, separated

1 In a large saucepan, melt butter. Whisk in flour until smooth; gradually add milk. Bring to a boil over medium heat; cook and stir for 1-2 minutes or until thickened. Reduce heat; stir in cheese until melted. Remove from the heat. Beat egg yolks. Stir a small amount of hot mixture into yolks; return all to the pan, stirring constantly. Cool slightly.

2 In a small bowl, beat egg whites until stiff peaks form. Fold into egg yolk mixture. Pour into two 8-oz. ramekins or custard cups coated with cooking spray.

3 Bake at 350° for 20-25 minutes or until a knife inserted near the center comes out clean. Serve immediately.

YIELD: 2 servings.

SPRING AND FALL PIE

LAURA COLLINS, RAPID CITY, SOUTH DAKOTA
Every spring, I have a good crop of rhubarb in my garden, and one of my favorite ways to use it is in this pie. I adapted this version from a recipe I received from our county Extension service.

PREP: 20 min. **BAKE:** 50 min. + cooling

1-1/2 cups sugar
3 tablespoons all-purpose flour
1-1/2 cups sliced fresh or frozen rhubarb, thawed and drained
1-1/2 cups fresh or frozen cranberries, thawed and halved
1-1/2 cups chopped peeled tart apples
Pastry for double-crust pie (9 inches)

1 In a large bowl, combine the sugar and flour; stir in the rhubarb, cranberries and apples. Line a 9-in. pie plate with bottom pastry; add filling.

2 Cover with a lattice crust; seal and flute edges. Bake at 450° for 10 minutes. Reduce heat to 350° bake 40 minutes longer or until filling is bubbly. Cover the edges loosely with foil to prevent overbrowning if necessary.

YIELD: 6-8 servings.

EDITOR'S NOTE: If using frozen rhubarb, measure rhubarb while still frozen, then thaw completely. Drain in a colander, but do not press liquid out.

EGGS BENEDICT CUPS

JENNIFER REISINGER, SHEBOYGAN, WISCONSIN
What a scrumptious way to jump start winter mornings! I use the leftover Hollandaise sauce from this savory breakfast treat to dress up broccoli at night.

PREP: 15 min. **BAKE:** 20 min.

2 slices white bread
1/3 cup shredded cheddar cheese
1 green onion, chopped
2 slices Canadian bacon, finely chopped
1/4 teaspoon garlic powder
1/4 teaspoon minced fresh basil
2 eggs, lightly beaten
2 tablespoons butter
2 tablespoons plus 2 teaspoons hollandaise sauce mix
1/2 cup water
Minced fresh parsley

1 Coat two 8-oz. ramekins or custard cups with cooking spray; line each with a slice of bread. Layer with cheese, onion, Canadian bacon, garlic powder and basil. Pour eggs into cups.

2 Place on a baking sheet. Bake at 350° for 20-25 minutes or until a thermometer reads 160°.

3 In a small saucepan, melt butter. Whisk in sauce mix; gradually stir in water. Bring to a boil; cook and stir for 1 minute or until thickened. Gently remove bread cups to serving plates; serve with hollandaise sauce and parsley.

YIELD: 2 servings.

EASY LATTE

TASTE OF HOME TEST KITCHEN
A latte has the same ingredients as a cappuccino, but is topped with just a thin layer of foamy milk. The techniques explained in this recipe result in a creamy cup of coffee as pleasing as any coffeehouse concoction.

PREP/TOTAL TIME: 10 min.
    1/2 cup milk
    1/3 cup hot brewed espresso

1 Place milk in a 1-cup microwave-safe measuring cup. Microwave, uncovered, on high for 1 minute or until milk is hot and small bubbles form around edge of cup.

2 Place a metal whisk in cup; whisk vigorously by holding whisk handle loosely between palms and quickly rubbing hands back and forth. Remove foam to a small measuring cup as it forms. Continue whisking until foam measures 1/8 to 1/4 cup; set aside.

3 Pour espresso into a cup; pour in remaining hot milk. Spoon foam over top and serve immediately.

YIELD: 1 serving.

EDITOR'S NOTE: You may also use a portable mixer with whisk attachment to froth the milk.

FRUIT-FILLED FRENCH TOAST WRAPS

DAWN JARVIS, BRECKENRIDGE, MINNESOTA
Here's a delicious way to add fiber to your diet. This pretty dish makes an amazing breakfast or brunch entree. It's easy to make but looks so special.

PREP/TOTAL TIME: 25 min.
      1 egg
    1/4 cup 2% milk
      1 teaspoon ground cinnamon
    1/2 teaspoon ground nutmeg
      2 whole wheat tortillas (8 inches)
      2 teaspoons butter
    2/3 cup sliced fresh strawberries
    2/3 cup fresh blueberries
    2/3 cup sliced ripe banana
      1 carton (6 ounces) vanilla yogurt
    1/4 cup granola
      1 teaspoon confectioners' sugar

1 In a shallow bowl, whisk the egg, milk, cinnamon and nutmeg. Dip both sides of tortillas in egg mixture. In a nonstick skillet, cook tortillas in butter over medium-high heat for 2 minutes on each side or until golden brown.

2 In a small bowl, combine the berries, banana, yogurt and granola. Spoon down the center of tortillas. Roll up; sprinkle with confectioners' sugar. Serve immediately.

YIELD: 2 servings.

YES, WE HAVE BANANAS
Look for plump bananas that are evenly yellow-colored. Green bananas are under-ripe, while a flecking of brown flecks indicates ripeness. If bananas are too green, place in a paper bag until ripe. Adding an apple to the bag will speed the process. Store ripe bananas at room temperature.

Summer brings blue skies, lazy days and warm-weather recipes that are perfect for backyard grilling, picnics, potlucks and beach getaways. You'll find cool relief from the heat with refreshing salads, cold beverages and ice cream treats. And don't forget about the beautifully bright market finds that make their debut during this time of the year. Whether it's berries, peaches, cherries, corn, tomatoes or melon that you love to eat, be sure to take advantage of summer's gifts while they're here.

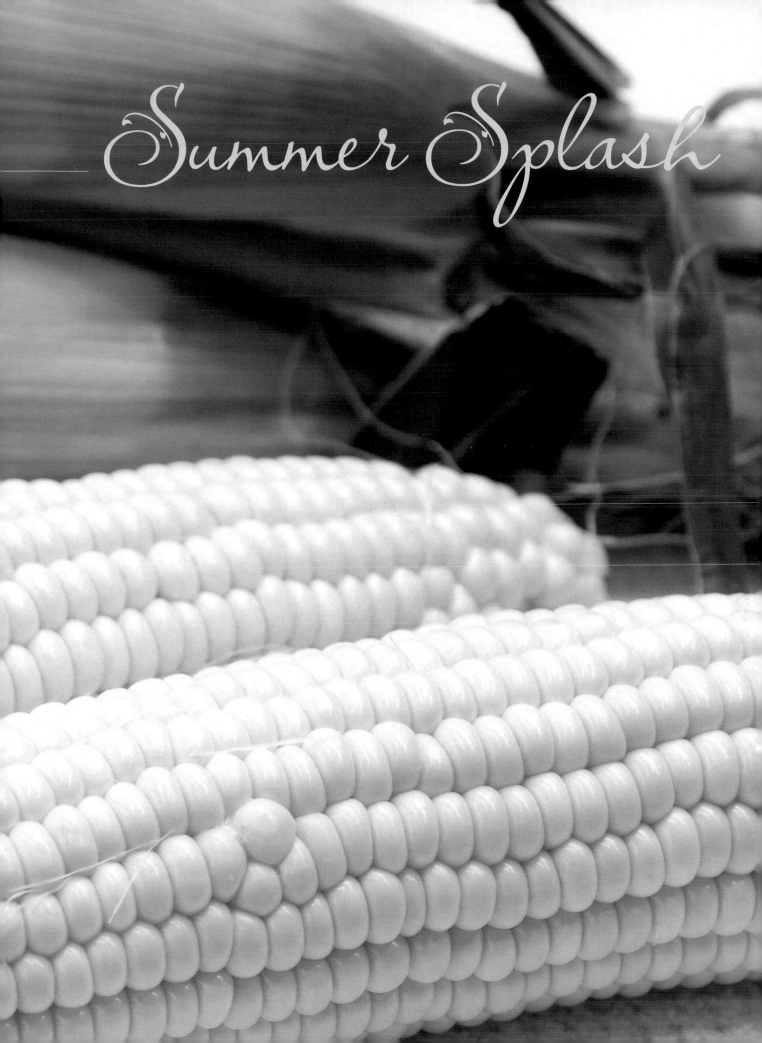

Summer Splash

APPETIZERS & BEVERAGES

CAESAR SALSA BAGUETTE SLICES

JODIE GHARBI, SHREVEPORT, LOUISIANA
I love throwing themed get-togethers. This appetizer was the hit of "Mediterranean Night." The fresh garden flavors in the tomatoey salsa are outstanding with a crusty baguette.

PREP/TOTAL TIME: 25 min.
   2 cups chopped seeded tomatoes
   3 tablespoons minced fresh chervil or
      1 tablespoon dried chervil
   1 tablespoon minced fresh cilantro
   1 tablespoon minced fresh parsley
   1 tablespoon capers, drained
 1/2 teaspoon hot pepper sauce
   2 tablespoons plus 1-1/2 teaspoons olive oil
4-1/2 teaspoons lemon juice
2-1/2 teaspoons red wine vinegar
   1 shallot, finely chopped
   1 garlic clove, minced
 1/2 teaspoon anchovy paste
 1/8 teaspoon grated lemon peel
   1 loaf (10-1/2 ounces) French bread baguette,
      cut into 1/2-inch slices and toasted

1 In a small bowl, combine the tomatoes, chervil, cilantro, parsley, capers and hot pepper sauce.

2 In another bowl, whisk the oil, lemon juice, vinegar, shallot, garlic, anchovy paste and lemon peel. Drizzle over tomato mixture; toss to coat. Serve with toasted baguette slices.

YIELD: 32 appetizers.

OLD-FASHIONED LEMONADE

TAMMI SIMPSON, GREENSBURG, KENTUCKY
Fourth of July gatherings just wouldn't be the same without homemade lemonade. The fresh-squeezed flavor of this sweet-tart beverage makes it a winner.

PREP: 15 min. + chilling
   2 to 2-1/2 cups sugar
   5 cups water, divided
   1 tablespoon grated lemon peel
1-3/4 cups lemon juice (about 6 lemons)

1 In a large saucepan, combine sugar, 1 cup water and lemon peel. Cook and stir over medium heat until sugar is dissolved, about 4 minutes.

2 Remove from heat. Stir in lemon juice and remaining water. Pour into a pitcher and refrigerate until chilled. Serve over ice.

YIELD: 2 quarts.

BERRY YOGURT SHAKES

JACQUIE ADAMS, COLQUITLAM, BRITISH COLUMBIA
We have a few raspberry bushes in our backyard. If my grandchildren don't get the berries first, I use them in recipes like this one. Of course, the kids love the mellow flavor of these shakes. So either way, they win!

PREP/TOTAL TIME: 5 min.
   2 cartons (8 ounces each) reduced-fat lemon yogurt
1-1/2 cups fat-free milk

1 cup unsweetened raspberries
Sugar substitute equivalent to 2 tablespoons sugar

1 Place all ingredients in a blender; cover and process until smooth. Pour into chilled glasses; serve immediately.

YIELD: 4 servings.

MIXED BERRY PIZZA

GRETCHEN WIDNER, SUN CITY WEST, ARIZONA
The fresh fruit shines through in this colorful dessert pizza. It's also a tempting appetizer at parties because it's a sweet change of pace from the usual savory dips.

PREP: 10 min. BAKE: 10 min. + chilling
   1 tube (8 ounces) refrigerated reduced-fat crescent rolls
  11 ounces reduced-fat cream cheese
 1/2 cup apricot preserves
   2 tablespoons confectioners' sugar
   2 cups sliced fresh strawberries
   1 cup fresh blueberries
   1 cup fresh raspberries

1 Unroll crescent roll dough and place in a 15-in. x 10-in. x 1-in. baking pan coated with cooking spray. Press onto the bottom and 1 in. up the sides of pan to form a crust; seal seams and perforations. Bake at 375° for 8-10 minutes or until golden. Cool completely.

2 In a large bowl, beat cream cheese until smooth. Beat in the preserves and confectioners' sugar; spread over crust. Cover and refrigerate for 1-2 hours.

3 Just before serving, arrange berries on top. Cut into 20 pieces.

YIELD: 20 servings.

LONG ISLAND ICED TEA

TASTE OF HOME TEST KITCHEN
Smooth but potent describes this drink. Adjust the tequila to suit your taste. If you like a bolder flavor, use one ounce. If you would prefer a more mellow drink, use a half ounce.

PREP/TOTAL TIME: 5 min.
   1 to 1-1/4 cups ice cubes
   1 ounce vodka
 1/2 to 1 ounce tequila
   1 ounce light rum
   1 ounce sour mix
   1 ounce triple sec
 1/2 ounce cola

1 Place ice in a Collins or highball glass. Pour the remaining ingredients into the glass; stir.

YIELD: 1 serving.

> **GARNISHES FOR SUMMER SIPPERS**
> To decorate a spritzer or cocktail, pierce a maraschino cherry and an orange slice with a toothpick. Cut partway through the orange slice so it can rest on the edge of the glass. Or, skewer berries, grapes, cherries, melon chunks and/or pineapple, then perch the fruit kabobs across the top of the glass.

CAPPUCCINO SMOOTHIES

MICHELLE CLUNEY, LAKE MARY, FLORIDA
Topped with miniature marshmallows, this icy beverage is a twist on traditional fruit smoothies. It's a nice drink to fix in hot weather when you're craving cappuccino.

PREP/TOTAL TIME: 5 min.
- 1 cup (8 ounces) cappuccino or coffee yogurt
- 1/3 cup milk
- 3 tablespoons confectioners' sugar, optional
- 1 tablespoon chocolate syrup
- 1-1/2 cups ice cubes
- 1/2 cup miniature marshmallows, divided

1 In a blender, combine the yogurt, milk, sugar if desired and chocolate syrup. Add ice cubes and 1/4 cup marshmallows; cover and process until blended. Pour into chilled glasses; top with the remaining marshmallows. Serve immediately.

YIELD: 3 servings.

MARINATED MOZZARELLA

PEGGY CAIRO, KENOSHA, WISCONSIN
I've made this dish for years, and I always come home with an empty container when I bring it to a party or barbeque. It can be made ahead to free up time later.

PREP: 15 min. + marinating
- 1/3 cup olive oil
- 1 tablespoon chopped oil-packed sun-dried tomatoes
- 1 tablespoon minced fresh parsley
- 1 teaspoon crushed red pepper flakes
- 1 teaspoon dried basil

- 1 teaspoon minced chives
- 1/4 teaspoon garlic powder
- 1 pound cubed part-skim mozzarella cheese

1 In a large resealable plastic bag, combine the first seven ingredients; add cheese cubes. Seal bag and turn to coat; refrigerate for at least 30 minutes.

2 Transfer to a serving dish; serve with toothpicks.

YIELD: 8-10 servings.

AVOCADO TACO DIP

RUTH ANN STELFOX, RAYMOND, ALBERTA
This Mexican-inspired dip is guaranteed to disappear in a hurry. It's simple to make and so tasty. It's perfect for a summertime fiesta.

PREP/TOTAL TIME: 20 min.
- 1 can (16 ounces) refried beans
- 1 cup (8 ounces) sour cream
- 2/3 cup mayonnaise
- 1 envelope taco seasoning
- 1 can (4 ounces) chopped green chilies, drained
- 4 medium ripe avocados, halved, pitted and peeled
- 2 teaspoons lime juice
- 1/4 teaspoon salt
- 1/4 teaspoon garlic powder
- 1 cup (4 ounces) shredded sharp cheddar cheese
- 1/2 cup thinly sliced green onions
- 1/2 cup chopped fresh tomato
- 1 can (2-1/4 ounces) sliced ripe olives, drained

Tortilla chips

1 Spread beans in a shallow 2-1/2-qt. dish. In a small bowl, combine sour cream, mayonnaise and taco seasoning; spread over beans. Sprinkle with chilies.

2 In a large bowl, mash avocados with the lime juice, salt and garlic powder. Spread over the chilies. Sprinkle with the cheese, onions, tomato and olives. Cover and refrigerate until serving. Serve with tortilla chips.

YIELD: 12-14 servings.

BOTTOMS-UP CHERRY LIMEADE

AWYNNE THURSTENSON, SILOAM SPRINGS, ARKANSAS
My guests enjoy this refreshing cherry-topped drink. It always hits the sweet spot on warm summer evenings. And it's pretty, too.

PREP/TOTAL TIME: 10 min.
- 3/4 cup lime juice
- 1 cup sugar
- 2 liters lime carbonated water, chilled
- 1/2 cup maraschino cherry juice
- Crushed ice
- 8 maraschino cherries with stems
- 8 lime slices

1 In a large bowl, combine lime juice and sugar. Cover and refrigerate. Just before serving, stir carbonated water into lime juice mixture.

2 For each serving, place 1 tablespoon cherry juice in a glass. Add crushed ice and about 1 cup of lime juice mixture. Garnish with a maraschino cherry and a lime slice.

YIELD: 8 servings.

SUMMER TEA SANDWICHES

TASTE OF HOME TEST KITCHEN
Our home economists prepared these dainty finger sandwiches that are perfect for casual picnics or ladies' luncheons. Tarragon-seasoned chicken complements cucumber and cantaloupe slices.

PREP: 45 min. BAKE: 20 min. + cooling
- 1/2 teaspoon dried tarragon
- 1/2 teaspoon salt, divided
- 1/4 teaspoon pepper
- 1 pound boneless skinless chicken breasts
- 1/2 cup reduced-fat mayonnaise
- 1 tablespoon finely chopped red onion
- 1 teaspoon dill weed
- 1/2 teaspoon lemon juice
- 24 slices soft multigrain bread, crusts removed
- 1 medium cucumber, thinly sliced
- 1/4 medium cantaloupe, cut into 12 thin slices

1 Combine the tarragon, 1/4 teaspoon salt and pepper; rub over chicken. Place on a baking sheet coated with cooking spray. Bake at 350° for 20-25 minutes or until juices run clear. Cool to room temperature; thinly slice.

2 Combine the mayonnaise, onion, dill, lemon juice and remaining salt; spread over one side of 12 slices of bread. Top with cucumber, chicken, cantaloupe and remaining bread. Cut sandwiches in half diagonally. Serve immediately.

YIELD: 12 servings.

SUMMER TIP
Dried herbs don't spoil, but they do lose flavor and potency over time. For maximum flavor, replace herbs that are over a year old. Store dried herbs in airtight containers away from heat and light. To substitute dried with fresh herbs, use three times the amount. So, for 1 teaspoon of dried herbs, use 3 teaspoons of fresh.

APPETIZER CHICKEN KABOBS

GAIL PONAK, VISCOUNT, SASKATCHEWAN
These little chicken kabobs are a scrumptious appetizer. They're quick and easy to prepare, which means I can spend more time having fun with guests outdoors.

PREP: 15 min. + marinating **BAKE:** 10 min.

- 3/4 cup soy sauce
- 1/4 cup sugar
- 1 tablespoon canola oil
- 1/4 teaspoon garlic powder
- 1/2 teaspoon ground ginger
- 2 boneless skinless chicken breasts, cut into 1-inch chunks
- 6 to 8 green onions, cut into 1-inch pieces
- 1/2 pound medium fresh mushrooms, stems removed

1 In a large bowl, combine first five ingredients. Pour half into a large resealable plastic bag; add chicken. Seal bag and turn to coat. Pour remaining marinade into another large plastic bag; add onions. Seal bag and toss to coat. Marinate for 30 minutes.

2 Drain and discard marinade from chicken. Drain and reserve marinade from onions. On soaked wooden skewers, thread a piece of chicken, onion, mushroom and another chicken piece.

3 Place on a broiler rack. Broil 5 in. from the heat, turning and basting with reserved marinade after 3 minutes. Broil for 3 minutes longer or until chicken is no longer pink.

YIELD: 20-24 appetizers.

EASY GREEN ONIONS
When a recipe calls for green onions, an easy and fast way to cut them is with kitchen scissors, rather than with a knife. If the recipe calls for quite a few, grab a bunch at one time and snip away. You're done before you know it, and this saves you from washing a knife and cutting board.

GOAT CHEESE 'N' VEGGIE QUESADILLAS

SARA LONGWORTH, BRISTOL, CONNECTICUT
The roasted veggies and goat cheese make this a unique party food. We love to top them with our favorite salsa for an extra kick!

PREP: 55 min. **BAKE:** 5 min.

- 1 small eggplant, peeled, quartered and cut into 1/2-inch slices
- 1 medium zucchini, cut into 1/4-inch slices
- 1 medium sweet red pepper, chopped
- 1 medium onion, chopped
- 1/4 cup chopped ripe olives
- 2 garlic cloves, minced
- 2 tablespoons olive oil
- 1 tablespoon lemon juice
- 1/2 teaspoon chili powder
- 1/2 teaspoon cayenne pepper
- 1 tablespoon minced fresh cilantro
- 1/2 cup semi-soft goat cheese
- 8 whole wheat tortillas (8 inches)

1 Place the first six ingredients in an ungreased 15-in. x 10-in. x 1-in. baking pan. Combine the oil, lemon juice, chili powder and cayenne; drizzle over vegetables and toss to coat. Bake, uncovered, at 400° for 35-40 minutes or until tender, stirring once. Stir in cilantro.

2 Spread 1 tablespoon goat cheese over one side of each tortilla. Place two tortillas, plain side down, on an ungreased baking sheet; spread each with 2/3 cup vegetable mixture. Top each with another tortilla. Repeat. Bake at 400° for 5-10 minutes or until golden brown. Cut each quesadilla into six wedges. Serve warm.

YIELD: 2 dozen appetizers.

GRILLED GLAZED DRUMMIES

LAURA MAHAFFEY, ANNAPOLIS, MARYLAND
My family prefers these mild grilled chicken wings over traditional hot wings. I make them for picnics, barbeques and even casual nights when we want a light supper.

PREP: 10 min. + marinating **GRILL:** 15 min.

- 1 cup ketchup
- 1/3 cup soy sauce
- 4 teaspoons honey
- 3/4 teaspoon ground ginger
- 1/2 teaspoon garlic powder
- 3 pounds fresh or frozen chicken drumettes, thawed

1 In a small bowl, combine the ketchup, soy sauce, honey, ginger and garlic powder. Pour 1 cup marinade into a large resealable plastic bag; add the chicken. Seal bag and turn to coat; refrigerate for at least 4 hours or overnight. Cover and refrigerate remaining marinade for basting.

2 Drain chicken and discard marinade. Grill, covered, over medium heat for 15-20 minutes or until juices run clear, turning and basting occasionally with reserved marinade.

YIELD: about 2 dozen.

TROPICAL FRUIT DIP

SUZANNE STROCSHER, BOTHELL, WASHINGTON
This refreshing snack is perfect for a summer luau. I love coconut and look for any excuse to make this yummy dip.

PREP: 15 min. + chilling

- 2 cups (16 ounces) 4% cottage cheese
- 1/4 cup lemon yogurt or flavor of your choice
- 3 to 4 tablespoons honey
- 1 teaspoon grated orange peel
- 2 tablespoons flaked coconut, toasted
  Assorted fresh fruit

1 Place the cottage cheese and yogurt in a blender; cover and process until smooth. Stir in honey and orange peel. Pour into a serving dish. Cover and refrigerate for at least 1 hour. Sprinkle with coconut. Serve with fruit.

YIELD: about 1-1/2 cups.

RASPBERRY SWEET TEA

TASTE OF HOME TEST KITCHEN
You only need a handful of ingredients to stir together this refreshing summer sipper. Its brilliant color and flavor make a popular thirst-quencher as the weather turns warm.

PREP: 20 min. + chilling

- 4 quarts water, divided
- 1 cup sugar
- 10 individual tea bags
- 1 package (12 ounces) frozen unsweetened raspberries, thawed and undrained
- 3 tablespoons lime juice

1 In a large saucepan, bring 2 qts. of water to a boil. Stir in sugar until dissolved. Remove from the heat.

2 Add tea bags; steep for 5-8 minutes. Discard tea bags.

3 In another saucepan, bring raspberries and remaining water to a boil. Reduce heat; simmer, uncovered, for 3 minutes. Strain and discard the pulp. Add raspberry juice and lime juice to the tea.

4 Transfer to a large pitcher. Refrigerate until chilled.

YIELD: 15 servings.

MINI BURGERS WITH THE WORKS

LINDA LANE, BENNINGTON, VERMONT

These mini burgers are great to serve at barbeques where guests can experiment with different toppings on each one.

PREP/TOTAL TIME: 30 min.

- 1/4 pound ground beef
- 3 slices process American cheese
- 4 slices white bread (heels of loaf recommended)
- 2 tablespoons prepared Thousand Island salad dressing
- 2 pearl onions, thinly sliced
- 4 baby dill pickles, thinly sliced
- 3 cherry tomatoes, thinly sliced

1 Shape beef into twelve 1-in. patties. Place on a microwave-safe plate lined with paper towels. Cover with another paper towel; microwave on high for 1 minute or until meat is no longer pink. Cut each slice of cheese into fourths; set aside.

2 Using a 1-in. round cookie cutter, cut out six circles from each slice of bread. Spread half of the bread circles with dressing. Layer with the burgers, cheese, onions, pickles and tomatoes. Top with the remaining bread circles; secure with toothpicks. Serve immediately.

YIELD: 1 dozen.

WHERE'S THE BEEF?

Ground beef is labeled according to the cut of meat from which it is ground, such as ground chuck or ground round. It is also labeled by its fat content or the percentage of lean meat to fat, such as 85% or 90% lean. A higher percentage equals leaner meat. Select bright red ground beef that is in a tightly sealed package.

BLT BITES

ELIZABETH BORGEMENKE, MASON, OHIO

I've put a twist on one of America's favorite sandwiches. These little bites have big flavor!

PREP: 30 min. + chilling

- 28 cherry tomatoes
- 7 bacon strips, cooked and crumbled
- 1/2 cup fat-free mayonnaise
- 1/3 cup chopped green onions
- 3 tablespoons grated Parmesan cheese
- 2 tablespoons finely chopped celery
- 2 tablespoons minced fresh parsley

1 Cut a thin slice off the top of each tomato. Scoop out and discard pulp; invert tomatoes onto paper towels to drain. In a small bowl, combine the bacon, mayonnaise, onions, cheese, celery and parsley. Spoon into tomatoes. Cover and refrigerate for at least 2 hours.

YIELD: 28 appetizers.

PARLOUR CHOCOLATE SODA

DAWN SAMS, GRAYSLAKE, ILLINOIS

We enjoy making this old-fashioned soda-fountain specialty at home. Besides being a favorite treat for my grandchildren, it's entertaining to watch it being prepared. They love the "magic" of the soda foaming up as they urge me to add more and more whipped topping.

PREP/TOTAL TIME: 10 min.

- 6 tablespoons chocolate syrup
- 2 tablespoons whipped cream in a can
- 2-1/2 cups cold carbonated water
- 4 scoops ice cream of your choice

Additional whipped cream, optional

1 For each serving, place 3 tablespoons chocolate syrup in a 16-oz. glass. Stir in 1 tablespoon of whipped cream and 1-1/4 cups water until foamy. Add two scoops of ice cream. Top with additional whipped cream if desired.

YIELD: 2 servings.

GRILLED POTATO SKINS

STEPHANIE MOON, GREEN BAY, WISCONSIN

The creamy topping on these potato skins is one of my husband's delicious creations. These appetizers make an excellent summertime treat alongside your favorite grilled meat. We like them with barbecue ribs. If you're not grilling your meal, you can bake the potato skins in a 375° oven for 18-20 minutes.

PREP/TOTAL TIME: 30 min.

- 2 medium potatoes
- 1-1/2 teaspoons butter, melted
- 2 tablespoons picante sauce
- 1/4 cup shredded cheddar cheese
- 1 tablespoon real bacon bits
- 1/4 cup chopped tomato
- 2 tablespoons chopped green onion

TOPPING:

- 3 tablespoons mayonnaise
- 2 tablespoons sour cream
- 1 tablespoon prepared ranch salad dressing
- 1-1/2 teaspoons real bacon bits
- 1/4 teaspoon garlic powder

1 Cut each potato lengthwise into four wedges. Cut away the white portion, leaving 1/4 in. on the potato skins. Place skins on a microwave-safe plate.

2 Microwave, uncovered, on high for 8-10 minutes or until tender. Brush butter over shells; top with picante sauce, cheese and bacon bits.

3 Grill the potatoes, skin side down, uncovered, over medium heat for 4-6 minutes or until lightly browned. Cover and grill 2-3 minutes longer or until cheese is melted. Sprinkle with the tomato and onion. In a small bowl, combine topping ingredients. Serve with potato skins.

YIELD: 4-5 servings.

CHERRY MALTS

TASTE OF HOME TEST KITCHEN

White chocolate and cherry ice cream are a luscious combination in this delightfully frosty malt. For a thicker, fruitier malt, add some frozen sweet cherries to the blender before processing.

PREP/TOTAL TIME: 5 min.

- 1 cup milk
- 3 cups cherry ice cream
- 3 tablespoons malted milk powder
- 1 square (1 ounce) white baking chocolate, chopped

1 In a blender, combine milk, ice cream, malted milk powder and chocolate; cover and process until blended. Pour into chilled glasses.

YIELD: 2 servings.

MINTED ICED TEA COOLER

DEBBIE TERENZINI-WILKERSON, LUSBY, MARYLAND

This cool rose-colored tea quenches your thirst in the most delightful way. It's a pleasant blend of fruit and mint flavors. It's very easy to make and a fun twist from traditional iced tea.

PREP: 10 min. + chilling

- 3 peppermint-flavored tea bags
- 7 cups boiling water
- 1 cup cranberry juice
- 3/4 cup pink lemonade concentrate

1 Steep tea bags in boiling water for 5-10 minutes. Discard tea bags. Pour tea into a pitcher or large bowl; stir in cranberry juice and lemonade concentrate. Cover and refrigerate overnight. Serve over ice.

YIELD: 8 servings.

OLD TAVERN CORN FRITTERS

LAURA LAGASSE, UNIONVILLE, OHIO

Two co-workers who also subscribe to Taste of Home *helped me convince the owners of The Old Tavern to share their recipe. It has been a family secret for nearly 200 years.*

PREP/TOTAL TIME: 30 min.

    1 cup all-purpose flour
1-1/2 teaspoons baking powder
    2 eggs
  1/3 cup milk
    1 can (15-1/4 ounces) whole kernel corn, drained
    1 tablespoon butter, melted
Oil for deep-fat frying
Confectioners' sugar
Maple syrup, warmed

1 In a large bowl, combine flour and baking powder; set aside. In another bowl, beat the eggs and milk; stir in corn and butter. Stir into dry ingredients just until blended.

2 In a deep-fat fryer or electric skillet, heat oil to 375°. Drop batter by heaping teaspoonfuls into hot oil; fry for 2-3 minutes or until golden brown. Drain on paper towels. Dust with confectioners' sugar. Serve with syrup.

YIELD: about 2 dozen.

TOMATO BASIL SNACKERS

TASTE OF HOME TEST KITCHEN

Fresh basil, summer-ripe tomatoes and melted mozzarella cheese top toasted English muffins in this fabulous afternoon snack from our home economists.

PREP/TOTAL TIME: 15 min.

    2 English muffins, split and toasted
    2 tablespoons fat-free mayonnaise
    3 plum tomatoes, cut into 1/4-inch slices
    6 fresh basil leaves, thinly sliced
  1/8 teaspoon pepper
  1/2 cup shredded part-skim mozzarella cheese

GRILLED SHRIMP WITH CILANTRO SAUCE

TASTE OF HOME TEST KITCHEN

Make this zippy, change-of-pace recipe from our home economists for a lip-smacking cilantro sauce that really dresses up grilled shrimp.

PREP/TOTAL TIME: 25 min.

1-1/2 cups fresh cilantro leaves
    4 teaspoons minced fresh gingerroot
    2 garlic cloves, peeled
    3 tablespoons plus 1-1/2 teaspoons canola oil
1-1/2 teaspoons lemon juice
    6 uncooked jumbo shrimp (about 1/3 pound), peeled and deveined
    1 teaspoon lemon-pepper seasoning

1 In a small food processor, combine the cilantro, ginger and garlic; cover and process until cilantro and garlic are chopped. While processing, gradually add oil and lemon juice in a steady stream until smooth. Transfer to a small serving bowl; set aside.

2 Coat grill rack with cooking spray before starting the grill. Thread shrimp onto two metal or soaked wooden skewers. Sprinkle with lemon-pepper. Grill, uncovered, over medium heat for 5-8 minutes on each side or until shrimp turn pink. Serve with cilantro sauce.

YIELD: 2 servings.

1 Place English muffin halves on an ungreased baking sheet; spread with mayonnaise. Top with the tomatoes, basil, pepper and cheese. Broil 4 in. from the heat for 3-4 minutes or until cheese is melted.

YIELD: 4 servings.

SWEET BERRY BRUSCHETTA

PATRICIA NIEH, PORTOLA VALLEY, CALIFORNIA
I've made this recipe by toasting the bread on a grill at cookouts, but any way I serve it, I never have any leftovers. Guests are pleasantly surprised when they find the bruschetta is sweet instead of savory.

PREP/TOTAL TIME: 20 min.
- 10 slices French bread (1/2 inch thick)
- 5 teaspoons sugar, divided
- 6 ounces cream cheese
- 1/2 teaspoon almond extract
- 3/4 cup fresh blackberries
- 3/4 cup fresh raspberries
- 1/4 cup slivered almonds, toasted
- 2 teaspoons confectioners' sugar

1 Place bread on an ungreased baking sheet; lightly coat with cooking spray. Sprinkle with 2 teaspoons sugar. Broil 3-4 in. from the heat for 1-2 minutes or until lightly browned.

2 In a small bowl, combine the cream cheese, almond extract and remaining sugar. Spread over toasted bread. Top with berries and almonds; dust with confectioners' sugar.

YIELD: 10 pieces.

> **SUMMER BERRIES**
> Purchase berries that are brightly colored without the hulls attached. One-half pint equals about 1 cup. When you get home, discard any that are soft, shriveled or moldy. Quickly rinse remaining berries in water, then place in a single layer in a paper towel-lined bowl. They'll stay fresh in the refrigerator for up to 3 days.

PEPPER STEAK QUESADILLAS

BARBARA MOORE, FARMINGTON, NEW MEXICO
I came up with this delicious snack when my family needed a quick lunch before running off in several directions. I threw together what I had in the fridge, and it was a big hit!

PREP/TOTAL TIME: 30 min.
- 1/2 pound boneless beef sirloin steak
- 1/2 each medium green, sweet red and yellow pepper, julienned
- 1 tablespoon chopped red onion
- 1 garlic clove, minced
- 1 tablespoon minced fresh cilantro
- 1/4 teaspoon dried rosemary, crushed
- 4 flour tortillas (6 inches)
- 6 cherry tomatoes, halved
- 1/4 cup sliced fresh mushrooms
- 1 cup (4 ounces) shredded part-skim mozzarella cheese

1 If grilling the steak, coat grill rack with cooking spray before starting the grill. Grill steak, covered, over medium heat or broil 4 in. from the heat for 4-6 minutes on each side or until meat reaches desired doneness (for medium-rare, a meat thermometer should read 145°; medium, 160°; well-done, 170°). Let stand for 10 minutes.

2 Meanwhile, in a large skillet coated with cooking spray, saute the peppers, onion and garlic for 5-6 minutes or until tender. Sprinkle with cilantro and rosemary.

3 Place two tortillas on a baking sheet coated with cooking spray. Cut the steak into thin strips; place on tortillas. Using a slotted spoon, place pepper mixture over steak. Top with the tomatoes, mushrooms, cheese and remaining tortillas; lightly spray top of tortillas with cooking spray.

4 Bake at 425° for 5-10 minutes or until golden brown and cheese is melted. Cut each quesadilla into four wedges.

YIELD: 4 servings.

104   101   106   100

SOUPS & SANDWICHES

102

SWISS CHARD BEAN SOUP

TASTE OF HOME TEST KITCHEN
This hearty soup combines nutritious Swiss chard with other garden vegetables. Its light broth is surprisingly rich in flavor and the grated Parmesan packs an additional punch. If you can't find yellow squash, just use more zucchini.

PREP: 25 min. **COOK:** 30 min.
- 1 medium carrot, coarsely chopped
- 1 small zucchini, coarsely chopped
- 1 small yellow summer squash, coarsely chopped
- 1 small red onion, chopped
- 2 tablespoons olive oil
- 2 garlic cloves, minced
- 3 cans (14-1/2 ounces each) reduced-sodium chicken broth
- 4 cups chopped Swiss chard
- 1 can (15-1/2 ounces) great northern beans, rinsed and drained
- 1 can (14-1/2 ounces) diced tomatoes, undrained
- 1 teaspoon dried thyme
- 1/2 teaspoon salt
- 1/2 teaspoon dried oregano
- 1/4 teaspoon pepper
- 1/4 cup grated Parmesan cheese

1 In a Dutch oven or soup kettle, saute the carrot, zucchini, yellow squash and onion in oil until tender. Add garlic; saute 1 minute longer. Add the broth, Swiss chard, beans, tomatoes, thyme, salt, oregano and pepper.

2 Bring to a boil. Reduce heat; simmer, uncovered, for 15 minutes or until chard is tender. Just before serving, sprinkle with Parmesan cheese.

YIELD: 10 servings (2-1/2 quarts).

SUMMER SQUASH SOUP

SANDRA PICHON, SLIDELL, LOUISIANA
With its delicate taste, this creamy concoction makes an easy but elegant first course for a company dinner.

PREP: 40 min. **COOK:** 20 min.
- 5 small yellow summer squash, seeded and cubed
- 2 green onions, cut into 3-inch pieces
- 2 tablespoons butter
- 1 can (14-1/2 ounces) chicken or vegetable broth
- 1/2 teaspoon salt
- 1/8 to 1/4 teaspoon white pepper
- 1-1/2 cups heavy whipping cream

1 In a large saucepan, saute squash and onions in butter until tender. Stir in the broth, salt and pepper; bring to a boil. Reduce heat; cover and simmer for 20-25 minutes or until vegetables are tender.

2 Cool slightly. Process in batches in a blender; return all to the pan. Stir in cream and heat through.

YIELD: 6 servings.

YOU AIN'T NOTHIN' BUT A HOUND DOGS

JUDY NIX, TOCCOA, GEORGIA
Planning a Fabulous '50s party to surprise my sister for her birthday got me humming. Recalling popular songs from the decade gave me the idea for a clever name for the chili dogs I served. Like Elvis' tune, they were a big hit!

PREP/TOTAL TIME: 20 min.
- 1/2 pound ground beef
- 2 tablespoons chopped onion
- 3/4 cup ketchup
- 1/4 cup water
- 1-1/2 teaspoons Worcestershire sauce
- 3/4 teaspoon chili powder
- 1/4 teaspoon pepper
- 1/8 teaspoon cayenne pepper
- 8 hot dogs, cooked
- 8 hot dog buns, split

1 In a large saucepan, cook the beef and onion over medium heat until meat is no longer pink; drain. Stir in the ketchup, water, Worcestershire sauce, chili powder, pepper and cayenne. Bring to a boil. Reduce heat; simmer, uncovered, for 5 minutes or until mixture reaches desired thickness.

2 Place hot dogs in buns; top each with about 2 tablespoons beef mixture.

YIELD: 8 servings.

HEARTY MUFFULETTA

RUTH HAYWARD, LAKE CHARLES, LOUISIANA
Famous in Louisiana, muffulettas are cold cuts, cheese and olive salad layered into an Italian bread shell. I was delighted when a friend gave me this recipe so I could try her delicious version. It's an easy sandwich to transport for a picnic—just wrap it tightly in plastic wrap.

PREP: 55 min. + chilling

- 1/2 cup finely chopped celery
- 1/2 cup sliced pimiento-stuffed olives, drained
- 1/2 cup sliced ripe olives, drained
- 1/2 cup giardiniera
- 1/3 cup finely chopped onion
- 1/3 cup olive oil
- 1/4 cup finely chopped green onions
- 1/4 cup minced fresh parsley
- 3 tablespoons lemon juice
- 1 teaspoon dried oregano
- 1 garlic clove, minced
- 1/8 teaspoon pepper
- 1 round loaf (24 ounces) unsliced Italian bread
- 1/4 pound thinly sliced hard salami
- 1/4 pound provolone cheese
- 1/4 pound thinly sliced deli ham

1 In a large bowl, combine the first 12 ingredients. Cover and refrigerate for at least 8 hours. Drain, reserving 2 tablespoons of the liquid.

2 Cut loaf of bread in half; hollow out the top and bottom, leaving a 1-in. shell (discard removed bread or save for another use). Brush the cut sides of bread with reserved liquid. Layer the bottom of bread shell with salami, half of the olive mixture, cheese, remaining olive mixture and ham. Replace bread top. Cut into wedges.

YIELD: 8-10 servings.

EDITOR'S NOTE: Giardiniera is a vegetable mixture available in mild and hot varieties. Look for it in the Italian or pickle section of your local grocery store.

MEATLESS MUFFULETTA
If you prefer, make Hearty Muffuletta without meat. Replace the salami and ham with grilled portobello mushroom caps, fresh tomato slices and spinach leaves. You could also sprinkle some drained and rinsed cannellini beans on top.

CHILLED BEAN SOUP

BETTY NICKELS, TAMPA, FLORIDA
I combine crunchy fresh veggies with black beans and a splash of hot pepper sauce to create this spicy chilled soup. I often serve this during the warm summer months, when tomatoes are in season. It tastes best when you let it mellow overnight in the refrigerator.

PREP: 15 min. + chilling

- 4 cups chopped seeded tomatoes
- 2 cups picante V8 juice
- 1 can (15 ounces) black beans, rinsed and drained
- 1 cup chopped cucumber
- 1 cup chopped sweet red or yellow pepper
- 1/2 cup chopped red onion
- 2 tablespoons balsamic vinegar
- 1 teaspoon sugar
- 1/4 to 1/2 teaspoon hot pepper sauce
- 1/4 teaspoon ground cumin
- 1/4 teapoon salt
- 1/4 teaspoon pepper
- 7 tablespoons reduced-fat sour cream

Sliced cucumber, optional

1 In a blender, combine tomatoes and V8 juice; cover and process just until blended.

2 Transfer to a large bowl. Stir in beans, chopped cucumber, sweet pepper, onion, vinegar, sugar and seasonings.

3 Cover and refrigerate for at least 4 hours or overnight. Serve with sour cream. Garnish with sliced cucumber if desired.

YIELD: 7 servings.

BROILED VEGETABLE SANDWICHES

JANE JACKSON, RANDOLPH, IOWA
Tender and crispy vegetables shine in this palate-pleasing sandwich. Served on a warm toasted bun with fresh basil, mayonnaise and a dash of jalapeno pepper, these veggies never had it so good!

PREP/TOTAL TIME: 30 min.

    6 slices peeled eggplant (1/4 inch thick)
  1/2 cup sliced yellow summer squash (1/4 inch thick)
  1/3 cup sliced zucchini (1/4 inch thick)
    2 slices red onion (1/4 inch thick)
    1 teaspoon Italian seasoning
Dash cayenne pepper
    2 hard rolls, split
    5 teaspoons reduced-fat mayonnaise
    2 fresh basil leaves
    2 fresh spinach leaves
    1 cup julienned roasted sweet red peppers
    2 slices tomato
    2 teaspoons minced seeded jalapeno pepper
  1/8 teaspoon pepper

1 Place the eggplant, yellow squash, zucchini and onion in a 15-in. x 10-in. x 1-in. baking pan coated with cooking spray. Coat vegetables with cooking spray; sprinkle with Italian seasoning and cayenne. Broil 4-6 in. from the heat for 5-7 minutes on each side or until tender and lightly browned.

2 Place rolls, cut side up, on an ungreased baking sheet. Broil for 2 minutes or until lightly browned. Spread roll bottoms with mayonnaise; layer with the basil, spinach, red peppers, tomato and jalapeno. Sprinkle with pepper. Top with broiled vegetables; replace roll tops.

YIELD: 2 servings.

EDITOR'S NOTE: When cutting hot peppers, disposable gloves are recommended. Avoid touching your face.

RED PEPPER SOUP

BARB NELSON, VICTORIA, BRITISH COLUMBIA
For a pretty touch, top the soup with grated cheese and parsley. We enjoy it with jalapeno cheese buns, but it's also good with warm garlic bread.

PREP: 35 min. **COOK:** 20 min. + cooling

    6 medium sweet red peppers, chopped
    2 medium carrots, chopped
    2 medium onions, chopped
    1 celery rib, chopped
    4 garlic cloves, minced
    1 tablespoon olive oil
    2 cans (one 49-1/2 ounces, one 14-1/2 ounces) chicken broth
  1/2 cup uncooked long grain rice
    2 tablespoons minced fresh thyme or 2 teaspoons dried thyme
1-1/2 teaspoons salt
  1/4 teaspoon pepper
  1/8 to 1/4 teaspoon cayenne pepper
  1/8 to 1/4 teaspoon crushed red pepper flakes

1 In a large Dutch oven or soup kettle, saute red peppers, carrots, onions, celery and garlic in oil until tender.

2 Stir in broth, rice, thyme, salt, pepper and cayenne; bring to a boil. Reduce heat; cover and simmer for 20-25 minutes or until the vegetables and rice are tender.

3 Cool for 30 minutes. Puree in small batches in a blender; return to pan. Add red pepper flakes; heat through.

YIELD: 10-12 servings (about 3 quarts).

CORN CHOWDER

MARCI INGRAM, OMAHA, NEBRASKA
Here in the "Cornhusker State," we make lots of dishes with corn! This thick chowder is great served with a fresh green salad.

PREP: 10 min. **COOK:** 40 min.

    6 ears fresh corn (about 3-1/2 cups)
Milk
    1 small onion, chopped
    1 small green pepper, chopped

1 celery rib, chopped
1 jalapeno pepper, seeded and chopped
1 tablespoon canola oil
3 tomatoes, peeled and chopped
2 potatoes, peeled and chopped
1 bay leaf
1 teaspoon salt
1/4 teaspoon pepper
1/4 teaspoon sugar
1/8 teaspoon ground allspice
2 cups half-and-half cream
Chopped fresh parsley, optional
Additional pepper, optional
6 bacon strips, cooked and crumbled, optional

1 Cut corn off cob. Rub the edge of a knife over each cob to "milk" it; add enough milk to cob juice to equal 1 cup. Set corn and liquid aside.

2 In a large saucepan, saute the onion, green pepper, celery and jalapeno in oil until soft. Add the tomatoes, potatoes, bay leaf, salt, pepper, sugar and allspice; bring to a boil.

3 Reduce heat; add the cream, reserved corn and milk mixture. Simmer for 30-40 minutes. Discard bay leaf. Garnish with the parsley, pepper and bacon if desired.

YIELD: 6-8 servings (2 quarts).

EDITOR'S NOTE: When cutting hot peppers, disposable gloves are recommended. Avoid touching your face.

ZUCCHINI BISQUE

MRS. OTTO (GERMAINE) STANK, POUND, WISCONSIN
Looking for a different way to serve a bounty of zucchini? Try this soup. A food processor hurries along preparation of the thick, full-flavored blend that's accented with just a hint of nutmeg.

PREP/TOTAL TIME: 30 min.
4 medium zucchini, shredded
1 medium onion, chopped
1/2 cup butter, cubed
2-1/2 cups chicken broth
1 cup heavy whipping cream
3/4 teaspoon salt
1/2 teaspoon minced fresh basil
1/2 teaspoon pepper
1/4 teaspoon ground nutmeg
Sour cream and additional nutmeg, optional

1 In a large saucepan, saute zucchini and onion in butter for 5-6 minutes or until tender. Stir in broth. Bring to a boil. Reduce heat; cover and simmer for 12-15 minutes. Cool slightly.

2 Transfer to a food processor; cover and process on low until smooth. Return to the pan. Stir in the cream, salt, basil, pepper and nutmeg. Bring to a boil. Reduce heat; simmer, uncovered, for 1-2 minutes or until heated through. Garnish with sour cream and additional nutmeg if desired.

YIELD: 6 servings.

TURKEY BURGERS WITH JALAPENO CHEESE SAUCE

VICKI SCHURK, HAMDEN, CONNECTICUT
This is a lighter version of a delicious burger that got rave reviews. I substitute the beef with turkey and use low-fat cheese, but the results are tastier than the original crowd-pleaser.

PREP/TOTAL TIME: 25 min.
3 slices whole wheat bread, torn
1 cup fat-free milk, divided
6 garlic cloves, minced
1-1/2 teaspoons ground mustard
1/4 teaspoon salt
1/4 teaspoon pepper
1-1/2 pounds lean ground turkey
1-1/4 teaspoons all-purpose flour
3/4 cup shredded reduced-fat cheddar cheese
1 jalapeno pepper, seeded and chopped
6 whole wheat hamburger buns, split
6 lettuce leaves
6 slices tomato

1 In a large bowl, soak bread in 1/2 cup milk for 1 minute. Add the garlic, mustard, salt and pepper. Crumble the turkey over mixture and mix well. Shape into six patties; set aside.

2 In a small saucepan, combine flour and remaining milk until smooth. Bring to a boil; cook and stir for 1-2 minutes or until thickened. Remove from the heat. Add cheese and jalapeno; stir until cheese is melted. Keep warm.

3 Coat grill rack with cooking spray before starting the grill. Grill patties, covered, over medium heat for 5-7 minutes on each side or until a meat thermometer reads 165° and juices run clear. Serve on buns with lettuce, tomato and jalapeno cheese sauce.

YIELD: 6 servings.

EDITOR'S NOTE: When cutting hot peppers, disposable gloves are recommended. Avoid touching your face.

TANGY CHICKEN SANDWICHES

JOE SLATE, PORT ST. JOE, FLORIDA
I love grilling chicken because it's a healthier choice. I put my "Joe-style" twist on this sandwich with a spicy-sweet marinade and a homemade blue cheese dressing.

PREP: 25 min. + marinating **GRILL:** 10 min.

- 3/4 cup Louisiana-style hot sauce
- 1/3 cup packed brown sugar
- 3 tablespoons butter
- 4-1/2 teaspoons cider vinegar
- 3/4 teaspoon Mexican seasoning
- 2 boneless skinless chicken breast halves (5 ounces each)
- 2 tablespoons crumbled blue cheese
- 2 tablespoons buttermilk
- 2 tablespoons mayonnaise
- 1-1/2 teaspoons shredded Parmesan cheese
- 1-1/2 teaspoons minced chives
- 3/4 teaspoon lemon juice
- 1/4 teaspoon balsamic vinegar
- 1/8 teaspoon minced garlic
- 1/8 teaspoon pepper
- 2 onion rolls, split and toasted
- 2 cooked bacon strips
- 2 slices Colby cheese (3/4 ounce each)
- 2 lettuce leaves
- 2 slices tomato
- 2 slices red onion

1 In a small saucepan over medium heat, bring the first five ingredients to a boil; boil, uncovered, for 1 minute. Cool for 10 minutes; set aside 1/4 cup for basting. Flatten chicken to 1/2-in. thickness. Pour the remaining marinade into a large resealable plastic bag; add chicken. Seal bag and turn to coat; refrigerate for at least 2 hours.

2 Drain and discard the marinade from chicken. Grill the chicken, covered, over medium heat or broil 4 in. from heat for 5-6 minutes on each side or until no longer pink, basting occasionally with reserved marinade.

3 Combine the blue cheese, buttermilk, mayonnaise, Parmesan cheese, chives, lemon juice, vinegar, garlic and pepper. Spread

over roll bottoms; top with the chicken, bacon, cheese, lettuce, tomato and onion. Replace roll tops.

YIELD: 2 servings.

COOL RASPBERRY SOUP

JANET MOOBERRY, PEORIA, ILLINOIS
An exquisite combination of spices and a rich berry flavor make this beautiful soup so refreshing. It's a lovely way to begin a luncheon. Your guests will rave about the special treat.

PREP: 10 min. + chilling

- 1 package (20 ounces) frozen unsweetened raspberries, thawed
- 1-1/4 cups water
- 1/4 cup white wine, optional
- 1 cup cran-raspberry juice
- 1/2 cup sugar
- 1-1/2 teaspoons ground cinnamon
- 3 whole cloves
- 1 tablespoon lemon juice
- 1 carton (8 ounces) raspberry flavor yogurt
- 1/2 cup sour cream

1 In a blender, puree raspberries, water and wine if desired. Transfer to a large saucepan; add the cran-raspberry juice, sugar, cinnamon and cloves. Bring just to a boil over medium heat. Remove from the heat; strain and allow to cool.

2 Whisk in lemon juice and yogurt. Refrigerate. To serve, pour into small bowls and top with a dollop of sour cream.

YIELD: 4-6 servings.

SUMMER VEGETABLE SOUP

EDITH RUTH MULDOON, BALDWIN, NEW YORK
This vegetable soup is chock-full of garden goodness, from zucchini and green beans to celery and potato. But it's the turmeric that gives it a tasty new twist.

PREP/TOTAL TIME: 30 min.

- 1 small onion, quartered and thinly sliced
- 1 tablespoon olive oil

4 cups reduced-sodium chicken or vegetable broth
1 cup sliced zucchini
1 can (15-1/2 ounces) navy beans, rinsed and drained
1/2 cup diced peeled red potato
1/2 cup cut fresh green beans (2-inch pieces)
1/2 cup chopped peeled tomato
1/4 teaspoon pepper
1/8 teaspoon ground turmeric
1/4 cup chopped celery leaves
2 tablespoons tomato paste

1 In a large saucepan, saute onion in oil until tender. Add the next eight ingredients. Bring to a boil. Reduce heat; cover and simmer for 20-30 minutes or until vegetables are tender.

2 Stir in celery leaves and tomato paste. Cover and let stand for 5 minutes before serving.

YIELD: 4 servings.

FAMILY-PLEASING SLOPPY JOES

JILL ZOSEL, SEATTLE, WASHINGTON
My grandma gave me this classic recipe years ago, and I made a few adjustments to give the sandwiches more pizzazz.

PREP/TOTAL TIME: 30 min.
1 pound lean ground turkey
1/2 cup chopped onion
2 garlic cloves, minced
1 tablespoon sugar
1 tablespoon all-purpose flour
1/4 teaspoon pepper
1 cup ketchup
1 tablespoon prepared mustard
1 tablespoon barbecue sauce
1 tablespoon Worcestershire sauce
6 sandwich buns, split

1 In a large nonstick skillet, cook the turkey and onion over medium heat until turkey is no longer pink; drain if necessary. Add garlic; cook for 1-2 minutes or until tender.

2 Stir in the sugar, flour and pepper. Add the ketchup, mustard, barbecue sauce and Worcestershire sauce. Bring to a boil. Reduce heat; cover and simmer for 5-10 minutes or until heated through. Serve on buns.

YIELD: 6 servings.

OPEN-FACED SWORDFISH SANDWICHES

ALICIA MONTALVO PAGAN, NEW BEDFORD, MASSACHUSETTS
Topped with mellow blue cheese salad dressing and a festive combination of carrots, red onion and lime juice, these warm sandwiches are a special way to welcome dinnertime.

PREP: 20 min. + chilling GRILL: 10 min.
1 cup canned bean sprouts, rinsed and drained
3/4 cup julienned carrots
1/4 cup thinly sliced red onion
1 tablespoon lime juice
1 teaspoon sugar
1/2 teaspoon minced fresh gingerroot
4 swordfish steaks (5 ounces each)
1 tablespoon olive oil
1/2 teaspoon salt
1/8 teaspoon cayenne pepper
4 slices sourdough bread (1/2 inch thick), toasted
8 teaspoons fat-free blue cheese salad dressing

1 In a small bowl, combine the bean sprouts, carrots and onion. Combine the lime juice, sugar and ginger; stir into vegetable mixture. Cover and refrigerate for 30 minutes.

2 Brush both sides of swordfish steaks with oil; sprinkle with salt and cayenne. If grilling the fish, coat grill rack with cooking spray before starting the grill. Grill fish, uncovered, over medium-hot heat or broil 4-6 in. from the heat for 6 minutes. Turn; grill or broil 4-7 minutes longer or until fish flakes easily with a fork.

3 Place a grilled swordfish steak on each piece of toasted bread; top with 2 teaspoons blue cheese dressing and about 1/2 cup bean sprout mixture.

YIELD: 4 servings.

ALOHA BURGERS

JOI MCKIM-JONES, WAIKOLOA, HAWAII
I love hamburgers and pineapple, so it just seemed natural for me to combine them. My family frequently requests these unique burgers. It's nice in place of the same old boring hamburger.

PREP/TOTAL TIME: 30 min.

    1 can (8 ounces) sliced pineapple
3/4 cup teriyaki sauce
    1 pound ground beef
    1 large sweet onion, sliced
    1 tablespoon butter
    4 lettuce leaves
    4 sesame seed or onion buns, split and toasted
    4 slices Swiss cheese
    4 bacon strips, cooked

1 Drain pineapple juice into a small bowl; add teriyaki sauce. Place 3 tablespoons in a resealable plastic bag. Add pineapple; toss to coat and set aside. Shape beef into four patties; place in an 8-in. square baking dish. Pour the remaining teriyaki sauce mixture over the beef patties; marinate for 5-10 minutes, turning once.

2 Drain and discard teriyaki marinade from patties. Grill, covered, over medium heat or broil 4 in. from heat for 6-9 minutes on each side or until no longer pink. Meanwhile, in a small skillet, saute onion in butter until tender, about 5 minutes; set aside.

3 Drain and discard pineapple marinade. Place pineapple on grill or under broiler to heat through. Layer lettuce and onion on bottom of buns. Top with burgers, cheese, pineapple and bacon. Replace tops; serve immediately.

YIELD: 4 servings.

BACON ON THE GRILL
If you've pulled out the grill for burgers, no need to smoke up the house to cook bacon. Place bacon strips in a disposable aluminum pie plate and place on the grill. Cook as you would on the stovetop. This allows you to enjoy the weather, plus, cleanup is easy. Dispose of the pie plate after the bacon grease has cooled.

GAZPACHO

TASTE OF HOME TEST KITCHEN
Healthy vegetables are the basis of this cold, tasty soup. For a bolder version, use spicy V8 juice.

PREP: 20 min. + chilling

    6 medium tomatoes, seeded and chopped
    1 medium green pepper, chopped
    1 cup chopped peeled cucumber
    1 cup chopped red onion
    4 cups tomato juice
    1 teaspoon dried oregano
    1 teaspoon dried basil
1/2 teaspoon salt
1/2 teaspoon minced garlic
1/4 teaspoon pepper
Dash hot pepper sauce
    3 tablespoons minced chives
Chopped sweet yellow pepper, optional

1 In a large bowl, combine the tomatoes, green pepper, cucumber and onion. In another large bowl, combine the tomato juice, oregano, basil, salt, garlic, pepper and hot pepper sauce; pour over the vegetables. Cover and refrigerate for at least 4 hours or overnight. Sprinkle with the minced chives and sweet yellow pepper if desired.

YIELD: 6 servings.

FRESH TOMATO SOUP

ROSEMARIE JOHNSON, NORRIDGE, ILLINOIS
This recipe makes the best tomato soup that I've ever eaten. Most people don't expect a tomato soup to be chunky, but everyone who has tried it finds it to be a pleasant change of pace from the smooth, creamy variety. It's an ideal way to use ripe tomatoes and other fresh garden produce.

PREP: 15 min. **COOK:** 20 min.

    1 cup chopped celery
    1 small onion, chopped
    1 medium carrot, grated
1/2 cup chopped green pepper
1/4 cup butter, cubed

4-1/2 cups chicken broth, divided
   1 quart fresh tomatoes, peeled and chopped
   4 teaspoons sugar
1/2 teaspoon salt
1/2 teaspoon curry powder
1/4 teaspoon pepper
1/4 cup all-purpose flour

1 In large saucepan, saute the celery, onion, carrot and green pepper in butter. Add 4 cups broth, tomatoes, sugar, salt, curry and pepper.

2 Bring to a boil. Reduce the heat; cover and simmer for 20 minutes. Combine flour and remaining broth until smooth. Gradually stir into the soup. Cook soup until slightly thickened, stirring frequently.

YIELD: 2 quarts.

SUMMERTIME MELON SOUP

VALERIE BLACK, FAIRFIELD BAY, ARKANSAS
This summertime soup always elicits a sweet response. Guests never fail to request the recipe. To make it look even better, I often serve it in cantaloupe "bowls."

PREP: 15 min. + chilling
   5 cups seeded cubed watermelon
   1 pint fresh strawberries, hulled and cut in half
1/4 cup sour cream
   2 tablespoons milk
   2 tablespoon sugar
   3 to 4 cantaloupes, optional
Additional fresh strawberries, optional

1 In a small bowl, combine watermelon and strawberries. Puree in batches in a blender, adding the sour cream, milk and sugar to the last batch. Pour into a 2-qt. container and mix well. Cover and chill at least 3 hours.

2 To serve soup in cantaloupe bowls, cut cantaloupes in half; hollow out melon and seeds, leaving about a 1-1/2-in. shell if desired. Cut a decorative edge if desired. Add soup; garnish with a strawberry if desired.

YIELD: 6-8 servings.

MINESTRONE WITH ITALIAN SAUSAGE

LINDA REIS, SALEM, OREGON
This zippy, satisfying soup is my dad's favorite, so I make it all the time. The recipe yields a lot, and I have found that it freezes well and tastes just as great reheated.

PREP: 25 min. COOK: 1 hour
   1 pound bulk Italian sausage
   1 large onion, chopped
   2 large carrots, chopped
   2 celery ribs, chopped
   1 medium leek (white portion only), chopped
   3 garlic cloves, minced
   1 medium zucchini, cut into 1/2-inch pieces
1/4 pound fresh green beans, trimmed and cut into 1/2-inch pieces
   6 cups beef broth
   2 cans (14-1/2 ounces each) diced tomatoes with basil, oregano and garlic
   3 cups shredded cabbage
   1 teaspoon dried basil
   1 teaspoon dried oregano
1/4 teaspoon pepper
   1 can (15 ounces) garbanzo beans or chickpeas, rinsed and drained
1/2 cup uncooked small pasta shells
   3 tablespoons minced fresh parsley
1/3 cup grated Parmesan cheese

1 In a soup kettle, cook sausage and onion over medium heat until meat is no longer pink; drain. Stir in the carrots, celery, leek and garlic; cook for 3 minutes. Add zucchini and green beans; cook 2 minutes longer.

2 Stir in the broth, tomatoes, cabbage, basil, oregano and pepper. Bring to a boil. Reduce heat; cover and simmer for 45 minutes.

3 Return to a boil. Stir in the garbanzo beans, pasta and parsley. Cook for 6-9 minutes or until pasta is tender. Serve with cheese.

YIELD: 11 servings (about 3 quarts).

SIDES & SALADS

ANTIPASTO PICNIC SALAD

MICHELE LARSON, BADEN, PENNSYLVANIA
Everybody just loves this tempting blend of meats, veggies and pasta. It goes together in no time, serves a crowd and tastes as delicious at room temperature as it does cold. Also, it's chunky enough for the kids to pick out any individual ingredient they might not like!

PREP: 30 min. COOK: 15 min.
- 1 package (16 ounces) medium pasta shells
- 2 jars (16 ounces each) giardiniera
- 1 pound fresh broccoli florets
- 1/2 pound cubed part-skim mozzarella cheese
- 1/2 pound hard salami, cubed
- 1/2 pound deli ham, cubed
- 2 packages (3-1/2 ounces each) sliced pepperoni, halved
- 1 large green pepper, cut into chunks
- 1 can (6 ounces) pitted ripe olives, drained

DRESSING:
- 1/2 cup olive oil
- 1/4 cup red wine vinegar
- 2 tablespoons lemon juice
- 1 teaspoon Italian seasoning
- 1 teaspoon coarsely ground pepper
- 1/2 teaspoon salt

1 Cook pasta according to package directions. Meanwhile, drain giardiniera, reserving 3/4 cup liquid. In a large bowl, combine the giardiniera, broccoli, mozzarella, salami, ham, pepperoni, green pepper and olives. Drain pasta and rinse in cold water; stir into meat mixture.

2 For dressing, in a small bowl, whisk oil, vinegar, lemon juice, Italian seasoning, pepper, salt and reserved giardiniera liquid. Pour over salad and toss to coat. Refrigerate until serving.

YIELD: 25 servings.

EDITOR'S NOTE: Giardiniera, a pickled vegetable mixture, is available in mild and hot varieties and can be found in the Italian or pickle section of your grocery store.

VANILLA YOGURT AMBROSIA

SHERRY HULSMAN, LOUISVILLE, KENTUCKY
This simple fruit salad is so yummy. I have served it many times, and it's always one of the first dishes to go. Fat-free vanilla yogurt also works well as the dressing.

PREP: 15 min. + chilling
- 1 can (20 ounces) pineapple tidbits, drained
- 1 can (11 ounces) mandarin oranges, drained
- 1-1/2 cups green grapes
- 1 cup miniature marshmallows
- 1/2 cup flaked coconut
- 1 carton (6 ounces) reduced-fat vanilla yogurt
- 1/4 cup chopped pecans, toasted

1 In a serving bowl, combine the pineapple, oranges, grapes, marshmallows and coconut. Fold in the yogurt. Cover and refrigerate for at least 1 hour. Just before serving, stir in pecans.

YIELD: 6 servings.

COCONUT SAVER
To soften shredded coconut that's turned hard, soak it in milk for 30 minutes. Drain it and pat it dry on paper towels before using. The leftover coconut-flavored milk can be used within 5 days in baked goods or blended with fresh fruit for a tasty beverage.

PEPPER AVOCADO SALSA

THERESA MULLENS, GILL, MASSACHUSETTS
Much of our summer menu is done on the grill, and peppers and avocados are favorites in my family. That led me to create this recipe to help spice up our barbecued entrees. I have also served it as an appetizer on thin wedges of bread and as a topping for easy country-style dishes like chicken and rice pilaf.

PREP: 15 min. + chilling

   2 medium tomatoes, diced
1/4 cup each diced green, sweet red and yellow pepper
1/4 cup diced red onion
   2 tablespoons olive oil
   2 tablespoons lime juice
   1 tablespoon white wine vinegar
   1 garlic clove, minced
   1 tablespoon minced fresh basil or 1 teaspoon dried basil
   1 tablespoon minced fresh dill or 1 teaspoon dill weed
   1 teaspoon sugar
3/4 teaspoon minced fresh thyme or 1/4 teaspoon dried thyme
Dash hot pepper sauce
   1 large ripe avocado

1 In a large bowl, combine the first 12 ingredients. Cover and refrigerate. Just before serving, peel and chop the avocado; stir into the salsa.

YIELD: 3-1/2 cups.

TEXAS TWO-STEP SLAW

SHARON WENCEL, AUSTIN, TEXAS
This quick and colorful slaw is laced with ranch dressing. It's a family favorite and comes together in minutes, but chilling for an hour helps to blend the flavors.

PREP/TOTAL TIME: 20 min.

   3 cups coleslaw mix
1/4 cup Mexicorn, drained
   1 jalapeno pepper, seeded and chopped
   2 tablespoons chopped red onion
   1 tablespoon minced fresh cilantro

1/2 cup shredded cheddar cheese
1/2 cup ranch salad dressing
1-1/2 teaspoons lime juice
1/2 teaspoon ground cumin

1 In a large bowl, combine the first six ingredients. In a small bowl, combine the salad dressing, lime juice and cumin. Pour over the coleslaw and toss to coat. Refrigerate until serving.

YIELD: 8 servings.

EDITOR'S NOTE: When cutting hot peppers, disposable gloves are recommended. Avoid touching your face.

CHERRY TOMATO CORN SALAD

TASTE OF HOME TEST KITCHEN
In the summer, use fresh sweet corn off the cob for this recipe. Saute the corn for 5 minutes in a skillet before adding it to the salad.

PREP/TOTAL TIME: 15 min.

1/4 cup minced fresh basil
   3 tablespoons olive oil
   2 teaspoons lime juice
   1 teaspoon sugar
1/2 teaspoon salt
1/4 teaspoon pepper
   2 cups frozen corn, thawed
   2 cups cherry tomatoes, halved
   1 cup chopped seeded peeled cucumber

1 In a jar with a tight-fitting lid, combine the basil, oil, lime juice, sugar, salt and pepper; shake well.

2 In a large bowl, combine the corn, tomatoes and cucumber. Drizzle with dressing; toss to coat. Refrigerate until serving.

YIELD: 6 servings.

SUMMER MELON SALSA

SUE GRONHOLZ, BEAVER DAM, WISCONSIN

I've been experimenting with lots of different fruit salsa recipes, and this one is so good. The refreshing blend of melons is complemented by a slight jalapeno kick. We like it with lime-flavored tortilla chips, but it's also delicious over grilled chicken.

PREP/TOTAL TIME: 15 min.

- 1/2 cup each cubed cantaloupe, honeydew and seedless watermelon
- 1/4 cup chopped red onion
- 1 jalapeno pepper, seeded and chopped
- 2 tablespoons minced fresh cilantro
- 1 tablespoon lime juice
- 1/4 teaspoon pepper
- 1/8 teaspoon salt

Tortilla chips

1 Combine the melon, onion, jalapeno, cilantro, lime juice, pepper and salt. Serve with chips. Refrigerate leftovers.

YIELD: 1-3/4 cups.

EDITOR'S NOTE: When cutting hot peppers, disposable gloves are recommended. Avoid touching your face.

> **THE LARGEST WATERMELONS IN THE WORLD**
> The Watermelon Festival in Hope, Arkansas is home to some of the world's largest watermelons. In the summer of 2005, Lloyd Bright and his family broke the world record for the largest watermelon in the world, with a monster melon that weighed in at 268.8 pounds!

BLACK-AND-WHITE BEAN SALAD

MARGARET ANDERSEN, GREELEY, COLORADO

This zippy bean salad goes perfectly with a barbecued meal and is also great for a buffet or potluck. Best of all, it can be prepared in no time at all.

PREP: 15 min. + chilling

- 1 can (16 ounces) great northern beans, rinsed and drained
- 1 can (15 ounces) black beans, rinsed and drained
- 1-1/4 cups chopped seeded tomato
- 1-1/2 cups diced sweet red or yellow pepper
- 3/4 cup thinly sliced green onions
- 1/2 cup salsa
- 3 tablespoons red wine or cider vinegar
- 2 tablespoons minced fresh parsley or cilantro
- 1/4 teaspoon salt
- 1/8 teaspoon pepper

1 In a large bowl combine the first five ingredients. In a small bowl, combine the salsa, vinegar, parsley, salt and pepper. Pour over bean mixture; toss to coat. Cover and refrigerate for at least 1 hour.

YIELD: 6-8 servings.

CHILI SAUCE

VIRGINIA LANPHIER, OMAHA, NEBRASKA

If you want a great way to use up your garden tomatoes, this sweet and tangy sauce goes great on just about any savory dish. I like it with home-style potatoes.

PREP: 2 hours PROCESS: 15 min.

- 4 quarts chopped peeled tomatoes (about 24 large)
- 2 cups chopped onions
- 2 cups chopped sweet red peppers (about 4 medium)
- 1 serrano pepper, finely chopped
- 1 cup sugar
- 3 tablespoons salt
- 3 tablespoons mixed pickling spices
- 1 tablespoon celery seed
- 1 tablespoon mustard seed
- 2-1/2 cups white vinegar

1 In a stock pot, combine tomatoes, onions, peppers, sugar and salt; simmer, uncovered, for 45 minutes.

2 Place the pickling spices, celery seed and mustard seed on a double thickness of cheesecloth; bring up corners of cloth and tie with string to form a bag; add to tomato mixture. Cook for 45 minutes or until very thick, stirring frequently.

3 Add vinegar; cook to desired thickness. Discard spice bag. Carefully ladle hot mixture into hot pint jars, leaving 1/2-in. headspace. Adjust caps. Process for 15 minutes in a boiling-water canner.

YIELD: about 6 pints.

EDITOR'S NOTE: When cutting hot peppers, disposable gloves are recommended. Avoid touching your face. The processing time listed is for altitudes of 1,000 feet or less. For altitudes up to 3,000 feet, add 5 minutes; 6,000 feet, add 10 minutes; 8,000 feet, add 15 minutes; 10,000 feet, add 20 minutes.

GOURMET GARDEN TOMATO SALAD

STACY KIBLER, CENTERVILLE, OHIO
I came up with this invigorating salad at our weekly pool gatherings with friends. Each of us brings our own meat to grill and a side to share. This dish was definitely a hit.

PREP/TOTAL TIME: 15 min.
 1-1/2 pounds red, yellow and/or orange tomatoes, cut into 1/4-inch slices
 1/3 cup olive oil
 1/3 cup balsamic vinegar
 1 tablespoon sugar
 1/4 teaspoon salt
 1/4 teaspoon pepper
 1/2 cup crumbled feta cheese
 1/3 cup fresh basil leaves, thinly sliced

1 Arrange tomatoes on a serving platter. In a bowl, whisk the oil, vinegar, sugar, salt and pepper. Drizzle over the tomatoes. Sprinkle with cheese and basil.

YIELD: 6 servings.

GRILLED CORN PASTA SALAD

TASTE OF HOME TEST KITCHEN
A perfect warm-weather salad, this colorful dish is especially tasty when sweet corn, tomatoes, and zucchini are in season. The garden-fresh ingredients are lightly dressed in mild basil vinegar and oil, plus a blend of other herbs and seasonings.

PREP: 20 min. + soaking GRILL: 25 min. + cooling
 4 large ears sweet corn in husks
 1-1/2 cups uncooked penne pasta
 2 cups cherry tomatoes
 1 medium zucchini, thinly sliced
 1 can (2-1/4 ounces) sliced ripe olives, drained
 1/3 cup white wine vinegar
 2 tablespoons olive oil
 1 tablespoon minced fresh basil or 1 teaspoon dried basil
 1 teaspoon sugar
 1 teaspoon salt
 1/2 teaspoon ground mustard
 1/4 teaspoon garlic powder
 1/4 teaspoon pepper

1 Carefully peel back the corn husks to within 1 in. of bottom; remove silk. Rewrap the corn in husks and secure with kitchen string. Place in a large kettle; cover with cold water. Soak for 20 minutes; drain. Grill the corn, covered, over medium heat for 25-30 minutes or until tender, turning often.

2 Meanwhile, cook pasta according to package directions; drain and rinse in cold water. When corn is cool enough to handle, remove kernels from cobs and place in a large bowl. Add the pasta, tomatoes, zucchini and olives.

3 In a jar with a tight-fitting lid, combine remaining ingredients; shake well. Pour over salad and toss gently to coat. Cover and refrigerate until serving.

YIELD: 8 servings.

WATERMELON TOMATO SALAD

MATTHEW DENTON, SEATTLE, WASHINGTON
Watermelon and tomatoes may seem an unlikely pair, but they team up to make a winning combination in this eye-catching salad dressed with parsley, basil and fresh-squeezed lime. Slice up leftover watermelon for summery snacks.

PREP/TOTAL TIME: 25 min.
- 10 cups cubed seedless watermelon
- 2 pints yellow grape or pear tomatoes
- 1 medium red onion, chopped
- 1/2 cup minced fresh parsley
- 1/2 cup minced fresh basil
- 1/4 cup lime juice

1 In a large bowl, combine the watermelon, tomatoes and onion. In a small bowl, combine the parsley, basil and lime juice. Pour over watermelon mixture and toss to coat. Refrigerate until serving.

YIELD: 16-18 servings.

ZESTY GRILLED CORN

DEB MCCAFFERY, DANVILLE, PENNSYLVANIA
This recipe is a definite crowd-pleaser at summer gatherings. It's easy to make the day before and just pop on the grill during the picnic.

PREP/TOTAL TIME: 30 min.
- 1/3 cup butter, cubed
- 2 tablespoons prepared mustard
- 2 tablespoons prepared horseradish
- 1 teaspoon Worcestershire sauce
- 1/4 to 1/2 teaspoon lemon-pepper seasoning
- 6 ears sweet corn, husked

1 In a small saucepan, melt the butter; add the mustard, horseradish, Worcestershire sauce and lemon-pepper. Place each ear of corn on a 13-in. x 12-in. piece of heavy-duty foil. Drizzle with the butter mixture. Fold in edges of foil and seal, leaving space for expansion of steam.

2 Grill, uncovered, over medium heat for 5-6 minutes on each side or until corn is tender. Carefully unwrap foil.

YIELD: 6 servings.

CALICO PEPPER SALAD

JENNIFER MOTTASHED, SIMCOE, ONTARIO
You can pep up all sorts of events with this pretty salad. It's easy on the cook, too. Not only is it ideal for mixing up ahead of time, it can be sized right for any gathering.

PREP: 15 min. + chilling
- 1 each medium green, sweet yellow, sweet red and purple pepper, julienned
- 1 small red onion, julienned
- 1/3 cup vinegar
- 1/4 cup canola oil
- 1 tablespoon sugar
- 1 tablespoon minced fresh basil or 1 teaspoon dried basil
- 1/4 teaspoon salt, optional

Dash pepper

1 In a large bowl, combine peppers and onion. Combine remaining ingredients. Pour over vegetables; toss to coat. Cover and refrigerate 6 hours or overnight.

YIELD: 10 servings.

EDITOR'S NOTE: This recipe may be easily doubled.

> **FREEZER PEPPERS**
> Diced green, sweet red and yellow peppers can be frozen without blanching, so there's no need to put them in boiling water. Simply wash and dry the peppers, remove the stems and seeds and chop as desired. Pack into freezer bags and label and date each package. The peppers will keep for 3 to 6 months.

GREEK POTATO SALAD

ROBERTA WEBSTER, HAMPTON, FLORIDA
I love the herby flavor of this easy-to-make potato salad. It's great for outdoor gatherings and covered-dish parties.

PREP: 25 min. COOK: 15 min. + cooling
- 5 cups cubed peeled potatoes
- 1/2 cup white wine vinegar
- 1/3 cup sugar
- 1 tablespoon olive oil
- 3-1/2 teaspoons dried oregano, divided
- 1-1/2 cups mayonnaise
- 1/2 teaspoon salt
- 1 bunch leaf lettuce, shredded
Cherry tomatoes, halved, optional

1 Place potatoes in a large saucepan and cover with water. Bring to a boil. Reduce heat; cover and cook for 10-15 minutes or until tender. Drain and cool to room temperature.

2 In a small bowl, combine vinegar, sugar, oil and 1/2 teaspoon oregano; set aside. In a large bowl, combine the mayonnaise, salt and remaining oregano. Add potatoes and toss to coat. Cover and refrigerate until chilled.

3 Just before serving, toss lettuce with the vinegar mixture; place on a serving platter. Top with potato salad. Garnish with cherry tomatoes if desired.

YIELD: 10 servings.

CHOPPED SALAD

ANN BUEGE, WINONA, MINNESOTA
This dish has traveled with me to many potlucks and picnics, where it's always met with rave reviews. It's one of my favorite salads because it's so simple to prepare.

PREP/TOTAL TIME: 10 min.
- 1 can (6 ounces) pitted ripe olives, drained and chopped
- 1 jar (5 ounces) pimiento-stuffed olives, drained and chopped
- 1 large cucumber, seeded and chopped
- 1 large green pepper, chopped
- 1 large tomato, chopped
- 1 small onion, chopped
- 1 bottle (8 ounces) Catalina salad dressing

1 In a large bowl, combine all ingredients. Serve immediately or cover and refrigerate until serving.

YIELD: 8-10 servings.

VEGETABLE-STUFFED EGGPLANT

DORIS HEATH, FRANKLIN, NORTH CAROLINA
A friend of mine who raised eggplants shared this recipe with me. This fast and delicious side will complement most any entree.

PREP: 20 min. BAKE: 30 min.
- 1 small eggplant
- 1 medium ear sweet corn, husk removed
- 1 small onion, finely chopped
- 1 small tomato, chopped
- 1 garlic clove, minced
- 4-1/2 teaspoons canola oil
- 2 tablespoons minced fresh parsley
- 1/2 teaspoon salt
- 1/4 teaspoon minced fresh oregano
- 1/4 teaspoon pepper
- 1/2 cup water
- 1/3 cup shredded cheddar cheese

1 Cut the eggplant in half lengthwise; remove pulp, leaving a 1/4-in. shell. Cut the removed pulp into cubes; set shells aside. Cut corn off the cob.

2 In a large nonstick skillet, saute the eggplant pulp, corn, onion, tomato and garlic in oil until onion is tender. Stir in seasonings. Spoon mixture into reserved shells. Place in an ungreased 11-in. x 7-in. baking dish; pour water into dish.

3 Cover and bake at 350° for 25-30 minutes or until heated through. Uncover; sprinkle with cheese. Bake 5 minutes longer or until cheese is melted.

YIELD: 2 servings.

FIT-FOR-A-KING BAKED BEANS

BEAN EDUCATION AND AWARENESS NETWORK,
SCOTTSBLUFF, NEBRASKA

These nicely seasoned, savory baked beans really live up to their name. They're extra special and make a perfect side dish for any potluck, church supper or family picnic.

PREP: 20 min. BAKE: 2-1/2 hours

- 3 bacon strips, diced
- 2 small onions, chopped
- 3 garlic cloves, minced
- 2-1/4 teaspoons ground ginger
- 4 cans (15-1/4 ounces each) great northern beans, rinsed and drained
- 1/2 cup apple cider or juice
- 1/2 cup salsa
- 1/2 cup molasses
- 1/2 cup packed brown sugar
- 1/2 cup gingersnaps, optional
- 1 tablespoon Dijon mustard
- 1/2 teaspoon dried thyme
- 1/2 teaspoon ground allspice
- 2 bay leaves

1 In a large skillet, cook the bacon until crisp. Remove with a slotted spoon to paper towels. Drain, reserving 1 teaspoon of the drippings. In the drippings, saute onions, garlic and ginger until tender.

2 In a large bowl, combine the remaining ingredients. Stir in the onion mixture and the cooked bacon. Transfer to a greased 2-qt. baking dish.

3 Cover and bake at 300° for 2 hours. Uncover; bake 30-35 minutes longer or until beans reach desired thickness. Discard bay leaves.

YIELD: 12-14 servings.

MARVELOUS MELON

JILLIAN SURMAN, WISCONSIN DELLS, WISCONSIN

Kids love these cantaloupe wedges filled with fruit-flavored gelatin and fresh strawberries. Even guests are impressed with this colorful dish. For different looks, I experiment with other combinations of melons, gelatin and fruit.

PREP: 15 min. + chilling

- 1 large cantaloupe
- 1 package (3 ounces) strawberry banana gelatin
- 1 cup boiling water
- 1/2 cup unsweetened applesauce
- 1 cup sliced fresh strawberries

1 Cut melon in half lengthwise from bud to stem end; discard seeds. Cut a thin slice off the bottom of each half so melon sits level; pat dry.

2 In a large bowl, dissolve gelatin in boiling water. Stir in applesauce and strawberries. Pour into melon halves (discard any remaining gelatin mixture or save for another use).

3 Cover with plastic wrap and refrigerate overnight. Just before serving, slice each melon half into three wedges.

YIELD: 6 servings.

ZUCCHINI PICKLES

DAVID HORSTE, PORTLAND, OREGON

I can never have enough recipes for zucchini after harvesting them from my garden every summer. Here's a great way to enjoy summer in a jar all year long.

PREP: 25 min. + standing PROCESS: 15 min.

- 2 pounds firm fresh zucchini, cut into 1/4-inch slices
- 2 small onions, sliced
- 1/4 cup canning salt
- 3 cups white vinegar
- 2 cups sugar
- 2 teaspoons mustard seed
- 1 teaspoon celery seed
- 1 teaspoon turmeric

1 Combine zucchini and onions in a large bowl; sprinkle with canning salt and cover with cold water. Let stand for 2 hours; rinse and drain.

2 In a large saucepan, bring the remaining ingredients to a boil. Pour over zucchini and onions; cover and let stand for 2 hours.

3 Transfer to a large saucepan. Bring to a boil; reduce heat and simmer for 5 minutes. Carefully pack hot mixture into hot half-pint jars, leaving 1/2-in. headspace. Remove air bubbles; wipe rims and adjust lids. Process for 15 minutes in a boiling-water canner.

YIELD: about 4 half-pints.

EDITOR'S NOTE: The processing time listed is for altitudes of 1,000 feet or less. For altitudes up to 3,000 feet, add 5 minutes; 6,000 feet, add 10 minutes; 8,000 feet, add 15 minutes; 10,000 feet, add 20 minutes.

VEGETABLE BARLEY SALAD

PATRICIA LEWANDOWSKI, WARWICK, MASSACHUSETTS
I often serve this salad as an entree on summer nights when it's too hot to eat a heavy meal. The recipe makes a big batch, which is terrific for potlucks and family reunions.

PREP: 20 min. **COOK:** 40 min. + chilling
    4 cups water
    2 cups uncooked medium pearl barley
    2 cups fresh broccoli florets
    2 cups diced carrots
    1 cup halved cherry or grape tomatoes
  1/2 cup chopped green onions
  1/2 cup julienned sweet red or green pepper
  1/2 cup sunflower kernels
  1/2 cup lemon juice
  1/2 cup olive oil
  1/4 cup white wine vinegar
    2 teaspoons grated lemon peel
    2 garlic cloves, peeled
  1/2 teaspoon salt
  1/4 to 1/2 teaspoon pepper
    1 tablespoon grated Parmesan cheese

1 In a large saucepan, bring water to a boil. Add barley. Reduce heat; cover and cook for 30-35 minutes or until tender. Rinse with cold water; drain well.

2 Place broccoli in a steamer basket. Place in a saucepan over 1 in. of water; bring to a boil. Cover and steam for 3-4 minutes or until crisp-tender. Rinse with cold water; drain.

3 In a large salad bowl, combine the barley, broccoli, carrots, tomatoes, onions, red pepper and sunflower kernels.

4 In a blender, combine the lemon juice, olive oil, vinegar, lemon peel, garlic, salt and pepper; cover and process until ingredients are combined.

5 Pour over barley mixture and stir to coat. Refrigerate for at least 1 hour. Just before serving, sprinkle with Parmesan cheese.

YIELD: 14 servings.

ASIAN BULGUR RICE SALAD

BRENDA TEW, SHELLEY, IDAHO
Some people call me the "Queen of Wheat" because I'm always telling them how to use it in creative ways. This tasty salad is a hit with my family. I often add cooked chicken or seafood to turn it into a main dish.

PREP: 15 min. + standing
  1/2 cup uncooked bulgur
1-1/2 cups boiling water
1-1/2 cups cooked long grain rice
  1/2 cup thinly sliced celery
  1/2 cup coarsely grated carrot
  1/2 cup sliced green pepper
  1/4 cup dried cranberries
SALAD DRESSING:
  1/4 cup minced fresh parsley
  1/4 cup rice vinegar
    2 tablespoons olive oil
    1 tablespoon finely chopped onion
    1 tablespoon water
    1 teaspoon sesame oil
    1 teaspoon honey
    1 garlic clove, minced
  1/2 teaspoon each salt, ground mustard and Chinese five-spice powder
  1/4 teaspoon pepper
    9 cups torn mixed salad greens
  1/4 cup sliced almonds, toasted

1 Place bulgur in a small bowl. Stir in boiling water. Cover and let stand for 30 minutes or until most of the liquid is absorbed. Drain and squeeze dry.

2 In a large bowl, combine rice, celery, carrot, green pepper, cranberries and bulgur. For dressing, in a jar with a tight-fitting lid, combine the parsley, vinegar, olive oil, onion, water, sesame oil, honey, garlic and seasonings; shake well.

3 Pour over rice mixture; toss gently to coat. Arrange greens on salad plates. Top with rice mixture; sprinkle with almonds.

YIELD: 6 servings.

CHERRY WALDORF SALAD

MARIE HATTRUP, THE DALLES, OREGON
I combine apples with cherries and cranberries to give a new twist to the classic Waldorf salad.

PREP: 10 min. + chilling

  2 large apples (about 1 pound), chopped
  1 tablespoon lemon juice
  2 celery ribs, chopped
  1 cup fresh or frozen pitted tart cherries, thawed
1/2 cup dried cranberries
1/2 cup slivered almonds, toasted
1/4 cup mayonnaise
1/4 cup sour cream
  2 tablespoons honey
1/8 teaspoon salt

1 In a large salad bowl, toss apples with lemon juice. Add the celery, cherries, cranberries and almonds.

2 In a small bowl, whisk the mayonnaise, sour cream, honey and salt until well blended. Pour over salad and toss to coat.

3 Cover and refrigerate for 1 hour before serving.

YIELD: 6-8 servings.

PICNIC MACARONI SALAD

JUDITH HUNT, GOLDSBORO, NORTH CAROLINA
This is the best-tasting macaroni salad ever! When I fix a batch, I serve myself a portion right away because if I wait until I get to the table, I know it will all be gone.

PREP: 15 min. + chilling

  2 packages (16 ounces each) elbow macaroni, cooked and drained
  8 medium carrots, chopped

  2 medium tart green apples, chopped
  2 medium green peppers, chopped
  2 small onions, chopped
  3 cups mayonnaise
1/3 cup prepared mustard
1/4 cup cider vinegar
1/4 cup sugar
  2 teaspoons garlic salt
  2 teaspoons salt
  1 teaspoon pepper
12 hard-cooked eggs, sliced
  1 teaspoon seafood seasoning

1 In a large bowl, combine the first five ingredients. In a small bowl, whisk the mayonnaise, mustard, vinegar, sugar, garlic salt, salt and pepper. Pour over macaroni mixture; toss to coat.

2 Top with egg slices; sprinkle with seafood seasoning. Cover and refrigerate for at least 3 hours.

YIELD: 30-32 servings.

RANCH-STYLE BUTTERMILK DRESSING

SHIRLEY FRANCEY, ST. CATHARINES, ONTARIO
This creamy quick-to-fix dressing is pleasantly seasoned with dill and minced parsley...and it whisks together in no time.

PREP/TOTAL TIME: 10 min.

2/3 cup buttermilk
1/3 cup reduced-fat mayonnaise
1/4 cup reduced-fat sour cream
  2 tablespoons minced fresh parsley
  1 garlic clove, minced
1/2 teaspoon sugar
1/2 teaspoon dill weed

1/4 teaspoon salt
1/4 teaspoon ground mustard
1/8 teaspoon pepper

1 In a bowl, combine all of the ingredients. Whisk until smooth. Cover and refrigerate until serving.

YIELD: 1 cup.

WILD RICE SEAFOOD SALAD

KATHLEEN ZUSAN, SCANDIA, MINNESOTA
With the rich Native American heritage of our state, a Minnesota wild rice recipe is in order. Wild rice grows naturally in our shallow lakes and was a staple of Indian diets.

PREP: 10 min. + chilling

3 cups cooked wild rice
2 packages (5 ounces each) frozen cooked salad shrimp, thawed
2 cups flaked imitation crabmeat
1/2 cup each chopped sweet yellow, green and red peppers
1/2 cup chopped onion
1/2 cup red wine vinegar
1/4 cup olive oil
2 teaspoons minced fresh marjoram or 1/2 teaspoon dried marjoram
2 teaspoons minced fresh tarragon or 1/2 teaspoon dried tarragon
2 teaspoons minced fresh thyme or 1/2 teaspoon dried thyme
1 teaspoon salt
1/4 teaspoon pepper

1 In a large serving bowl, combine rice, shrimp, crab, peppers and onion.

2 In a jar with a tight-fitting lid, combine the remaining ingredients; shake well. Pour over rice mixture and toss to coat. Cover and refrigerate for at least 2 hours before serving.

YIELD: 4-5 servings.

BLUSHING PEACH JAM

CHERYL HALL, OSCEOLA, INDIANA
Our family lives on 10 acres where we tend a large garden. We love this jam so much we've started growing raspberries, too.

PREP: 20 min. **PROCESS:** 10 min.

2 cups crushed peeled peaches
2 cups red raspberries, crushed
1/4 cup bottled lemon juice
7 cups sugar
2 pouches (3 ounces each) liquid fruit pectin
1/8 teaspoon almond extract

1 In a Dutch oven, combine the peaches, raspberries and lemon juice. Stir in sugar; mix well. Bring to a full rolling boil, stirring constantly. Boil for 1 minute.

2 Remove from the heat. Quickly stir in pectin; return to a full rolling boil. Boil for 1 minute, stirring constantly. Remove from the heat; skim off foam. Add extract.

3 Carefully ladle hot mixture into hot pint jars, leaving 1/4-in. headspace. Remove air bubbles; wipe rims and adjust lids. Process for 10 minutes in a boiling-water canner.

YIELD: 4 pints.

EDITOR'S NOTE: The processing time listed is for altitudes of 1,000 feet or less. Add 1 minute to the processing time for each 1,000 feet of additional altitude.

> **PECTIN KNOW-HOW**
> Both powdered and liquid pectin are made from naturally occurring pectin in apples and citrus fruits. But they are not interchangeable. Always use the type of pectin called for. Usually, powdered pectin is stirred into the fruit and brought to a boil before the sugar is added. Liquid pectin, on the other hand, is added to the mixture after all other ingredients have been brought to a boil.

TROPICAL FRUIT SALAD

TERI LINDQUIST, GURNEE, ILLINOIS

I needed a speedy salad for a luncheon recently. I used what I had available and everyone loved it! Light, fluffy and full of fruit, this salad could double as a healthy dessert. It's also a great dish to bring along on family picnics or trips to the beach.

PREP/TOTAL TIME: 15 min.

     2 cans (15-1/4 ounces each) mixed tropical fruit, drained
     1 can (11 ounces) mandarin oranges, drained
     1 medium banana, sliced
     1 cup miniature marshmallows
     2 cartons (6 ounces each) vanilla yogurt
 1/4 cup flaked coconut
 1/4 cup slivered almonds, toasted

1 In a large salad bowl, combine the tropical fruit, oranges, banana and marshmallows. Add yogurt; toss gently to coat. Sprinkle with coconut and almonds. Refrigerate until serving.

YIELD: 6 servings.

CHERRY PINEAPPLE SALAD

LEONA LUECKING, WEST BURLINGTON, IOWA

This recipe makes a really pretty salad. My sister-in-law often brings it to our family get-togethers during the summer.

PREP: 20 min. + chilling

     3 packages (3 ounces each) cherry gelatin
2-1/3 cups boiling water
     2 cans (16-1/2 ounces each) pitted dark sweet cherries
     1 can (20 ounces) pineapple tidbits
 1/3 cup lemon juice
 1/3 cup heavy whipping cream

 1/3 cup mayonnaise
     2 packages (3 ounces each) cream cheese, softened
Dash salt
 1/2 cup coarsely chopped nuts

1 In a large bowl, dissolve gelatin in water. Drain and reserve enough cherry and pineapple juices to measure 2-1/2 cups; add to gelatin with lemon juice. Set fruits aside.

2 Divide gelatin in half. Set aside one portion of gelatin at room temperature; chill the other portion until partially set. Fold pineapple into chilled gelatin; pour into a 13-in. x 9-in. dish. Chill until almost firm.

3 In a small bowl, beat the cream, mayonnaise, cream cheese and salt until light and fluffy. Spread over chilled gelatin layer. Refrigerate until firm. Chill the reserved gelatin mixture until partially set. Fold in cherries and nuts; spread over cream cheese layer. Chill for at least 3 hours.

YIELD: 12-16 servings.

BROCCOLI SALAD SUPREME

TERRI TWYMAN, BONANZA, OREGON

People can't get enough of the sweet grapes and crunchy broccoli in this colorful salad. I appreciate its make-ahead convenience.

PREP/TOTAL TIME: 10 min.

    10 cups broccoli florets (about 3-1/2 pounds)
     6 cups seedless red grapes (about 3 pounds)
     1 cup sliced celery
     6 green onions, sliced
     2 cups mayonnaise
 2/3 cup sugar
     2 tablespoons cider vinegar
     1 pound sliced bacon, cooked and crumbled
1-1/3 cups slivered almonds, toasted

1 In a large salad bowl, combine the broccoli, grapes, celery and onions. In a small bowl, combine the mayonnaise, sugar and vinegar. Pour over broccoli mixture and toss to coat.

2 Cover and refrigerate for at least 4 hours or overnight. Just before serving, gently stir in bacon and almonds.

YIELD: about 20 servings.

COLORFUL TOMATO 'N' MOZZARELLA SALAD

TARI AMBLER, SHOREWOOD, ILLINOIS
This is my twist on the popular tomato-mozzarella salad. Since the rest of the salad is so light, you can splurge with the fresh mozzarella!

PREP: 20 min. + standing
- 1 cup fresh baby spinach
- 2 medium yellow tomatoes, sliced
- 2 medium red tomatoes, sliced
- 4 ounces fresh mozzarella cheese, sliced
- 2 tablespoons thinly sliced fresh basil leaves
- 1/4 teaspoon salt
- 1/4 teaspoon pepper
- 1 tablespoon balsamic vinegar
- 2 teaspoons olive oil

1 Arrange spinach on a platter; top with tomato and cheese slices. Sprinkle with basil, salt and pepper. Drizzle with vinegar and oil. Let stand for 15 minutes before serving.

YIELD: 4 servings.

WILD BERRY FREEZER JAM

BARBARA HOHMANN, PETAWAWA, ONTARIO
One summer, I wanted to make a wild berry jam but couldn't find a recipe—so I invented my own and have been enjoying it ever since.

PREP: 15 min. + freezing
- 1 cup saskatoon berries
- 1 cup raspberries
- 1 cup strawberries
- 1 cup blackberries
- 1 cup blueberries
- 4 cups sugar
- 1 pouch (3 ounces) liquid fruit pectin
- 1 tablespoon lemon juice

1 In a large bowl, crush all of the berries. Stir in sugar; let stand for 10 minutes. Combine pectin and lemon juice; add to fruit, stirring constantly until sugar is dissolved, about 3 minutes.

2 Pour into jars or freezer containers, leaving 1/2-in. headspace. Cover tightly. Let stand at room temperature until set, up to 24 hours. Freeze or store in the refrigerator up to 3 weeks.

YIELD: 6 half-pints.

CRAB-STUFFED AVOCADOS

GAIL VANGUNDY, PARKER, COLORADO
We enjoy having this creamy and crunchy salad out on our deck on summer evenings. It goes together in no time flat!

PREP/TOTAL TIME: 20 min.
- 1 can (6 ounces) crabmeat, drained, flaked and cartilage removed
- 1/2 cup sliced celery
- 1/2 cup shredded lettuce
- 3 tablespoons mayonnaise
- 1 teaspoon finely chopped onion
- 1/2 teaspoon lemon juice
- 1/8 to 1/4 teaspoon seafood seasoning
- 1/8 teaspoon paprika
- 1 medium ripe avocado, halved and pitted

1 In a bowl, combine the crab, celery, lettuce, mayonnaise, onion, lemon juice and seasonings. Spoon into avocado halves. Serve immediately.

YIELD: 2 servings.

CELERY STORAGE AND STRINGS
To store celery, remove it from the bag and wrap first in a paper towel, then in aluminum foil. Store in the refrigerator. When you need some, break off what you need, rewrap the rest and return to the refrigerator. To remove the strings from celery, run a potato peeler along the curved outside of the stalk.

124 125 128 126

ENTREES

130

JALAPENO RIBS

SHIRLEY MANTHEY, OMAHA, NEBRASKA

These ribs are unique because of the spicy rub and the combination of sweet brown sugar and spicy jalapeno peppers in the sauce. I always make them for my husband's birthday.

PREP: 1 hour 35 min. **GRILL:** 10 min.

- 4 teaspoons brown sugar
- 2 teaspoons chili powder
- 1 teaspoon salt
- 1 teaspoon paprika
- 1 teaspoon pepper
- 1/8 teaspoon garlic powder
- 3-1/2 to 4 pounds pork spareribs

JALAPENO BARBECUE SAUCE:

- 2 cans (8 ounces each) tomato sauce
- 2/3 cup packed brown sugar
- 1/3 cup lemon juice
- 1/4 cup Worcestershire sauce
- 1 small onion, finely chopped
- 2 jalapeno peppers, seeded and finely chopped
- 2 teaspoons beef bouillon granules

1 Combine the first six ingredients; rub onto both sides of ribs. Place ribs, meat side up, on a rack in a foil-lined roasting pan. Bake at 325° for 1-1/2 to 1-3/4 hours or until tender.

2 Meanwhile, in a large saucepan, combine sauce ingredients; simmer, uncovered, for 30-40 minutes or until thickened.

3 Transfer ribs to grill. Grill, uncovered, over medium heat for 10-15 minutes, basting with sauce and turning several times. Reheat remaining sauce and serve with ribs.

YIELD: 4 servings.

EDITOR'S NOTE: Ribs may be baked and sauce may be prepared a day ahead and refrigerated. Then grill and baste for 15 minutes or until heated through and nicely glazed. When cutting hot peppers, disposable gloves are recommended. Avoid touching your face.

RUSTIC VEGETARIAN PIZZA

PRISCILLA GILBERT, INDIAN HARBOUR BEACH, FLORIDA

While my husband was stationed in the service in Naples, Italy, we tried all kinds of pizzas with fresh ingredients. This veggie pizza is delicious, but not complicated to prepare.

PREP: 20 min. **BAKE:** 30 min. + standing

- 1 tablespoon cornmeal
- 1 tube (13.8 ounces) refrigerated pizza crust
- 1-1/2 teaspoons olive oil, divided
- 11 slices part-skim mozzarella cheese, divided
- 1 small zucchini, cut into 1/8-inch slices, patted dry, divided
- 1 small onion, sliced
- 4 plum tomatoes, cut into 1/4-inch slices
- 1/4 teaspoon salt
- 1/4 teaspoon pepper
- 1/4 cup torn fresh basil

1 Sprinkle cornmeal over a greased baking sheet. Unroll pizza crust; shape into a 12-in. square. Place on the baking sheet. Brush with 1 teaspoon oil. Arrange nine slices of cheese over dough to within 1 in. of edges. Cut each remaining cheese slice into four pieces; set aside.

2 Place half of the zucchini, about 2 in. apart, around edges of cheese. Fold edges of dough about 1 in. over zucchini. Bake at 400° for 6 minutes. Layer with onion and remaining zucchini; top with tomatoes. Sprinkle with salt and pepper. Bake for 16 minutes or until crust is golden brown.

3 Arrange reserved cheese over the tomatoes; bake 4 minutes longer or until cheese is melted. Drizzle with remaining oil. Sprinkle with basil. Let stand for 10 minutes before slicing.

YIELD: 4-6 servings.

FREEZING ZUCCHINI

You can freeze zucchini with a bit of preparation. First, shred the zucchini, then steam it for 1 to 2 minutes or until translucent; drain well. Pack in measured amounts into freezer containers, leaving 1/2 inch of space at the top, or in heavy-duty resealable bags. Cool, seal and freeze.

PORK ROAST WITH MANGO SALSA

B.J. WALL, LANEXA, VIRGINIA
I served this special roast at my son and daughter-in-law's rehearsal dinner. It can be prepared on the grill or in the oven, but grilling enhances the flavors. The fruit salsa perfectly complements the pork's tasty herbal rub.

PREP: 25 min. + marinating **GRILL:** 1-1/4 hours + standing

- 3 tablespoons paprika
- 1 tablespoon garlic powder
- 2 teaspoons dried oregano
- 2 teaspoons dried thyme
- 3/4 teaspoon cayenne pepper
- 1/2 teaspoon salt
- 1/2 teaspoon ground cumin
- 1/2 teaspoon pepper
- 1/4 teaspoon ground nutmeg
- 1 boneless whole pork loin roast (2-1/2 pounds)

SALSA:

- 1 medium mango, peeled and chopped
- 1/2 cup chopped seeded plum tomatoes
- 1/2 cup chopped red onion
- 1/2 cup chopped peeled cucumber
- 1/4 cup lime juice
- 2 tablespoons minced fresh cilantro
- 1 tablespoon olive oil
- 1 tablespoon dry red wine or cider vinegar
- 1 teaspoon ground cumin

1 Combine the first nine ingredients; rub over the roast. Place in a shallow baking dish; cover and refrigerate for 3 hours or overnight. In a large bowl, combine the salsa ingredients; cover and refrigerate until serving.

2 If grilling the roast, coat grill rack with cooking spray before starting the grill. Prepare grill for indirect heat. If baking the roast, place on a rack in a shallow roasting pan.

3 Grill pork, covered, over indirect medium heat for 1-1/4 hours or bake, uncovered, at 350° for 1-1/2 hours or until a meat thermometer reads 160°.

4 Cover loosely with foil and let stand for 15 minutes before slicing. Serve with salsa.

YIELD: 8 servings.

VEGGIE KABOBS WITH GINGERED YOGURT

MARIE RIZZIO, TRAVERSE CITY, MICHIGAN
This is a great way to serve vegetables for a colorful, summery meal. They're eye-appealing, tasty and easy to make!

PREP: 20 min. **GRILL:** 15 min.

- 1 carton (8 ounces) reduced-fat plain yogurt
- 2 green onions, finely chopped
- 1 teaspoon grated fresh gingerroot
- 1 teaspoon honey
- 1/2 teaspoon ground mustard
- 1 garlic clove, minced
- 1/4 teaspoon salt
- 2 large sweet red peppers, cut into eight pieces
- 1 large zucchini, cut into eight slices
- 1 medium eggplant, peeled and cut into eight slices
- 1 large green pepper, cut into eight pieces
- 4 teaspoons canola oil

1 In a small bowl, combine the yogurt, onions, ginger, honey, mustard, garlic and salt. Cover and refrigerate until serving.

2 On four metal or soaked wooden skewers, alternately thread red peppers, zucchini, eggplant and green pepper; brush with oil. Grill, covered, over medium heat for 15-18 minutes or until vegetables are tender, turning occasionally. Serve with yogurt sauce.

YIELD: 4 servings.

VEGGIE-STUFFED EGGPLANT

RUBY WILLIAMS, BOGALUSA, LOUISIANA
For years, I cooked for my husband and our five children. Now it's just me and my great-grandson. This hearty and nutritious dish is one we both enjoy.

PREP: 25 min. **BAKE:** 20 min.

- 1 medium eggplant
- 1/2 cup chopped onion
- 2 garlic cloves, minced
- 1/2 cup chopped fresh mushrooms
- 1/2 cup chopped zucchini
- 1/2 cup chopped sweet red pepper
- 3/4 cup seeded chopped tomatoes
- 1/4 cup toasted wheat germ
- 2 tablespoons minced fresh parsley
- 1/2 teaspoon dried thyme
- 1/4 teaspoon salt
- 1/4 teaspoon pepper
- Dash crushed red pepper flakes
- 1 tablespoon grated Parmesan cheese

1 Cut eggplant in half lengthwise; remove pulp, leaving a 1/4-in.-thick shell. Cube pulp; set shells and pulp aside.

2 In a large nonstick skillet coated with cooking spray, saute onion and garlic until onion is tender. Add the mushrooms, zucchini, red pepper and eggplant pulp; saute for 4-6 minutes or until vegetables are crisp-tender. Stir in the tomatoes, wheat germ, parsley, thyme, salt, pepper and pepper flakes; cook for 1 minute.

3 Divide mixture evenly between the eggplant shells; sprinkle with Parmesan cheese. Place on a baking sheet. Bake at 400° for 20-25 minutes or until shells are tender.

YIELD: 2 servings.

SAUCY BARBECUED CHICKEN

CHARLOTTE WITHERSPOON, DETROIT, MICHIGAN
My aunt was affectionately called "The Barbecue Queen." As the aroma of her grilled chicken filled the air, folks in town would stop by just to sample her scrumptious food.

PREP: 65 min. **GRILL:** 45 min.

- 2 cups ketchup
- 1/2 cup water
- 1/2 cup tomato sauce
- 1/2 cup corn syrup
- 1/2 cup cola
- 1/4 cup cider vinegar
- 1/4 cup butter, cubed
- 1/4 cup steak sauce
- 2 tablespoons soy sauce
- 1-1/2 teaspoons sugar
- 1 teaspoon seasoned salt
- 1 teaspoon hot pepper sauce
- 1/2 teaspoon garlic powder
- 1/2 teaspoon onion powder
- 1/2 teaspoon Liquid Smoke, optional
- 1 broiler/fryer chicken (3 to 3-1/2 pounds) cut up

1 In a large saucepan, combine the first 15 ingredients. Bring to a boil, stirring constantly. Reduce heat; simmer, uncovered, for 1 hour, stirring frequently.

2 Set aside 1 cup for basting. Store remaining sauce in the refrigerator for another use.

3 Grill chicken, covered, over medium heat for 30 minutes, turning occasionally. Baste with marinade; grill 5-10 minutes longer or until juices run clear, turning and basting frequently with marinade.

YIELD: 4 servings.

BARBECUED CHUCK ROAST

ARDIS GAUTIER, LAMONT, OKLAHOMA
Whether I serve this roast for church dinners, company or family, it is always a hit. To go along with it, my family likes scalloped potatoes, tossed salad and pie. Leftovers make great sandwiches.

PREP: 25 min. + marinating **GRILL:** 1 hour 20 min.

- 2/3 cup cider vinegar
- 1/2 cup ketchup
- 1/4 cup canola oil
- 1/4 cup soy sauce
- 2 tablespoons Worcestershire sauce
- 2 teaspoons garlic powder
- 2 teaspoons salt
- 2 teaspoons prepared mustard
- 1/2 teaspoon pepper
- 1 boneless beef chuck roast (2-1/2 to 3 pounds)
- 1/2 cup unsweetened applesauce

1 In a large bowl, combine the the first nine ingredients. Pour half of the marinade into a large resealable plastic bag; add roast. Seal bag and turn to coat; refrigerate for at least 3 hours. Cover and refrigerate remaining marinade.

2 Drain and discard the marinade. Grill roast, covered, over indirect heat for 20 minutes, turning occasionally.

3 Add the applesauce to the reserved marinade; brush over roast. Continue basting and turning the roast several times for 1 to 1-1/2 hours or until the meat reaches desired doneness (for medium-rare, a meat thermometer should read 145°; medium, 160°; well-done, 170°).

YIELD: 6-8 servings.

PREPARING A GRILL FOR INDIRECT HEAT
For a charcoal grill, bank half of the coals on one side of the grill and the other half on the other side. Place a foil drip pan in the center of the grill, replace the cooking grate and place the meat over the drip pan. Cover and grill according to recipe directions.

CHEESE RAVIOLI WITH ZUCCHINI

MARIA REGAKIS, SOMERVILLE, MASSACHUSETTS
Whipping cream lends rich flavor to the sauce for this colorful pasta and vegetable medley.

PREP: 15 min. **COOK:** 20 min.

- 1 cup heavy whipping cream
- 1/2 cup chicken broth
- 1 package (9 ounces) refrigerated cheese ravioli
- 1 small onion, finely chopped
- 1 tablespoon butter
- 1 medium sweet red pepper, julienned
- 3 cups julienned zucchini
- 1/2 teaspoon salt
- 1/4 teaspoon garlic powder
- 3/4 cup grated Parmesan cheese, divided
- 1 to 2 tablespoons minced fresh basil
- 1 tablespoon minced fresh parsley

1 In a large saucepan, bring the cream and broth to a boil. Reduce the heat; simmer, uncovered, for 10-15 minutes or until reduced to 1 cup. Meanwhile, cook ravioli according to package directions.

2 In a large skillet, saute onion in butter for 2 minutes. Add red pepper; cook 2 minutes longer. Stir in the zucchini, salt and garlic powder; cook for 1-2 minutes or until the vegetables are crisp-tender. Keep warm.

3 Stir 1/2 cup cheese, basil and parsley into cream sauce; cook for 1 minute. Drain ravioli; add to skillet with cream sauce. Toss to coat. Sprinkle with remaining cheese.

YIELD: 4 servings.

INDIVIDUAL GRILLED PIZZAS

MARTHA HASEMAN, HINCKLEY, ILLINOIS
This is one of my favorite grilled dishes. Featuring garden-fresh vegetables and a light pesto sauce, the pizzas are especially popular because each family member can add whatever toppings he or she prefers. This way everyone is happy.

PREP/TOTAL TIME: 30 min.
- 1-1/2 cups all-purpose flour
- 1/2 cup whole wheat flour
- 1 package (1/4 ounce) quick-rise yeast
- 1/2 teaspoon salt
- 1/2 teaspoon sugar
- 3/4 cup warm water (120° to 130°)
- 1 tablespoon olive oil

PESTO:
- 1 cup chopped fresh basil
- 1/4 cup fat-free plain yogurt
- 2 tablespoons unsalted sunflower kernels
- 1 tablespoon olive oil
- 1 garlic clove, minced
- 1/8 teaspoon salt
- 1/8 teaspoon pepper

TOPPINGS:
- 1 cup (4 ounces) shredded part-skim mozzarella cheese, divided
- 2 medium tomatoes, thinly sliced
- 2 green onions, finely chopped
- Coarsely ground pepper
- 2 tablespoons grated Parmesan cheese

1 In a large bowl, combine the flours, yeast, salt and sugar. Add water and oil; mix just until a soft dough forms. Turn onto a floured surface; knead until smooth and elastic, about 5-7 minutes. Cover and let stand for 10-15 minutes.

2 Meanwhile, in a blender, combine the pesto ingredients. Cover and process until smooth, scraping sides often. Set aside.

3 Divide dough into fourths. Roll each portion into a 6-in. circle. Coat grill rack with cooking spray before starting the grill. Prepare grill for indirect medium heat.

4 Grill dough over the direct heat area. Cover and cook for 1 minute or until puffed and golden. Turn; place over indirect heat. Spread pesto over crusts. Top with 2/3 cup mozzarella cheese, tomatoes, onions, pepper, Parmesan and remaining mozzarella. Grill, covered, for 3-5 minutes or until the cheese is melted and crust is lightly browned.

YIELD: 4 servings.

EDITOR'S NOTE: Individual prebaked Italian bread shells may be substituted for the homemade crust.

LEMON-PEPPER CATFISH

REGINA ROSENBERRY, GREENCASTLE, PENNSYLVANIA
Nothing beats a late supper of grilled catfish after a hard day's work. It's a favorite of our family during the summertime.

PREP: 5 min. + marinating GRILL: 10 min.
- 6 tablespoons lemon juice
- 1/4 cup butter, melted
- 2 teaspoons Worcestershire sauce
- 4 catfish fillets (about 5 ounces each)
- 1/2 teaspoon salt
- 1/2 teaspoon lemon-pepper seasoning

1 In a large resealable plastic bag, combine lemon juice, butter and Worcestershire sauce. Add the fish; seal bag and turn to coat. Cover and refrigerate for 30 minutes, turning occasionally.

2 Coat grill rack with cooking spray before starting the grill. Drain and discard the marinade. Sprinkle the fish with salt and lemon-pepper. Grill, covered, over medium heat for 4-6 minutes on each side or until fish flakes easily with a fork.

YIELD: 4 servings.

GREASING A GRILL
Never spray a grilling grate directly over the flame (gas or coal) as this can cause a fire. To grease, fold a paper towel into a small pad. Holding the pad with long-handled tongs, dip the paper towel in vegetable oil and rub over the grate.

GRILLED FLANK STEAK

JENNY REECE, FARWELL, MINNESOTA

This recipe is from my sister, and it's a favorite of mine when serving company. The meat and vegetables can be prepared ahead of time. When the company arrives, I just fire up the grill and serve a meaty main meal in minutes!

PREP: 20 min. + marinating GRILL: 15 min.

- 1/4 cup soy sauce
- 2 tablespoons white vinegar
- 1 green onion, sliced
- 1-1/2 teaspoons garlic powder
- 1-1/2 teaspoons ground ginger
- 3 tablespoons honey
- 3/4 cup canola oil
- 1 beef flank steak (about 1-1/2 pounds)
- 1 pound fresh mushrooms, sliced
- 1 green pepper, cut into thin strips
- 1 yellow or sweet red pepper, cut into thin strips
- 3 carrots, cut into julienned strips

1 In a bowl, combine the first seven ingredients. Pour 3/4 cup marinade into a large resealable plastic bag; add the beef. Seal bag and turn to coat; refrigerate for up to 24 hours. Cover and refrigerate remaining marinade.

2 Drain and discard marinade. Grill flank steak, uncovered, over medium heat for 6-8 minutes on each side or until meat reaches desired doneness (for medium-rare, a meat thermometer should read 145°; medium, 160°; well-done, 170°).

3 Meanwhile, in a skillet, saute vegetables in reserved marinade until crisp-tender. Thinly slice steak across the grain. Serve with vegetables.

YIELD: 5 servings.

TERIYAKI SHISH KABOBS

SUZANNE PELEGRIN, OCALA, FLORIDA

The tender beef, tangy sauce, sweet pineapple and flavorful vegetables make this main dish a memorable one. When I was a teenager in the 1960s, my father worked for an airline, and my family lived on the island of Guam in the South Pacific. A friend of Mother's there gave her this wonderful recipe. We ate this delicious warm-weather dish often, and now I prepare it for my family.

PREP: 20 min. + marinating GRILL: 15 min.

- 1 cup ketchup
- 1 cup sugar
- 1 cup soy sauce
- 2 teaspoons garlic powder
- 2 teaspoons ground ginger
- 1 beef top sirloin steak (1-1/2 inches thick and 2 pounds), cut into 1-1/2-inch cubes
- 1/2 fresh pineapple, trimmed and cut into 1-inch chunks
- 2 to 3 small zucchini, cut into 1-inch chunks
- 1/2 pound medium fresh mushrooms
- 1/2 pound pearl onions
- 1 large green or sweet red pepper, cut into 1-inch pieces

1 Combine first five ingredients in a large resealable plastic bag; reserving half the marinade. Add the beef. Seal the bag and turn to coat the beef; refrigerate overnight. Cover and refrigerate reserved marinade.

2 Drain and discard marinade from beef. Thread the meat, pineapple and vegetables alternately on metal or soaked wooden skewers.

3 Grill over hot heat for 15-20 minutes, turning often, or until meat reaches desired doneness and vegetables are tender.

4 In a saucepan, bring reserved marinade to a boil; boil for 1 minute. Remove the meat and vegetables from skewers; serve with marinade.

YIELD: 6-8 servings.

GLAZED SALMON FILLET

JERILYN COLVIN, FOXBORO, MASSACHUSETTS

*My husband caught a lot of salmon when we lived in Alaska, so I had
to learn how to cook it. Basted with a sweet glaze, this tasty fillet is a
staple in our house. Our children absolutely love it.*

PREP/TOTAL TIME: 30 min.

- 1-1/2 cups packed brown sugar
- 6 tablespoons butter, melted
- 3 to 6 tablespoons lemon juice
- 2-1/4 teaspoons dill weed
- 3/4 teaspoon cayenne pepper
- 1 salmon fillet (about 2 pounds)

Lemon-pepper seasoning

1 In a small bowl, combine the first five ingredients; mix well.
Remove 1/2 cup to a saucepan; simmer until heated through.
Set aside remaining mixture for basting.

2 Sprinkle salmon with lemon-pepper. Place on grill with skin
side down. Grill, covered, over medium heat for 5 minutes. Brush
with the reserved brown sugar mixture. Grill 10-15 minutes longer
or until fish flakes easily with a fork, basting occasionally. Serve
with the warmed sauce.

YIELD: 6-8 servings.

SWEET AND SOUR PORK KABOBS

BARBARA FOSSEN, LA CRESCENT, MINNESOTA

*Making these zesty pork kabobs is as much fun as eating them. My
husband enjoys grilling our kabobs outdoors. On rainy days, he broils
them up juicy and tender in the oven. Either way, I always make sure
to make enough for seconds.*

PREP: 20 min. + marinating **GRILL:** 10 min.

- 2 medium carrots, cut into 1-inch pieces
- 1 can (8 ounces) pineapple chunks
- 1/4 cup red wine vinegar
- 1 tablespoon canola oil
- 1 tablespoon soy sauce

- 1 teaspoon sugar
- 1 garlic clove, crushed
- 3/4 pound boneless pork, cut into 1-inch pieces

Small green pepper, cut into 1-inch pieces

Small red pepper, cut into 1-inch pieces

Hot cooked rice

1 In a small saucepan, bring 1 in. of water to a boil; add carrots.
Cover and cook for 10-12 minutes or until almost tender; drain
well. Drain pineapple, reserving 1/4 cup juice. Set pineapple aside.

2 In a small bowl, combine the vinegar, oil, soy sauce, sugar,
garlic and reserved pineapple juice. Pour over cubed pork; let
stand for 30 minutes.

3 On four metal or soaked wooden skewers, alternate the pork,
carrots, peppers and reserved pineapple. Grill over medium-
hot heat for 5-6 minutes or until meat is tender, basting with
reserved marinade. Serve with rice.

YIELD: 4 servings.

POTATO CHICKEN PACKETS

PAM HALL, ELIZABETH CITY, NORTH CAROLINA

*I season chicken breasts with a delightful combination of herbs
before topping each with veggies. Servings are individually wrapped
in foil, so I can enjoy nature's beauty in my backyard while the
packets cook on the grill.*

PREP: 15 min. **GRILL:** 30 min.

- 4 boneless skinless chicken breast halves (4 ounces each)
- 1/4 cup olive oil
- 3 teaspoons dried rosemary, crushed
- 1 teaspoon dried thyme
- 1/2 teaspoon dried basil
- 1 garlic clove, minced
- 8 to 10 small red potatoes, quartered
- 2 medium yellow summer squash, cut into 1/4-inch slices
- 1 large onion, chopped
- 2 tablespoons butter, cubed

Salt and pepper to taste

1 Place each chicken breast on a double thickness of heavy-
duty foil (about 12 in. square). Combine oil, rosemary, thyme,
basil and garlic; drizzle over chicken. Top with potatoes, squash,

onion and butter. Sprinkle with salt and pepper. Fold foil over mixture and seal tightly.

2 Grill, covered, over medium heat for 30 minutes or until a meat thermometer reads 160°. Open foil carefully to allow steam to escape.

YIELD: 4 servings.

CAN-CAN CHICKEN

STEVE BATH, LINCOLN, NEBRASKA
I spray my chicken with a mixture of 2 cups apple cider and 1 tablespoon balsamic vinegar. This adds moisture to the crisp skin but requires an additional 15 to 30 minutes of cooking time.

PREP: 30 min. + chillng **GRILL:** 1-1/4 hours
    1 tablespoon kosher salt
    1 teaspoon sugar
    1 teaspoon onion powder
    1 teaspoon garlic powder
    1 teaspoon cayenne pepper
    1 teaspoon paprika
    1 teaspoon ground mustard
    1 broiler/fryer chicken (3-1/2 to 4 pounds)
    1 can (12 ounces) beer

1 In a small bowl, combine the first seven ingredients. Loosen skin from around the chicken breast, thighs and legs. Rub the spice mixture onto and under skin. Tuck wing tips behind the back. Refrigerate for 1 hour.

2 Prepare grill for indirect grilling, using a drip pan. Pour out half of the beer, reserving for another use. Poke additional holes in top of the can with a can opener. Holding the chicken with legs pointed down, lower chicken over can so it fills the body cavity.

3 Place chicken over drip pan; grill, covered, over indirect medium heat for 1-1/4 to 1-1/2 hours or until a meat thermometer inserted into a thigh reads 180°. Remove chicken from grill; cover and let stand for 10 minutes. Remove chicken from can.

YIELD: 6 servings.

MOLASSES-GLAZED BABY BACK RIBS

KIM BRALEY, DUNEDIN, FLORIDA
My husband sizzles up his luscious ribs recipe for our large family at least once a month in the summer. The sweet-and-sour barbecue sauce is the perfect condiment for the moist, tender meat. We enjoy these ribs with corn on the cob.

PREP: 20 min. + marinating **GRILL:** 70 min.
4-1/2 pounds pork baby back ribs
    2 liters cola
  1/2 teaspoon salt
  1/2 teaspoon pepper
  1/4 teaspoon garlic salt
  1/4 teaspoon dried oregano
  1/4 teaspoon onion powder
  1/8 teaspoon cayenne pepper
BARBECUE SAUCE:
  1/4 cup ketchup
  1/4 cup honey
  1/4 cup molasses
    1 tablespoon prepared mustard
  1/2 teaspoon cayenne pepper
  1/2 teaspoon salt

1 Place the ribs in large resealable plastic bags; add cola. Seal bags and turn to coat; refrigerate for 8 hours or overnight.

2 Drain and discard cola. Pat ribs dry with paper towels. Combine the seasonings; rub over ribs.

3 Prepare grill for indirect heat, using a drip pan. Place the ribs over pan; grill, covered, over indirect medium heat for 1 hour, turning occasionally.

4 In a small bowl, combine barbecue sauce ingredients. Brush over ribs; grill 10-20 minutes longer or until meat is tender.

YIELD: 4 servings.

FABULOUS TACO SALAD

ANNA YEATTS, KERNERSVILLE, NORTH CAROLINA
Everyone loves this recipe. It's like eating decadent Mexican food while keeping the calories under control.

PREP/TOTAL TIME: 30 min.

  1 pound extra-lean ground turkey
  1 medium onion, finely chopped
  3 garlic cloves, minced
  1 teaspoon olive oil
  4 plum tomatoes, chopped
  1/4 teaspoon salt
  1/4 teaspoon pepper
  1/4 cup minced fresh cilantro
  6 cups torn romaine
  1/2 cup shredded reduced-fat Mexican cheese blend
  1/2 cup salsa

1 In a large nonstick skillet over medium heat, cook the turkey, onion and garlic in oil until meat is no longer pink. Stir in the tomatoes, salt and pepper; cook for 3-4 minutes or until tomatoes are tender. Remove from the heat; stir in cilantro.

2 Divide romaine among four plates; top each with 3/4 cup turkey mixture, 2 tablespoons cheese and 2 tablespoons salsa.

YIELD: 4 servings.

TACO SALAD WHILE CAMPING

To adapt any taco salad recipe for camping, first cook the meat at home. Combine lettuce, cheese and diced tomatoes in a resealable bag. At the campground, simmer the meat with a can of chili beans, then add seasonings and a touch of water. Come time to eat, serve the meat mixture and toppings in small bags of corn chips.

BEEF FAJITAS WITH CILANTRO SAUCE

REBECCA SODERGREN, WICHITA FALLS, TEXAS
I found this recipe in the newspaper and made some variations. The jalapeno pepper gives just the slightest bit of zing to the otherwise cool, refreshing sauce.

PREP: 15 min. + marinating GRILL: 25 min.

  4 tablespoons lime juice, divided
  3 tablespoons olive oil, divided
  2 tablespoons minced fresh thyme
  1 tablespoon hot pepper sauce
  1 boneless beef sirloin steak (1-1/2 pounds)
1-1/2 cups fat-free plain yogurt
  1/2 cup fresh cilantro leaves
  1 jalapeno pepper, seeded
  2 large green peppers, halved
  2 large onions, thickly sliced
  8 flour tortillas (6 inches), warmed
Shredded lettuce, tomato wedges and sliced ripe olives, optional

1 In a large resealable plastic bag, combine 3 tablespoons lime juice, 2 tablespoons oil, thyme and hot pepper sauce. Add the beef; seal bag and turn to coat. Refrigerate for at least 2 hours.

2 For sauce, place yogurt, cilantro, jalapeno and remaining lime juice in a blender; cover and process until smooth. Transfer to a small bowl; refrigerate until serving. Brush green peppers and onions with remaining oil; set aside.

3 Drain and discard the marinade. Grill beef, uncovered, over medium-hot heat for 6-7 minutes on each side or until meat reaches desired doneness (for medium-rare, a meat thermometer should read 145°; medium, 160°; well-done, 170°). Let stand for 10 minutes before slicing.

4 Meanwhile, grill the green peppers and onions, uncovered, over medium-hot heat for 5 minutes on each side or until crisp-tender. Cut into strips; spoon onto tortillas. Top with sliced beef. Serve with cilantro sauce. Garnish with lettuce, tomatoes and olives if desired. Fold in sides.

YIELD: 8 servings.

EDITOR'S NOTE: When cutting hot peppers, disposable gloves are recommended. Avoid touching your face.

EXOTIC GRILLED CHICKEN

TASTE OF HOME TEST KITCHEN
The marinade makes a savory statement in this grilled chicken recipe from our home economists. It smells so good when cooking, your guests will be eager to try a piece.

PREP: 15 min. + marinating GRILL: 45 min.
  1/4 cup soy sauce
    3 tablespoons canola oil
    2 tablespoons water
    1 tablespoon dried minced onion
    1 tablespoon sesame seeds
1-1/2 tablespoons sugar
    2 garlic cloves, minced
  1/2 teaspoon ground ginger
  1/2 teaspoon salt
  1/8 teaspoon cayenne pepper
    1 broiler/fryer chicken (3 to 4 pounds), cut up

1 In a large resealable plastic bag, combine first 10 ingredients. Set aside 1/4 cup for basting; cover and refrigerate. Add the chicken to bag; seal bag and turn to coat. Refrigerate for 8 hours or overnight.

2 Drain and discard marinade from chicken. Grill chicken, skin side down, uncovered, over medium heat for 15 minutes on each side. Brush with reserved marinade. Grill for 5 minutes. Turn and baste again; grill 5 minutes longer or until meat juices run clear. Discard unused marinade.

YIELD: 4-6 servings.

PINEAPPLE SHRIMP PACKETS

NANCY ZIMMERMAN, CAPE MAY COURT HOUSE, NEW JERSEY
Your family and friends will delight in receiving these individual grilled shrimp packets. The foil makes cleanup a breeze.

PREP/TOTAL TIME: 25 min.
    6 canned pineapple slices
1-1/2 pounds uncooked medium shrimp, peeled and deveined
  1/3 cup chopped sweet red pepper
  1/3 cup packed brown sugar
    1 tablespoon seafood seasoning
    3 tablespoons butter, cubed

1 For each packet, place a pineapple slice on a double thickness of heavy-duty foil (about 12 in. square). Top with shrimp and red pepper. Combine brown sugar and seafood seasoning; sprinkle over shrimp. Dot with butter. Fold foil around mixture and seal tightly.

2 Grill, covered, over medium heat for 10-15 minutes or until shrimp turn pink.

YIELD: 6 servings.

GRILLED CHICKEN CUCUMBER SALAD

PATRICIA VATTA, NORWOOD, ONTARIO
I often increase the amount that this quick, light and nourishing grilled salad serves to accommodate company.

PREP: 25 min. GRILL: 15 min.
  1/2 cup cucumber ranch salad dressing
  1/4 teaspoon dill weed
    2 boneless skinless chicken breast halves (6 ounces each)
    1 medium apple, cored and cut into 1/4-inch rings
    2 cups mixed salad greens
1-1/4 cups sliced cucumber

1 In a small bowl, combine salad dressing and dill. Pour 1/4 cup into a large resealable plastic bag; add chicken. Seal bag and turn to coat; refrigerate for 20 minutes. Refrigerate remaining dressing.

2 Drain and discard marinade. Coat grill rack with cooking spray before starting the grill. Grill chicken, covered, over medium heat for 6 minutes on each side or until a meat thermometer reads 170°. Keep warm.

3 Brush 1 tablespoon dressing over apple rings; grill for 1 minute on each side. Divide salad greens and cucumber between two serving plates. Slice chicken; arrange chicken and apple rings over greens. Serve with remaining dressing.

YIELD: 2 servings.

SPICY GRILLED CHICKEN SALAD

BRENDA EICHELBERGER, WILLIAMSPORT, MARYLAND
After working in the garden all day, I don't feel much like spending hours in the kitchen. So I'll frequently prepare this quick-to-fix salad for supper. It's filling and good for you, too.

PREP/TOTAL TIME: 30 min.

- 1 can (8 ounces) sliced pineapple
- 3 tablespoons vegetable oil
- 2 tablespoons soy sauce
- 1 tablespoon cider vinegar
- 1 tablespoon honey
- 1/4 teaspoon ground ginger
- 1/4 teaspoon cayenne pepper
- 4 boneless skinless chicken breast halves (1 pound)
- 1/2 to 1 teaspoon seasoned pepper
- 5 cups torn salad greens
- 1 small green pepper, julienned
- 1 small sweet red pepper, julienned
- 1 cup sliced fresh mushrooms
- 1 small onion, sliced into rings

1 Drain pineapple, reserving 2 tablespoons juice. Set the pineapple slices aside. In a jar with tight-fitting lid, combine the juice, oil, soy sauce, vinegar, honey, ginger and cayenne; shake well. Brush some over pineapple slices; set aside.

2 Sprinkle both sides of chicken with pepper; grill or broil for 4-5 minutes on each side or until juices run clear. Cut into strips.

3 Grill or broil pineapple for 2-3 minutes, turning often until browned. To serve, place the greens, peppers, mushrooms and onion in a large bowl; top with chicken and pineapple. Drizzle with remaining dressing.

YIELD: 4 servings.

BRATS IN BEER

JILL HAZELTON, HAMLET, INDIANA
The secret to this delicious bratwurst recipe is the flavorful marinade, which really comes through in the grilled onions. We like to serve it on cool summer evenings while watching the ball game.

PREP: 10 min. + marinating GRILL: 15 min.

- 1 can (12 ounces) beer or nonalcoholic beer
- 2 tablespoons brown sugar
- 2 tablespoons soy sauce
- 1 tablespoon chili powder
- 1 tablespoon prepared mustard
- 1/8 teaspoon garlic powder
- 8 uncooked bratwurst links
- 1 large onion, thinly sliced
- 8 brat or hot dog buns, split

1 In a small bowl, combine the first six ingredients. Pour 1-3/4 cups into a large resealable plastic bag; add bratwurst. Seal bag and turn to coat; refrigerate for 4 hours or overnight. Cover and refrigerate remaining marinade.

2 Add onion to remaining marinade; toss to coat. Place on a double thickness of heavy-duty foil (about 18 in. square). Fold foil around onion mixture and seal tightly. Drain and discard marinade from bratwurst.

3 Grill the bratwurst and onion, covered, over medium heat or broil 4 in. from the heat for 15-20 minutes or until meat is no longer pink and onion is tender, turning frequently. Open foil carefully to allow steam to escape. Serve the brats in buns with onion mixture.

YIELD: 8 servings.

TWO-TOMATO PASTA

MARY ANN HANSEN, ST. CLOUD, MINNESOTA
Plum and cherry tomatoes are put to delicious use in this breezy pasta combination. This is my favorite summer dish with fresh tomatoes. It's speedy and makes very simple fare with grilled meat.

PREP/TOTAL TIME: 25 min.

- 8 ounces uncooked bow tie pasta
- 1/2 cup chopped onion
- 1 tablespoon olive oil
- 2 teaspoons minced garlic
- 2 teaspoons all-purpose flour
- 1 can (5-1/2 ounces) evaporated milk
- 6 plum tomatoes, cut into quarters
- 2 cups cherry tomatoes, halved
- 1/2 cup shredded Parmesan cheese
- 1/2 teaspoon salt
- 1/4 teaspoon pepper
- 6 fresh basil leaves, torn

1 Cook pasta according to package directions. Meanwhile, in a large skillet, saute onion in oil until tender. Add garlic; saute 1-2 minutes longer.

2 Combine flour and milk until smooth; gradually add to skillet. Bring to a boil; cook and stir for 2 minutes or until thickened. Add the tomatoes, Parmesan cheese, salt and pepper. Reduce heat; cook and stir until cheese is melted. Drain pasta; stir into tomato mixture. Sprinkle with basil.

YIELD: 9 servings.

CORN DOGS

RUBY WILLIAMS, BOGALUSA, LOUISIANA
Have a hankering for county fair corn dogs? Prepare them at home in no time flat. Everyone will enjoy this hearty treat.

PREP/TOTAL TIME: 25 min.
- 3/4 cup yellow cornmeal
- 3/4 cup self-rising flour
- 1 egg, lightly beaten
- 2/3 cup milk
- 10 Popsicle sticks
- 10 hot dogs
Oil for deep-fat frying

1 In a large bowl, combine cornmeal, flour and egg. Stir in milk to make a thick batter; let stand 4 minutes. Insert sticks into hot dogs; dip in batter.

2 In an electric skillet or deep-fat fryer, heat oil to 375°. Fry corn dogs, a few at a time, about 6-8 minutes or until golden brown, turning occasionally. Drain on paper towels.

YIELD: 10 servings.

EDITOR'S NOTE: As a substitute for self-rising flour, place 1 teaspoon baking powder and 1/4 teaspoon salt in a measuring cup. Add all-purpose flour to measure 3/4 cup.

CURRIED PEANUT CHICKEN

JENNIFER MYERS, HAVERTOWN, PENNSYLVANIA
This is a nice change from traditional grilled items. I sprinkle coconut and currants over a tasty combination of chicken and peppers.

PREP: 15 min. + marinating GRILL: 10 min.
- 1-1/2 cups orange juice
- 3/4 cup peanut butter
- 2 tablespoons curry powder
- 4 boneless skinless chicken breast halves (6 ounces each)
- 2 medium sweet red peppers, cut in half
- 1/4 cup flaked coconut, toasted
- 1/4 cup dried currants
Hot cooked rice

1 Combine the orange juice, peanut butter and curry powder. Pour 2/3 cup marinade into a large resealable plastic bag; add chicken. Seal bag and turn to coat; refrigerate for 8 hours or overnight. Cover and refrigerate remaining marinade.

2 Drain chicken and discard the marinade. Grill chicken and peppers, covered, over medium heat for 5-8 minutes on each side or until chicken juices run clear and peppers are tender. Warm the reserved marinade. Cut the chicken and peppers into 1/2-in. strips; sprinkle with coconut and currants. Serve with rice and reserved marinade.

YIELD: 4 servings.

DIJON PORK CHOPS

VIVIAN KELBY, CROWN POINT, INDIANA
My children, grandchildren and great-grandchildren have enjoyed these simply delicious chops for years. They're super easy to prepare, and we know you'll like them too.

PREP/TOTAL TIME: 20 min.
- 1/4 cup red wine vinegar
- 2 tablespoons vegetable oil
- 2 tablespoons Dijon mustard
- 2 teaspoons minced fresh parsley
- 1/2 teaspoon minced chives
- 1/4 teaspoon dried tarragon
- 4 boneless butterflied pork chops (4 ounces each), trimmed
Additional chives, optional

1 Combine the vinegar, oil, mustard and herbs; set aside.

2 Grill chops, uncovered, over medium heat for 2 minutes per side for 1/2-in. chops (4 minutes on each side for 1-in. chops). Brush with mustard mixture and grill 2 minutes longer. Turn; baste and grill 2 minutes longer or until juices run clear. Sprinkle with chives if desired.

YIELD: 4 servings.

GRILLED VEGGIE WRAPS

BRITANI SEPANSKI, INDIANAPOLIS, INDIANA
I love this vegetable marinade, but the key to this recipe's success is the three-cheese spread. My father is a meat-and-potatoes eater, but the grilled wraps pass his test!

PREP: 15 min. + marinating GRILL: 15 min.

- 2 tablespoons balsamic vinegar
- 1-1/2 teaspoons minced fresh basil
- 1-1/2 teaspoons olive oil
- 1-1/2 teaspoons molasses
- 3/4 teaspoon minced fresh thyme
- 1/8 teaspoon salt
- 1/8 teaspoon pepper
- 1 medium zucchini, cut lengthwise into 1/4-inch slices
- 1 medium sweet red pepper, cut into 1-inch pieces
- 1 medium red onion, cut into 1/2-inch slices
- 4 ounces whole fresh mushrooms, cut into 1/2-inch pieces
- 4 ounces fresh sugar snap peas
- 1/2 cup crumbled feta cheese
- 3 tablespoons reduced-fat cream cheese
- 2 tablespoons grated Parmesan cheese
- 1 tablespoon reduced-fat mayonnaise
- 4 flour tortillas (8 inches)
- 4 romaine leaves

1 In a large resealable plastic bag, combine the first seven ingredients; add the vegetables. Seal the bag and turn to coat; refrigerate for 2 hours, turning once.

2 Drain and reserve marinade. In a small bowl, combine cheeses and mayonnaise; set aside. Place vegetables in a grill basket or disposable foil pan with slits cut in the bottom. Grill, uncovered, over medium-high heat for 5 minutes.

3 Set aside 1 teaspoon marinade. Turn vegetables; baste with remaining marinade. Grill 5-8 minutes longer or until tender. Brush one side of each tortilla with reserved marinade. Place the tortillas, marinade side down, on grill for 1-3 minutes or until lightly toasted.

4 Spread 3 tablespoons of cheese mixture over ungrilled side of each tortilla. Top with romaine and 1 cup grilled vegetables; roll up.

YIELD: 4 servings.

PESTO SAUCE

SUE JURACK, MEQUON, WISCONSIN
I like to serve this pesto sauce over buttered gnocchi with an extra sprinkle of Parmesan cheese. You can also serve it over any pasta of your choice or use it to marinate a grilled chicken breast. The pesto can be frozen and used later.

PREP/TOTAL TIME: 15 min.

- 2/3 cup packed coarsely chopped fresh basil
- 1/3 cup grated Parmesan cheese
- 1/3 cup olive oil
- 2 tablespoons pine nuts or sunflower kernels
- 1/2 teaspoon salt
- 1/8 teaspoon pepper
- 1 garlic clove, peeled

1 In a food processor, combine all the ingredients; cover and process until blended. Cover and freeze for up to 3 months.

YIELD: 1/2 cup.

EDITOR'S NOTE: When freezing the pesto, leave about 3/4 inch in the top of the container, then cover the top with a thin layer of olive oil, so the pesto doesn't brown during freezing.

BASIL TUNA STEAKS

LINDA MCLYMAN, SYRACUSE, NEW YORK
One of my favorite creations is this five-ingredient recipe. Tuna is delicious, is good for you and can be grilled in no time.

- 6 tuna steaks (6 ounces each)
- 4-1/2 teaspoons olive oil
- 3 tablespoons minced fresh basil
- 3/4 teaspoon salt
- 1/4 teaspoon pepper

1 Drizzle both sides of tuna steaks with oil. Sprinkle with the basil, salt and pepper.

2 Coat grill rack with cooking spray before starting the grill. Grill tuna, covered, over medium heat for 6-8 minutes on each side or until fish flakes easily with a fork.

YIELD: 6 servings.

BLACK BEAN TORTILLA PIE

WENDY KELLY, VOORHEESVILLE, NEW YORK

I found this Southwestern entree awhile ago but decreased the cheese and increased the herbs originally called for. It's one of my daughter's favorite meals and she always smiles when she sees it on the table. It's a great entree to fix when you want a break from meat dishes. To cut back on calories, use reduced-fat cheese. For toppings, I like to use fresh salsa and light sour cream.

PREP: 50 min. **BAKE:** 15 min.

- 1 medium onion, chopped
- 1 medium green pepper, chopped
- 3 garlic cloves, minced
- 1 teaspoon ground cumin
- 1/4 teaspoon pepper
- 1 tablespoon olive oil
- 2 cans (15 ounces each) black beans, rinsed and drained
- 1 can (14-1/2 ounces) vegetable broth
- 1 package (10 ounces) frozen corn, thawed
- 4 green onions, thinly sliced
- 4 flour tortillas (8 inches)
- 1 cup (4 ounces) shredded cheddar cheese, divided

1 In a large skillet, saute the onion, green pepper, garlic, cumin and pepper in oil. Add beans and broth. Bring to a boil; cook until liquid is reduced to about 1/3 cup. Stir in corn and green onions; remove from the heat.

2 Place one tortilla in a 9-in. springform pan coated with cooking spray. Layer with 1-1/2 cups bean mixture and 1/4 cup cheese. Repeat layers twice. Top with remaining tortilla. Place pan on a baking sheet.

3 Bake, uncovered, at 400° for 15-20 minutes or until heated through. Remove sides of pan. Sprinkle with remaining cheese. Cut into wedges.

YIELD: 6 servings.

MINI HAM 'N' CHEESE FRITTATAS

SUSAN WATT, BASKING RIDGE, NEW JERSEY

I found this recipe a few years ago and tried to make it with a few changes. I'm diabetic, and this fits into my low-carb and low-fat diet. Every time I serve a brunch, the frittatas are the first thing to disappear, and nobody knows they are lower in fat!

PREP: 15 min. **BAKE:** 25 min.

- 1/4 pound cubed fully cooked lean ham
- 1 cup (4 ounces) shredded reduced-fat cheddar cheese
- 6 eggs
- 4 egg whites
- 3 tablespoons minced chives
- 2 tablespoons fat-free milk
- 1/4 teaspoon salt
- 1/4 teaspoon pepper

1 Divide ham evenly among eight muffin cups coated with cooking spray; top with cheese. In a large bowl, beat eggs and whites. Beat in the chives, milk, salt and pepper. Pour over cheese, filling each muffin cup three-fourths full.

2 Bake at 375° for 22-25 minutes or until a knife inserted near the center comes out clean. Carefully run a knife around edges to loosen; remove from pan. Serve warm.

YIELD: 8 frittatas.

SHREDDED CHEESE TO GO

It's usually less expensive to buy cheese in blocks than in shredded form. Purchase large quantities of cheddar, Monterey Jack and mozzarella, then shred them in a food processor. Store the shredded cheese in the freezer in heavy-duty resealable plastic bags so that it's available whenever it's needed.

141

140

145

144

DESSERTS

150

SUMMER CELEBRATION ICE CREAM CAKE

KRISTA FRANK, RHODODENDRON, OREGON
I wanted to make my youngest son an ice cream cake one year for his summer birthday, as he prefers ice cream to the traditional cake. He picked the flavors and I decided to try my favorite brownie recipe as a crust. It worked!

PREP: 15 min. BAKE: 20 min. + freezing

- 1 cup sugar
- 3 tablespoons butter, melted
- 3 tablespoons orange yogurt
- 1 egg
- 1 teaspoon grated orange peel
- 1 teaspoon vanilla extract
- 3/4 cup all-purpose flour
- 1/3 cup baking cocoa
- 1 cup (6 ounces) semisweet chocolate chips
- 1-3/4 quarts vanilla ice cream, softened
- 4 to 6 squares (1 ounce each) semisweet chocolate
- 1 tablespoon shortening
Mixed fresh berries

1 Line an 8-in. square baking dish with foil and grease the foil; set aside. In a large bowl, combine the sugar, butter, yogurt, egg, orange peel and vanilla until blended. Combine flour and cocoa; stir into sugar mixture. Add chocolate chips.

2 Spread into prepared dish. Bake at 325° for 20-25 minutes or until a toothpick inserted near the center comes out with moist crumbs. Cool on a wire rack.

3 Spread ice cream over cake. Cover and freeze for 3 hours or until firm.

4 Remove from the freezer 10 minutes before serving. In a microwave-safe bowl, melt the chocolate and shortening; stir until smooth. Using foil, lift the dessert out of the dish; gently peel off foil. Cut into squares. Garnish with the berries and drizzle with chocolate.

YIELD: 9 servings.

ZUCCHINI CHIP CUPCAKES

DEBRA FORSHEE, STOCKTON, KANSAS
My three girls love these moist, nut-topped cupcakes even without frosting. They're a great way to use up zucchini, and they freeze well for a quick snack.

PREP: 15 min. BAKE: 20 min.

- 1/2 cup butter, softened
- 1/2 cup canola oil
- 1-3/4 cups sugar
- 2 eggs
- 1/2 cup milk
- 1 teaspoon vanilla extract
- 2-1/2 cups all-purpose flour
- 1/4 cup baking cocoa
- 1 teaspoon baking soda
- 1/2 teaspoon salt
- 1/2 teaspoon ground cinnamon
- 2 cups shredded zucchini
- 1/4 cup miniature semisweet chocolate chips
- 1/4 cup chopped pecans

1 In a large bowl, cream the butter, oil and sugar until light and fluffy. Beat in the eggs, milk and vanilla. Combine the flour, cocoa, baking soda, salt and cinnamon; gradually add to creamed mixture. Fold in zucchini and chocolate chips.

2 Fill greased or paper-lined muffin cups two-thirds full. Top with pecans. Bake at 375° for 20-25 minutes or until a toothpick comes out clean. Cool for 10 minutes before removing from pans to wire racks to cool completely.

YIELD: about 2 dozen.

STRIPED FRUIT POPS

TASTE OF HOME TEST KITCHEN
These frosty favorites are thrice as nice, lusciously layered with fresh strawberries, kiwifruit and peaches. A touch of honey adds to their natural sweetness. Plus, the pops' bright stripes are sure to light up kids' eyes!

PREP: 15 min. + freezing

  3/4 cup honey, divided
    2 cups sliced fresh strawberries
  12 plastic cups or Popsicle molds (3 ounces each)
    6 kiwifruit, peeled and sliced
  12 Popsicle sticks
1-1/3 cups sliced fresh ripe peaches

1 In a blender, combine 1/4 cup honey and strawberries; cover and process until blended. Pour into cups or molds. Freeze for 30 minutes or until firm.

2 In a blender, combine 1/4 cup honey and kiwi; cover and process until blended. Pour over frozen strawberry layer; insert Popsicle sticks. Freeze until firm.

3 Repeat with peaches and remaining honey; pour over the kiwi layer. Freeze until firm.

YIELD: 1 dozen.

EVERYTHING IS JUST PEACHY
The peak season for fresh peaches is June through September. However, you can always substitute frozen peaches (thawed and drained) or well-drained canned peaches in equal amounts for fresh peaches. One pound of frozen or canned peaches is equal to approximately three medium peaches.

PUFFY OVEN PANCAKES

LILLIAN JULOW, GAINESVILLE, FLORIDA
Puffy and pretty, with a refreshing hint of lemon, this berry-topped pancake is a cherished favorite. It makes a wonderful morning wake-up meal or addition to a special brunch.

PREP/TOTAL TIME: 30 min.

    2 tablespoons butter
    2 eggs
  1/2 cup 2% milk
    1 teaspoon grated lemon peel
  1/2 teaspoon vanilla extract
  1/2 cup all-purpose flour
  1/4 cup fresh blueberries
  1/4 cup fresh raspberries
  1/4 cup sliced fresh strawberries
    1 teaspoon confectioners' sugar

1 Divide butter between two 2-cup round baking dishes. Place on a baking sheet. Heat in a 400° oven until butter is melted.

2 In a small bowl, whisk the eggs, milk, lemon peel and vanilla. Whisk in flour until blended. Pour over butter. Bake, uncovered, for 14-16 minutes or until golden brown and puffy.

3 In a small bowl, gently combine berries. Spoon onto pancakes; sprinkle with confectioners' sugar. Serve immediately.

YIELD: 2 servings.

BLUEBERRY PEACH COBBLER

RONI GOODELL, SPANISH FORK, UTAH
This delicious cobbler smells so good while it's in the oven, your mouth will be watering before it's finished baking. Believe me—there will be no leftovers! My family likes it served warm with cream or ice cream.

PREP: 20 min. **BAKE:** 25 min.
- 1/2 cup packed brown sugar
- 3 tablespoons cornstarch
- 1/4 teaspoon ground mace
- 1/4 cup sherry or unsweetened apple juice
- 5 cups sliced peeled peaches
- 1 cup fresh or frozen blueberries
- 1/2 cup chopped pecans
- 1 tablespoon butter
- 1 tablespoon lemon juice

TOPPING:
- 1 cup all-purpose flour
- 1/3 cup sugar
- 1-1/2 teaspoons baking powder
- Dash salt
- 1/4 cup cold butter, cubed
- 1/4 cup milk
- 1 egg, lightly beaten

1 In a large saucepan, combine the brown sugar, cornstarch and mace. Stir in sherry or juice until blended. Bring to a boil; cook and stir for 1-2 minutes or until thickened. Add the peaches, blueberries, pecans, butter and lemon juice. Pour into a greased shallow 2-qt. baking dish.

2 For topping, in a small bowl, combine flour, sugar, baking powder and salt. Cut in butter until coarse crumbs form. Stir in milk and egg. Spoon over fruit mixture.

3 Bake at 400° for 25-30 minutes or until bubbly and a toothpick inserted in the topping comes out clean. Serve warm.

YIELD: 6-8 servings.

CREAMY MOCHA FROZEN DESSERT

LAUNA SHOEMAKER, MIDLAND CITY, ALABAMA
Light as a feather, this cool, satisfying dessert is delicious and impressive to serve. It's an excellent dessert to take to a potluck because it can be made ahead and stored in the freezer.

PREP: 20 min. + freezing
- 2 teaspoons instant coffee granules
- 1 tablespoon hot water
- 1 cup cream-filled chocolate cookie crumbs
- 3/4 cup chopped pecans, divided
- 1/4 cup butter, melted
- 2 packages (8 ounces each) cream cheese, softened
- 1 can (14 ounces) sweetened condensed milk
- 1/2 cup chocolate-flavored syrup
- 1 carton (8 ounces) frozen whipped topping, thawed

1 In a small bowl, dissolve coffee granules in hot water; set aside. In another bowl, combine cookie crumbs, 1/2 cup pecans and butter. Pat into a 13-in. x 9-in. dish.

2 In a large bowl, beat cream cheese until light and fluffy. Blend in coffee mixture, milk and chocolate syrup. Fold in whipped topping and spread over crust. Sprinkle remaining pecans on top. Freeze.

YIELD: 24 servings.

BROWNIE FOR ICE CREAM SANDWICHES

LUCIE FITZGERALD, SPRING HILL, FLORIDA
This brownie recipe is perfect for creating ice cream sandwiches. All you need is 4 cups softened ice cream. Cut the brownie in half widthwise; spread one half with ice cream and top with the other half of the brownie. Wrap in plastic and freeze, then cut into desired shapes—you'll have a treat everyone will enjoy!

PREP: 10 min. **BAKE:** 10 min. + cooling
- 1/2 cup butter, cubed
- 4 squares (1 ounce each) semisweet chocolate

2 eggs
1 cup sugar
1 teaspoon vanilla extract
3/4 cup all-purpose flour
1/4 teaspoon salt
1/2 cup chopped pecans, optional

1 In a microwave, melt butter and chocolate; stir until smooth. Cool slightly. In a large bowl, beat the eggs and sugar. Stir in the vanilla and chocolate mixture. Combine the flour and salt; gradually add to chocolate mixture.

2 Pour into a parchment paper-lined 15-in. x 10-in. x 1-in. baking pan; sprinkle with pecans if desired. Bake at 400° for 10-12 minutes or until center is set (do not overbake). Cool completely on a wire rack. Invert brownie onto a work surface and remove parchment paper.

3 Prepare according to recipe directions for Banana Split Ice Cream Sandwiches.

YIELD: enough to make 12-15 ice cream sandwiches.

BANANA SPLIT ICE CREAM SANDWICHES

TASTE OF HOME TEST KITCHEN
Enjoy a banana split without the spoon! Our Test Kitchen captures the flavors of this popular sundae, serving it up sandwich-style.

PREP: 25 min. **BAKE:** 10 min. + freezing
Brownie for Ice Cream Sandwiches
    1/2 cup hot fudge ice cream topping, warmed
      4 cups strawberry ice cream, softened
      1 medium firm banana, thinly sliced

1 Prepare the batter for Brownie for Ice Cream Sandwiches. Bake and cool according to recipe directions.

2 Cut the brownie in half widthwise. Spread hot fudge topping over one brownie half; spread with ice cream and layer with banana slices. Turn over remaining brownie half; place over bananas. Cover and freeze for 2 hours or until firm.

3 Cut into bars, squares or desired shapes. Wrap in plastic wrap. Freeze until serving.

YIELD: 12-15 servings.

GERMAN PLUM TART

HELGA SCHLAPE, FLORHAM PARK, NEW JERSEY
The buttery crust of this fruit-filled treat melts in your mouth. You can substitute sliced apples or peaches for the plums with great results. I've used this crust with blueberries, too.

PREP: 10 min. **BAKE:** 35 min.
    1/2 cup butter, softened
      4 tablespoons sugar, divided
      1 egg yolk
    3/4 to 1 cup all-purpose flour
      2 pounds plums, quartered (about 4 cups)

1 In a small bowl, cream butter and 3 tablespoons sugar until light and fluffy. Beat in egg yolk. Gradually add flour, 1/4 cup at a time, until the mixture forms a soft dough. Press onto the bottom and up the sides of a 10-in. pie plate.

2 Arrange plums, skin side up with edges overlapping, in crust; sprinkle with remaining sugar. Bake at 350° for 35-45 minutes or until crust is golden brown and fruit is tender.

YIELD: 6-8 servings.

CHERRY-BERRY PEACH PIE

AMY HARTKE, ELGIN, ILLINOIS
I had an overabundant supply of cherries one year, so I adapted several recipes to use them up. I knew this one was a keeper when I received phone calls from my mother and grandmother complimenting me on this pie.

PREP: 30 min. **BAKE:** 50 min. + cooling

2-1/2 cups all-purpose flour
2 tablespoons sugar
1/2 teaspoon salt
1 cup cold butter, cubed
4 to 6 tablespoons cold water

FILLING:
2 cups fresh or frozen sliced peaches, thawed
1-3/4 cups pitted fresh dark sweet cherries or 1 can (15 ounces) pitted dark sweet cherries, drained
1 cup fresh or frozen blueberries, thawed
1 teaspoon almond extract
1 teaspoon vanilla extract
1-1/2 cups sugar
1/4 cup all-purpose flour
1/4 cup quick-cooking tapioca
1/2 teaspoon salt
1/2 teaspoon ground nutmeg
1 tablespoon butter

1 In a large bowl, combine flour, sugar and salt; cut in butter until crumbly. Gradually add water, tossing with a fork until dough forms a ball. Divide dough in half. Roll out one portion to fit a 9-in. deep-dish pie plate; transfer to pie plate. Trim the pastry even with edge of plate; set aside.

2 For filling, in a large bowl, combine the peaches, cherries, blueberries and extracts. Combine sugar, flour, tapioca, salt and nutmeg; sprinkle over the fruit and gently toss to coat. Let stand for 15 minutes.

3 Spoon filling into crust. Dot with butter. Roll out remaining pastry; make a lattice crust. Seal and flute edges.

4 Bake at 375° for 50-55 minutes or until the crust is golden brown and filling is bubbly. Cover edges with foil during the last 15 minutes to prevent overbrowning if necessary. Cool on a wire rack.

YIELD: 6-8 servings.

SHERBET WATERMELON

MARGARET RILEY, TALLAHASSEE, FLORIDA
I usually double this recipe so I can have one dessert on hand for family and friends who stop by unexpectedly in summer. Each refreshing wedge comes complete with chocolate chip "seeds."

PREP: 20 min. + freezing

About 1 pint lime sherbet, slightly softened
About 1 pint pineapple sherbet, slightly softened
About 1-1/2 pints raspberry sherbet, slightly softened
1/4 cup miniature semisweet chocolate chips

1 Line a 1-1/2-qt. round metal bowl with plastic wrap. Press a thin layer of lime sherbet against the bottom and sides of bowl. Freeze, uncovered, until firm. Spread a thin layer of pineapple sherbet evenly over the lime sherbet layer. Freeze until firm. Pack raspberry sherbet into center of sherbet-lined bowl. Smooth the top to resemble a cut watermelon. Cover and freeze until firm, about 8 hours.

2 Just before serving, remove the bowl from the freezer and uncover. Invert onto a serving plate. Remove the bowl and plastic wrap. Cut into wedges; press a few chocolate chips into the raspberry sherbet section of each wedge to resemble watermelon seeds.

YIELD: 8 servings.

RASPBERRY TRIFLE

MARCY CELLA, L'ANSE, MICHIGAN

Beautiful and luscious, this trifle is an impressive way to use your fresh raspberries. Plus, people will never know how nice and easy it is to prepare if you use purchased pound cake or lady fingers.

PREP: 25 minutes + chilling

    1 package (16 ounces) pound cake, cut into 18 slices or
    2 packages (3 ounces each) ladyfingers
    2 packages (3.4 ounces each) instant vanilla pudding mix
    1 jar (18 ounces) raspberry jam
 1-1/2 pints fresh raspberries
    Whipped cream and fresh raspberries, for garnish

1 Arrange one-third of sliced cake in the bottom of a trifle dish or large decorative bowl.

2 Prepare the pudding according to package directions. Place one-third more cake pieces around inside of bowl, using half of pudding to hold them in place.

3 Gently stir together the jam and raspberries; spoon half over pudding. Cover with the remaining cake pieces. Layer remaining pudding and raspberry mixture. Chill. Garnish with whipped cream and fresh raspberries.

YIELD: 8-10 servings.

TRIFLES GALORE

It's easy to vary the recipe above to suit your individual taste. Along with raspberries, you can use other types of fruit, such as strawberries, kiwis, blackberries or blueberries. If you're a chocolate lover, sprinkle the top of the trifle with semisweet chocolate chips. If you want to double the chocolate flavor, in addition to chocolate chips, substitute the vanilla pudding with chocolate pudding.

COUNTRY-STYLE VANILLA ICE CREAM

CYNDI FYNAARDT, OSKALOOSA, IOWA

The creamy texture of this old-fashioned ice cream, with its wonderful vanilla flavor, makes it a winner. Plus, it's simple to make.

PREP: 20 min. + chilling **FREEZE:** 2 hours

    6 cups milk, divided
    2 cups sugar
    4 eggs, beaten
    1 teaspoon vanilla extract
    2 packages (3.4 ounces each) instant vanilla pudding mix
    1 carton (8 ounces) frozen whipped topping, thawed

1 In a large saucepan, heat 2-1/2 cups milk to 175°; stir in sugar until dissolved. Whisk a small amount of hot mixture into the eggs. Return all to the pan, whisking constantly. Cook and stir over low heat until mixture reaches at least 160° and coats the back of a metal spoon. Remove from the heat. Cool quickly by placing the pan in a bowl of ice water; stir for 2 minutes. Stir in the vanilla.

2 Place remaining milk in a bowl; whisk in pudding mixes for 2 minutes. Let stand for 2 minutes or until soft-set. Stir into egg mixture. Stir in whipped topping. Press waxed paper onto surface of custard. Refrigerate for several hours or overnight.

3 Fill the cylinder of ice cream freezer two-thirds full; freeze according to the manufacturer's directions. Refrigerate the remaining mixture until ready to freeze. Transfer to a freezer container; freeze for 2-4 hours before serving.

YIELD: 2-1/2 quarts.

CREAMY PEACH PIE

MARY ANN BOSTIC, SINKS GROVE, WEST VIRGINIA
This pie always receives rave reviews and is especially good when peaches are in season.

PREP: 15 min. **BAKE:** 50 min.
Pastry for double-crust pie (9 inches)
- 3/4 cup plus 1 tablespoon sugar, divided
- 3 tablespoons cornstarch
- 1/2 teaspoon ground nutmeg
- 1/4 teaspoon ground ginger
- 1/4 teaspoon ground cinnamon
- 4 tablespoons heavy whipping cream, divided
- 1 tablespoon lemon juice
- 1/2 teaspoon almond extract
- 7 cups sliced peeled peaches (about 7 medium)

1 Line a 9-in. pie plate with bottom pastry; trim even with edge of plate. Set aside. In a bowl, combine 3/4 cup sugar, cornstarch, nutmeg, ginger and cinnamon; stir in 3 tablespoons cream, lemon juice and extract. Add the peaches; toss gently. Pour into the crust.

2 Roll out remaining pastry to fit top of pie; make decorative cutouts in pastry. Place top crust over filling; trim, seal and flute edges. Brush pastry and cutouts with remaining cream. Place cutouts on top of pie; sprinkle with remaining sugar.

3 Cover edges loosely with foil. Bake at 400° for 40 minutes. Remove foil; bake 8-12 minutes longer or until crust is golden brown and filling is bubbly. Cool on a wire rack. Refrigerate the leftovers.

YIELD: 6-8 servings.

PEELING PEACHES
Place peaches in a large pot of boiling water for 10-20 seconds or until the skin splits. Remove with a slotted spoon. Place in an ice water bath to cool the peaches and stop the cooking process. Use a paring knife to peel the skin. If stubborn areas of skin won't peel off, return fruit to boiling water for a few more seconds.

FROSTED FUDGE BROWNIES

SUE SODERLUND, ELGIN, ILLINOIS
A neighbor brought over a pan of these rich brownies along with the recipe when I came home from the hospital with our baby daughter 12 years ago. I've made them ever since for family occasions, potlucks and parties.

PREP: 10 min. + cooling **BAKE:** 25 min. + cooling
- 1 cup plus 3 tablespoons butter, cubed
- 3/4 cup baking cocoa
- 4 eggs
- 2 cups sugar
- 1-1/2 cups all-purpose flour
- 1 teaspoon baking powder
- 1 teaspoon salt
- 1 teaspoon vanilla extract

FROSTING:
- 6 tablespoons butter, softened
- 2-2/3 cups confectioners' sugar
- 1/2 cup baking cocoa
- 1 teaspoon vanilla extract
- 1/4 to 1/3 cup milk

1 In a saucepan, melt butter. Remove from heat. Stir in cocoa; cool. In a large bowl, beat the eggs and sugar until blended. Combine flour, baking powder and salt; gradually add to egg mixture. Stir in vanilla and the cooled chocolate mixture until well blended.

2 Spread into a greased 13-in. x 9-in. baking pan. Bake at 350° for 25-28 minutes or until a toothpick inserted near the center comes out clean (do not overbake). Cool on a wire rack.

3 For frosting, in a large bowl, cream butter and confectioners' sugar until light and fluffy. Beat in cocoa and vanilla. Add enough milk until the frosting achieves spreading consistency. Spread over brownies. Cut into bars.

YIELD: 2 dozen.

WATERMELON SLUSH

ELIZABETH MONTGOMERY, CAMBRIDGE, MASSACHUSETTS
This frosty treat makes a refreshing ending to a summer meal. Simply scoop the slushy mixture into bowls or tall glasses and top with lemon-lime soda.

PREP: 5 min. + freezing
- 1/4 cup lime juice
- 8 cups cubed seedless watermelon
- 1/4 cup sugar
- 2 cups diet lemon-lime soda, chilled

1 In a blender, cover and process the lime juice, watermelon, and sugar in batches until smooth. Pour into a freezer-proof container. Cover and freeze for 30 minutes or until edges begin to freeze.

2 Stir and return to freezer. Repeat every 20 minutes or until slushy, about 90 minutes. Spoon 3/4 cup into bowls or glasses; add 1/4 cup soda.

YIELD: 8 servings.

VERY BERRY PEACH SAUCE

BRENDA WHITE, HAGERSTOWN, MARYLAND
Paired with ice cream, this colorful sauce makes a special after-dinner treat in no time. It's also delicious on chicken and pork.

PREP/TOTAL TIME: 20 min.
- 2 tablespoons sugar
- 4-1/2 teaspoons cornstarch
- 1/2 cup red currant jelly
- 2 medium peaches, peeled and sliced
- 1/2 cup fresh or frozen blueberries
- 1/2 cup fresh raspberries

1 In a small saucepan, combine sugar and cornstarch. Stir in jelly until smooth. Stir in peaches, blueberries and raspberries.

2 Cook and stir over medium heat until mixture comes to a boil. Cook 3-4 minutes longer or until thickened (some berries will remain whole).

YIELD: 6 servings.

FRESH FRUIT TARTS

DONA ERHART, STOCKBRIDGE, MICHIGAN
These luscious tarts are the jewels of the party whenever I serve them. I usually double this recipe. You can bake the shells ahead and freeze them, then fill and decorate the tarts the day of the gathering.

PREP: 20 min. + chilling **BAKE:** 15 min. + cooling
- 1-1/2 cups all-purpose flour
- 1/4 cup sugar
- 1/4 teaspoon salt
- 1/2 cup cold butter, cubed
- 1 egg, lightly beaten

FILLING:
- 4 ounces cream cheese, softened
- 1/4 cup sweetened condensed milk
- 2 tablespoons lemon juice

Assorted fresh berries
- 2 tablespoons apricot preserves

1 In a large bowl, combine flour, sugar and salt. Cut in butter until mixture resembles coarse crumbs. Add egg; mix with a fork until blended. Shape dough into a ball. Cover and refrigerate for 1 hour or until easy to handle.

2 Divide the dough into six portions. Press each portion into a greased 4-1/2-in. tart pan. Bake at 350° for 15-20 minutes or until edges are lightly browned. Cool for 10 minutes before removing from pans to wire racks to cool completely.

3 For filling, in a small bowl, beat cream cheese until smooth. Beat in sweetened condensed milk and lemon juice. Spoon 2 rounded tablespoonfuls into each cooled tart shell. Arrange berries over filling.

4 In a small saucepan, melt preserves over medium heat; stir until smooth. Brush over berries.

YIELD: 6 servings.

OZARK MOUNTAIN BERRY PIE

ELAINE MOODY, CLEVER, MISSOURI
I think the best berries in the world are grown in the Ozarks. We own a small berry farm, and this is one of my favorite recipes.

PREP: 15 min. **BAKE:** 45 min. + cooling

- 1 cup sugar
- 1/4 cup cornstarch
- 1/2 teaspoon ground cinnamon, optional

Dash salt

- 1/3 cup water
- 1 cup fresh blueberries

Pastry for a double-crust pie (9 inches)

- 1 cup fresh strawberries
- 1 cup fresh raspberries
- 3/4 cup fresh blackberries
- 1 tablespoon lemon juice
- 2 tablespoons butter

1 In a large saucepan, combine sugar, cornstarch, cinnamon, salt and water until smooth; add blueberries. Bring to a boil; cook and stir for 2 minutes or until thickened. Set aside to cool.

2 Line a 9-in. pie plate with bottom crust; trim pastry even with edge. Gently fold the remaining fresh berries and lemon juice into the blueberry mixture. Pour into pastry; dot with butter. Roll out the remaining pastry; make a lattice crust. Trim, seal and flute edges. Bake at 400° for 10 minutes. Reduce heat to 350°; bake for 45-50 or until the crust is golden brown and filling is bubbly. Cool on a wire rack. Store in the refrigerator.

YIELD: 8 servings.

NO-BAKE CHOCO-NUT CHEWS

ANDREA SU, BINGHAMTON, NEW YORK
We have a hard time keeping these tasty snacks in our house for long, so it's good that they're quick to make!

PREP: 20 min. + cooling

- 2 squares (1 ounce each) unsweetened chocolate
- 2 cups sugar
- 1/2 cup milk
- 1/2 cup butter, cubed
- 1/2 cup peanut butter
- 1 teaspoon vanilla extract
- 4 cups quick-cooking oats
- 1/3 cup chopped walnuts

1 In a large saucepan, bring chocolate, sugar and milk to a boil; boil for 1 minute, stirring constantly. Remove from the heat; add butter, peanut butter, vanilla, oats and nuts. Drop by tablespoonfuls onto waxed paper. Allow to harden, about 20 minutes, before peeling off paper.

YIELD: 3-4 dozen.

SOUR CHERRY SORBET

CAROL GAUS, ITASCA, ILLINOIS
My mother-in-law has a sour cherry tree in her yard that yields many quarts of cherries each June, and this is a great way to use some.

PREP: 10 min. + freezing

- 3 cups frozen pitted tart cherries
- 1 cup sugar
- 1/3 cup white wine or grape juice
- 1/2 teaspoon almond extract
- 1/2 teaspoon salt

1 Place cherries in a food processor; cover and process until smooth. Add remaining ingredients; cover and pulse until blended. Pour into a freezer container. Cover and freeze until firm.

YIELD: 6 servings.

NO-BAKE KIWI PINEAPPLE CHEESECAKE

KIMI TAZIRI, FORT COLLINS, COLORADO
When I was a teacher, this dessert was the one co-workers and my students requested most often. It's light, refreshing and easy to make.

PREP: 45 min. + chilling
1-3/4 cups crushed vanilla wafers (about 55 wafers)
  1/4 cup sugar
  1/2 cup butter, melted

FILLING:
  1 can (20 ounces) sliced pineapple
  1 envelope unflavored gelatin
  2 packages (8 ounces each) cream cheese, softened
  1 carton (15 ounces) ricotta cheese
  1 cup confectioners' sugar
  1 tablespoon grated orange peel
  1 teaspoon vanilla extract

TOPPING:
  1/2 cup orange marmalade
  1 kiwifruit, peeled, halved and sliced

1 In a bowl, combine the wafer crumbs and the sugar; stir in the butter. Press onto the bottom and 2 in. up the sides of a greased 9-in. springform pan. Bake at 350° for 8 minutes. Cool on a wire rack; refrigerate for 30 minutes.

2 Meanwhile, for filling, drain pineapple, reserving 1/2 cup juice (discard remaining juice or save for another use). In a small saucepan, sprinkle gelatin over reserved juice; let stand for 1 minute. Cook over low heat, stirring until gelatin is completely dissolved. Cool to room temperature, about 10 minutes.

3 In a bowl, beat the cream cheese, ricotta cheese and confectioners' sugar until smooth; gradually add gelatin mixture, orange peel and vanilla. Beat on low speed until well mixed. Spoon half into crust. Cut four pineapple rings in half; arrange in a spoke fashion over filling. Evenly spoon remaining filling over pineapple. Refrigerate for 6 hours or overnight.

4 For topping, beat marmalade until soft and spreadable; brush 6 tablespoons on top of cheesecake. Cut remaining pineapple rings in half; arrange over marmalade. Place the kiwi slices between pineapple rings. Brush with remaining marmalade. Just before serving, run a knife around edge of pan to loosen. Remove sides of pan. Refrigerate leftovers.

YIELD: 12-14 servings.

FROZEN MUD PIE

DEBBIE TERENZINI-WILKERSON, LUSBY, MARYLAND
Here's one of those "looks like you fussed" desserts that is so easy it's become a standard for me. The cookie crust is a snap to make.

PREP: 40 min. + freezing
1-1/2 cups cream-filled chocolate sandwich cookie crumbs
1-1/2 teaspoons sugar, optional
  1/4 cup butter, melted
  4 cups chocolate chip or coffee ice cream, softened
  1/4 cup chocolate syrup, divided
Additional cream-filled chocolate sandwich cookies, optional

1 In a small bowl, combine cookie crumbs and sugar if desired. Stir in butter. Press onto the bottom and up the sides of an ungreased 9-in. pie plate. Refrigerate for 30 minutes.

2 Spoon 2 cups ice cream into crust. Drizzle with half the chocolate syrup; swirl with knife. Carefully top with remaining ice cream. Drizzle with remaining syrup; swirl with a knife. Cover and freeze until firm.

3 Remove from freezer 10-15 minutes before serving. Garnish with whole cookies if desired.

YIELD: 8 servings.

BLUEBERRY CHEESECAKE ICE CREAM

MELISSA SYMINGTON, NECHE, NORTH DAKOTA
After sampling this flavor at an ice cream stand, I kept trying to duplicate it until it was just right.

PREP: 25 min. + freezing **BAKE:** 10 min. + cooling

- 1/2 cup sugar
- 1 tablespoon cornstarch
- 1/2 cup water
- 1-1/4 cups fresh or frozen blueberries
- 1 tablespoon lemon juice

GRAHAM CRACKER MIXTURE:

- 2-1/4 cups graham cracker crumbs (about 36 squares)
- 2 tablespoons sugar
- 1/2 teaspoon ground cinnamon
- 1/2 cup butter, melted

ICE CREAM:

- 1-1/2 cups sugar
- 1 package (3.4 ounces) instant cheesecake or vanilla pudding mix
- 1 quart heavy whipping cream
- 2 cups milk
- 2 teaspoons vanilla extract

1 In a small saucepan, combine the sugar and cornstarch. Gradually stir in water until smooth. Stir in blueberries and lemon juice. Bring to a boil. Reduce the heat; simmer, uncovered, for 5 minutes or until slightly thickened, stirring occasionally. Cover and refrigerate until chilled.

2 In a large bowl, combine cracker crumbs, sugar and cinnamon. Stir in butter. Pat into an ungreased 15-in. x 10-in. x 1-in. baking pan. Bake at 350° for 10-15 minutes or until lightly browned. Cool completely on a wire rack.

3 Meanwhile, in a large bowl, whisk the ice cream ingredients. Fill ice cream freezer cylinder two-thirds full; freeze according

to manufacturer's directions. Refrigerate remaining mixture until ready to freeze. Whisk before adding to ice cream freezer (mixture will have some lumps).

4 Crumble graham cracker mixture. In a large container, layer the ice cream, graham cracker mixture and blueberry sauce three times; swirl. Freeze.

YIELD: 2 quarts.

ICY SUMMER TREATS DESSERT

DARLENE BRENDEN, SALEM, OREGON
You won't break a sweat fixing these easy chillers! The frozen snack, made from fruity gelatin and powdered soft drink mix, can be whipped up in no time. My kids loved these when they were little, and although grown, they still request the treats when they visit.

PREP: 10 min. + freezing

- 1 cup sugar
- 1 package (3 ounces) cherry gelatin
- 1 package (.13 ounces) unsweetened cherry soft drink mix
- 2 cups boiling water
- 2 cups cold water
- 10 disposable plastic cups (5 ounces)
  Heavy-duty aluminum foil
- 10 Popsicle sticks

1 In a large bowl, combine the sugar, gelatin and soft drink mix in boiling water until dissolved. Add cold water. Pour into cups.

2 Cover each cup with foil; insert sticks through foil (foil will hold sticks upright). Place in a 13-in. x 9-in. pan; freeze. To serve, remove foil and plastic cups.

YIELD: 10 servings.

EDITOR'S NOTE: Any flavor gelatin and soft drink mix may be used.

RASPBERRY CRISP

DONNA CRAIK, VANCOUVER ISLAND, BRITISH COLUMBIA
This delicious crisp is sure to be a family pleaser.

PREP: 20 min. **BAKE:** 25 min.

- 4 cups fresh raspberries, divided
- 3/4 cup sugar
- 2 tablespoons cornstarch
- 1-3/4 cups quick-cooking oats
- 1 cup all-purpose flour
- 1 cup packed brown sugar
- 1/2 teaspoon baking soda
- 1/2 cup cold butter
  Whipped cream

1 Crush 1 cup raspberries; add enough water to measure 1 cup. In a saucepan, combine sugar and cornstarch; stir in raspberry mixture until well blended. Bring to a boil; cook and stir for 2 minutes or until thickened. Remove from the heat; stir in the remaining raspberries. Cool.

2 In a large bowl, combine the oats, flour, brown sugar and baking soda. Cut in the butter until mixture resembles coarse crumbs. Press half of the crumbs into a greased 9-in. square baking dish. Spread with the cooled berry mixture. Sprinkle with the remaining crumbs.

3 Bake at 350° for 25-30 minutes or until top is lightly browned. Serve warm with whipped cream.

YIELD: 8 servings.

FREEZER PEANUT BUTTER PIE

NINA RUFENER, MANSFIELD, OHIO
What a cool and creamy treat for the warm summer months! The easy-to-make dessert has two of my favorite flavors, peanut butter and chocolate.

PREP: 15 min. + freezing

    1 quart vanilla ice cream, softened
    1 graham cracker crust (9 inches)
    1/2 cup peanut butter
    1/3 cup light corn syrup
Chocolate syrup
Chopped walnuts

1 Spread half of the ice cream into crust. Combine peanut butter and corn syrup; spread over ice cream. Top with the remaining ice cream. Drizzle with chocolate syrup and sprinkle with nuts.

2 Cover and freeze for 3-4 hours. Remove from the freezer 15 minutes before serving.

YIELD: 6-8 servings.

SOFTENING ICE CREAM

Ice cream is often softened for use in recipes or when it is too hard to scoop for eating. To soften in the refrigerator, transfer ice cream from the freezer to the refrigerator 20-30 minutes before using. Or let it stand at room temperature for 10-15 minutes. Hard ice cream can also be microwaved at 30% power for about 30 seconds.

BLACKBERRY CUSTARD TORTE

ANN FOX, AUSTIN, TEXAS
Sour cream gives the custard an interesting flavor twist in this outstanding blackberry dessert.

PREP: 15 min. **BAKE:** 1-1/2 hours + cooling

    1 cup all-purpose flour
    1/2 cup sugar
    1-1/2 teaspoons baking powder
    1/2 cup cold butter
    1 egg
FILLING:
    3 egg yolks
    2 cups (16 ounces) sour cream
    1/2 cup sugar
    1/4 teaspoon vanilla extract
    4 cups fresh or frozen blackberries, drained, divided
Whipped cream

1 In a small bowl, combine the flour, sugar and baking powder; cut in butter until crumbly. Stir in egg until dough forms a ball. Press onto the bottom and 2 in. up the sides of an ungreased 9-in. springform pan.

2 For filling, beat egg yolks, sour cream, sugar and vanilla in another small bowl just until combined. Sprinkle 2 cups blackberries over crust. Carefully pour sour cream mixture over berries. Place pan on a baking sheet.

3 Bake at 325° for 1-1/2 hours or until center is almost set. Cool on a wire rack (center will fall).

4 Remove sides of pan. Top with the whipped cream and remaining blackberries. Refrigerate any leftovers.

YIELD: 12-14 servings.

EDITOR'S NOTE: This dessert is best eaten the same day it's prepared.

156

161

156

154

SPECIAL OCCASIONS

154

1 teaspoon Worcestershire sauce
1/2 teaspoon salt
Dash pepper

BURGER:
1 pound lean ground beef
4 hamburger buns, split
Optional toppings: sliced tomato, onion, pickles and condiments

1 Coat grill rack with cooking spray before starting the grill. In a large bowl, combine egg and seasonings. Crumble beef over mixture and mix well. Shape into four 3/4-in.-thick patties.

2 Grill, covered, over medium heat for 5-7 minutes on each side or until a meat thermometer reads 160° and juices run clear. Serve on buns with desired toppings.

YIELD: 4 servings.

CRISPY PICNIC CHICKEN

JOANIE ELBOURN, GARDNER, MASSACHUSETTS
Crackers, cheese and spices are all you need to create a coating that turns plain chicken into something special.

PREP: 15 min. **BAKE:** 50 min.
20 butter-flavored crackers, crushed
2/3 cup grated Parmesan cheese
2 teaspoons dried parsley flakes
3/4 teaspoon garlic powder
1/2 teaspoon paprika
1/8 teaspoon pepper
1/3 cup butter, melted
1 broiler/fryer chicken (3-1/2 to 4 pounds), cut up

1 In a large resealable plastic bag, combine first six ingredients. Place butter in a shallow bowl. Dip a few pieces of chicken at a time in butter, then place in bag; seal and shake to coat.

2 Bake, uncovered, at 350° for 50 minutes or until chicken is tender and juices run clear. Serve hot or chilled.

YIELD: 4-6 servings.

THE PERFECT HAMBURGER

SHIRLEY KIDD, NEW LONDON, MINNESOTA
Chili sauce and horseradish add zip to these hamburgers and make them a nice change from ordinary burgers. We think they're perfect and make them often for family and friends.

PREP/TOTAL TIME: 20 min.
1 egg, lightly beaten

SEASONINGS:
2 tablespoons chili sauce
1 teaspoon dried minced onion
1 teaspoon prepared horseradish

PICNIC POTATO SALAD

LOUISE KURTTI, FARGO, NORTH DAKOTA
The Red River Valley near where my family lives is a prime growing area for potatoes. They request this recipe not only in summer, but year-round.

PREP: 20 min. **COOK:** 20 min. + chilling
4 medium potatoes (about 1-1/2 pounds), peeled
1/2 medium cucumber, finely chopped
3/4 cup chopped fresh broccoli
1/2 cup finely chopped celery
2 hard-cooked eggs, chopped
3/4 cup mayonnaise
2 tablespoons milk
2 tablespoons finely chopped onion
1-1/2 teaspoons chopped fresh parsley
1-1/2 teaspoons prepared mustard

1 Combine the juices in a large container. Refrigerate. Just before serving, stir in ginger ale and orange slices.

YIELD: 5 quarts.

PICNIC BARS

FRANK BEE, EUGENE, OREGON

You'll score points with a crowd when you stir together these delicious fudge-like treats. They're very moist and rich. The chocolate chips and walnuts make a pretty topping.

PREP: 10 min. **BAKE:** 25 min.

- 1-3/4 cups all-purpose flour
- 1 cup sugar
- 1/4 cup baking cocoa
- 1/2 cup cold butter, cubed
- 2 eggs
- 1 can (14 ounces) sweetened condensed milk
- 2 cups (12 ounces) semisweet chocolate chips, divided
- 1 cup chopped walnuts

1 In a large bowl, combine the flour, sugar and cocoa; cut in butter until mixture resembles coarse crumbs. Stir in eggs. Set aside 1-1/2 cups for topping.

2 Press remaining crumb mixture into a greased 13-in. x 9-in. baking pan. Bake at 350° for 6-8 minutes or until set.

3 Meanwhile, in a saucepan, combine the milk and 1 cup of chocolate chips; cook and stir over low heat until melted. Carefully spread over crust. Combine reserved crumb mixture with nuts and remaining chips. Sprinkle over chocolate layer.

4 Bake for 15-20 minutes or until top is set (chips will not look melted). Cool before cutting.

YIELD: 3 dozen.

- 1-1/2 teaspoons white vinegar
- 3/4 teaspoon celery seed
- 1/2 teaspoon each salt, pepper and sugar

1 Place potatoes in a large saucepan and cover with water. Bring to a boil. Reduce heat; cover and cook for 15-20 minutes or until tender. Drain. Cool; cut into cubes.

2 In a large bowl, combine the potatoes with the cucumber, broccoli, celery and eggs. In a small bowl, combine remaining ingredients. Pour over salad and gently toss. Cover and chill 1 hour before serving. Store in refrigerator.

YIELD: 4-6 servings.

PICNIC FRUIT PUNCH

MARION LOWERY, MEDFORD, OREGON

This pink cooler is deliciously thirst-quenching on a warm day. Seeing its color, folks guess it might be pink lemonade. They're pleasantly surprised to discover the bubbly blend includes cranberry, pineapple, orange and lemon juices.

PREP/TOTAL TIME: 10 min.

- 8 cups cranberry juice
- 3 cups pineapple juice
- 3 cups orange juice
- 1/4 cup lemon juice
- 1 liter ginger ale, chilled
- 1 medium navel orange, sliced

GIANT PICNIC SANDWICH

ROXIE FAGER, IDAHO FALLS, IDAHO

I'm always looking for fun foods to prepare for company in the summer. This delicious sandwich travels well for a picnic or get-together held the same day it is made...plus it looks as good as it tastes.

PREP: 15 min. + rising BAKE: 20 min. + chilling

     1 package (16 ounces) hot roll mix
     1 teaspoon milk
     2 teaspoons sesame seeds
   1/2 cup creamy Italian salad dressing
     6 to 8 lettuce leaves
     6 ounces thinly sliced fully cooked ham
     6 ounces thinly sliced Genoa salami
     1 medium cucumber, sliced
     4 slices red onion, separated into rings
     6 ounces sliced Swiss cheese
     1 medium green pepper, sliced
     2 medium tomatoes, thinly sliced

1 Prepare hot roll mix according to package instructions. Pat or roll into a 12-in. circle; place on a greased 12-in. pizza pan. Cover and let rise in a warm place until doubled, about 30 minutes.

2 Brush with milk; sprinkle with sesame seeds. Bake at 375° for 20-25 minutes or until golden brown. Cool on a wire rack.

3 Cut in half horizontally; spread salad dressing on cut sides. On bottom half, layer the lettuce, ham, salami, cucumber, onion, cheese, green pepper and tomatoes. Replace the top half. Refrigerate until ready to serve. Cut into wedges.

YIELD: 6-8 servings.

STRAWBERRY CHEESECAKE ICE CREAM

KAREN MAUBACH, FAIRBURY, ILLINOIS

I found the recipe for this creamy and refreshing dessert in an old cookbook. Made in an ice cream freezer, it's wonderful for family gatherings. We love how it tastes like a berry-topped cheesecake.

PREP: 10 min. FREEZE: 30 min.

     3 cups sliced fresh strawberries
     6 ounces reduced-fat cream cheese
     2 cans (12 ounces each) fat-free evaporated milk
     1 can (14 ounces) fat-free sweetened condensed milk
     1 teaspoon vanilla extract
     1 cup reduced-fat whipped topping

1 Place strawberries in a blender; cover and process until smooth. In a large bowl, beat cream cheese until smooth. Beat in the evaporated milk, condensed milk, vanilla and pureed strawberries. Fold in whipped topping.

2 Fill the cylinder of the ice cream freezer two-thirds full; freeze according to manufacturer's directions. Refrigerate the remaining mixture until ready to freeze. Allow to ripen in ice cream freezer or firm up in your refrigerator freezer for 2-4 hours before serving.

YIELD: 2 quarts.

WE ALL SCREAM FOR ICE CREAM SANDWICHES
Homemade ice cream sandwiches are an easy treat to make. Place 1/2 cup of any flavor ice cream on the flat side of a 3-in. cookie of your choice. Place another cookie, bottom side down, on top of the ice cream. Gently press cookies together until ice cream is even with the edges. If desired, roll edges in toppings, like chopped nuts or sprinkles. Serve or wrap in plastic wrap and freeze.

PICNIC PASTA SALAD

FELICIA FIOCCHI, VINELAND, NEW JERSEY
My family's not big on traditional pasta salads made with mayonnaise, so when I served this colorful version that uses Italian dressing, it was a big hit. This crowd-pleaser is loaded with vegetables, beans and tricolor pasta.

PREP/TOTAL TIME: 25 min.

- 1 package (12 ounces) tricolor spiral pasta
- 1 package (10 ounces) refrigerated tricolor tortellini
- 1 jar (7-1/2 ounces) marinated artichoke hearts, undrained
- 1/2 pound fresh broccoli florets (about 1-3/4 cups)
- 12 ounces provolone cheese, cubed
- 12 ounces hard salami, cubed
- 1 medium sweet red pepper, chopped
- 1 medium green pepper, chopped
- 1 can (15 ounces) garbanzo beans or chickpeas, rinsed and drained
- 2 cans (2-1/4 ounces each) sliced ripe olives, drained
- 1 medium red onion, chopped
- 4 garlic cloves, minced
- 2 envelopes Italian salad dressing mix

1 Cook the spiral pasta and tortellini according to package directions. Drain and rinse in cold water. Place in a large bowl; add the artichokes, broccoli, provolone cheese, salami, peppers, beans, olives, onion and garlic.

2 Prepare salad dressing according to package directions; pour over salad and toss to coat. Serve immediately or cover and refrigerate.

YIELD: 14-16 servings.

RAINBOW GELATIN CUBES

DEANNA PIETROWICZ, BRIDGEPORT, CONNECTICUT
These perky gelatin cubes are fun to serve and to eat! I vary the colors to match the occasion—pink and blue for a baby shower, school colors for a graduation party, etc. Kids of all ages snap them up.

PREP: 30 min. + chilling

- 4 packages (3 ounces each) assorted flavored gelatin
- 6 envelopes unflavored gelatin, divided
- 5-3/4 cups boiling water, divided
- 1 can (14 ounces) sweetened condensed milk
- 1/4 cup cold water

1 In a small bowl, combine one package flavored gelatin and one envelope unflavored gelatin. Stir in 1 cup boiling water until dissolved. Pour into a 13-in. x 9-in. dish coated with cooking spray; refrigerate until set but not firm, about 20 minutes.

2 In small bowl, combine the condensed milk and 1 cup boiling water. In another bowl, sprinkle two envelopes unflavored gelatin over cold water; let stand for 1 minute. Stir in 3/4 cup boiling water. Add to milk mixture. Spoon 1 cup of the creamy gelatin mixture over the first flavored gelatin layer. Refrigerate until set but not firm, about 25 minutes.

3 Repeat from beginning of recipe twice alternating flavored gelatin with creamy gelatin layers. Chill each layer until set but not firm before spooning the next layer on top. Make final flavored gelatin; spoon over top. Refrigerate for at least 1 hour after completing last layer before cutting into 1-in. squares.

YIELD: about 9 dozen.

LOUISIANA BARBECUE BRISKET

ALLAN STACKHOUSE JR., JENNINGS, LOUISIANA
Turn to this dish when you need a special entree to feed a crowd. Don't be deterred by the length of this recipe...it has many make-ahead steps. Plus, it grills unattended for hours, so there's no last-minute fuss.

PREP: 20 min. + marinating **GRILL:** 4 hours

    3 tablespoons paprika

    2 teaspoons each salt, garlic powder and pepper

    1 teaspoon each cayenne pepper, dried oregano and
      ground mustard

1/2 teaspoon chili powder

    1 fresh beef brisket (4 to 6 pounds)

BARBECUE SAUCE:

    2 cups ketchup

    1 cup packed brown sugar

    1 cup unsweetened pineapple juice

2/3 cup light corn syrup

1/2 cup finely chopped onion

1/2 cup apple juice

1/4 cup chili powder

    2 to 4 tablespoons hot pepper sauce

    4 teaspoons Worcestershire sauce

    1 to 4 teaspoons Liquid Smoke, optional

1 In a small bowl, combine the seasonings. Rub 2 teaspoons over brisket. (Place remaining seasoning mixture in an airtight container; save for up to 3 months for another use.)

2 In a large bowl, combine the sauce ingredients; stir until brown sugar is dissolved. Pour 2 cups into a large resealable plastic bag; add the brisket. Seal bag and turn to coat; refrigerate for 8 hours or overnight, turning several times. Cover and refrigerate remaining sauce.

3 Prepare grill for indirect heat, using a drip pan. Drain and discard marinade from brisket; pat dry with paper towels. Place brisket over pan; grill, covered, over indirect low heat for 30-45 minutes on each side or until browned.

4 Transfer brisket to a heavy-duty disposable roasting pan. Pour 1-1/4 cups of reserved sauce over brisket. Cover with a double layer of heavy-duty foil and seal tightly.

5 Grill, covered, over indirect low heat for 3-4 hours or until meat is fork-tender. Slice brisket across the grain. Serve with remaining sauce.

YIELD: 12-16 servings.

EDITOR'S NOTE: This is a fresh beef brisket, not corned beef. This recipe is best when the brisket is untrimmed.

GRILLED POTATO SALAD WITH BALSAMIC DRESSING

ELAINE SWEET, DALLAS, TEXAS
A Texas-size family reunion requires a substantial salad like this one on the buffet table. Made with red potatoes, real bacon, tangy dressing and more, it's guaranteed to be gobbled up quickly.

PREP: 35 min. **GRILL:** 10 min.

    6 medium red potatoes (about 1-1/2 pounds), quartered

2-1/4 teaspoons canola oil

    3 cups fresh baby spinach

    1 cup fresh or frozen corn, thawed

1/2 medium sweet red pepper, julienned

1/2 poblano pepper, seeded and julienned

1/2 medium red onion, thinly sliced

    3 green onions, chopped

    6 bacon strips, diced

    3 garlic cloves, minced

    2 shallots, minced

1/2 cup balsamic vinegar

    2 tablespoons whole grain mustard

1 teaspoon pepper
2 hard-cooked eggs, coarsely chopped
1/4 cup sunflower kernels

1 Place potatoes in a large saucepan; cover with water. Bring to a boil. Reduce heat; cover and cook for 8-10 minutes or until crisp-tender. Drain; toss potatoes with oil.

2 Place potatoes in a grill wok or basket. Grill, covered, over medium heat for 8-12 minutes or golden brown, stirring frequently. Transfer to a large salad bowl; add the spinach, corn, peppers and onions. Set aside.

3 In a large skillet, cook the bacon over medium heat until partially cooked but not crisp. Add the garlic and shallots; cook for 1-2 minutes or until tender. Stir in the vinegar, mustard and pepper. Bring to a gentle boil; cook and stir for 2-3 minutes or until slightly thickened.

4 Drizzle over the potato mixture and gently toss to coat. Sprinkle with eggs and sunflower kernels. Serve immediately.

YIELD: 12 servings.

EDITOR'S NOTE: When cutting hot peppers, disposable gloves are recommended. Avoid touching your face.

BLUE CHEESE BACON DRESSING

MARION KARLIN, WATERLOO, IOWA
This dressing is absolutely fantastic—I've made it again and again. It has just about everything we like in it.

PREP: 10 min.
    1 cup mayonnaise
1/2 cup sour cream
    5 to 6 tablespoons milk
    1 tablespoon white wine vinegar
1/2 teaspoon sugar
1/4 teaspoon salt
1/4 teaspoon garlic powder
1/4 teaspoon white pepper
    1 cup (4 ounces) crumbled blue cheese

1/4 cup crumbled cooked bacon
1/4 cup minced chives

1 Whisk the mayonnaise, sour cream, milk, vinegar, sugar, salt, garlic powder and pepper until blended. Stir in blue cheese, bacon and chives. Cover and store in refrigerator.

YIELD: 2 cups.

FROZEN MOCHA TORTE

LISA KIVIRIST, BROWNTOWN, WISCONSIN
For an easy, make-ahead dessert that's elegant and luscious, try this recipe. The perfect blend of mocha and chocolate is in each cool, refreshing slice.

PREP: 20 min. + freezing
    1 cup chocolate wafer crumbs
1/4 cup sugar
1/4 cup butter, melted
    1 package (8 ounces) cream cheese, softened
    1 can (14 ounces) sweetened condensed milk
2/3 cup chocolate syrup
    2 tablespoons instant coffee granules
    1 tablespoon hot water
    1 cup heavy whipping cream, whipped
Chocolate-covered coffee beans, optional

1 In a small bowl, combine wafer crumbs, sugar and butter. Press onto the bottom and 1 in. up the sides of a greased 9-in. springform pan; set aside.

2 In a large bowl, beat the cream cheese, milk and chocolate syrup until smooth. Dissolve coffee granules in hot water; add to cream cheese mixture. Fold in whipped cream. Pour over crust. Cover and freeze for 8 hours or overnight.

3 Remove from freezer 10-15 minutes before serving. Carefully run a knife around edge of pan to loosen. Remove sides of pan. Garnish with coffee beans if desired.

YIELD: 10-12 servings.

PATRIOTIC PIZZAS

TASTE OF HOME TEST KITCHEN

Here's a pizza you decorate like a high-flyin' flag! You can decorate it in two ways: With stripes for the U.S. or with a maple leaf for Canada. Both designs consist of tangy fruit and smooth cream cheese over a tender crust. Since each version is simple to make, you can quickly make either one for a summer picnic or patriotic party.

PREP: 20 min. **BAKE:** 10 min. + cooling

CRUST:
- 1 cup all-purpose flour
- 1/2 cup confectioners' sugar
- 1/2 cup cold butter

AMERICAN FLAG:
- 2 packages (8 ounces each) cream cheese, softened
- 1 cup sugar
- 1 teaspoon vanilla extract
- 1/2 teaspoon lemon juice
- 2 cups halved fresh strawberries
- 1/2 cup fresh or frozen blueberries

Star pastry tip #21

CANADIAN FLAG:
- 1 package (8 ounces) cream cheese, softened
- 1/2 cup sugar
- 1/2 teaspoon vanilla extract
- 1/4 teaspoon lemon juice
- 3 cups halved fresh strawberries

Round pastry tip #5

1 Pizza Crust: In a bowl, combine flour and confectioners' sugar. Cut the butter into the dry ingredients until crumbly. Press the mixture onto a greased 12-in. pizza pan. Bake at 325° for 10-15 minutes or until the crust is lightly browned. Let cool.

2 American flag: In a bowl, beat the cream cheese and sugar. Add the vanilla and lemon juice, mixing until smooth. Spread 1 cup cream cheese mixture over the crust. Set the remaining cream cheese mixture aside.

3 Referring to the photo for position, arrange five rows of fresh strawberries on top of the pizza to create the red stripes of flag. Place the blueberries in the upper left corner.

4 Cut a hole in the corner of the plastic or pastry bag and insert the star tip. Fill the bag with the reserved cream cheese mixture. For the white stripes, pipe a zigzag pattern between the rows of strawberries.

5 Canadian flag: In a bowl, beat the cream cheese and sugar. Add the vanilla and lemon juice, mixing until smooth. Spread 3/4 cup cream cheese mixture over the crust. Set remaining mixture aside. Arrange strawberries in the shape of a maple leaf on top of the pizza. Cut a hole in the corner of the plastic of pastry bag and insert the round tip. Fill the bag with the reserved cream cheese mixture. Pipe veins on the maple leaf.

YIELD: 1 pizza.

CRAFTER THOUGHT: Interested in making a different flag that celebrates your heritage? You'll need fruit in other colors. Try kiwi for green, pineapple for gold, etc. Or, use M&M candies instead. The finished size of each pizza measures about 12 inches across.

ALL-AMERICAN HAMBURGERS

DIANE HIXON, NICEVILLE, FLORIDA

We do a lot of camping and outdoor cooking. Hamburgers are on our menu more than any other food.

PREP/TOTAL TIME: 20 min.
- 2 tablespoons finely chopped onion
- 2 tablespoons chili sauce

2 teaspoons Worcestershire sauce
2 teaspoons prepared mustard
1 pound ground beef
4 slices American or cheddar cheese, halved diagonally
2 slices Swiss cheese, halved diagonally
4 hamburger buns, split and toasted

Lettuce leaves, sliced tomato and onion, cooked bacon, ketchup and mustard, optional

1 In a large bowl, combine the first four ingredients. Crumble beef over mixture and mix well. Shape into four patties.

2 Grill, covered, over medium heat for 6 minutes on each side or until a meat thermometer reads 160° and juices run clear.

3 During the last minute of cooking, top each patty with two triangles of American cheese and one triangle of Swiss cheese. Serve on buns with the lettuce, tomato, onion, bacon, ketchup and mustard if desired.

YIELD: 4 servings.

PRETZEL SPARKLERS

RENEE SCHWEBACH, DUMONT, MINNESOTA
These irresistible treats are simple enough for kids to make, and they sell well at bazaars. You can use different candy sprinkles to reflect other holiday themes.

PREP/TOTAL TIME: 30 min.
8 squares (1 ounce each) white baking chocolate
1 package (10 ounces) pretzel rods

Colored candy stars or sprinkles

1 In a microwave-safe bowl; melt the chocolate at 70% power for 1 minute; stir. Microwave at additional 10- to 20-second intervals, stirring until smooth.

2 Dip each pretzel rod about halfway into chocolate; allow the excess to drip off. Sprinkle with stars. Dry on waxed paper.

YIELD: about 2 dozen.

FOURTH OF JULY BEAN CASSEROLE

DONNA FANCHER, LAWRENCE, INDIANA
The outstanding barbecue taste of these beans makes them a favorite for cookouts all summer and into the fall. It's a popular dish with everyone—even kids. Having meat in with the beans is so much better than plain pork and beans.

PREP: 20 min. **BAKE:** 1 hour
1/2 pound sliced bacon, diced
1/2 pound ground beef
1 cup chopped onion
1 can (28 ounces) pork and beans
1 can (16 ounces) kidney beans, rinsed and drained
1 can (15-1/4 ounces) lima beans
1/2 cup barbecue sauce

1/2 cup ketchup
1/2 cup sugar
1/2 cup packed brown sugar
2 tablespoons prepared mustard
2 tablespoons molasses
1 teaspoon salt
1/2 teaspoon chili powder

1 In a large skillet, cook bacon, beef and onion until meat is no longer pink and onion is tender; drain.

2 Transfer to a greased 2-1/2-qt. baking dish; add all of the beans and mix well. In a small bowl, combine the remaining ingredients; stir into beef and bean mixture. Cover and bake at 350° for 45 minutes. Uncover; bake 15 minutes longer.

YIELD: 12 servings.

RED, WHITE AND BLEU SLAW

BONNIE HAWKINS, ELKHORN, WISCONSIN
One of my favorite all-time recipes is this refreshing salad perfect for Fourth of July celebrations—or any time at all. The blend of flavors is wonderful. I use this recipe as often as I can...it's just simply the best!

PREP/TOTAL TIME: 10 min.
6 cups angel hair coleslaw
12 cherry tomatoes, halved
3/4 cup coleslaw salad dressing
3/4 cup crumbled blue cheese, divided
1/2 cup real bacon bits

1 In a large bowl, combine the coleslaw, tomatoes, salad dressing and 1/2 cup blue cheese. Cover and refrigerate until serving. Just before serving, sprinkle with the bacon bits and remaining cheese.

YIELD: 6 servings.

The days of Autumn are heralded
by backpacks, pencils, apple cider,
brightly colored leaves tumbling to
the ground and cool, crisp winds.
Snow may just be around the corner,
and chilly-weather fare is back in
style with spiced apple desserts,
homemade bread, robust soups
and hot, heartwarming meals.
And, if you enjoy using fresh
pumpkin in soups, stews, breads
or homebaked pies, this is the only
time of year that farm-grown
cooking pumpkins are for sale at
local markets and grocery stores.

Autumn Harvest

167 172 169 171

APPETIZERS & BEVERAGES

170

SAUSAGE-STUFFED MUSHROOMS

KATHY DEEZIK, HARTSTOWN, PENNSYLVANIA
A few years back, I was looking for a snack that would suit my family's tastes. I combined three different recipes and came up with this one. They love the rich Parmesan flavor.

PREP/TOTAL TIME: 30 min.

    20 to 24 large fresh mushrooms
    2 tablespoons finely chopped onion
    2 to 3 garlic cloves, minced
    1 tablespoon butter
    1/4 pound bulk pork sausage, cooked, crumbled and drained
    3 tablespoons seasoned bread crumbs
    3 tablespoons grated Parmesan cheese
    1 tablespoon dried parsley flakes
    1 egg white

1 Remove mushroom stems from caps. Set caps aside (discard stems or save for another use). In a small skillet, saute onion and garlic in butter until tender.

2 In a large bowl, combine sausage, bread crumbs, Parmesan, parsley and egg white. Stir in the onion mixture. Fill mushroom caps; place in a lightly greased 15-in. x 10-in. x 1-in. baking pan.

3 Bake at 350° for 10-15 minutes or until the mushrooms are tender and tops are browned.

YIELD: about 2 dozen.

DELICIOUS STUFFED MUSHROOMS
To ensure the mushrooms are completely cooked after baking, first, place the caps on a paper towel-lined plate and microwave on high in 30-second intervals, up to 2 minutes. This removes some of the moisture and ensures they become tender when baked.

CRANBERRY SLUSH

SHAREN CHRISTENSEN, SALEM, UTAH
One taste of this sweet icy treat leads to another...and another. My mother-in-law makes it for family gatherings, and it never lasts long. Often, my husband and twin daughters request it as a snack or dessert. It's a refreshing party beverage as well.

PREP: 10 min. COOK: 15 min. + freezing

    1 pound fresh or frozen cranberries
    2-1/2 cups cold water, divided
    3-1/2 cups fresh or frozen unsweetened raspberries
    1 envelope unflavored gelatin
    2 cups sugar
    2 cups ginger ale
    1-3/4 cups raspberry ginger ale or additional ginger ale

1 In a large saucepan, cook the cranberries and 1-1/2 cups water over medium heat until the berries pop, about 15 minutes. Stir in raspberries.

2 Transfer to a blender; cover and process until smooth. Strain and discard seeds, reserving juice. Pour the juice into a 2-qt. freezer-proof container; set aside.

3 In a small saucepan, sprinkle gelatin over remaining water. Let stand for 1 minute. Stir in sugar. Cook and stir over medium heat until gelatin and sugar are dissolved. Add to berry juice. Stir in ginger ale; cover and freeze.

4 **To use frozen slush:** Remove from the freezer 1 hour before serving. For each serving, combine 1 cup cranberry slush with 1/4 cup raspberry ginger ale in a glass; stir well.

YIELD: 7 servings.

ZUCCHINI-HERB PATE

MELISSA SULLIVAN, IUKA, KANSAS
A friend gave me the recipe for this pate after she'd served it at a formal wedding reception. But I make it most often to spread on crackers at potlucks and other casual get-togethers.

PREP: 1-1/4 hours + chilling
- 4 medium zucchini (about 1 pound)
- 2 teaspoons tarragon vinegar
- 2 teaspoons sugar
- 2 teaspoons salt, divided
- 1/2 cup packed fresh parsley sprigs
- 1/2 cup minced chives
- 1 package (8 ounces) cream cheese, softened
- 1/2 teaspoon pepper

Crackers

1 Line a bowl with a double thickness of cheese cloth. Coarsely shred zucchini into prepared bowl. Sprinkle with the vinegar, sugar and 1 teaspoon salt. Toss gently; cover with a towel and set aside for 1 hour.

2 Meanwhile, in a food processor with the chopping blade, mince parsley and chives. Gather ends of cheesecloth, squeezing out as much liquid from the shredded zucchini as possible. Add drained zucchini to food processor and process until pureed. Add the cream cheese, pepper and remaining salt; process until smooth.

3 Press pate into a small bowl. Cover and refrigerate overnight. Serve with crackers.

YIELD: 1-1/2 cups.

MAPLE CREAM COFFEE

TASTE OF HOME TEST KITCHEN
On a crisp autumn day, this creamy drink is perfect for after dinner. Even non-coffee drinkers will enjoy the hint of maple and lighter coffee flavor.

PREP/TOTAL TIME: 10 min.
- 3/4 cup half-and-half cream
- 1/4 cup maple syrup
- 1-1/4 cups brewed coffee
- 1/4 cup whipped cream

1 In a small saucepan, cook and stir the cream and syrup over medium heat until heated through. (Do not boil.) Divide evenly between two cups. Stir in the brewed coffee. Top with whipped cream.

YIELD: 2 servings.

AUSSIE SAUSAGE ROLLS

MELISSA LANDON, PORT CHARLOTTE, FLORIDA
I was born and raised in Australia, but moved to the United States when I married my husband. When I long for a taste of home, I bake up a batch of these sausage rolls and share them with my neighbors and co-workers.

PREP: 15 min. **BAKE:** 20 min.
- 1-1/4 pounds bulk pork sausage
- 1 medium onion, finely chopped
- 2 teaspoons minced chives
- 2 teaspoons minced fresh basil or 1/2 teaspoon dried basil
- 2 garlic cloves, minced
- 1 teaspoon paprika, divided
- 1/2 teaspoon salt
- 1/4 teaspoon pepper
- 1 package (17.3 ounces) frozen puff pastry, thawed

1 In a large bowl, combine the sausage, onion, chives, basil, garlic, 3/4 teaspoon paprika, salt and pepper. Unfold pastry onto a lightly floured surface. Roll each pastry sheet into an 11-in. x 10-1/2-in. rectangle. Cut widthwise into 3-1/2-in. strips.

2 Spread 1/2 cup of sausage mixture down the center of each strip. Fold pastry over and press edges together to seal. Cut each roll into six pieces.

3 Place seam side down on a rack in a shallow baking pan. Sprinkle with remaining paprika. Bake at 350° for 20-25 minutes or until golden brown.

YIELD: 3 dozen.

SLOW COOKER CIDER

ALPHA WILSON, ROSWELL, NEW MEXICO
There's no last-minute rush when you slowly simmer this punch.

PREP: 5 min. **COOK:** 2 hours

    2 cinnamon sticks (3 inches)
    1 teaspoon whole cloves
    1 teaspoon whole allspice
    2 quarts apple cider
  1/2 cup packed brown sugar
    1 orange, sliced

1 Place cinnamon, cloves and allspice in a double thickness of cheesecloth; bring up corners of cloth and tie with a string to form a bag.

2 Place cider and brown sugar in a 3-qt. slow cooker; stir until sugar dissolves. Add spice bag. Place the orange slices on top. Cover and cook on low for 2-3 hours or until heated through. Discard spice bag.

YIELD: 2 quarts.

WARM BROCCOLI CHEESE DIP

BARBARA MAIOL, CONYERS, GEORGIA
When my family gathers for a party, this flavorful, creamy dip is served. Everyone loves its zip from the jalapeno pepper and the crunch of the broccoli.

PREP: 15 min. **COOK:** 2-1/2 hours

    2 jars (8 ounces each) process cheese sauce
    1 can (10-3/4 ounces) condensed cream of chicken soup, undiluted
    3 cups frozen chopped broccoli, thawed and drained
  1/2 pound fresh mushrooms, chopped
    2 tablespoons chopped seeded jalapeno pepper
Assorted fresh vegetables

1 In a 1-1/2-qt. slow cooker, combine the cheese sauce and soup. Cover and cook on low for 30 minutes or until cheese is melted, stirring occasionally. Stir in the broccoli, mushrooms and jalapeno. Cover and cook on low for 2 hours or until heated through. Serve with vegetables.

YIELD: 5-1/2 cups.

EDITOR'S NOTE: When cutting hot peppers, disposable gloves are recommended. Avoid touching your face.

APPLE-GOAT CHEESE BRUSCHETTA

LAURA PERRY, CHESTER SPRINGS, PENNSYLVANIA
It takes just six ingredients and 20 minutes to put together this beautiful bruschetta. Crunchy apple and warm goat cheese top these crispy autumn treats.

PREP/TOTAL TIME: 20 min.

   16 slices French bread (1/2 inch thick)
    1 medium Fuji apple, chopped
  1/4 cup crumbled goat cheese
  3/4 teaspoon minced fresh thyme
  1/2 teaspoon minced fresh oregano
  1/4 teaspoon coarsely ground pepper

1 Place bread slices on an ungreased baking sheet. Broil 3-4 in. from the heat for 1-2 minutes or until golden brown. Combine the apple, goat cheese, thyme, oregano and pepper; sprinkle over bread. Broil 1 minute longer or until cheese is softened.

YIELD: 16 appetizers.

POTATO 'N' ROASTED PEPPER QUESADILLAS

JILL HEATWOLE, PITTSVILLE, MARYLAND
This is a nice change of pace from other meatless meals. Using reduced-fat cheese trims calories without cutting flavor in the mouthwatering quesadillas.

PREP: 40 min. **BAKE:** 10 min.

    1 medium sweet red pepper
    1 jalapeno pepper
    3 medium potatoes, peeled, cooked and cut into 1/8-inch slices
  1/2 cup chopped onion
    2 teaspoons canola oil
    1 tablespoon lime juice
    1 tablespoon minced fresh cilantro
  1/2 teaspoon salt
  1/4 teaspoon pepper
  1/2 cup shredded reduced-fat cheddar cheese
    6 flour tortillas (6 inches)

1 Cut red pepper and jalapeno in half; remove and discard seeds. Place peppers cut side down on a foil-lined baking sheet. Broil 4 in. from the heat for 15-20 minutes or until skins are blistered and blackened. Immediately place peppers in a bowl; cover and let stand for 15-20 minutes. Peel off and discard charred skin. Chop peppers; set aside.

2 In a nonstick skillet coated with cooking spray, cook potatoes and onion in oil for 8 minutes or until potatoes are lightly browned and onion is tender. Remove from the heat. Add the lime juice, cilantro, salt and pepper. Stir in cheese and roasted peppers.

3 Place three tortillas on a baking sheet coated with cooking spray. Spoon potato mixture onto each; top with remaining tortillas and press down firmly.

4 Bake at 450° for 5 minutes. Spritz top of tortillas with cooking spray. Carefully turn over; bake 5 minutes longer or until the cheese is melted and tortillas are lightly browned. Cut each into four wedges.

YIELD: 4 servings.

EDITOR'S NOTE: When cutting hot peppers, disposable gloves are recommended. Avoid touching your face.

FESTIVE APPETIZER SPREAD

EDITH HOWE, WOBURN, MASSACHUSETTS
Our state is known for its cranberries, and there are many bogs in our area. I won first place with this recipe in a contest sponsored by our local newspaper.

PREP: 20 min. + cooling

   1 cup water
   1 cup sugar
   1 package (12 ounces) fresh or frozen cranberries
 1/2 cup apricot preserves
   2 tablespoons lemon juice
 1/3 cup slivered almonds, toasted
   1 package (8 ounces) cream cheese
Assorted crackers

1 In a large saucepan over medium heat, bring the water and sugar to a boil without stirring; boil for 5 minutes. Add the cranberries, cook until berries pop and sauce is thickened, about 10 minutes. Remove from the heat.

2 Cut apricots in the preserves into small pieces; add to the cranberry mixture. Stir in lemon juice. Cool. Add almonds.

3 Spoon over cream cheese; serve with crackers. Store leftovers in the refrigerator.

YIELD: about 3 cups.

EDITOR'S NOTE: This sauce may also be served as an accompaniment to poultry or pork.

AUTUMN TEA

SANDRA MCKENZIE, BRAHAM, MINNESOTA
I've served beverages made with various flavors of tea at several gatherings, and people are always surprised by the results. This blend features flavors we associate with fall—apple, cranberry and pumpkin pie spice. Serve it either warm or cold.

PREP/TOTAL TIME: 15 min.

   5 individual tea bags
   5 cups boiling water
   5 cups unsweetened apple juice
   2 cups cranberry juice
 1/2 cup sugar
 1/3 cup lemon juice
 1/4 teaspoon pumpkin pie spice

1 Place tea bags in a large heat-proof bowl; add boiling water. Cover and steep for 8 minutes. Discard tea bags. Add the remaining ingredients to tea; stir until the sugar is dissolved. Serve warm or over ice.

YIELD: 3 quarts.

PUMPKIN PIE DIP

LAURIE LACLAIR, NORTH RICHLAND HILLS, TEXAS
I came up with this rich creamy dip when I had a small amount of canned pumpkin left in the fridge after my holiday baking. It is also great served with sliced pears and apples, or as a spread on zucchini bread or any other nut bread.

PREP/TOTAL TIME: 10 min.
  1 package (8 ounces) cream cheese, softened
  2 cups confectioners' sugar
  1 cup canned pumpkin
1/2 cup sour cream
  1 teaspoon ground cinnamon
  1 teaspoon pumpkin pie spice
1/2 teaspoon ground ginger
Gingersnap cookies

1 In a large bowl, beat cream cheese and confectioners' sugar until smooth. Beat in the pumpkin, sour cream, cinnamon, pumpkin pie spice and ginger until blended. Serve with the gingersnaps. Refrigerate leftovers.

YIELD: 4 cups.

PEAR PISTACHIO PITA

STEPHANIE MARCHESE, WHITEFISH BAY, WISCONSIN
This recipe makes a fun and deliciously different appetizer or snack! Pears and pistachio nuts are a surprising and satisfying combination.

PREP/TOTAL TIME: 20 min.
  2 tablespoons olive oil
  2 teaspoons crushed garlic
  4 whole pita breads (6 inches each)
  1 cup (4 ounces) crumbled blue cheese
  2 medium pears, peeled and sliced
1/2 cup chopped pistachios

1 In a bowl, combine oil and garlic; brush on top of each pita. Arrange oil side up on an ungreased baking sheet. Sprinkle with cheese, pears and pistachios.

2 Bake at 375° for 8-10 minutes or until pears are tender. Cut into wedges.

YIELD: 24 appetizers.

SQUASH APPETIZER CUPS

LORI BOWES, WATERFORD, MICHIGAN
These cheesy, moist bites always go fast! If I'm in a hurry, I bake the mixture in a greased 9 x 13-in. pan and cut into squares.

PREP: 35 min. BAKE: 20 min.
1-1/2 cups shredded zucchini
1-1/2 cups shredded yellow summer squash
1/2 cup diced onion
1/4 cup shredded Parmesan cheese
1/4 cup shredded Colby cheese
  2 tablespoons minced fresh parsley
1-1/2 teaspoons minced fresh marjoram or
     1/2 teaspoon dried marjoram
  1 garlic clove, minced
  1 cup biscuit/baking mix
1/2 teaspoon seasoned salt
Dash pepper
  4 eggs, lightly beaten
1/2 cup canola oil

1 In a large skillet, saute the zucchini and yellow squash over medium heat until reduced to about 1-1/2 cups, about 10 minutes. Transfer to a small bowl. Add onion, cheeses, parsley, marjoram and garlic.

2 In a large bowl, combine the biscuit mix, seasoned salt and pepper. Stir in the eggs and oil just until combined. Fold in the squash mixture.

3 Fill greased miniature muffin cups three-fourths full. Bake at 350° for 20-25 minutes or until golden brown and a toothpick inserted near the muffin centers comes out clean. Cool for 5 minutes before removing from the pans to wire racks. Serve warm. Refrigerate any leftovers.

YIELD: about 3 dozen.

HARVEST SNACK MIX

MARLENE HARGUTH, MAYNARD, MINNESOTA
Candy corn makes this a natural snack for autumn gatherings. The sweet and salty flavors are irresistible. If you like, use other types of Halloween candy in place of the candy corn.

PREP: 20 min. **BAKE:** 30 min. + cooling

- 2 cups pretzel sticks
- 1 cup mixed nuts
- 1/2 cup sunflower kernels
- 6 tablespoons butter, melted
- 1/2 teaspoon ground cinnamon
- 1/8 teaspoon ground cloves
- 8 cups popped popcorn
- 1 cup candy corn
- 1 cup chocolate bridge mix

1 In a large bowl, combine pretzels, nuts and sunflower kernels. Combine butter, cinnamon and cloves. Drizzle a third of butter mixture over pretzel mixture; toss to coat. Transfer to a greased 15-in. x 10-in. x 1-in. baking pan. Bake at 300° for 15 minutes.

2 Place popcorn in a large bowl; drizzle with remaining butter mixture and toss to coat. Stir into the pretzel mixture. Bake 15 minutes longer or until heated through. Cool; transfer to a large bowl. Add candy corn and bridge mix; toss to combine.

YIELD: 3 quarts.

HIGHBUSH CRANBERRY TEA

TASTE OF HOME TEST KITCHEN
The highbush cranberry shrub doesn't produce true cranberries, but the berries it produces look and taste similar to cranberries. The two fruits and be used interchangeably.

PREP/TOTAL TIME: 25 min.

- 4 cups highbush cranberries
- 10 cups water, divided
- 2 to 3 cups sugar
- 1 cup red-hot candies
- 15 whole cloves
- 1 cup thawed orange juice concentrate
- 1/2 cup lemon juice

1 In a large saucepan, bring cranberries and 4 cups water to a boil. Reduce heat; simmer for 4 minutes or until berries pop. Press through a strainer; discard skins and seeds. Juice should measure about 4-1/2 cups; set aside.

2 In another saucepan, combine the sugar, candies, cloves and remaining water; bring to a boil. Reduce heat; simmer for 5 minutes or until candies dissolve. Strain and discard cloves. Stir in the orange juice concentrate, lemon juice and reserved cranberry juice. Serve hot or chilled.

YIELD: 3-1/4 quarts.

EDITOR'S NOTE: Regular cranberries may be substituted.

BEER CHEESE

PAT WARTMAN, BETHLEHEM, PENNSYLVANIA
I like to serve this zesty cheese spread with crackers and vegetable dippers. It's a great snack to take along to picnics.

PREP: 30 min. + chilling

- 1/3 cup beer or nonalcoholic beer
- 4 ounces cream cheese, cubed
- 3 ounces crumbled blue cheese
- 1/4 cup Dijon mustard
- 2 tablespoons grated onion
- 1/2 to 1 teaspoon hot pepper sauce
- 1 garlic clove, minced
- 3 cups (12 ounces) shredded cheddar cheese

Assorted crackers

1 In a small saucepan, bring beer to a boil. Remove from the heat and cool to room temperature.

2 In a food processor, combine the beer, cream cheese, blue cheese, mustard, onion, pepper sauce and garlic. Add the cheddar cheese; cover and process until well blended. Transfer to a bowl. Cover and refrigerate overnight.

3 Let cheese stand at room temperature for 30 minutes before serving. Serve with crackers.

YIELD: 3 cups.

PEANUT BUTTER POPCORN BALLS

BETTY CLAYCOMB, ALVERTON, PENNSYLVANIA
Trick-or-treaters are always happy to receive these tasty popcorn balls. I love making them as well as eating them!

PREP: 20 min. + standing

- 5 cups popped popcorn
- 1 cup dry roasted peanuts
- 1/2 cup sugar
- 1/2 cup light corn syrup
- 1/2 cup chunky peanut butter
- 1/2 teaspoon vanilla extract

1 Place popcorn and peanuts in a large bowl; set aside. In a large heavy saucepan over medium heat, bring sugar and corn syrup to a rolling boil, stirring occasionally. Remove from the heat; stir in peanut butter and vanilla. Quickly pour over the popcorn mixture and mix well.

2 When cool enough to handle, quickly shape the popcorn mixture into ten 2-1/2-in. balls. Let stand at room temperature until firm; wrap in plastic wrap.

YIELD: 10 popcorn balls.

HARVESTTIME CHEESE BALL

SUZANNE CLEVELAND, LYONS, GEORGIA
Everyone will get a kick out of this creamy, savory spread. The zippy cheddar ball can be made a day ahead.

PREP: 20 min. + chilling

- 1 package (8 ounces) cream cheese, softened
- 1 carton (8 ounces) spreadable chive and onion cream cheese
- 2 cups (8 ounces) shredded sharp cheddar cheese
- 2 teaspoons paprika
- 1/2 teaspoon cayenne pepper
- 1 celery rib or broccoli stalk

Sliced apples and assorted crackers

1 In a small bowl, beat the cream cheeses until smooth. Stir in the cheddar cheese, paprika and cayenne. Shape the cheese mixture into a ball; wrap in plastic wrap. Refrigerate for 4 hours or until firm.

2 With the opposite side of a knife blade, add vertical lines to the cheese ball to resemble a pumpkin; insert half of a celery rib with leaves or broccoli stalk for the stem. Serve with apples and assorted crackers.

YIELD: 2-1/2 cups.

MINI SPINACH FRITTATAS

NANCY STATKEVICUS, TUCSON, ARIZONA
These mini frittatas are a cinch to make and just delicious. Their pared-down size makes for perfect cocktail party appetizers. For added convenience, the recipe can be doubled or tripled easily for a crowd. To make ahead, let cool, place in resealable plastic bags and store in the freezer.

PREP/TOTAL TIME: 30 min.

- 1 cup ricotta cheese
- 3/4 cup grated Parmesan cheese
- 2/3 cup chopped fresh mushrooms
- 1 package (10 ounces) frozen chopped spinach, thawed and squeezed dry
- 1 egg
- 1/2 teaspoon dried oregano
- 1/4 teaspoon salt
- 1/4 teaspoon pepper
- 24 slices pepperoni

1 In a small bowl, combine the cheeses, mushrooms, spinach, egg and seasonings. Place a slice of pepperoni in each of 24 greased miniature muffin cups. Fill the muffin cups three-fourths full with the cheese mixture.

2 Bake at 375° for 20-25 minutes or until a toothpick comes out clean. Carefully run a knife around edges of muffin cups to loosen. Serve warm.

YIELD: 2 dozen.

CINNAMON APPLE SHAKES

NATALIE CARTER, AUSTIN, TEXAS
Autumn flavor is abundant in this rich beverage. Simply blend applesauce, caramel topping, ice cream and a couple other ingredients for a sweet and velvety fall treat.

PREP/TOTAL TIME: 10 min.

    3 cups vanilla ice cream
  3/4 cup milk
  1/2 cup cinnamon applesauce
  1/4 cup caramel ice cream topping
  1/2 teaspoon rum extract

1 In a blender, combine all the ingredients; cover and process until smooth. Pour into chilled glasses; serve immediately.

YIELD: 4 servings.

FIERY PUMPKIN SEEDS

TASTE OF HOME TEST KITCHEN
These spicy seeds from our Test Kitchen will warm you when cooler temperatures come to call. Take note: little ones may find them too spicy for their liking.

PREP: 5 min. **BAKE:** 45 min. + cooling

    1 cup fresh pumpkin seeds
    2 teaspoons Louisiana-style hot sauce
    1 teaspoon chili powder
  1/2 teaspoon salt
  1/2 teaspoon ground cumin
  1/4 teaspoon cayenne pepper
  1/4 teaspoon pepper

1 In a small bowl, toss pumpkin seeds with hot sauce. Combine the chili powder, salt, cumin, cayenne and pepper; sprinkle over seeds and toss to coat. Spread into a greased foil-lined 15-in. x 10-in. x 1-in. baking pan.

2 Bake, uncovered, at 250° for 45-50 minutes or until seeds are lightly browned and dry, stirring occasionally. Cool completely. Store in an airtight container.

YIELD: 1 cup.

CHAI

TERESE BLOCK, WAUKESHA, WISCONSIN
Chai (rhymes with "pie") is the word for tea in some parts of the world...but in India, it's a spiced milk tea that's becoming more popular in North America. This recipe is just as tasty as any coffee-house chai.

PREP/TOTAL TIME: 25 min.

      2 cups water
      2 individual tea bags
      1 cinnamon stick
      6 cardamom seeds, crushed
      1 whole clove
    1/4 teaspoon ground ginger
  2-1/2 cups milk
    1/3 cup sugar
Sweetened whipped cream, ground cinnamon and
    cinnamon sticks, optional

1 In a small saucepan, combine the first six ingredients. Bring to a boil. Reduce heat; cover and simmer for 5 minutes.

2 Stir in milk. Return to a boil; boil for 1 minute, then strain. Stir in sugar until dissolved. Pour into mugs. Top each with whipped cream, cinnamon and a cinnamon stick if desired.

YIELD: 4 servings.

183   179   185   179

SOUPS, STEWS & SANDWICHES

181

ITALIAN BEEF HOAGIES

LORI PIATT, DANVILLE, ILLINOIS
You'll need just five ingredients to feed a crowd these tender tangy sandwiches. On weekends, I start the roast the night before, so I can shred it in the morning.

PREP: 25 min. **COOK:** 8 hours

  1 beef sirloin tip roast (4 pounds), halved
  2 envelopes Italian salad dressing mix
  2 cups water
  1 jar (16 ounces) mild pickled pepper rings, undrained
 18 hoagie buns, split

1 Place roast in a 5-qt. slow cooker. Combine salad dressing mix and water; pour over roast. Cover and cook on low for 8 hours or until meat is tender. Remove meat; shred with a fork and return to slow cooker. Add pepper rings; heat through. Spoon 1/2 cup meat mixture onto each bun.

YIELD: 18 servings.

THANKSGIVING SANDWICHES

ROBYN LIMBERG-CHILD, ST. CLAIR, MICHIGAN
This sandwich tastes like Thanksgiving, with turkey, stuffing and cranberry sauce rolled into one. I'm always asked for this recipe, and people are surprised at how simple it is!

PREP/TOTAL TIME: 10 min.

  2 cups cubed cooked turkey
3/4 cup dried cranberries
  1 celery rib, chopped
1/2 cup chopped pecans, toasted
3/4 cup honey-mustard salad dressing
  4 whole wheat pita breads (6 inches), halved
Lettuce leaves, optional

1 In a bowl, combine the turkey, cranberries, celery and pecans. Add dressing and toss to coat. If desired, line pita halves with lettuce; fill with turkey mixture.

YIELD: 4-8 servings.

APPLE CIDER BEEF STEW

MARGARET WILSON, SUN CITY, CALIFORNIA
I created this slow-cooker recipe using convenience products to save time chopping vegetables and browning beef. Apple cider and cinnamon are the unique additions that give a down-home flavor to this easy and economical stew.

PREP: 20 min. **COOK:** 6-1/4 hours

  4 cups frozen vegetables for stew (about 24 ounces), thawed
  1 can (8 ounces) sliced water chestnuts, drained
  1 jar (4-1/2 ounces) sliced mushrooms, drained
  1 tablespoon dried minced onion
  2 envelopes brown gravy mix
  2 tablespoons onion soup mix
  2 teaspoons steak seasoning
1/8 teaspoon ground cinnamon
  2 pounds beef stew meat, cut into 1-inch cubes
  1 can (14-1/2 ounces) beef broth
1-1/4 cups apple cider or unsweetened apple juice
  1 can (8 ounces) tomato sauce
  1 bay leaf
  3 tablespoons cornstarch
1/3 cup cold water

1 Place vegetables, water chestnuts, mushrooms and onion in a 5-qt. slow cooker. In a large resealable plastic bag, combine gravy mix, soup mix, steak seasoning and cinnamon; add beef, a few pieces at a time, and shake to coat. Add to slow cooker.

2 Combine the broth, cider and tomato sauce; pour over beef. Add bay leaf. Cover and cook on low for 6-7 hours or until meat is tender.

3 Combine cornstarch and water until smooth; stir into stew. Cover and cook on high for 15 minutes or until thickened. Discard bay leaf.

YIELD: 12 servings.

EDITOR'S NOTE: This recipe was tested with McCormick's Montreal Steak Seasoning. Look for it in the spice aisle.

HEARTY PORK STEW

REBECCA OVERY, EVANSTON, WYOMING
This spicy slow-cooked stew combines tender chunks of pork with colorful tomatoes and green peppers. I garnish bowls of it with chopped hard-cooked eggs and green onions.

PREP: 10 min. COOK: 8-1/2 hours

1-1/2 to 2 pounds boneless pork, cut into 1-inch cubes
   4 cups water
   1 can (14-1/2 ounces) stewed tomatoes
   1 medium onion, chopped
   1 medium green pepper, chopped
1/3 cup soy sauce
   1 to 2 tablespoons chili powder
   1 tablespoon dried celery flakes
1/2 teaspoon garlic powder
1/2 teaspoon pepper
1/3 cup cornstarch
1/3 cup cold water
Hot cooked noodles

1 In a 3-qt. slow cooker, combine the first 10 ingredients. Cover and cook on low for 8 hours.

2 Combine cornstarch and water until smooth; gradually stir into slow cooker. Cover and cook on high for 30 minutes or until slightly thickened. Serve in bowls over noodles.

YIELD: 8 servings.

SOY SAUCE SUBSTITUTE
If soy sauce isn't for you, here's a substitute. Dissolve 3 tablespoons beef bouillon granules in 1-1/2 cups boiling water. Stir in 1/4 cup plus 1 teaspoon cider vinegar, 2 tablespoons sesame oil, 1 tablespoon dark molasses and a dash of pepper. Pour into a jar with a tight-fitting lid and refrigerate. Shake well before using.

UPPER PENINSULA PASTIES

CAROLE LYNN DERIFIELD, VALDEZ, ALASKA
I grew up in Michigan's Upper Peninsula, where many people are of English ancestry. Pasties, which are traditional meat pies and often eaten by hand, are popular in this region.

PREP: 35 min. + chilling BAKE: 1 hour
   2 cups shortening
   2 cups boiling water
5-1/2 to 6 cups all-purpose flour
   2 teaspoons salt

FILLING:
  12 large red potatoes (about 6 pounds), peeled
   4 medium rutabagas (about 3 pounds), peeled
   2 medium onions, chopped
   2 pounds ground beef
   1 pound ground pork
   1 tablespoon salt
   2 teaspoons pepper
   2 teaspoons garlic powder
1/4 cup butter
Half-and-half cream, optional

1 In a large bowl, stir shortening and water until shortening is melted. Gradually stir in flour and salt until a very soft dough is formed; cover and refrigerate for 1-1/2 hours.

2 Quarter and thinly slice potatoes and rutabagas; place in a large bowl with onions, beef, pork and seasonings.

3 Divide dough into 12 equal portions. On a floured surface, roll out one portion at a time into a 10-in. circle. Mound about 2 cups filling on half of each circle; dot with 1 teaspoon butter. Moisten edges with water; fold dough over filling and press edges with a fork to seal.

4 Place on ungreased baking sheets. Cut several slits in top of pasties. Brush with cream if desired. Bake at 350° for 1 hour or until golden brown. Cool on wire racks. Serve hot or cold. Store in the refrigerator.

YIELD: 12 servings.

PUMPKIN SLOPPY JOES

DONNA MUSSER, PEARL CITY, ILLINOIS

Here's a wonderful harvest version of an old standby—sloppy joes made with pumpkin! I add cloves, nutmeg and chili powder for extra zest and suggest serving with dill pickle slices on the side.

PREP/TOTAL TIME: 30 min.

- 1/2 pound lean ground beef
- 3 tablespoons finely chopped onion
- 1/4 cup ketchup
- 2 tablespoons tomato juice
- 1/4 teaspoon chili powder
- Dash ground cloves and nutmeg
- Dash pepper
- 2/3 cup canned pumpkin
- 2 hamburger buns, split

1 In a large skillet, cook beef and onion over medium heat until meat is no longer pink; drain.

2 Add the ketchup, tomato juice, chili powder, cloves, nutmeg and pepper. Bring to a boil. Stir in the pumpkin. Reduce heat; cover and simmer for 15-20 minutes or until heated through. Serve on buns.

YIELD: 2 servings.

LAMB CURRY

LORNA IRVING, HOLBERG, BRITISH COLUMBIA

This is without a doubt the yummiest stew I've ever tasted. My mom often made it for special occasions when I was growing up. It's been popular with our family for over 40 years. You can make it ahead and reheat before serving.

PREP: 15 min. **COOK:** 1 hour 25 min.

- 2 pounds lean lamb stew meat, cut into 3/4-inch cubes
- 4 teaspoons olive oil
- 1 medium onion, chopped
- 2 garlic cloves, minced
- 1 tablespoon curry powder
- 1 teaspoon salt
- 1/4 teaspoon pepper
- 1/8 teaspoon each ground coriander, cumin and cinnamon

- 1/8 teaspoon cayenne pepper
- 1/4 cup all-purpose flour
- 1-1/4 cups water
- 1 cup unsweetened pineapple juice
- 1 medium tart apple, peeled and chopped
- 1/4 cup tomato sauce
- 1/2 cup sour cream
- Hot cooked noodles or rice, optional

1 In a Dutch oven, brown meat in oil in batches on all sides; remove from pan and keep warm. Cook onion and garlic in drippings until onion is tender. Add the curry, salt, pepper, coriander, cumin, cinnamon and cayenne; cook and stir for 2 minutes. Sprinkle with flour; cook and stir for 2-3 minutes. Stir in the water, pineapple juice, apple and tomato sauce.

2 Return meat to Dutch oven. Bring to boil. Reduce the heat; cover and simmer for 1 hour or until meat is tender. Remove from the heat. Stir in the sour cream. Serve with noodles or rice if desired.

YIELD: 6 servings.

SQUASH 'N' CHICKEN STEW

TASTE OF HOME TEST KITCHEN

Our Test Kitchen created this satisfying stew that's colorful, full-flavored and family-friendly. Chicken thighs are slowly simmered with stewed tomatoes, butternut squash, green peppers and onion for meal-in-one convenience.

PREP: 15 min. **COOK:** 6 hours

- 2 pounds boneless skinless chicken thighs, cut into 1/2-inch pieces
- 1 can (28 ounces) stewed tomatoes, cut up
- 3 cups cubed butternut squash
- 2 medium green peppers, cut into 1/2-inch pieces
- 1 small onion, sliced and separated into rings
- 1 cup water
- 1 teaspoon salt
- 1 teaspoon ground cumin
- 1/2 teaspoon ground coriander
- 1/2 teaspoon pepper
- 2 tablespoons minced fresh parsley
- Hot cooked couscous, optional

1 In a 5-qt. slow cooker, combine the first 10 ingredients. Cover and cook on low for 6-7 hours or until chicken juices run clear. Sprinkle with parsley. Serve with couscous if desired.

YIELD: 5 servings.

ANYTIME TURKEY CHILI

BRAD BAILEY, CARY, NORTH CAROLINA
I created this dish to grab the voters' attention at a chili contest we held in our backyard. With pumpkin, brown sugar and cooked turkey, it's like an entire Thanksgiving dinner in one bowl.

PREP: 15 min. **COOK:** 1-1/4 hours

- 2/3 cup chopped sweet onion
- 1/2 cup chopped green pepper
- 1-1/2 teaspoons dried oregano
- 2 garlic cloves, minced
- 1 teaspoon ground cumin
- 1 teaspoon olive oil
- 1 can (16 ounces) kidney beans, rinsed and drained
- 1 can (15-1/2 ounces) great northern beans, rinsed and drained
- 1 can (15 ounces) solid-pack pumpkin
- 1 can (15 ounces) crushed tomatoes
- 1 can (14-1/2 ounces) reduced-sodium chicken broth
- 1/2 cup water
- 2 tablespoons brown sugar
- 2 tablespoons chili powder
- 1/2 teaspoon pepper
- 3 cups cubed cooked turkey breast

1 In a large saucepan, saute the onion, green pepper, oregano, garlic and cumin in oil until vegetables are tender. Stir in the beans, pumpkin, tomatoes, broth, water, brown sugar, chili powder and pepper; bring to a boil. Reduce heat; cover and simmer for 1 hour. Add turkey; heat through.

YIELD: 8 servings (2 quarts).

FORGOTTEN MINESTRONE

MARSHA RANSOM, SOUTH HAVEN, MICHIGAN
This soup gets its name because the broth simmers for hours, allowing me to work on my free-lance writing. After one taste, you'll agree this full-flavored soup is truly unforgettable!

PREP: 15 min. **COOK:** 7-1/2 hours

- 1 pound beef stew meat, cut into 1/2-inch cubes
- 1 can (28 ounces) diced tomatoes, undrained
- 1 medium onion, chopped
- 2 tablespoons minced dried parsley
- 2-1/2 teaspoons salt, optional
- 1-1/2 teaspoons ground thyme
- 1 beef bouillon cube
- 1/2 teaspoon pepper
- 6 cups water
- 1 medium zucchini, halved and thinly sliced
- 2 cups chopped cabbage
- 1 can (15 ounces) garbanzo beans or chickpeas, rinsed and drained
- 1 cup uncooked elbow macaroni
- 1/4 cup grated Parmesan cheese, optional

1 In a 5-qt. slow cooker, combine the first nine ingredients. Cover and cook on low for 7-9 hours or until meat is tender.

2 Add the zucchini, cabbage, beans and macaroni; cover and cook on high for 30-45 minutes or until vegetables are tender. Sprinkle each serving with cheese if desired.

YIELD: 8 servings.

> **SLOW COOKER TIPS**
> Choose the correct size slow cooker for your recipe. A slow cooker should be from half to two-thirds full. Unless the recipe instructs you to add ingredients, refrain from lifting the lid while the slow cooker is cooking. The loss of steam can mean an additional 15 to 30 minutes of cooking each time you lift the lid. Be sure the lid is sealed properly—not tilted or askew. The steam creates a seal.

SWEET POTATO AND PEAR SOUP

CRISTY SHANK, SUMMERSVILLE, WEST VIRGINIA
I'm a family physician who loves to try new recipes. This tasty cold-weather soup has garnered many warm compliments from family and friends. They rave over it.

PREP: 15 min. **COOK:** 30 min.

- 1-3/4 pounds sweet potatoes (about 4 medium), peeled and cubed
- 1-3/4 cups water
- 1 teaspoon salt, divided
- 1/4 teaspoon ground cinnamon
- 2 large pears, peeled and sliced
- 1 large onion, chopped
- 2 tablespoons butter
- 1/2 cup white grape juice
- 1 cup half-and-half cream
- 1/4 teaspoon white pepper

1 In a large saucepan, combine the sweet potatoes, water, 3/4 teaspoon salt and cinnamon. Bring to a boil. Reduce heat; simmer, uncovered, for 20 minutes.

2 Meanwhile, in another large saucepan, cook and stir the pears and onion in butter over medium heat for 5 minutes. Stir in grape juice; bring to a boil. Reduce heat; simmer, uncovered, for 5 minutes. Stir into the sweet potato mixture. Cool slightly.

3 In a blender, cover and puree soup in batches; return to the pan. Stir in the cream, pepper and remaining salt; heat through (do not boil).

YIELD: 5 servings.

CHEESY SAUSAGE STROMBOLI

VADA MCROBERTS, SILVER LAKE, KANSAS
I've had a hundred requests for this recipe over the years. Perfect for brunch or as an evening snack, this sausage-filled bread is not tricky to make...and I never have to worry about storing leftovers!

PREP: 30 min. + rising **BAKE:** 20 min.

- 5 cups all-purpose flour
- 2 tablespoons sugar
- 2 teaspoons salt
- 2 packages (1/4 ounce each) active dry yeast
- 1-1/2 cups warm water (120° to 130°)
- 1/2 cup warm milk (120° to 130°)
- 2 tablespoons butter, melted
- 2 pounds bulk pork sausage
- 4 cups (16 ounces) shredded part-skim mozzarella cheese
- 3 eggs
- 1 teaspoon minced fresh basil or 1/4 teaspoon dried basil
- 2 tablespoons grated Parmesan cheese

1 In a large bowl, combine flour, sugar, salt and yeast. Add water, milk and butter; beat on low until well combined. Turn onto a well-floured surface; knead until smooth and elastic, about 6-8 minutes. Place in a greased bowl, turning once to grease top. Cover and let rise in a warm place until doubled, about 1 hour.

2 Meanwhile, in a skillet, cook sausage until no longer pink; drain and cool. Stir in mozzarella, 2 eggs and basil; set aside.

3 Punch dough down; divide in half. Roll one portion into a 15-in. x 10-in. rectangle on a greased baking sheet. Spoon half of the sausage mixture lengthwise down one side of rectangle to within 1 in. of edges.

4 Fold the dough over filling; pinch edges to seal. Cut four diagonal slits on top of the stromboli. Repeat with remaining dough and filling. Beat the remaining egg; brush over loaves. Sprinkle with Parmesan cheese. Cover and let rise until doubled, about 45 minutes.

5 Bake at 375° for 20-25 minutes or until golden brown. Slice; serve warm.

YIELD: 2 loaves (16 slices each).

APPLE 'N' PROSCIUTTO SANDWICHES

ELIZABETH BENNETT, MILL CREEK, WASHINGTON
Prepared on an indoor grill, these Italian-style sandwiches are spread with homemade rosemary pesto. They're wonderful on a cool day with a bowl of butternut squash soup.

PREP/TOTAL TIME: 20 min.

- 1/4 cup olive oil
- 1/2 cup chopped walnuts
- 2 tablespoons grated Parmesan cheese
- 2 tablespoons minced fresh rosemary
- 1 loaf (12 ounces) focaccia bread

8 thin slices prosciutto
1 medium apple, sliced
6 ounces Brie cheese, rind removed and sliced

1 In a blender, combine the oil, walnuts, Parmesan cheese and rosemary; cover and process until blended and nuts are finely chopped. With a bread knife, split focaccia into two horizontal layers. Spread rosemary mixture over cut sides of bread.

2 On bottom of bread, layer prosciutto, apple and Brie; replace bread top. Cut into quarters.

3 Cook on an indoor grill for 2-3 minutes or until bread is browned and cheese is melted. To serve, cut each wedge in half.

YIELD: 8 servings.

HARVEST STEW

TASTE OF HOME TEST KITCHEN
This warming stew features tasty golden squash, moist tender pork and sweet apples for an interesting change of pace from traditional beef stew.

PREP: 20 min. **COOK:** 40 min.
1-1/2 pounds boneless pork, cut into 1-inch cubes
1 medium onion, chopped
2 garlic cloves, minced
2 tablespoons butter
3 cups chicken broth
3/4 teaspoon salt
1/4 teaspoon dried rosemary, crushed
1/4 teaspoon rubbed sage
1 bay leaf
1 medium butternut squash, peeled and cubed (3 cups)
2 medium apples, peeled and cubed

1 In a large saucepan, cook the pork, onion and garlic in butter until meat is no longer pink; drain. Add the broth, salt, rosemary, sage and bay leaf.

2 Cover and simmer for 20 minutes. Add squash and apples; simmer, uncovered, for 20 minutes or until squash and apples are tender. Discard bay leaf.

YIELD: 6 servings.

HEARTY HUNTER'S STEW

JOYCE WORSECH, CATAWBA, WISCONSIN
After hunting season, this is my go-to stew recipe because it's a great way to use up venison. If you don't eat game meat, then just use beef. Either way, it's a delicious cold-weather recipe.

PREP: 25 min. **COOK:** 2 hours 50 min.
2 pounds boneless venison or beef chuck roast, cut in 1-inch cubes
2 tablespoons canola oil
4-1/4 cups water, divided
1/2 cup tomato juice
2 medium onions, cut in wedges
2 celery ribs, sliced
1 teaspoon Worcestershire sauce
2 bay leaves
2 to 3 teaspoons salt
1/2 teaspoon pepper
6 medium carrots, quartered
1 large rutabaga, peeled and cubed
6 medium potatoes, peeled and quartered
1 cup frozen peas
1 tablespoon cornstarch

1 In a Dutch oven, brown meat in oil over medium heat. Add 4 cups water and scrape to loosen browned drippings from pan. Add the tomato juice, onions, celery, Worcestershire sauce, bay leaves, salt and pepper. Bring to a boil. Reduce heat; cover and cook for 2 hours, stirring occasionally.

2 Discard bay leaves; add the carrots, rutabaga and potatoes. Cover and cook for 40-60 minutes.

3 Stir in the peas; cook for 10 minutes. Combine cornstarch and remaining water until smooth; stir into stew. Bring to a boil. Cook and stir for 2 minutes or until thickened.

YIELD: 8 servings.

CALICO CHILI

CAMILLE GOULDSBOROUGH, GROSS ISLE, MANITOBA

I developed this recipe myself when I was 16. It freezes well and almost tastes better the day after you make it. The variety of vegetables make it colorful to serve and give it the calico name.

PREP: 15 min. **COOK:** 25 min.

- 1 pound ground beef
- 1 medium green pepper, chopped
- 1 medium onion, chopped
- 1 celery rib, chopped
- 2 garlic cloves, minced
- 1 can (28 ounces) diced tomatoes, undrained
- 1 can (28 ounces) kidney beans, rinsed and drained
- 1 can (15-1/4 ounces) whole kernel corn, drained
- 1 cup cooked rice
- 1 cup diced zucchini, optional
- 1 cup water
- 2 tablespoons cider vinegar
- 1 tablespoon dried parsley flakes
- 1 tablespoon chili powder
- 1 tablespoon Worcestershire sauce
- 1/4 teaspoon each dried oregano, thyme and rosemary, crushed

Salt and pepper to taste

1 In a Dutch oven, cook the beef, green pepper, onion, celery and garlic over medium heat until beef is no longer pink; drain.

2 Stir in the remaining ingredients. Bring to a boil. Reduce heat; simmer, uncovered, for 20 minutes or until thickened and heated through, stirring occasionally.

YIELD: 8-10 servings (10 cups).

BRATS WITH SAUERKRAUT

DARLENE DIXON, HANOVER, MINNESOTA

I've made many variations of this excellent main dish. The bratwurst can be plain, smoked or cheese-flavored, served whole or cut in slices, with a bun or without. It would be popular at a party or potluck.

PREP: 10 min. **COOK:** 6 hours

- 8 uncooked bratwurst links
- 1 can (14 ounces) sauerkraut, rinsed and well drained

- 2 medium apples, peeled and finely chopped
- 3 bacon strips, cooked and crumbled
- 1/4 cup packed brown sugar
- 1/4 cup finely chopped onion
- 1 teaspoon ground mustard
- 8 brat buns, split

1 Place the bratwurst in a 5-qt. slow cooker. In a large bowl, combine the sauerkraut, apples, bacon, brown sugar, onion and mustard; spoon over bratwurst.

2 Cover and cook on low for 6-7 hours or until sausage is no longer pink. Place brats in buns; using a slotted spoon, top with sauerkraut mixture.

YIELD: 8 servings.

FALL VEGETABLE SOUP

HELEN VAIL, GLENSIDE, PENNSYLVANIA

This hearty soup comes together quickly. If you plan to have leftovers the next day, cook the pasta separately and add it to the soup. To store the pasta, after draining, toss it with a little oil, place in a covered container and refrigerate.

PREP: 15 min. **COOK:** 20 min.

- 4 cans (14-1/2 ounces each) reduced-sodium beef or vegetable broth
- 3 cups water
- 2 medium sweet potatoes, peeled and cubed
- 1 medium onion, chopped
- 4 garlic cloves, minced
- 2 teaspoons Italian seasoning
- 6 cups shredded cabbage
- 1 package (7 ounces) small pasta shells
- 2 cups frozen peas

1 In a soup kettle or Dutch oven, combine the broth, water, sweet potatoes, onion, garlic and Italian seasoning; bring to a boil. Reduce heat; cover and simmer for 10 minutes.

2 Return to a boil. Add the cabbage, pasta and peas; cook for 8-10 minutes or until the pasta and vegetables are tender.

YIELD: 14 servings (about 3-1/2 quarts).

APPLE-SWISS TURKEY SANDWICHES

GLORIA UPDYKE, FRONT ROYAL, VIRGINIA
Honey mustard adds a sweet tang to this hearty concoction. Apple slices, Swiss cheese, cucumber and turkey are layered between slices of nutritious multigrain bread. These delicious sandwiches pack well to take to the office or on the trail.

PREP/TOTAL TIME: 15 min.
- 3 tablespoons honey mustard
- 8 slices multi-grain bread, toasted
- 2 medium unpeeled apples, thinly sliced
- 8 slices reduced-fat Swiss cheese
- 1/2 cup thinly sliced cucumber
- 8 ounces thinly sliced cooked turkey breast

1 Lightly spread mustard on each slice of toast; set aside. Place apples on a microwave-safe plate and microwave, uncovered, on high for 1 minute or until slightly softened.

2 Arrange half of the apple slices and cheese on 4 slices of toast. Top with cucumber and turkey. Add remaining apple and cheese slices. Top with remaining toast, mustard side down.

YIELD: 4 servings.

BASQUE VEGETABLE SOUP

NORMAN CHEGWYN, RICHMOND, CALIFORNIA
This is a hearty soup widely served here, especially at the many restaurants specializing in Basque cuisine. It's a nice way to use the abundant vegetables that are available this time of year. Give it a try this harvest season.

PREP: 25 min. **COOK:** 2-1/4 hours + cooling
- 1 broiler/fryer chicken (2 to 3 pounds)
- 8 cups water
- 2 medium leeks, sliced
- 2 medium carrots, sliced
- 1 large turnip, peeled and cubed
- 1 large onion, chopped
- 1 large potato, peeled and cubed
- 1 garlic clove, minced
- 1-1/2 teaspoons salt
- 1/2 teaspoon pepper
- 1 tablespoon snipped fresh parsley
- 1 teaspoon dried thyme
- 3/4 pound fresh Polish sausage links
- 2 cups navy beans, rinsed and drained
- 1 cup shredded cabbage
- 1 can (15 ounces) tomato sauce

1 In Dutch oven, slowly bring chicken and water to a boil; skim foam. Reduce heat; cover and simmer for 45-60 minutes or until tender. Remove chicken; set aside until cool enough to handle.

2 Strain broth and skim fat. Return broth to Dutch oven. Add the leeks, carrots, turnip, onion, potato, garlic, salt, pepper, parsley and thyme. Bring to a boil. Reduce heat; cover and simmer for 30 minutes.

3 In a large skillet, cook sausage over medium heat until no longer pink. Drain on paper towels; set aside.

4 Meanwhile, remove chicken from bones; discard bones and skin. Cut chicken into bite-size pieces; add to the Dutch oven. Add beans, cabbage and cooked sausage. Simmer, uncovered, for 30 minutes or until vegetables are tender. Stir in tomato sauce; heat through.

YIELD: 10-12 servings (3 quarts).

PUMPKIN SOUP

KIMBERLY KNEPPER, EULESS, TEXAS

I whipped up this satisfying soup last Thanksgiving for my family, and everyone was crazy about it! Even my brother, who is one of the pickiest eaters I know, asked for seconds.

PREP/TOTAL TIME: 20 min.

- 1/2 pound fresh mushrooms, sliced
- 1/2 cup chopped onion
- 2 tablespoons butter
- 2 tablespoons all-purpose flour
- 1/2 to 1 teaspoon curry powder
- 3 cups vegetable broth
- 1 can (15 ounces) solid-pack pumpkin
- 1 can (12 ounces) evaporated milk
- 1 tablespoon honey
- 1/2 teaspoon salt
- 1/4 teaspoon pepper
- 1/4 teaspoon ground nutmeg

Minced chives

1 In a large saucepan, saute the mushrooms and onion in butter until tender. Stir in the flour and curry powder until blended. Gradually add the broth. Bring to a boil; cook and stir for 2 minutes or until thickened. Add the pumpkin, milk, honey, salt, pepper and nutmeg; heat through. Garnish with minced chives if desired.

YIELD: 7 servings.

CURRIED LENTIL SOUP

CHRISTINA TILL, SOUTH HAVEN, MICHIGAN

Curry gives a different taste sensation to this chili-like soup. It's delicious with a dollop of sour cream. My family welcomes it with open arms...and watering mouths.

PREP: 15 min. **COOK:** 8 hours

- 4 cups hot water
- 1 can (28 ounces) crushed tomatoes

- 3 medium potatoes, peeled and diced
- 3 medium carrots, thinly sliced
- 1 large onion, chopped
- 1 celery rib, chopped
- 1 cup dried lentils, rinsed
- 2 garlic cloves, minced
- 2 bay leaves
- 4 teaspoons curry powder
- 1-1/2 teaspoons salt, optional

1 In a 3-qt. slow cooker, combine all the ingredients. Cover and cook on low for 8 hours or until the vegetables and lentils are tender. Discard bay leaves.

YIELD: 10 servings (2-1/2 quarts).

APPLE CHICKEN STEW

CAROL MATHIAS, LINCOLN, NEBRASKA

My husband and I enjoy visiting the apple orchards in nearby Nebraska City. We always buy cider to use in this sensational slow-cooked stew.

PREP: 10 min. **COOK:** 4 hours

- 4 medium potatoes, cubed
- 4 medium carrots, cut into 1/4-inch slices
- 1 medium red onion, halved and sliced
- 1 celery rib, thinly sliced
- 1-1/2 teaspoons salt
- 3/4 teaspoon dried thyme
- 1/2 teaspoon pepper
- 1/4 to 1/2 teaspoon caraway seeds
- 2 pounds boneless skinless chicken breasts, cubed
- 2 tablespoons olive oil
- 1 large tart apple, peeled and cubed
- 1-1/4 cups apple cider or juice
- 1 tablespoon cider vinegar
- 1 bay leaf

Minced fresh parsley

1 In a 5-qt. slow cooker, layer the potatoes, carrots, onion and celery. Combine the salt, thyme, pepper and caraway; sprinkle half over vegetables.

2 In a skillet, saute chicken in oil until browned; transfer to slow cooker. Top with apple. Combine apple cider and vinegar; pour over chicken and apple. Sprinkle with remaining salt mixture. Top with bay leaf.

3 Cover and cook on high for 4-5 hours or until vegetables are tender and chicken is no longer pink. Discard bay leaf. Stir before serving. Sprinkle with parsley.

YIELD: 6-8 servings.

AUTUMN CHOWDER

SHEENA HOFFMAN, NORTH VANCOUVER, BRITISH COLUMBIA
When the weather gets chilly, we enjoy comfort foods like this hearty chowder. It's easy to prepare, and the aroma of it as it simmers makes my mouth water.

PREP: 10 min. **COOK:** 35 min.

- 2 bacon strips, diced
- 1/4 cup chopped onion
- 1 medium red potato, cubed
- 1 small carrot, halved lengthwise and thinly sliced
- 1/2 cup water
- 3/4 teaspoon chicken bouillon granules
- 1 cup milk
- 2/3 cup frozen corn
- 1/8 teaspoon pepper
- 2-1/2 teaspoons all-purpose flour
- 2 tablespoons cold water
- 3/4 cup shredded cheddar cheese

1 In a large saucepan, cook bacon over medium heat until crisp; remove to paper towels. Drain, reserving 1 teaspoon drippings. In drippings, saute onion until tender. Add potato, carrot, water and bouillon. Bring to a boil. Reduce heat; cover and simmer for 15-20 minutes or until the vegetables are almost tender.

2 Stir in the milk, corn and pepper. Cook 5 minutes longer. Combine the flour and cold water until smooth; gradually whisk into soup. Bring to a boil; cook and stir for 1-2 minutes or until thickened. Remove from the heat; stir in cheese until melted. Sprinkle with bacon.

YIELD: 2 servings.

BEEF-STUFFED FRENCH BREAD

ERIN GEE, FORT COLLINS, COLORADO
A wonderful lady from Utah shared this recipe with me—it fed her large farm family, and now I serve it to my family and friends. Using Colorado beef and an Idaho potato makes this hearty sandwich a real Western meal! If you have a leftover baked potato from dinner, this is a perfect way to use it.

PREP: 25 min. **BAKE:** 20 min. + chilling

- 1 pound ground beef
- 1/2 cup chopped onion
- 1 large baked potato, peeled and cubed
- 1 can (10-3/4 ounces) condensed cream of mushroom soup, undiluted
- 1 can (4 ounces) mushroom stems and pieces, drained
- 1 teaspoon dried parsley flakes
- 1/4 teaspoon garlic powder
- 1/8 teaspoon pepper
- Dash hot pepper sauce
- 1 loaf (1 pound) French bread
- 1 cup (4 ounces) shredded cheddar cheese

1 In a large skillet, cook the beef and onion over medium heat until meat is no longer pink; drain. Add the potato, soup, mushrooms, parsley, garlic powder, pepper and hot pepper sauce; cover and simmer for 10 minutes.

2 Meanwhile, cut the loaf of bread in half lengthwise. Hollow out bottom of loaf, leaving a 3/4-in. shell; set aside. Place the removed bread in a blender; cover and process until crumbled. Add 1 cup of crumbs to beef mixture (save remaining crumbs for another use). Stir in cheese.

3 Spoon beef mixture into bread shell; replace bread top. Wrap in heavy-duty foil; place on a baking sheet. Bake at 350° for 20 minutes. Let stand for 5 minutes before slicing.

YIELD: 6-8 servings.

BEEF BARLEY STEW

BARB SMITH, REGINA, SASKATCHEWAN
On cool days, which we get plenty of here, I like to get out my slow cooker and make up a batch of this comforting stew. Trying to appeal to 10 picky eaters in our large household is not too easy, but with this recipe, everyone asks for seconds.

PREP: 20 min. COOK: 6 hours
- 1-1/2 pounds beef stew meat, cut into 1-inch pieces
- 1 medium onion, chopped
- 2 tablespoons canola oil
- 4 cups water
- 1 can (15 ounces) tomato sauce
- 5 medium carrots, cut into 1/2-inch pieces
- 1 celery rib, thinly sliced
- 2 teaspoons salt
- 1/2 teaspoon dried oregano
- 1/2 teaspoon paprika
- 1/4 teaspoon pepper
- 2 cups fresh or frozen green beans, thawed
- 2 cups fresh or frozen corn, thawed
- 3/4 cup medium pearl barley

1 In a large skillet, brown beef and onion in oil until meat is no longer pink; drain. Transfer to a 5-qt. slow cooker. Add water, tomato sauce, carrots, celery, salt, oregano, paprika and pepper.

2 Cover and cook on low for 4-5 hours. Add beans, corn and barley; cover and cook on low 2 hours longer or until barley, beef and vegetables are tender.

YIELD: 6-8 servings.

PORK BARBECUE SANDWICHES

GEORGE HASCHER, PHOENICIA, NEW YORK
We were happy when there was pork roast on the menu because we were sure that, within the next few days, we'd be feasting on leftover pork in these tasty sandwiches.

PREP/TOTAL TIME: 30 min.
- 2 celery ribs, finely chopped
- 1 medium onion, finely chopped
- 1 teaspoon canola oil
- 1 cup ketchup
- 1 to 1-1/2 teaspoons salt
- 1 teaspoon ground mustard
- 2 cups shredded cooked pork
- 2 to 3 kaiser rolls or hamburger buns, split

1 In a large saucepan, saute celery and onion in oil until tender. Stir in the ketchup, salt and mustard. Add pork. Bring to a boil. Reduce heat; cover and simmer for 20-30 minutes or until heated through. Serve on rolls.

YIELD: 2-3 servings.

RED CABBAGE AND APPLE SLAW
A crisp slaw is a natural pairing with the Pork Barbecue Sandwiches. In a bowl, toss 3/4 cup cubed, peeled tart apple with 1 tablespoon lemon juice. Add 1-3/4 cups shredded red cabbage, 2 tablespoons each mayonnaise and plain yogurt, and a dash each onion salt, white pepper and celery seed. Toss to coat.

BUTTERNUT SQUASH SOUP

LINDA ROSE PROUDFOOT, HUNTINGTON, CONNECTICUT
This deep golden soup is as pretty as it is yummy. If you'd like, you can intensify the garlic flavor by adding an extra bulb. The garlic is what really flavors this soup.

PREP: 25 min. **BAKE:** 1-1/2 hours + standing

    3 pounds unpeeled butternut squash, halved and seeded
    2 large unpeeled onions
    1 small garlic bulb
 1/4 cup olive oil
    2 tablespoons minced fresh thyme or 2 teaspoons
       dried thyme
    3 to 3-1/2 cups chicken or vegetable broth
 1/2 cup heavy whipping cream
    3 tablespoons minced fresh parsley
 1/2 teaspoon salt
 1/4 teaspoon pepper
Sprigs fresh thyme, optional

1 Cut the squash into eight large pieces. Place cut side up in a 15-in. x 10-in. x 1-in. baking pan. Cut 1/4 in. off tops of onion and garlic bulbs (the end that comes to a closed point).

2 Place the cut side up in baking pans. Brush with oil; sprinkle with thyme. Cover tightly and bake at 350° for 1-1/2 to 2 hours or until the vegetables are very tender. Uncover and let stand until lukewarm.

3 Remove peel from squash and onions; remove soft garlic from skins. In a large bowl, combine the vegetables, broth and cream. Puree in small batches in a blender until smooth; transfer to a large saucepan. Add the parsley, salt and pepper; heat through (do not boil). Garnish with thyme if desired.

YIELD: 8 servings (2 quarts).

SAUERKRAUT SAUSAGE SOUP

YVONNE KETT, APPLETON, WISCONSIN
My husband and I make our own sauerkraut and grow many of the vegetables in this easy slow cooker soup. It cooks all day and smells delicious when we come home from work.

PREP: 20 min. **COOK:** 5 hours

    4 cups chicken broth
    1 pound smoked Polish sausage, cut into 1/2-inch slices
    1 can (16 ounces) sauerkraut, rinsed and well drained
    2 cups sliced fresh mushrooms
 1-1/2 cups cubed peeled potatoes
    1 can (10-3/4 ounces) condensed cream of mushroom soup,
       undiluted
 1-1/4 cups chopped onions
    2 large carrots, sliced
    2 celery ribs, chopped
    2 tablespoons white vinegar
    2 teaspoons dill weed
    1 teaspoon sugar
 1/4 teaspoon pepper

1 In a 5-qt. slow cooker, combine all ingredients. Cover and cook on low for 5-6 hours or until vegetables are tender.

YIELD: 10 servings.

193   198   190   192

SIDES, SALADS & BREADS

190

CHALLAH

TASTE OF HOME TEST KITCHEN

This traditional Jewish bread is often called egg bread because it uses more eggs than most. The attractive golden color and delicious flavor make it hard to resist.

PREP: 30 min. **BAKE:** 30 min.

    2 packages (1/4 ounce each) active dry yeast
    1 cup warm water (110° to 115°)
1/2 cup canola oil
1/3 cup sugar
    1 tablespoon salt
    4 eggs
    6 to 6-1/2 cups all-purpose flour

TOPPING:

    1 egg
    1 teaspoon cold water
    1 tablespoon sesame or poppy seeds, optional

1 In a large bowl, dissolve yeast in warm water. Add oil, sugar, salt, eggs and 4 cups flour. Beat until smooth. Stir in enough remaining flour to form a firm dough. Turn onto a floured surface; knead until smooth and elastic, about 6-8 minutes. Place in a greased bowl, turning once to grease top. Cover and let rise in a warm place until doubled, about 1 hour.

2 Punch dough down. Turn onto a lightly floured surface; divide in half. Divide each portion into thirds. Shape each piece into a 15-in. rope. Place three ropes on a greased baking sheet and braid; pinch ends to seal and tuck under. Repeat with remaining dough. Cover and let rise until doubled, about 1 hour.

3 Beat egg and cold water; brush over braids. Sprinkle with the sesame or poppy seeds if desired. Bake at 350° for 30-35 minutes or until golden brown. Remove to wire racks to cool.

YIELD: 2 loaves (16 slices each).

HARVEST POTATO CASSEROLE

MRS. ROBERT CODY, DALLAS, TEXAS

Sour cream and cream of chicken soup lend to the creamy texture of this tried-and-true casserole. My family prefers this to traditional mashed potatoes.

PREP: 40 min. + chilling **BAKE:** 45 min.

    8 large potatoes
    2 bay leaves
1/4 cup butter, melted
1/2 teaspoon salt
1/4 teaspoon pepper
    2 cups (16 ounces) sour cream
    1 can (10-3/4 ounces) condensed cream of chicken soup, undiluted
    2 cups (8 ounces) shredded cheddar cheese, divided
    1 jar (2 ounces) diced pimientos, drained
    4 green onions, chopped
1/2 cup crushed cornflakes

1 Place potatoes and bay leaves in a Dutch oven or large kettle; cover with water. Bring to a boil. Reduce heat; cover and simmer for 15-20 minutes or until tender. Remove from the heat; cool to room temperature. Place in the freezer (still covered by the cooking water) for 1 hour.

2 Drain potatoes; peel and grate. Place in a greased 13-in. x 9-in. baking dish. Drizzle with butter. Sprinkle with salt and pepper; toss to coat.

3 In a large bowl, combine the sour cream, soup, 1 cup cheese, pimientos and onion; spread over potatoes. Sprinkle with the remaining cheese; top with cornflakes (dish will be full).

4 Bake, uncovered, at 350° for 45-50 minutes or until bubbly.

YIELD: 12-15 servings.

WARM PEAR SALAD

MARJORIE ZALEWSKI, TOLEDO, OHIO
Pear slices tossed with salad greens, red onion and blue cheese are drizzled with tangy raspberry vinaigrette in this refreshing salad. After enjoying a similar dish at a restaurant, I came home and worked up my own version. My family declared it a winner.

PREP/TOTAL TIME: 15 min.

- 3 large ripe pears, cut into 1/4-inch slices
- 6 cups torn mixed salad greens
- 6 slices red onion, separated into rings
- 2 ounces crumbled blue cheese
- 1/4 cup sunflower kernels

RASPBERRY VINAIGRETTE:
- 1/2 cup olive oil
- 1/2 cup honey
- 1/3 cup white wine vinegar
- 1 tablespoon Dijon mustard
- 1-1/2 teaspoons lemon juice
- 1 cup fresh or frozen raspberries, thawed
- 1/4 teaspoon salt

Pepper to taste

1 In a nonstick skillet, saute pear slices for 2-3 minutes on each side or until tender. On salad plates, arrange the greens, pears, onion, blue cheese and sunflower kernels.

2 In a blender, combine the vinaigrette ingredients; cover and process until smooth. Drizzle over salads.

YIELD: 8-10 servings.

CINNAMON-SWIRL PEAR BREAD

JOAN ANDERSON, WINNIPEG, MANITOBA
Pears add moisture to this delightful bread. I've been making it for over 20 years, and it's become a favorite of my family and friends. Try slices toasted to go along with Sunday brunch.

PREP: 50 min. + rising BAKE: 35 min.
- 3 cups chopped peeled ripe pears (about 3 medium)
- 1/2 cup water

- 1-1/4 cups plus 1 teaspoon sugar, divided
- 3 packages (1/4 ounce each) active dry yeast
- 1/2 cup warm water (110° to 115°)
- 4 eggs, lightly beaten
- 1/2 cup butter, softened
- 1/2 cup honey
- 2 teaspoons salt
- 1 teaspoon almond extract
- 10 to 11 cups all-purpose flour
- 1 tablespoon ground cinnamon

1 In a large saucepan, combine the pears, water and 1/2 cup sugar. Simmer, uncovered, for 10-12 minutes or until tender. Drain well, reserving syrup. Add cold water if necessary to syrup to measure 1 cup; set aside.

2 In a large bowl, dissolve yeast in warm water. Add 1 teaspoon sugar; let stand for 10 minutes. Add the eggs, butter, honey, salt, extract, 4 cups flour and reserved pears and syrup. Beat until smooth. Add enough remaining flour to form a soft dough.

3 Turn onto a floured surface; knead until smooth and elastic, about 6-8 minutes. Place in a greased bowl, turning once to grease top. Cover and let rise in a warm place until doubled, about 1-1/4 hours.

4 Punch dough down; divide into thirds. Roll each portion into a 16-in. x 8-in. rectangle. Combine cinnamon and remaining 3/4 cup sugar; sprinkle over dough to within 1/2 in. of edges.

5 Roll up, jelly-roll style, starting with a short side; pinch seams to seal. Place, seam side down, in three greased 9-in. x 5-in. loaf pans. Cover and let rise until doubled, about 45 minutes.

6 Bake at 375° for 20 minutes. Cover loosely with foil. Bake 15-20 minutes longer or until bread tests done. Remove from pans to wire rack to cool.

YIELD: 3 loaves (16 slices each).

MORNING MAPLE MUFFINS

ELIZABETH TALBOT, LEXINGTON, KENTUCKY
Maple combines with a subtle touch of cinnamon and nuts to give these muffins the flavor of a hearty pancake breakfast.

PREP/TOTAL TIME: 30 min.

- 2 cups all-purpose flour
- 1/2 cup packed brown sugar
- 2 teaspoons baking powder
- 1/2 teaspoon salt
- 3/4 cup milk
- 1/2 cup butter, melted
- 1/2 cup maple syrup
- 1/4 cup sour cream
- 1 egg
- 1/2 teaspoon vanilla extract

TOPPING:

- 3 tablespoons all-purpose flour
- 3 tablespoons sugar
- 2 tablespoons chopped nuts
- 1/2 teaspoon ground cinnamon
- 2 tablespoons cold butter

1 In a large bowl, combine the flour, brown sugar, baking powder and salt. In another bowl, combine the milk, butter, syrup, sour cream, egg and vanilla. Stir into the dry ingredients just until moistened.

2 Fill greased or paper-lined muffin cups two-thirds full. For topping, combine the flour, sugar, nuts and cinnamon; cut in butter until crumbly. Sprinkle over batter.

3 Bake at 400° for 16-20 minutes or until a toothpick inserted near the center comes out clean. Cool for 5 minutes before removing from pans to wire racks. Serve warm.

YIELD: 16 muffins.

CRUNCHY APPLE SALAD

JULIE PEARSALL, UNION SPRINGS, NEW YORK
This old-fashioned salad is part of my favorite meal that Mom used to make. Crunchy apples, celery and walnuts blend well with the creamy mayonnaise.

PREP/TOTAL TIME: 10 min.

- 4 large red apples, diced
- 1 cup chopped celery
- 1 cup raisins
- 1 cup chopped walnuts
- 1/2 cup mayonnaise

1 In a large bowl, combine apples, celery, raisins and walnuts. Add mayonnaise; toss to coat. Cover and refrigerate until serving.

YIELD: 16 servings.

SWEET POTATO BREAD

SALLY GIESBRECHT, ORLAND, CALIFORNIA
This recipe originally started from my favorite banana bread recipe. I substituted sweet potatoes and made a few other adjustments to come up with this delicious quick bread.

PREP: 20 min. **BAKE:** 70 min. + cooling

- 3/4 cup butter, softened
- 1 cup sugar
- 3 eggs
- 1/2 cup honey
- 1-1/2 cups mashed sweet potatoes
- 1 package (3.4 ounces) instant vanilla pudding mix
- 2-1/4 cups all-purpose flour
- 1 teaspoon baking powder
- 1 teaspoon baking soda
- 1/2 teaspoon salt
- 1/2 cup buttermilk
- 1 cup chopped pecans
- 2/3 cup raisins

ICING:

- 1 cup confectioners' sugar
- 1 tablespoon milk
- 2 teaspoons butter, melted
- 1 teaspoon lemon juice

1 In a large bowl, cream butter and sugar until light and fluffy. Add eggs, one at a time, beating well after each addition. Add the honey, sweet potatoes and dry pudding mix and mix well. Combine the flour, baking powder, baking soda and salt; add to creamed mixture alternately with buttermilk, beating well after each addition. Fold in pecans and raisins.

2 Pour into two greased 9-in. x 5-in. loaf pans. Bake at 350° for 70-80 minutes or until a toothpick inserted near the center comes out clean. Cool for 10 minutes before removing from pans to wire racks.

3 In a small bowl, combine icing ingredients until smooth; drizzle over cooled bread.

YIELD: 2 loaves (16 slices each).

VEGETABLE NOODLE CASSEROLE

TARA BRICCO, COVINGTON, TENNESSEE
I found the recipe for this vegetable casserole in an old magazine I bought at a yard sale right after I got married. It's my husband Rory's favorite, and has stood the test of time! It's a wonderful side dish for meat.

PREP: 15 min. **BAKE:** 30 min.

- 1 can (10-3/4 ounces) condensed cream of mushroom soup, undiluted
- 1 cup (8 ounces) sour cream
- 3/4 cup chopped onion
- 1 teaspoon salt
- 1/4 teaspoon pepper
- 3 cups frozen chopped broccoli, thawed
- 1-3/4 cups frozen cauliflower, thawed and cut into bite-size pieces
- 8 ounces wide egg noodles, cooked and drained
- 1-1/2 cups (6 ounces) shredded Swiss cheese, divided

1 In a large bowl, combine the soup, sour cream, onion, salt and pepper. Add the broccoli, cauliflower, noodles and 1/4 cup of cheese; mix gently.

2 Pour into a greased 13-in. x 9-in. baking dish. Top with the remaining cheese. Bake, uncovered, at 350° for 30 minutes or until heated through.

YIELD: 6-8 servings.

BUTTERCUP YEAST BREAD

KELLY KIRBY, WESTVILLE, NOVA SCOTIA
Just by tasting it, you'd never know there was squash in this delicious, fluffy bread. People love the colorful slices, even though they have a hard time guessing where the pretty orange tint comes from!

PREP: 40 min. + rising **BAKE:** 35 min. + cooling

- 3 packages (1/4 ounce each) active dry yeast
- 1/2 cup warm water (110° to 115°)
- 2 tablespoons sugar
- 2-1/2 cups mashed cooked buttercup or butternut squash
- 2 cups milk
- 2/3 cup packed brown sugar
- 2/3 cup butter, softened
- 2 eggs, lightly beaten
- 3 teaspoons salt
- 13 cups all-purpose flour

1 In a very large bowl, dissolve yeast in warm water. Add sugar; let stand for 5 minutes. Add the squash, milk, brown sugar, butter, eggs and salt; mix well. Add 6 cups flour. Beat on medium speed for 3 minutes. Stir in enough remaining flour to form a soft dough.

2 Turn onto a floured surface; knead until smooth and elastic, about 10 minutes. Place in a greased bowl, turning once to grease top. Cover and let rise in a warm place until doubled, about 1-1/4 hours.

3 Punch dough down. Divide into three portions; shape into loaves. Place in three greased 9-in. x 5-in. loaf pans. Cover and let rise until doubled, about 45 minutes.

4 Bake at 350° for 35-40 minutes or until golden brown. Cool for 10 minutes before removing from pans to wire racks to cool completely.

YIELD: 3 loaves (16 slices each).

APPLE CREAM COFFEE CAKE

ORIANA CHURCHILL, LONDONDERRY, NEW HAMPSHIRE
This tried-and-true recipe tastes wonderful. The apple filling makes it moist, while the crispy nut mixture adds a bit of crunch.

PREP: 20 min. BAKE: 40 min. + cooling
- 1/2 cup butter, softened
- 1-1/2 cups sugar, divided
- 2 eggs
- 1 teaspoon vanilla extract
- 2 cups all-purpose flour
- 1 teaspoon baking powder
- 1/2 teaspoon baking soda
- 1/2 teaspoon salt
- 1 cup (8 ounces) sour cream
- 1/2 cup chopped walnuts
- 2 teaspoons ground cinnamon
- 1 medium apple, peeled and thinly sliced

1 In a large bowl, cream butter and 1 cup sugar until light and fluffy. Add eggs, one at a time, beating well after each addition. Blend in vanilla. Combine the flour, baking powder, baking soda and salt; add to creamed mixture alternately with sour cream, beating well after each addition. In a small bowl, combine the nuts, cinnamon and remaining sugar.

2 Spread half of the batter in a well-greased 10-in. tube pan with a removable bottom. Top with apple slices; sprinkle with half of the nut mixture. Top with remaining batter, then with remaining nut mixture.

3 Bake at 375° for 40-45 minutes or until a toothpick inserted near the center comes out clean. Cool in pan for 30 minutes. Carefully run a knife around edge of pan to loosen. Lift cake with removable bottom from pan. Cool completely. Before serving, carefully lift cake from pan bottom.

YIELD: 12-16 servings.

GNOCCHI IN SAGE BUTTER

TASTE OF HOME TEST KITCHEN
Buttery garlic and sage sauce adds melt-in-your-mouth flavor to these feather-light but filling and oh-so-easy, homemade potato puffs from our Test Kitchen.

PREP: 70 min. COOK: 5 min.
- 1 pound russet potatoes, peeled and quartered
- 3 quarts water
- 2/3 cup all-purpose flour
- 1 egg
- 1/2 teaspoon salt
- Dash ground nutmeg
- 2 tablespoons butter
- 2 garlic cloves, thinly sliced
- 4 fresh sage leaves, thinly sliced

1 Place potatoes in a saucepan and cover with water. Bring to a boil. Reduce heat; cover and simmer for 15-20 minutes or until tender. Drain.

2 Over a warm burner or very low heat, stir the potatoes for 1-2 minutes or until the steam is evaporated. Press through a potato ricer or strainer into a small bowl; cool slightly. In a Dutch oven, bring water to a boil.

3 Using a fork, make a well in the riced potatoes. Sprinkle flour over the potatoes and into the well. Whisk the egg, salt and nutmeg; pour into well. Stir until blended. Knead 10-12 times, forming a soft dough.

4 Divide dough into four portions. On a floured surface, roll portions into 1/2-in.-thick ropes; cut into 3/4-in. pieces. Press and roll each piece with a lightly floured fork. Cook gnocchi in boiling water in batches for 30-60 seconds or until they float. Remove with a strainer and keep warm.

5 In a large heavy saucepan, cook butter over medium heat for 3 minutes. Add garlic and sage; cook for 2-4 minutes or until butter and garlic are golden brown. Add gnocchi; stir gently to coat. Serve immediately.

YIELD: 4 servings.

WILD RICE SALAD

ELAINE SABACKY, LITCHFIELD, MINNESOTA

You're in for a treat if you've never tasted wild rice from Minnesota! Wild rice is actually a cereal grain that's full of fiber and minerals. It's not only healthful, but delicious, especially when prepared in this dish.

PREP: 20 min. **COOK:** 35 min. + chilling

- 2 cups water
- 2/3 cup wild rice
- 2 medium tart apples, chopped
- 2 celery ribs, sliced
- 2 tablespoons brown sugar
- 1 tablespoon lemon juice

DRESSING:

- 1/2 cup reduced-fat plain yogurt
- 1/2 cup reduced-fat mayonnaise

1 In a large saucepan, bring the water and rice to a boil. Reduce heat; cover and simmer for 45-60 minutes or until rice is tender. Fluff with a fork. Drain if necessary.

2 In a large bowl, combine rice, apples, celery, brown sugar and lemon juice. Combine the dressing ingredients; pour over rice mixture; toss to coat. Cover and refrigerate for at least 2 hours before serving.

YIELD: 6-8 servings.

PISTACHIO PUMPKIN BREAD

KATHY KITTELL, LENEXA, KANSAS

These cute little loaves blend pumpkin, pistachio, rum and raisins with festive results. A few years ago during the holiday season, a friend shared this delightful recipe with me. Since then, I've made it every holiday and shared it with family and friends.

PREP: 15 min. **BAKE:** 30 min. + cooling

- 1 package (14 ounces) pumpkin quick bread/muffin mix
- 2 eggs
- 1 cup water
- 3 tablespoons canola oil
- 1/4 to 1/2 teaspoon rum extract
- 1/2 cup raisins
- 1/2 cup chopped pistachios

GLAZE:

- 1/4 cup sugar
- 2 tablespoons water
- 1 tablespoon butter
- 1/4 teaspoon rum extract

1 In a large bowl, combine the bread mix, eggs, water, oil and extract just until blended. Stir in raisins and pistachios. Transfer to three greased 5-3/4-in. x 3-in. x 2-in. loaf pans.

2 Bake at 375° for 30-35 minutes or until a toothpick inserted near the center comes out clean. Cool for 5 minutes.

3 Meanwhile, for glaze, in small saucepan, combine sugar, water and butter. Bring to a boil; cook and stir for 3 minutes or until sugar is dissolved. Remove from heat; stir in extract.

4 Remove the loaves from the pans to wire racks. With a toothpick, poke holes in the top of each loaf; brush with the glaze. Cool completely.

YIELD: 3 mini loaves (4 slices each).

MUENSTER BREAD

MELANIE MERO, IDA, MICHIGAN

The recipe makes a beautiful round loaf. With a layer of cheese peeking out of every slice, it's definitely worth the effort.

PREP: 20 min. + rising **BAKE:** 45 min. + cooling

- 2 packages (1/4 ounce each) active dry yeast
- 1 cup warm milk (110° to 115°)
- 1/2 cup butter, softened
- 2 tablespoons sugar
- 1 teaspoon salt
- 3-1/4 to 3-3/4 cups all-purpose flour
- 1 egg plus 1 egg yolk
- 4 cups (1 pound) shredded Muenster cheese
- 1 egg white, beaten

1 In a large bowl, dissolve yeast in milk. Add butter, sugar, salt and 2 cups flour; beat until smooth. Stir in enough remaining flour to form a soft dough.

2 Turn onto a floured surface; knead until smooth and elastic, about 6-8 minutes. Place in a greased bowl, turning once to grease top. Cover and let rise in a warm place until doubled, about 1 hour.

3 In a large bowl, beat egg and yolk; stir in cheese. Punch down dough; roll into a 16-in. circle.

4 Place in a greased 9-in. round baking pan, letting dough drape over the edges. Spoon the cheese mixture into center of dough. Gather dough up over filling in 1-1/2-in. pleats. Gently squeeze pleats together at top and twist to make a top knot. Allow to rise 10-15 minutes.

5 Brush loaf with egg white. Bake at 375° for 40-45 minutes. Cool on a wire rack for 20 minutes. Serve warm.

YIELD: 1 loaf (16 slices).

HARVEST FRUIT BREAD

SANDY VIAS, SAN LEANDRO, CALIFORNIA

My sister is raising two little girls but always makes time to bake homemade bread. They like this loaf best. It's studded with fruit and nuts, and terrific toasted and spread with butter.

PREP: 10 min. BAKE: 3 hours

- 1 cup plus 2 tablespoons water (70° to 80°)
- 1 egg
- 3 tablespoons butter, softened
- 1/4 cup packed brown sugar
- 1-1/2 teaspoons salt
- 1/4 teaspoon ground nutmeg
- Dash allspice
- 3-3/4 cups plus 1 tablespoon bread flour
- 2 teaspoons active dry yeast
- 1 cup dried fruit (dried cherries, cranberries and/or raisins)
- 1/3 cup chopped pecans

1 In bread machine pan, place the first nine ingredients in order suggested by manufacturer. Select basic bread setting. Choose crust color and loaf size if available. Bake according to bread machine directions (check dough after 5 minutes of mixing; add 1 to 2 tablespoons water or flour if needed). Just before final kneading (your machine may audibly signal this), add fruit and pecans.

YIELD: 1 loaf (12 slices).

EDITOR'S NOTE: We recommend you do not use a bread machine's time-delay feature for this recipe.

BUTTERCUP SQUASH COFFEE CAKE

MARY JONES, CUMBERLAND, MAINE

My father grows a large squash patch, so each fall, I get an ample amount of his harvest. I make this treat to share with my co-workers. They rave about the moist cake, the crunchy streusel and the applesauce between the layers.

PREP: 15 min. BAKE: 55 min.

CRUMB MIXTURE:
- 1/4 cup packed brown sugar
- 1/4 cup sugar
- 1/4 cup all-purpose flour
- 1/4 cup quick-cooking oats
- 1/4 cup chopped nuts
- 1-1/2 teaspoons ground cinnamon
- 3 tablespoons cold butter

CAKE:
- 1/2 cup butter-flavored shortening
- 1 cup sugar
- 2 eggs
- 1 cup mashed cooked buttercup squash
- 1 teaspoon vanilla extract
- 2 cups all-purpose flour
- 2 teaspoons baking powder
- 1-1/2 teaspoons ground cinnamon
- 1/2 teaspoon baking soda
- 1/2 teaspoon salt
- 1/4 teaspoon ground ginger
- 1/4 teaspoon ground nutmeg
- Pinch ground cloves
- 1/2 cup unsweetened applesauce

GLAZE:
- 1/2 cup confectioners' sugar
- 1/4 teaspoon vanilla extract
- 1-1/2 teaspoons hot water

1 In a small bowl, combine the first six ingredients. Cut in butter until crumbly; set aside. For cake, in a large bowl, cream shortening and sugar until light and fluffy. Beat in eggs, one at a time, beating well after each addition. Beat in squash and vanilla. Combine dry ingredients; gradually add to creamed mixture and mix well. Spoon half into a greased 9-in. springform pan.

2 Spread applesauce over batter. Sprinkle with half of the crumb mixture. Spoon remaining batter evenly over crumb mixture. Top with remaining crumb mixture.

3 Bake at 350° for 50-55 minutes or until a toothpick inserted near the center comes out clean. Cool for 10 minutes before removing sides of pan.

4 For glaze, combine the confectioners' sugar, extract and enough water to achieve desired consistency; drizzle over the coffee cake.

YIELD: 10-12 servings.

HOMEMADE NOODLES

ALVINIA KING, RUDOLPH, WISCONSIN
When our son Conrad married Erin on our dairy farm, family and friends helped me prepare food for 400. To go with grilled pork and chicken, we fixed an array of side dishes, including these wonderful noodles. At this Polish wedding, we wanted to be sure no one went home hungry.

PREP: 30 min. + standing **COOK:** 5 min.

    6 to 7 cups all-purpose flour
1-1/2 teaspoons salt
    6 eggs, lightly beaten
    1 cup water
    1 tablespoon canola oil
Melted butter and minced fresh parsley, optional

1 In a large bowl, combine 6 cups flour and salt. Make a well in the center. Beat eggs and water; pour into well. Stir together, forming a dough. Turn dough onto a floured surface; knead 8-10 times.

2 Divide dough into eight portions. On a lightly floured surface, roll each portion into a 1/16-in.-thick square. Let stand, uncovered, for 10 minutes.

3 Roll up, jelly-roll style. Using a sharp knife, cut into 1/4-in. slices. Unroll noodles and dry in a single layer on paper towels for 1 hour before cooking.

4 To cook, bring salted water to a rapid boil. Add noodles and oil to boiling water; cook for 2 minutes or until tender but not soft. Drain; toss with butter and parsley if desired.

YIELD: 24 servings.

MEASURING DRY INGREDIENTS
For dry ingredients such as flour, sugar or cornmeal, spoon ingredients into a dry measuring cup over a canister or waxed paper. Fill cup to overflowing, then level by sweeping a metal spatula or flat side of a knife across the top.

APPLE PIE JAM

AUDREY GODELL, STANTON, MICHIGAN
Although I've been canning for years, I've never found a good apple jam recipe, so I created this one. My husband of 41 years and I love this jam so much because it tastes just like apple pie....without the crust!

PREP: 30 min. **PROCESS:** 10 min.

    4 to 5 large Golden Delicious apples, peeled and sliced (about 2 pounds)
    1 cup water
    5 cups sugar
1/2 teaspoon butter
    1 pouch (3 ounces) liquid fruit pectin
1-1/2 teaspoons ground cinnamon
    1 teaspoon ground nutmeg
1/4 teaspoon ground mace, optional

1 In a Dutch oven, combine apples and water. Cover and cook slowly until tender. Measure 4-1/2 cups apples; return to the pan. (Save remaining apple mixture for another use or discard.)

2 Add the sugar and butter to pan; bring to a full rolling boil, stirring constantly. Quickly stir in pectin; return to a full rolling boil. Boil 1 minute, stirring constantly.

3 Remove from the heat; skim off foam. Stir in the spices. Carefully ladle hot mixture into hot half-pint jars, leaving 1/4-in. headspace. Remove air bubbles; wipe rims and adjust lids. Process for 10 minutes in a boiling-water canner.

YIELD: 7 half-pints.

EDITOR'S NOTE: The processing time listed is for altitudes of 1,000 feet or less. Add 1 minute to the processing time for each 1,000 feet of additional altitude.

HARVEST GREEN SALAD

BETH ROYALS, RICHMOND, VIRGINIA
This salad always gets rave reviews. Guests say that it fills them up without weighing them down.

PREP: 25 min. **BAKE:** 1 hour + cooling
- 3 whole medium fresh beets
- 1 large sweet potato, peeled and cubed
- 2 tablespoons water
- 1/2 cup reduced-fat balsamic vinaigrette
- 2 tablespoons jellied cranberry sauce
- 1 package (5 ounces) spring mix salad greens
- 1/2 cup dried cranberries
- 4 ounces crumbled Gorgonzola cheese

1 Wash beets; trim stem and leave root intact. Wrap beets in aluminum foil. Place on a baking sheet. Bake at 400° for 1 hour or until tender. Remove foil and cool.

2 In a microwave-safe bowl, combine the sweet potato and water. Cover and microwave on high for 4-5 minutes or until tender. Cool.

3 In a blender, combine the vinaigrette and cranberry sauce; cover and process until smooth. Peel the beets and cut into slices. On six salad plates, arrange the greens, beets and sweet potatoes. Sprinkle with the cranberries and cheese. Drizzle with dressing.

YIELD: 6 servings.

EDITOR'S NOTE: Use plastic gloves when peeling beets to avoid stains.

BACON SCALLOPED POTATOES

VALERIE BELLEY, ST. LOUIS, MISSOURI
I enhance this pared-down potato dish by adding a layer of sliced onions and sprinkling of crumbled bacon. The onions and bacon make the potatoes seem more special. The recipe can easily be doubled for company, too.

PREP: 15 min. **BAKE:** 65 min.
- 2 tablespoons butter
- 2 tablespoons all-purpose flour
- 1/4 teaspoon salt
- 3/4 cup milk
- 2 medium potatoes, peeled and sliced
- 2 small onions, sliced
- 3 bacon strips, cooked and crumbled

1 In a small saucepan, melt butter. Stir in flour and salt until smooth. Gradually add milk. Bring to a boil; cook and stir for 2 minutes or until thickened.

2 In a greased 1-qt. baking dish, layer the potatoes and onions. Pour white sauce over the top. Cover and bake at 350° for 65-75 minutes or until potatoes are tender. Sprinkle with bacon.

YIELD: 2 servings.

CRAN-RASPBERRY JAM

MARJILEE BOOTH, CHINO HILLS, CALIFORNIA
I'm sure to pick up extra bags of cranberries for the freezer in fall so that I can make this lovely, delicious jam all year-round. My kids love it on peanut butter sandwiches. Jars of this pretty ruby-colored jam also make great gifts.

PREP: 20 min. **PROCESS:** 10 min.
- 2 packages (10 ounces each) frozen sweetened raspberries, thawed
- 4 cups fresh or frozen cranberries
- 1 package (1-3/4 ounces) powdered fruit pectin
- 5 cups sugar

1 Drain the raspberries, reserving juice; add enough water to juice to measure 1-1/2 cups. Pour into a Dutch oven. Add raspberries, cranberries and pectin; bring to a full rolling boil, stirring constantly. Stir in sugar; return to a full rolling boil. Boil for 1 minute, stirring constantly.

2 Remove from the heat; skim off foam. Carefully ladle hot mixture into hot half-pint jars, leaving 1/4-in. headspace. Remove air bubbles; wipe rims and adjust lids. Process for 10 minutes in a boiling-water canner.

YIELD: 6 half-pints.

EDITOR'S NOTE: The processing time listed is for altitudes of 1,000 feet or less. Add 1 minute to the processing time for each 1,000 feet of additional altitude.

ORANGE CRANBERRY BREAD

RON GARDNER, GRAND HAVEN, MICHIGAN
With this, you can enjoy two moist loaves of bread that are packed with the zesty taste of cranberries and orange peel. I suggest toasting the slices and serving them with butter or cream cheese.

PREP: 20 min. **BAKE:** 50 min. + cooling

2-3/4 cups all-purpose flour
2/3 cup sugar
2/3 cup packed brown sugar
3-1/2 teaspoons baking powder
1 teaspoon salt
1/2 teaspoon ground cinnamon
1/4 teaspoon ground nutmeg
1 egg
1 cup milk
1/2 cup orange juice
3 tablespoons canola oil
2 to 3 teaspoons grated orange peel
2 cups coarsely chopped fresh or frozen cranberries
1 large apple, peeled and chopped

1 In a large bowl, combine the flour, sugars, baking powder, salt, cinnamon and nutmeg. Whisk the egg, milk, orange juice, oil and orange peel; stir into dry ingredients just until blended. Fold in the cranberries and apple.

2 Pour into two greased 8-in. x 4-in. loaf pans. Bake at 350° for 50-55 minutes or until a toothpick inserted near the center comes out clean. Cool for 10 minutes before removing from pans to wire racks.

YIELD: 2 loaves (16 slices each).

MUSHROOM PILAF

GENE BROFKA, AUSTIN, TEXAS
While combing through my grandmother's recipes, I ran across something I hadn't seen since childhood. I prepared what Grandma called her "pretty pilaf." It was just as I remembered.

PREP: 10 min. **COOK:** 30 min. + standing

1 cup chopped onion
1 cup uncooked long grain rice
1 ounce uncooked spaghetti, broken into 1-inch pieces (about 1/2 cup)
1/4 cup butter
1 can (14-1/2 ounces) chicken broth
1 jar (6 ounces) sliced mushrooms, drained
1/2 cup water
1/4 teaspoon salt
1/4 cup minced fresh parsley

1 In a large saucepan, saute the onion, rice and spaghetti in butter until onion is tender and spaghetti is golden brown.

2 Stir in the broth, mushrooms, water and salt. Bring to a boil. Reduce heat; cover and simmer for 20 minutes or until rice is tender. Remove from the heat; let stand for 10 minutes. Fluff with a fork; stir in parsley.

YIELD: 6-8 servings.

APPLE-WALNUT TOSSED SALAD

MARY WALTON, KELSO, WASHINGTON
The pretty, flavorful cranberry dressing for this fall salad is also good for gift-giving.

PREP/TOTAL TIME: 25 min.

1/4 cup red wine vinegar
1/4 cup fresh cranberries
2 tablespoons honey
1 tablespoon sugar
1 tablespoon chopped red onion
1/4 teaspoon salt
1/4 teaspoon pepper
3/4 cup vegetable oil
2 packages (5 ounces each) spring mix salad greens
3 medium Red Delicious apples, thinly sliced
1 cup chopped walnuts, toasted

1 For cranberry vinaigrette, combine the first seven ingredients in a blender; cover and process until blended. While processing, gradually add oil in a steady stream.

2 Transfer to a serving dish. In a large bowl, toss the salad greens, apples and walnuts. Serve with vinaigrette.

YIELD: 8 servings.

NO-COOK CRANBERRY RELISH

ELEANOR SLIMAK, CHICAGO, ILLINOIS
This relish is a tangy addition when it's served with chicken or ham, and makes a plate look so pretty! To make more than one serving, simply multiply the recipe by the amount of servings desired.

PREP: 5 min. + chilling
    1/2 cup fresh or frozen cranberries
    1/4 medium orange, peeled
      1 tablespoon sugar

1 In a blender, combine all the ingredients; cover and process until coarsely chopped. Cover and chill for 30 minutes or until ready to serve.

YIELD: 1 serving.

CREAMED CAULIFLOWER

PEGGIE DE CHICK, AUBURN, NEW YORK
This is a Hungarian recipe from my mother. It's easy to make and flavorful. Even those who don't normally care for cauliflower can't pass it up prepared this way.

PREP: 15 min. BAKE: 25 min.
      1 medium head cauliflower, broken into florets
        (about 7 cups)
  1-1/2 teaspoons salt, divided
    1/2 cup dry bread crumbs, divided
      1 cup half-and-half cream
      1 tablespoon butter
Minced fresh parsley, optional

1 Place the cauliflower in a saucepan; add 1 in of water and 1 teaspoon salt. Bring to a boil. Reduce heat. Cover and simmer for 6-7 minutes or until crisp-tender; drain.

2 Grease the bottom and sides of a 2-qt. baking dish; sprinkle with 2 tablespoons bread crumbs. Add cauliflower. Pour cream over top. Dot with butter; sprinkle with remaining salt and bread crumbs.

3 Bake, uncovered, at 350° for 25-30 minutes or until the cauliflower is tender. Garnish with parsley if desired.

YIELD: 6-8 servings.

HERB POTATO ROLLS

LONNA SMITH, WOODRUFF, WISCONSIN
My grandma always made these rolls. She herself enjoyed them as a child in Germany. I practiced for years before I finally perfected the recipe! It's a real winner!

PREP: 30 min. + rising BAKE: 30 min.
      5 to 5-1/2 cups all-purpose flour
      1 cup mashed potato flakes
      2 packages (1/4 ounce each) active dry yeast
      1 tablespoon sugar
      1 tablespoon minced chives
      2 teaspoons salt
      2 teaspoons minced fresh parsley
      2 cups milk
    1/2 cup sour cream
      2 eggs

1 In a large bowl, combine 3 cups flour, potato flakes, yeast, sugar, chives, salt and parsley. In a small saucepan, heat milk and sour cream to 120°-130° add to dry ingredients. Beat on medium speed for 2 minutes. Add eggs and 1/2 cup flour; beat 2 minutes longer. Stir in enough remaining flour to form a soft dough.

2 Turn onto a floured surface; knead until smooth and elastic, about 6-8 minutes. Place in a greased bowl, turning once to grease top. Cover and let rise in a warm place until doubled, about 45 minutes.

3 Punch dough down. Turn onto a lightly floured surface; divide into 24 pieces. Shape each into a roll. Place in a greased 13-in. x 9-in. baking pan. Cover and let rise until doubled, about 35 minutes.

4 Bake at 375° for 30-35 minutes or until golden brown. Remove to wire racks.

YIELD: 2 dozen.

AUTUMN TOSSED SALAD

EDIE DESPAIN, LOGAN, UTAH

When you take this wonderful salad to a holiday gathering or serve it at home, you will get rave reviews and many requests for the recipe. The lemon- and mustard-flavored vinaigrette is delicious, and the cashews add delicous crunch. And the fall flavor of apple, pear and cranberries are a natural combination. The dressing keeps for up to a week in the refrigerator.

PREP: 30 min. + chilling

- 1/2 cup lemon juice
- 1/2 cup sugar
- 2 teaspoons finely chopped onion
- 1 teaspoon Dijon mustard
- 1/2 teaspoon salt
- 2/3 cup vegetable oil
- 1 tablespoon poppy seeds
- 1 bunch romaine, torn
- 1 cup (4 ounces) shredded Swiss cheese
- 1 cup unsalted cashews
- 1 medium apple, chopped
- 1 medium pear, chopped
- 1/4 cup dried cranberries

1 In a blender, combine the lemon juice, sugar, finely chopped onion, Dijon mustard and salt. While processing, gradually add the oil in a steady stream. Stir in the poppy seeds. Transfer to a small pitcher or bowl. Cover and refrigerate for 1 hour or until chilled.

2 In a large salad bowl, combine the romaine, Swiss cheese, cashews, apple, pear and cranberries. Drizzle with the dressing and toss to coat.

YIELD: 10 servings.

SWEET POTATO BAKE

PAM HOLLOWAY, MARION, LOUISIANA

This is an easy dish to prepare and is a perfect addition to that special holiday meal. The topping is flavorful and adds a nice contrast of textures.

PREP: 35 min. **BAKE:** 20 min. + standing

- 7 large sweet potatoes (about 6 pounds), peeled and cubed
- 1/4 cup butter
- 1/2 cup orange marmalade
- 1/4 cup orange juice
- 1/4 cup packed brown sugar
- 2 teaspoons salt
- 1 teaspoon ground ginger

TOPPING:
- 12 oatmeal cookies, crumbled
- 6 tablespoons butter, softened

1 Place sweet potatoes in a Dutch oven and cover with water. Bring to a boil. Reduce heat; cover and cook just for 10-15 minutes or until tender. Drain

2 Mash potatoes with butter. Add the marmalade, orange juice, brown sugar, salt and ginger. Transfer to a greased 13-in. x 9-in. baking dish. Toss cookie crumbs with butter; sprinkle over the top.

3 Bake, uncovered, at 400° for 20 minutes or until browned. Let stand for 15 minutes before serving.

YIELD: 10-12 servings.

CRANBERRY WALDORF SALAD

BARBARA MCFETERS, WILSONVILLE, OREGON

A touch of honey gives this simple salad a bit of sweetness while chopped apple and celery provide crunch. Best of all, it takes mere minutes to toss together for a quick lunch or side dish.

PREP: 15 min. + chilling

- 1 large apple, chopped
- 2/3 cup dried cranberries
- 1 celery rib, diced
- 2 tablespoons mayonnaise
- 1 tablespoon honey

1 In a small bowl, combine the apple, cranberries and celery. Combine mayonnaise and honey; pour over apple mixture and toss to coat. Cover and refrigerate for 30 minutes or until serving.

YIELD: 2 servings.

HARVEST SQUASH MEDLEY

RUTH COWLEY, PIPE CREEK, TEXAS

To me, cooking is an art, and I love trying new recipes. This one dresses up baked butternut squash, sweet potatoes and apples with citrus and spices.

PREP: 25 min. **BAKE:** 1 hour

- 6 cups water
- 1 butternut squash, peeled, seeded and cut into 3/4-inch pieces
- 2 medium sweet potatoes, peeled and cut into 3/4-inch pieces
- 1/4 cup honey
- 1/4 cup orange juice
- 3 tablespoons butter
- 1 tablespoon grated orange peel
- 1/2 teaspoon ground cinnamon
- 1/8 teaspoon ground nutmeg
- 2 small apples, peeled and sliced
- 1/2 cup chopped walnuts, toasted

1 In a large saucepan, bring water to a boil. Add the squash and return to a boil. Reduce the heat; cover and simmer for 10 minutes. Drain. Place squash and sweet potatoes in a greased 13-in. x 9-in. baking dish.

2 In a small saucepan, combine the honey, orange juice, butter, orange peel, cinnamon and nutmeg. Bring to a boil, stirring constantly. Pour over squash and potatoes.

3 Cover and bake at 350° for 30 minutes, stirring occasionally. Uncover; stir in apples. Bake 30-35 minutes longer or until tender, stirring occasionally. Sprinkle with walnuts.

YIELD: 10 servings.

CREAMY BROCCOLI WITH CASHEWS

KAREN ANN BLAND, GOVE, KANSAS

Looking for a holiday side dish that's something special? The sour-cream sauce in this broccoli casserole makes it a little different from the usual, and the cashews lend a nice crunch. It's great with a variety of entrees.

PREP/TOTAL TIME: 20 min.

- 9 cups fresh broccoli florets
- 1/4 cup chopped onion
- 2 tablespoons butter
- 1 cup (8 ounces) sour cream
- 2 teaspoons honey
- 1 teaspoon cider vinegar
- 1/2 teaspoon salt
- 1/2 teaspoon paprika
- 1/2 cup coarsely chopped cashews

1 Place the broccoli in a steamer basket; place in a large saucepan over 1 in. of water. Bring to a boil; cover and steam for 3-4 minutes or until crisp-tender.

2 Meanwhile, in a small skillet, saute onion in butter until tender. Remove from the heat; stir in the sour cream, honey, vinegar, salt and paprika.

3 Transfer broccoli to a serving bowl. Add sour cream mixture and toss to coat. Sprinkle with cashews.

YIELD: 6 servings.

GRANOLA RAISIN BREAD

PATRICIA NELSON, KENOSHA, WISCONSIN
Made with granola, oats, raisins and honey, this bread has a subtle sweetness. It's so delightful that friends often request the recipe. Slices of the crusty loaf are especially good toasted. If you prefer a softer crust, rub margarine or butter on the loaf while it's warm.

PREP: 10 min. BAKE: 3-4 hours
1-2/3 cups water (70° to 80°)
1/3 cup honey
2 tablespoons butter
1-1/2 teaspoons salt
3-1/2 cups bread flour
1 cup quick-cooking oats
1 tablespoon active dry yeast
1 cup granola
3/4 cup golden raisins

1 In bread machine pan, place the first seven ingredients in order suggested by manufacturer. Select basic bread setting. Choose crust color and loaf size if available.

2 Bake according to bread machine directions (check dough after 5 minutes of mixing; add 1 to 2 tablespoons of water or flour if needed). Just before the final kneading (your machine may audibly signal this), add the granola and raisins.

YIELD: 1 loaf (2 pounds, 16 slices each).

APPLE CABBAGE SLAW

LUCILE PROCTOR, PANGUITCH, UTAH
Chopped apple adds fruity sweetness, color and crunch to the tangy cabbage in this flavorful slaw. It's a refreshing side dish anytime of the year. Mom stored apples and cabbage in the root cellar, so she fixed this dish frequently to feed our big family. It's simple to make, and always goes over well at potlucks.

PREP/TOTAL TIME: 15 min.
6 cups shredded cabbage
3 medium red apples, chopped
1 can (5 ounces) evaporated milk
1/4 cup lemon juice
2 tablespoons sugar
2 teaspoons grated onion
1 teaspoon celery seed
1/2 teaspoon salt, optional
Dash pepper

1 In a large bowl, toss the cabbage and apples. In a small bowl, combine the remaining ingredients. Pour over cabbage mixture and toss to coat. Refrigerate until serving.

YIELD: 10 servings.

LENTIL BREAD

MIKE BUESCHER, FT. WAYNE, INDIANA
Lentils pack a little extra protein and fiber to this fragrant and flavorful bread. I grew up on a farm where bread was baked weekly...and have been making my own bread for over 20 years. I like to experiment with all types of grains and flours to make very hearty loaves. This is a favorite.

PREP: 70 min. + rising BAKE: 35 min.
3/4 cup lentils, rinsed
1-1/2 cups water
4-1/2 teaspoons finely chopped onion
1 garlic clove, minced
2 packages (1/4 ounce each) active dry yeast
1 cup warm water (110° to 115°)
1-1/2 cups warm fat-free milk (110° to 115°)
1/4 cup olive oil
1/4 cup sugar
1 tablespoon grated Parmesan cheese
1 tablespoon salt
1 cup whole wheat flour
6 to 7 cups bread flour

1 In a saucepan, combine lentils, water, onion and garlic; bring to a boil. Reduce heat; cover and simmer for 30 minutes or until lentils are tender. Cool slightly. Transfer mixture to a blender or food processor; process until smooth. Cool to 110°-115°.

2 In a large bowl, dissolve yeast in warm water. Add the milk, lentil mixture, oil, sugar, Parmesan, salt, whole wheat flour and 3 cups bread flour. Beat until smooth. Stir in enough remaining bread flour to form a soft dough. Turn onto a floured surface; knead until smooth and elastic, about 6-8 minutes. Place in a greased bowl, turning once to grease top. Cover and let rise in a warm place until doubled, about 1 hour.

3 Punch dough down. Turn onto a lightly floured surface. Divide into thirds; shape into loaves. Place in three greased 9-in. x 5-in. loaf pans. Cover and let rise until doubled, about 30 minutes. Bake at 375° for 35-45 minutes or until golden brown. Remove from pans to wire racks to cool.

YIELD: 3 loaves (12 slices each).

210 207 214 206

ENTREES

213

TURKEY LEG POT ROAST

RICK AND VEGAS PEARSON, CADILLAC, MICHIGAN
Well-seasoned turkey legs and a variety of tender vegetables make this meal ideal for a crisp fall day. Moist and satisfying, the recipe couldn't be more comforting!

PREP: 15 min. **COOK:** 5 hours
- 3 medium potatoes, peeled and quartered
- 2 cups fresh baby carrots
- 2 celery ribs, cut into 2-1/2-inch pieces
- 1 medium onion, peeled and quartered
- 3 garlic cloves, peeled and quartered
- 1/2 cup chicken broth
- 3 turkey drumsticks (about 1/2 pound each)
- 2 teaspoons seasoned salt
- 1 teaspoon dried thyme
- 1 teaspoon dried parsley flakes
- 1/4 teaspoon pepper

1 In a greased 5-qt. slow cooker, combine the first six ingredients. Place the drumsticks over the vegetables. Sprinkle with the seasoned salt, thyme, parsley and pepper. Cover; cook on low for 5 to 5-1/2 hours or until a meat thermometer reads 180°.

YIELD: 3 servings.

BUYING TURKEY DRUMSTICKS
Here are a few things to consider before purchasing fresh turkey legs at the grocery store. Make sure they are bright in color (not brown) and firm to the touch. Avoid ones with pin feathers, because they're difficult to remove. And be sure to purchase drumsticks that are similar in size so they finish cooking at the same time.

CRANBERRY PORK CHOPS

JOAN DOBBS, EVANSVILLE, ILLINOIS
This meal is a proven winner to fix. I never have leftovers. It combines two of my favorite flavors—pork and cranberries.

PREP: 30 min. **COOK:** 35 min.
- 1-1/2 cups sugar
- 1-3/4 cups water, divided
- 1 package (12 ounces) fresh or frozen cranberries
- 1/2 cup barbecue sauce
- 8 bone-in pork loin chops (1/2 to 3/4 inch thick and 8 ounces each)
- Salt and pepper to taste
- 2 tablespoons canola oil
- 2 tablespoons cornstarch
- 1/4 cup cold water

1 In a large saucepan, combine the sugar and 1-1/2 cups water. Cook and stir over medium heat until the sugar is dissolved. Bring to a boil; boil, uncovered, for 5 minutes. Add cranberries; cook 5 minutes longer or until the berries pop. Skim off foam if necessary. Stir in the barbecue sauce and remaining water; set aside.

2 Season the pork chops with salt and pepper. In a large skillet over medium heat, brown the chops on both sides in oil; drain. Pour the cranberry sauce over chops. Cover and simmer for 35-40 minutes or until a meat thermometer reads 160°. Remove chops and keep warm.

3 Combine the cornstarch and cold water until smooth; add to the skillet. Bring to a boil; cook and stir for 2 minutes or until thickened. Serve with pork chops.

YIELD: 8 servings.

EDITOR'S NOTE: One 14-ounce can of whole-berry cranberry sauce may be substituted for the sugar, cranberries and 1-1/2 cups water. Combine cranberry sauce with the barbecue sauce and 1/4 cup water; use as directed in recipe.

HEARTY PASTA CASSEROLE

TASTE OF HOME TEST KITCHEN
Loaded with colorful, flavorful roasted veggies, this recipe became an instant hit with us when it was developed in our Test Kitchen. This rustic, Italian-inspired casserole is also the perfect main dish "to go," because it transports easily and retains heat well. A great make-ahead meal, too!

PREP: 45 min. **BAKE:** 35 min.

    2   cups cubed peeled butternut squash
    1/2 pound fresh brussels sprouts, halved
    1   medium onion, cut into wedges
    2   teaspoons olive oil
    1   package (13-1/4 ounces) whole wheat penne pasta
    1   pound Italian turkey sausage links, casings removed
    2   garlic cloves, minced
    2   cans (14-1/2 ounces each) Italian stewed tomatoes
    2   tablespoons tomato paste
  1-1/2 cups (6 ounces) shredded part-skim mozzarella cheese,
         divided
    1/3 cup shredded Asiago cheese, divided

1 In a large bowl, combine the squash, brussels sprouts and onion; drizzle with oil and toss to coat. Spread vegetables in a single layer in two 15-in. x 10-in. x 1-in. baking pans coated with cooking spray. Bake, uncovered, at 425° for 30-40 minutes or until tender.

2 Meanwhile, cook pasta according to package directions. In a large nonstick skillet, cook sausage and garlic over medium heat until meat is no longer pink; drain. Add tomatoes and tomato paste; cook and stir over medium heat until slightly thickened, about 5 minutes.

3 Drain pasta and return to the pan. Add the sausage mixture, 1 cup mozzarella, 1/4 cup Asiago and roasted vegetables.

4 Transfer to a 13-in. x 9-in. baking dish coated with cooking spray. Cover and bake at 350° for 30-40 minutes or until heated through. Uncover; sprinkle with remaining cheeses. Bake 5 minutes longer or until cheese is melted.

YIELD: 8 servings.

AUTUMN BEEF POT ROAST

RACHEL KOISTINEN, HAYTI, SOUTH DAKOTA
Rely on your slow cooker to help prepare this moist pot roast. I thicken the juices to make a pleasing apple gravy that's wonderful over the beef slices and onions. It's a surefire recipe for a satisfying Sunday dinner.

PREP: 30 min. **COOK:** 5 hours + standing

    1   beef sirloin tip roast (3 pounds), cut in half
    1   cup water
    1   teaspoon seasoned salt
    1/2 teaspoon reduced-sodium soy sauce
    1/2 teaspoon Worcestershire sauce
    1/4 teaspoon garlic powder
    1   large tart apple, quartered
    1   large onion, sliced
    2   tablespoons cornstarch
    2   tablespoons cold water
    1/8 teaspoon browning sauce

1 In a large nonstick skillet coated with cooking spray, brown roast on all sides. Transfer to a 5-qt. slow cooker. Add water to the skillet, stirring to loosen any browned bits; pour over roast. Sprinkle with seasoned salt, soy sauce, Worcestershire sauce and garlic powder. Top with apple and onion.

2 Cover; cook on low for 5-6 hours or until the meat is tender.

3 Remove roast and onion; let stand for 15 minutes before slicing. Strain cooking liquid into a saucepan, discarding apple. Bring the liquid to a boil; cook until reduced to 2 cups, about 15 minutes. Combine cornstarch and cold water until smooth; stir in browning sauce. Stir into the cooking liquid. Bring to a boil; cook and stir for 2 minutes or until thickened. Serve with the beef and onion.

YIELD: 8 servings with leftovers.

VENISON POT ROAST

DEBBIE PHILLIPS, PITTSBURG, TEXAS

This hearty dish is full of tender meat and wonderful seasonings. Game is plentiful around our home, and my family could eat this satisfying meal weekly.

PREP: 20 min. **COOK:** 3 hours

- 3 tablespoons all-purpose flour
- 1/2 teaspoon salt
- 1/2 teaspoon pepper
- 1 boneless venison roast (3 to 4 pounds)
- 2 tablespoons canola oil
- 1 cup apple juice or cider
- 1 cup beef broth
- 1 medium onion, sliced
- 1 teaspoon dried thyme
- 1 bay leaf
- 8 small potatoes, peeled
- 6 medium carrots, cut into 2-inch pieces
- 4 celery ribs, cut into 2-inch pieces

1 Combine the first three ingredients; rub over roast. In a Dutch oven, brown roast on all sides in oil. Add apple juice, broth, onion, thyme and bay leaf. Bring to a boil; reduce heat. Cover and simmer for 2 hours.

2 Add the potatoes, carrots and celery; cover and simmer for 1 hour or until meat and vegetables are tender. Discard bay leaf. Thicken pan juices if desired.

YIELD: 6-8 servings.

COMPANY TURKEY POTPIE

TASTE OF HOME TEST KITCHEN

Do you enjoy serving comfort food to your friends and family? If so, you'll want to make this posh potpie, filled with cooked turkey breast and an unusual assortment of autumn vegetables combined in a creamy herb sauce. Best of all, there's no crust to make—just top with prepared phyllo dough.

PREP: 1 hour **BAKE:** 10 min.

- 1/2 pound sliced baby portobello mushrooms
- 2 shallots, chopped
- 2 teaspoons olive oil
- 2 cups cubed peeled butternut squash
- 1 cup chopped sweet red pepper
- 1/2 cup sliced fennel bulb
- 2 cups reduced-sodium chicken broth, divided
- 1/3 cup all-purpose flour
- 1/2 cup 2% milk
- 3 cups cubed cooked turkey breast
- 2 tablespoons sherry or additional reduced-sodium chicken broth
- 1 teaspoon rubbed sage
- 1/2 teaspoon salt
- 1/2 teaspoon dried thyme
- 1/4 teaspoon pepper
- 10 sheets phyllo dough (14 inches x 9 inches)

Refrigerated butter-flavored spray

1 In a large skillet, saute mushrooms and shallots in oil until tender. Add the squash, red pepper and fennel; saute 5 minutes longer. Add 1/4 cup broth. Cover and cook over medium-low heat until vegetables are tender, about 15 minutes.

2 Sprinkle flour over vegetables; cook and stir for 1 minute. Gradually add milk and remaining broth. Bring to a boil; cook and stir for 1-2 minutes or until thickened. Stir in turkey, sherry or additional broth, sage, salt, thyme and pepper. Transfer to a 2-qt. baking dish coated with cooking spray.

3 Stack all 10 phyllo sheets. Roll up, starting with a long side; cut into 1/2-in. strips. Place strips in a large bowl and toss to separate; spritz with butter-flavored spray. Arrange over turkey mixture; spritz again. Bake, uncovered, at 425° for 10-15 minutes or until golden brown.

YIELD: 6 servings.

BRAT SAUERKRAUT SUPPER

ANN CHRISTENSEN, MESA, ARIZONA

This stick-to-your-ribs German dish is sure to satisfy even the biggest appetite at your house. Sliced apple and apple juice lend mellowing sweetness to the tangy sauerkraut, flavorful bratwurst, red potatoes and bacon. Serve it with slices of hearty rye bread.

PREP: 15 min. **COOK:** 4 hours

- 1 jar (32 ounces) sauerkraut, rinsed and well drained
- 2 medium red potatoes, peeled, halved and cut into thin slices
- 1 medium tart apple, peeled and cut into thick slices
- 1 small onion, chopped
- 1/2 cup apple juice
- 1/4 cup water
- 2 tablespoons brown sugar
- 1 teaspoon chicken bouillon granules
- 1 teaspoon caraway seeds
- 1 garlic clove, minced
- 1 bay leaf
- 1 pound fully cooked bratwurst links
- 6 bacon strips, cooked and crumbled

1 In a 5-qt. slow cooker, combine the first 11 ingredients. Top with bratwurst. Cover and cook on high for 4-5 hours or until potatoes are tender. Discard bay leaf. Sprinkle with bacon.

YIELD: 6 servings.

HOORAY FOR SAUERKRAUT

The Ohio Sauerkraut Festival in Waynesville, Ohio is held the second week in October every year and attracts about 250,000 people from every state in the nation. Over seven tons of sauerkraut are served, along with other delicious foods. The festival is also well-known for its excellent craft booths and entertainment.

CIDER-BAKED COUNTRY HAM

MARION LOWERY, MEDFORD, OREGON

This is the best ham I've ever made. I serve it often to family and friends, and each time I get requests for the recipe.

PREP: 1-1/4 hours **BAKE:** 1 hour + standing

- 1/2 bone-in fully cooked ham (5 to 7 pounds)
- 2 quarts apple cider or apple juice
- 1-1/2 teaspoons whole peppercorns
- 1 bay leaf
- Whole cloves
- 1 cup applesauce
- 1 tablespoon prepared horseradish
- 2 teaspoons ground mustard

1 Place the ham in a Dutch oven or large kettle. Add cider, peppercorns and bay leaf. Add enough water just to cover; bring to a boil. Reduce heat; cover and simmer for 1 hour.

2 Drain, reserving 3 cups cooking liquid; discard peppercorns and bay leaf. Remove skin from ham if desired; score surface with shallow cuts, making diamond shapes. Insert whole cloves in the center of each diamond. Combine the applesauce, horseradish and mustard; rub over ham.

3 Place ham on a rack in shallow roasting pan; pour reserved liquid into pan. Bake, uncovered, at 350° for 1 hour or until a meat thermometer reads 140°. Remove from the oven; cover with foil and let stand for 10-15 minutes before slicing.

YIELD: 16-20 servings.

RATATOUILLE WITH SAUSAGE

DIANE HALFERTY, TUCSON, ARIZONA

We've enjoyed this hearty and flavorful dish for years. I concocted it when we lived on a large farm and had lots of fresh veggies and sausage available. In a pinch, prepared spaghetti sauce can be used in place of the fresh tomatoes.

PREP: 25 min. **BAKE:** 30 min.

   1 medium eggplant, peeled
   4 small zucchini, cut into 1/2-inch slices
1/3 cup all-purpose flour
   2 to 4 tablespoons olive oil, divided
   2 large onions, sliced
   3 garlic cloves, minced
   8 uncooked Italian sausage links (about 2 pounds)
   4 medium green peppers, julienned
   4 medium tomatoes, coarsely chopped
1/4 cup water
1/2 cup minced fresh basil or 8 teaspoons dried basil
   2 tablespoons minced fresh oregano or 2 teaspoons dried oregano
   2 tablespoons minced fresh thyme or 2 teaspoons dried thyme
   1 teaspoon salt
1/4 teaspoon pepper
   1 cup (4 ounces) shredded part-skim mozzarella cheese

1 Cut eggplant into 2-in. x 1/2-in. strips; place in a bowl. Add zucchini and flour; toss to coat.

2 In a large skillet, heat 1 tablespoon of oil over medium heat; cook eggplant and zucchini in small batches until lightly browned, add oil as needed. Transfer vegetables to a greased shallow 3-qt. baking dish.

3 In the same skillet, saute onions and garlic until tender; spoon over eggplant mixture. Brown sausage in the skillet; drain. Cover and cook over low heat for 15-20 minutes or until no longer pink.

4 Meanwhile, in another skillet, saute the green peppers for 3 minutes. Add tomatoes, water and seasonings; cook on high for 2 minutes. Reduce heat; cover and simmer for 5 minutes. Drain sausage; place over onions. Top with green pepper mixture.

5 Bake, uncovered, at 350° for 20 minutes. Sprinkle with cheese; bake 10 minutes longer or until cheese is melted.

YIELD: 8 cups ratatouille and 8 sausages.

CHICKEN WITH CREAMY APPLE-MUSHROOM SAUCE

KATHERINE MAJOR, KINGSTON, ONTARIO

When I found this recipe, I lightened it up a bit by using evaporated milk instead of cream. Everyone who tries it loves the smooth sauce, tender chicken and mild apple flavor. They don't miss the heavy cream at all.

PREP: 15 min. **COOK:** 30 min.

   4 boneless skinless chicken breast halves (4 ounces each)
   1 tablespoon olive oil
   3 cups sliced fresh mushrooms
   1 medium onion, sliced
   2 garlic cloves, minced
1-1/2 cups reduced-sodium chicken broth
   1 teaspoon dried tarragon
1/2 teaspoon pepper
1/8 teaspoon salt
   2 cups thinly sliced peeled tart apples (about 2 medium)
   2 tablespoons cornstarch
3/4 reduced-fat evaporated milk, divided
   1 teaspoon minced fresh parsley

1 In a nonstick skillet, brown the chicken in olive oil on both sides. Remove and keep warm. In the same skillet, saute the sliced mushrooms, onion and garlic until tender. Stir in the broth, tarragon, pepper and salt; bring to a boil.

2 Add apples and reserved chicken. Reduce heat; cover and simmer until a meat thermometer reads 170°. Remove chicken to a serving platter.

3 Combine the cornstarch and 1/4 cup milk until smooth; stir in the remaining milk. Add to skillet. Bring to a boil; cook and stir for 2 minutes or until thickened. Serve with the chicken; sprinkle with parsley.

YIELD: 4 servings.

> **AN APPLE A DAY**
>
> Although apples are available all year-round, they each have their own peak season. Select apples that are firm and that have a smooth, unblemished skin free from bruises. Store unwashed apples in the refrigerator away from other vegetables with strong aromas. Apples can be refrigerated for up to 6 weeks.
>
> To prevent apple slices from turning brown, rub them with lemon or lime juice. This coats the apple slices and prevents the air from turning them brown. They store nicely in a resealable plastic bag in the refrigerator.

CRANBERRY MEAT LOAF

MARCIA HARRIS, STEVENSVILLE, MICHIGAN

Everyone in my family loves this unusual recipe, which features both cranberry sauce and cranberries. It's especially nice during fall and the Christmas season.

PREP: 15 min. **BAKE:** 1-1/4 hours

- 2 eggs
- 3/4 cup crushed saltines (about 22 crackers)
- 1/2 cup whole-berry cranberry sauce
- 1/4 cup fresh or frozen cranberries, thawed
- 1/4 cup packed brown sugar
- 2 tablespoons chopped onion
- 1-1/2 teaspoons salt
- 1/8 teaspoon pepper
- 1-1/2 pounds ground beef
- 1/2 pound ground ham
- 1/2 cup barbecue sauce, optional

Bay leaves and fresh cranberries, optional

1 In a large bowl, combine the first eight ingredients. Crumble beef and ham over mixture and mix well. Pat into a greased 9-in. x 5-in. loaf pan. Bake, uncovered, at 350° for 1-1/4 hours or until a meat thermometer reads 160°.

2 During the last 15 minutes of baking, baste the meat loaf with barbecue sauce if desired. Garnish with bay leaves and cranberries if desired. Discard bay leaves before slicing.

YIELD: 4-5 servings.

PORK WITH SAVORY QUINCE COMPOTE

TASTE OF HOME TEST KITCHEN

White wine boosts the warm flavors of quince and rosemary in this sweet, savory compote or chutney for pork tenderloin. This dressed-up dish from our Test Kitchen makes a sophisticated but simple entree for special guests.

PREP: 30 min. **COOK:** 40 min.

- 3/4 teaspoon salt
- 1/2 teaspoon dried thyme
- 1/4 teaspoon ground ginger
- 1/4 teaspoon pepper
- 2 pork tenderloins (1 pound each)

COMPOTE:

- 1 small onion, chopped
- 1 tablespoon butter
- 2 medium quinces, peeled and cut into 1/2-inch pieces
- 1 cup reduced-sodium chicken broth
- 1/2 cup white wine or additional reduced-sodium chicken broth
- 1/4 cup honey
- 2 teaspoons minced fresh rosemary or 1/2 teaspoon dried rosemary, crushed
- 1 bay leaf
- 1/2 teaspoon salt
- 1/4 teaspoon pepper

1 Combine the salt, thyme, ginger and pepper; sprinkle over pork. Place on a rack in a shallow roasting pan lined with heavy-duty foil. Bake, uncovered, at 425° for 30-35 minutes or until a meat thermometer reads 160°.

2 Meanwhile, for compote, in a large nonstick skillet over medium heat, saute the onion in butter until tender. Stir in remaining ingredients; bring to a boil. Reduce heat; cover and simmer for 8 minutes. Uncover; simmer 25-30 minutes longer or until quinces are tender and liquid is thickened. Discard bay leaf.

3 Let the pork stand for 5 minutes before slicing. Serve with the quince compote.

YIELD: 6 servings (1-1/2 cups compote).

ROASTED VEGGIE PASTA SALAD

TASTE OF HOME TEST KITCHEN
Oven-roasted vegetables mixed with pasta and salad dressing make a tasty meatless entree.

PREP: 20 min. **BAKE:** 30 min.

- 1 small butternut squash, peeled and cut into 1-inch pieces
- 2 cups water
- 1 medium eggplant, cut into 1-inch pieces
- 1 large zucchini, cut into 1-inch pieces
- 1 medium sweet red pepper, cut into 1-inch pieces
- 1 medium red onion, cut into 1-inch pieces
- 1/2 cup olive oil
- 1 teaspoon dried marjoram
- 1 package (16 ounces) tricolor spiral pasta
- 1/2 cup Italian salad dressing
- 1/4 cup minced fresh basil
- 1 teaspoon salt
- 1/2 teaspoon pepper

1 Place squash and water in a microwave-safe bowl. Cover and cook for 10 minutes or until tender; drain.

2 Arrange the squash, eggplant, zucchini, red pepper and onion in a greased 15-in. x 10-in. x 1-in. baking pan. In a small bowl, whisk the oil and marjoram until combined. Drizzle over the vegetables.

3 Bake, uncovered, at 450° for 30 minutes or until tender. Meanwhile, cook pasta according to package directions; drain.

4 In a large bowl, combine the pasta and roasted vegetables. Stir in the salad dressing, basil, salt and pepper. Serve warm or at room temperature.

YIELD: 8 servings.

GRANDPA'S AUTUMN WAFFLES

JUNE FORMANEK, BELLE PLAINE, IOWA
These waffles make a delicious breakfast on a cold Iowa morning. This is my father's original recipe, and I've used it all my life. I've handed it down to my seven children, and I'm sure they'll pass it on to their own children!

PREP/TOTAL TIME: 30 min.

- 2 tablespoons butter
- 1/4 cup packed brown sugar
- 2 medium tart apples, sliced
- 1/4 cup raisins
- 1/4 cup chopped pecans
- 2 cups all-purpose flour
- 2 teaspoons sugar
- 2 teaspoons baking powder
- 1/4 teaspoon salt
- 3 eggs
- 3/4 cup milk
- 3/4 cup half-and-half cream
- 5 tablespoons butter, melted

Maple syrup, warmed

1 In a large skillet, melt butter and brown sugar. Add the apples, raisins and pecans. Cook and stir over medium-low heat for 3-4 minutes or until apples are tender; keep warm.

2 In a large bowl, combine the flour, sugar, baking powder and salt. In another large bowl, whisk the eggs, milk, cream and butter; stir into dry ingredients just until moistened.

3 Bake in a preheated waffle iron according to manufacturer's directions until golden brown. Serve with the apple topping and maple syrup.

YIELD: 5 waffles (about 7-1/2 inches each).

PORK AND PEAR STIR-FRY

BETTY PHILLIPS, FRENCH CREEK, WEST VIRGINIA
I've served this full-flavored stir-fry for years, always to rave reviews. Tender pork and ripe pears make a sweet combination, and a spicy sauce adds plenty of zip. This dish is a must for help-yourself luncheons or fellowship dinners.

PREP/TOTAL TIME: 20 min.

- 1/2 cup plum preserves or preserves of your choice
- 3 tablespoons soy sauce
- 2 tablespoons lemon juice
- 1 tablespoon prepared horseradish
- 2 teaspoons cornstarch
- 1/4 teaspoon crushed red pepper flakes
- 1 medium sweet yellow or green pepper, julienned
- 1/2 to 1 teaspoon minced fresh gingerroot
- 1 tablespoon canola oil
- 3 medium ripe pears, peeled and sliced
- 1 pound pork tenderloin, cut into 1/4-inch strips
- 1 can (8 ounces) sliced water chestnuts, drained
- 1-1/2 cups fresh or frozen snow peas
- 1 tablespoon sliced almonds, toasted

Hot cooked rice

1 In a small bowl, combine the first six ingredients; set aside. In a skillet or wok, stir-fry yellow pepper and ginger in oil for 2 minutes. Add the pears; stir-fry for 1 minute or until pepper is crisp-tender. Remove and keep warm.

2 Stir-fry half of the pork at a time for 1-2 minutes or until meat is no longer pink. Return pear mixture and all of the pork to pan. Add water chestnuts and reserved sauce. Bring to a boil; cook and stir for 2 minutes. Add peas; heat through. Sprinkle with almonds. Serve with rice.

YIELD: 4 servings.

APPLE-DIJON PORK ROAST

CINDY STEFFEN, CEDARBURG, WISCONSIN
This is one of my family's favorite meals for cold-weather comfort. The recipe takes less than five minutes to assemble and is delicious. I like to serve the roast with cooked rice, then use the tangy sauce as a gravy for both.

PREP: 15 min. **COOK:** 4 hours

- 1 boneless whole pork loin roast (2 to 3 pounds)
- 1 can (14-1/2 ounces) chicken broth
- 1 cup unsweetened apple juice
- 1/2 cup Dijon mustard
- 6 tablespoons cornstarch
- 6 tablespoons cold water

1 Cut the roast in half; place in a 5-qt. slow cooker. Combine the broth, apple juice and mustard; pour over roast. Cover and cook on low for 4 to 4-1/2 hours or until a meat thermometer reads 160°.

2 Remove roast and keep warm. For gravy, strain cooking juices and skim fat. Pour juices into a small saucepan. Combine cornstarch and water until smooth; gradually stir into juices. Bring to a boil; cook and stir for 2 minutes or until thickened. Serve with the pork.

YIELD: 8 servings.

COOKING PORK

Fresh pork needs only to be cooked to an internal temperature of 160° to 170°. At 160°, the internal color of boneless roasts may be faint pink and bone-in roasts may be slightly pink near the bone. But if the juices run clear, the meat is properly cooked. Correctly cooked pork is juicy and tender.

AUTUMN SAUSAGE CASSEROLE

DIANE BRUNELL, WASHINGTON, MASSACHUSETTS
Apple, raisins and spices give this hearty sausage-rice casserole the taste of autumn. We enjoy it with a green salad on a cold fall day. It would be a nice potluck dish, too—just double the recipe if needed.

PREP: 20 min. BAKE: 25 min.

   1 pound bulk pork sausage
   1 medium apple, peeled and chopped
   1 medium onion, chopped
1/2 cup chopped celery
   3 cups cooked long grain rice
1/2 cup raisins
1/3 cup minced fresh parsley
   1 tablespoon brown sugar
1/2 teaspoon salt
1/4 teaspoon ground allspice
1/4 teaspoon ground cinnamon
1/8 teaspoon pepper

1 In a large skillet, cook the sausage, apple, onion and celery over medium heat until meat is no longer pink; drain. Stir in the remaining ingredients.

2 Transfer to a greased 2-qt. baking dish. Cover and bake at 350° for 25-30 minutes or until heated through.

YIELD: 4-6 servings.

HOMEMADE PORK SAUSAGE

It's easy to make your own pork sausage. It adds delicious flavor to recipes or is great cooked by itself. Simply combine 1 pound ground pork, 1 tablespoon maple syrup, a 1/2 teaspoon each of salt, onion powder, rubbed sage, dried thyme, poultry seasoning and ground nutmeg, and 1/4 teaspoon cayenne pepper.

FRENCH-STYLE CHICKEN

CATHERINE JOHNSTON, STAFFORD, NEW YORK
When I have friends over, I make this classy light recipe and serve with a tossed salad and crisp French bread. Toasted almond slices sprinkled on top add a crunchy, finishing touch.

PREP/TOTAL TIME: 25 min.

   6 boneless skinless chicken breast halves (4 ounces each)
3/4 teaspoon salt-free lemon-pepper seasoning
1-1/3 cups reduced-sodium chicken broth
   3 medium unpeeled apples, cut into wedges
   1 medium onion, thinly sliced
   4 tablespoons apple cider or juice, divided
1/4 teaspoon ground cinnamon
1/8 teaspoon ground nutmeg
   1 tablespoon cornstarch
Minced fresh parsley

1 Sprinkle chicken with lemon-pepper. In a large nonstick skillet coated with cooking spray, cook chicken for 5-6 minutes on each side or until a meat thermometer reads 170°. Remove and keep warm.

2 In same skillet, combine broth, apples, onion, 3 tablespoons cider, cinnamon and nutmeg. Bring to a boil. Combine the cornstarch and remaining cider until smooth; stir into apple mixture. Bring to a boil; cook and stir for 1-2 minutes or until thickened. Top with chicken; sprinkle with parsley.

YIELD: 6 servings.

APPLE-GLAZED PORK CHOPS

TASTE OF HOME TEST KITCHEN
Simple enough for weeknights yet impressive enough for guests, these juicy chops are topped with a glaze of herbs, apple cider and brown sugar. The cooked apple slices and onions will make it a fast favorite in your home.

PREP/TOTAL TIME: 30 min.

    4 bone-in center-cut pork loin chops (3/4 inch thick and 7 ounces each)
    2 tablespoons canola oil
    1 cup apple cider or apple juice
    2 tablespoons brown sugar, divided
    1 teaspoon salt
 1/4 teaspoon dried rosemary, crushed
 1/4 teaspoon dried thyme
    1 tablespoon cornstarch
    1 tablespoon cold water
    2 large tart apples, sliced
 1/2 cup sliced onion
    2 tablespoons butter

1 In a large skillet, brown the pork chops in the oil. Add the apple cider, 1 tablespoon brown sugar, salt, rosemary and thyme. Cover and cook for 7-8 minutes or until a meat thermometer reads 160°. Combine the cornstarch and water until smooth; add to the skillet. Bring to a boil; cook and stir for 1-2 minutes or until thickened.

2 Meanwhile, in small skillet, cook the apples, onion, butter and remaining brown sugar over medium heat for 3-4 minutes or until apples are softened. Serve with pork chops.

YIELD: 4 servings.

BRISKET WITH CRANBERRY GRAVY

NOELLE LABRECQUE, ROUND ROCK, TEXAS
With just a few minutes of hands-on work, this tender beef brisket simmers into a delectable entree. The meat and gravy are great for sandwiches and leftovers the next day.

PREP: 15 min. COOK: 5-1/2 hours

    1 medium onion, sliced
    1 fresh beef brisket (3 pounds), halved
    1 can (16 ounce) jellied cranberry sauce
 1/2 cup cranberry juice concentrate
    2 tablespoons cornstarch
 1/4 cup water

1 Place the sliced onion in a 5-qt. slow cooker; top with brisket. Combine the cranberry sauce and juice concentrate; pour over beef. Cover and cook on low for 5-1/2 to 6 hours or until meat is tender.

2 Remove the brisket and keep warm. Strain the cooking juices, discarding onion; skim fat.

3 In a small saucepan, stir the cornstarch and water together until smooth; stir in cooking juices. Bring to a boil over medium heat, stirring constantly. Cook and stir for 2 minutes or until thickened. Thinly slice the brisket across the grain; serve with the gravy.

YIELD: 12 servings.

CHOPS WITH FRUIT STUFFING

SUZANNE REYES, TUSTIN, CALIFORNIA
The aroma that fills the house as this pork dish simmers is fabulous. All you need to complete the meal is a green vegetable and maybe a loaf of bread. It's impressive enough for company.

PREP: 10 min. **COOK:** 3 hours

- 6 boneless pork loin chops (1/2 inch thick and 4 ounces each)
- 1 tablespoon canola oil
- 1 package (6 ounces) herb stuffing mix
- 2 celery ribs, chopped
- 1 medium tart apple, peeled and chopped
- 1 cup dried cherries or cranberries
- 1/2 cup chopped onion
- 2/3 cup chicken broth
- 1/4 cup butter, melted

1 In a large skillet, brown pork chops in oil on both sides. In a large bowl, combine the remaining ingredients.

2 Place half of the stuffing mixture in a 3-qt. slow cooker. Top with pork and remaining stuffing mixture. Cover and cook on low for 3 hours or until a meat thermometer reads 160°.

YIELD: 6 servings.

TAILGATE SAUSAGES

TASTE OF HOME TEST KITCHEN
You'll need just a handful of ingredients to fix these tasty sandwiches from our Test Kitchen. Fully cooked sausages are stuffed with cheese and a homemade relish, then wrapped in foil so they're easy to transport and a breeze to grill before the game.

PREP/TOTAL TIME: 20 min.

- 1/2 cup giardiniera
- 1/2 teaspoon sugar
- 4 cooked Italian sausage links
- 4 slices provolone cheese, cut into strips
- 4 brat buns or hot dog buns, split

1 In a small food processor, combine the giardiniera and sugar; cover and process until blended. Make a lengthwise slit three-fourths of the way through each sausage to within 1/2 in. of each end. Fill with giardiniera mixture and cheese.

2 Place the sausages in buns; wrap individually in a double thickness of heavy-duty foil (about 12 in. x 10 in.). Grill, uncovered, over medium-hot heat for 8-10 minutes or until heated through and cheese is melted.

YIELD: 4 servings.

EDITOR'S NOTE: Giardiniera, a pickled vegetable mixture, is available in mild and hot varieties and can be found in the Italian or pickle section of your grocery store.

SWEET POTATO HAM BAKE WITH APPLES

AMANDA DENTON, BARRE, VERMONT
A great use for leftover ham, this dish has been served at countless church suppers. A puffy topping covers a mixture of sweet potatoes, ham and apples.

PREP: 20 min. **BAKE:** 35 min.

- 3 medium tart apples, peeled and sliced
- 2 medium sweet potatoes, peeled and thinly sliced
- 3 cups cubed fully cooked ham
- 3 tablespoons brown sugar
- 1/2 teaspoon salt
- 1/4 teaspoon pepper
- 1/4 teaspoon curry powder
- 2 tablespoons cornstarch
- 1/3 cup apple juice
- 1 cup pancake mix
- 1 cup milk
- 2 tablespoons butter, melted
- 1/2 teaspoon ground mustard

1 In a large skillet, combine the apples, sweet potatoes, ham, brown sugar, salt, pepper and curry. Cook over medium heat until apples are crisp-tender; drain. Combine cornstarch and apple juice until smooth; stir into apple mixture. Bring to a boil; cook and stir for 1-2 minutes or until mixture is thickened.

2 Transfer to a greased 2-qt. baking dish. Cover and bake at 375° for 10 minutes or until the sweet potatoes are tender. Meanwhile, in a large bowl, whisk together the pancake mix, milk, butter and mustard; pour over ham mixture.

3 Bake, uncovered, for about 25 minutes or until puffed and golden brown.

YIELD: 8 servings.

TURKEY WITH CRANBERRY-GRAPE SAUCE

MARGUERITE SHAEFFER, SEWELL, NEW JERSEY
Our son-in-law brought home wild turkey, which inspired this delectable main dish. The sauce stirs up quickly...and you can grill the turkey in just minutes.

PREP: 15 min. + marinating BAKE: 15 min.

- 1 teaspoon cornstarch
- 1/2 cup orange juice
- 1/4 cup dried cranberries
- 4-1/2 teaspoons honey
- 1 tablespoon lemon juice
- 2 turkey breast tenderloins (12 ounces each), halved widthwise
- 2 teaspoons olive oil
- 1 teaspoon coarsely ground pepper
- 1/2 teaspoon salt
- 1-1/2 cups green grapes, halved

1 In a small saucepan, combine the first five ingredients until smooth. Bring to a boil; cook and stir for 1-2 minutes or until thickened. Cover and refrigerate.

2 If grilling, coat grill rack with cooking spray before starting the grill. Flatten turkey to 3/4-in. thickness. Combine oil, pepper and salt; rub over both sides of turkey. Grill turkey, covered, over direct medium heat or broil 4-6 in. from the heat for 5-7 minutes on each side or until a meat thermometer reads 170°. Just before serving, stir grapes into sauce. Serve turkey with cranberry-grape sauce.

YIELD: 4 servings.

APPLE PANCAKES WITH CIDER SYRUP

APRIL HARMON, GREENEVILLE, TENNESSEE
These tender pancakes filled with minced apple and raisins are delicious, especially when they are drizzled with apple cider syrup. They're wonderful in the summer or on a cool fall morning. Although they taste decadent, because they are made with whole wheat flour, buttermilk and fruit, it's a satisfying breakfast full of nutritious ingredients. It's a great start to any day!

PREP/TOTAL TIME: 30 min.

- 1/2 cup all-purpose flour
- 1/4 cup whole wheat flour
- 2 teaspoons sugar
- 1/4 teaspoon baking soda
- 1/4 teaspoon salt
- 1/4 teaspoon ground cinnamon
- 2/3 cup minced peeled apple
- 1/4 cup raisins
- 2/3 cup buttermilk
- 1 egg, separated
- 2 teaspoons butter, melted
- 1/4 teaspoon vanilla extract

SYRUP:
- 1/4 cup sugar
- 2 teaspoons cornstarch
- 2/3 cup apple cider or juice
- 1 cinnamon stick (1-1/2 inches)

Dash ground nutmeg
Additional butter, optional

1 In a small bowl, combine the first six ingredients; stir in the minced apple and raisins. Combine the buttermilk, egg yolk, butter and vanilla extract; stir into dry ingredients. In a small bowl, beat egg white until soft peaks form; fold into batter.

2 Pour the batter by heaping 1/4 cupfuls onto a hot griddle coated with cooking spray; turn when bubbles form on top. Cook until the second side is lightly browned.

3 Meanwhile, in a small saucepan, combine sugar, cornstarch and cider until smooth; add the cinnamon stick. Bring to a boil over medium heat; cook and stir for 2 minutes or until thickened. Discard cinnamon stick. Stir nutmeg into syrup. Serve pancakes with warm syrup and additional butter if desired.

YIELD: 6 pancakes (2/3 cup syrup).

STORING WHOLE WHEAT FLOUR
Because it contains the wheat germ, whole wheat flour has a higher oil content and can go rancid after 3-5 months if stored at room temperature. For longer storage and to maintain good quality, store whole wheat flour in an airtight container in the freezer. It can keep up to 1 year if stored this way.

229 222 220 222

DESSERTS

224

APPLE CRISP

JUNE SMITH, BYRON CENTER, MICHIGAN
Delicious with ice cream or plain for breakfast, this dessert serves a crowd. It's perfect for picnics and family gatherings.

PREP: 20 min. **BAKE:** 25 min.
- 3 quarts sliced peeled apples (about 12 medium)
- 2 cups sugar
- 2 teaspoons ground cinnamon
- 1/2 teaspoon ground nutmeg
- 1/2 cup shortening
- 1/2 cup butter, softened
- 1 cup packed brown sugar
- 1-1/2 cups all-purpose flour
- 1-1/2 cups old-fashioned oats
- 1/2 teaspoon baking soda
- 1/2 teaspoon salt

Ice cream, optional

1 In a Dutch oven, combine the apples, sugar, cinnamon and nutmeg; cook and stir over medium heat just until apples are tender. Set aside.

2 In a large bowl, cream the shortening, butter and brown sugar until light and fluffy. Combine the flour, oats, baking soda and salt; gradually add to creamed mixture and mix well.

3 Pat half of flour mixture into a greased 13-in. x 9-in. baking dish. Spread apples over top; crumble remaining flour mixture over apples.

4 Bake at 400° for 25-30 minutes or until golden brown. Serve warm with ice cream if desired.

YIELD: About 16 servings.

MAPLE CREAM PIE

EMMA MAGIELDA, AMSTERDAM, NEW YORK
This pie is delicious and I serve it often when I have guests over for dinner. New York is one of the nation's top producers of maple syrup.

PREP: 30 min. + chilling **BAKE:** 15 min. + cooling
Pastry for single-crust pie (9 inches)
- 1/4 cup cornstarch
- 1/4 teaspoon salt
- 1-3/4 cups milk, divided
- 3/4 cup plus 1 tablespoon maple syrup, divided
- 2 egg yolks, lightly beaten
- 2 tablespoons butter
- 1 cup heavy whipping cream

Sliced almonds, toasted

1 Line a 9-in. pie plate with pastry; trim to 1/2 in. beyond edge of plate. Flute edges. Line unpricked pastry shell with a double thickness of heavy-duty foil. Bake at 450° for 8 minutes. Remove foil; bake 5 minutes longer. Cool on a wire rack.

2 For filling, combine cornstarch and salt in a large saucepan. Stir in 1/2 cup milk until smooth. Gradually stir in the remaining milk and 3/4 cup maple syrup. Cook and stir over medium heat until thickened and bubbly. Reduce the heat; cook and stir 2 minutes longer. Remove from heat. Stir in a small amount of hot filling into egg yolks; return all to the pan, stirring constantly. Bring to a gentle boil; cook and stir 2 minutes longer. Remove from the heat. Gently stir in butter. Cool to room temperature without stirring.

3 In a chilled small bowl, beat cream on high speed until stiff peaks form. Fold 1 cup cream into cooled filling; spoon into crust. Fold remaining syrup into remaining cream; frost top of pie. Refrigerate overnight. Garnish with toasted almonds. Refrigerate leftovers.

YIELD: 8 servings.

UPSIDE-DOWN APPLE GINGERBREAD

FLORENCE PALMER, MARSHALL, ILLINOIS
Don't expect any leftovers when you take this moist cake to a potluck. People love it because it's a little different and has a wonderful flavor. Try it for your next gathering.

PREP: 15 min. **BAKE:** 45 min. + cooling

- 1/4 cup butter, melted
- 1/3 cup packed brown sugar
- 2 large apples, peeled and sliced

GINGERBREAD:

- 1/2 cup butter, melted
- 1/2 cup sugar
- 1/3 cup packed brown sugar
- 1 egg
- 1/2 cup molasses
- 2 cups all-purpose flour
- 1 teaspoon baking soda
- 1 teaspoon ground cinnamon
- 1 teaspoon ground ginger
- 1/2 teaspoon ground cloves
- 1/2 teaspoon salt
- 1/4 teaspoon ground nutmeg
- 3/4 cup hot tea

1 Pour the butter into a 9-in. square baking pan; sprinkle with brown sugar. Arrange apples cut side up in a single layer over sugar; set aside.

2 For gingerbread, in a large bowl, cream butter and sugars until light and fluffy. Beat in egg. Beat in molasses. Combine dry ingredients; add to sugar mixture alternately with hot tea, beating well after each.

3 Pour over apples. Bake at 350° for 45 to 50 minutes or until a toothpick inserted near the center comes out clean. Cool for 10 minutes before inverting onto a serving plate. Serve warm.

YIELD: 9 servings.

FALL FRUIT PIE

JANET MORGAN-CAVALLARO, PINCOURT, QUEBEC
Although it's my husband who's the cook at our house, I enjoy baking. A good friend passed along this recipe to me. The pie was an instant hit with my family, and I've been giving the recipe to other friends ever since.

PREP: 15 min. + cooling **BAKE:** 45 min.

- 2 cups fresh or frozen cranberries
- 1-3/4 cups sugar
- 1/3 cup quick-cooking tapioca
- 1/4 cup water
- 2 teaspoons grated orange peel
- 3 cups sliced peeled baking apples
- Pastry for double-crust pie (9 inches)
- 1 egg white, beaten
- 1 tablespoon water
- Additional sugar

1 In a large saucepan, combine the cranberries, sugar, tapioca, water and orange peel; let stand for 15 minutes. Bring to a boil, stirring occasionally. Remove from heat and stir in apples. Set saucepan in a pan of cold water for 10 minutes, stirring occasionally.

2 Meanwhile, line pie plate with the bottom pastry. Pour filling into crust. Top with remaining pastry or a lattice crust. If using a full top crust, cut a few slits in it.

3 Beat egg white and water until foamy; brush over top pastry. Sprinkle with sugar. Bake at 375° for 45-55 minutes or until crust is golden brown and filling is bubbly. Cool completely.

YIELD: 6-8 servings.

BOUNCE BERRIES
Cranberries are also called "bounce berries" because when ripe, they bounce. The chambers of air inside the berries also allow them to float in water, which helps farmers corral and harvest them from large bogs. Cranberries are put through a bounce test to determine the quality of each berry.

PUMPKIN SEED CRANBERRY BISCOTTI

NANCY RENNER, EUGENE, OREGON

A hint of pumpkin seed and almond gives this biscotti a wonderful flavor that's just right for fall. Try these with a cup of coffee or hot cocoa today!

PREP: 30 min. **BAKE:** 35 min. + cooling

- 3/4 cup sugar
- 2 eggs
- 1/4 cup canola oil
- 1-1/2 teaspoons vanilla extract
- 1/2 teaspoon almond extract
- 1-3/4 cups all-purpose flour
- 1 teaspoon baking powder
- 1/2 teaspoon salt
- 1 cup salted pumpkin seeds or pepitas, toasted
- 1/2 cup dried cranberries

1 In a small bowl, beat sugar, eggs, oil and extracts. Combine the flour, baking powder and salt; gradually add to the sugar mixture and mix well. Stir in pumpkin seeds and cranberries (dough will be sticky).

2 Divide dough in half; place on a baking sheet coated with cooking spray. With lightly floured hands, shape each portion into a 12-in. x 2-in. rectangle. Bake at 350° for 25-30 minutes or until golden brown.

3 Carefully remove to wire racks; cool for 10 minutes. Transfer to a cutting board; cut diagonally with a serrated knife into 3/4-in. slices. Place cut side down on ungreased baking sheets.

4 Bake for 5 minutes or until firm. Turn and bake 5-10 minutes longer or until lightly browned. Remove to wire racks to cool. Store in an airtight container.

YIELD: 2-1/2 dozen.

SPICED CAKE DOUGHNUTS

KATHERINE NELSON, CENTERVILLE, UTAH

As part of our family's Halloween tradition, I make these delicious frosted doughnuts to serve with warm, spiced cider. Grated apples give them a scrumptious flavor and texture.

PREP: 30 min. + chilling **COOK:** 5 min./batch + cooling

- 1/4 cup shortening
- 1 cup sugar
- 3 eggs
- 1 teaspoon vanilla extract
- 5 cups all-purpose flour
- 3 teaspoons baking powder
- 2 teaspoons salt
- 1 teaspoon baking soda
- 1 teaspoon ground cinnamon
- 1 teaspoon ground nutmeg
- 1/4 teaspoon ground mace
- 1/2 cup buttermilk
- 1 cup grated peeled apples
- Oil for deep-fat frying

BROWNED BUTTER FROSTING:
- 1/2 cup packed brown sugar
- 3 tablespoons butter
- 1/4 cup heavy whipping cream
- 1-3/4 cups confectioners' sugar
- Colored sprinkles

1 In a large bowl, cream shortening and sugar until light and fluffy. Beat in eggs and vanilla. Combine the flour, baking powder, salt, baking soda, cinnamon, nutmeg and mace; add to creamed mixture alternately with buttermilk, beating well after each addition. Fold in the apples. Cover and refrigerate for at least 2 hours.

2 On a lightly floured surface, roll dough to 1/2-in. thickness. Cut with a floured 2-1/2-in. doughnut cutter. In an electric skillet or deep-fat fryer, heat oil to 375°. Fry doughnuts, a few at a time, until golden brown on both sides. Drain on paper towels.

3 For frosting, in a small saucepan, bring brown sugar and butter to a boil. Cook and stir for 1 minute or until slightly thickened. Pour into a small bowl; let stand for 10 minutes. Add cream; beat until smooth. Gradually add confectioners' sugar, 1/4 cup at a time, beating well after each addition until frosting achieves desired consistency. Frost doughnuts; top with sprinkles.

YIELD: 22 doughnuts.

FUDGY PEANUT BUTTER CAKE

BONNIE EVANS, NORCROSS, GEORGIA
I clipped this recipe from a newspaper years ago. The house smells great while it's cooking. My husband and son enjoy this warm dessert with vanilla ice cream and nuts on top.

PREP: 10 min. **COOK:** 1-1/2 hours
    1/3 cup milk
    1/4 cup peanut butter
       1 tablespoon canola oil
    1/2 teaspoon vanilla extract
    3/4 cup sugar, divided
    1/2 cup all-purpose flour
    3/4 teaspoon baking powder
       2 tablespoons baking cocoa
       1 cup boiling water
Vanilla ice cream

1 In a large bowl, combine the milk, peanut butter, oil and vanilla, beat until well blended. In a small bowl, combine 1/4 cup sugar, flour and baking powder; gradually beat into peanut butter mixture until blended. Spread evenly into a 1-1/2-qt. slow cooker coated with cooking spray.

2 In a small bowl, combine the cocoa and remaining sugar; stir in boiling water. Pour into slow cooker (do not stir).

3 Cover and cook on high for 1-1/2 to 2 hours or until a toothpick inserted near center comes out clean. Serve warm with ice cream.

YIELD: 4 servings.

EDITOR'S NOTE: Reduced-fat or generic brands of peanut butter are not recommended for this recipe.

CHOCOLATE SWEET POTATO CAKE

SALLY GREEN, MOBILE, ALABAMA
This recipe was given to my mother in 1940. Mother had lost all of her recipes, collected during 7 years of marriage, in a house fire, so her friends gave her a recipe party. Each recipe was handwritten, and among them is this cake, which is one of our family's favorites.

PREP: 10 min. **BAKE:** 70 min. + cooling
    2/3 cup butter, softened
       2 cups sugar
       4 eggs
       2 cups all-purpose flour
       1 tablespoon baking cocoa
       1 teaspoon baking soda
       1 teaspoon baking powder
       1 teaspoon each ground cinnamon, nutmeg,
          allspice and cloves
    1/2 cup milk
       2 medium sweet potatoes, peeled, cooked,
          mashed and cooled
       1 teaspoon vanilla extract
       2 cups chopped pecans
    1/2 cup raisins
Confectioners' sugar, optional

1 In a large bowl, cream butter and sugar until light and fluffy. Add eggs, one at a time, beating well after each addition. Combine the flour, cocoa, baking soda, baking powder, and spices; gradually add to creamed mixture alternately with milk, beating well after each addition. Beat in sweet potatoes and vanilla until blended. Stir in pecans and raisins.

2 Transfer to a greased and floured 10-in. fluted tube pan. Bake at 350° for 70-80 minutes or until a toothpick inserted near the center comes out clean. Cool for 10 minutes before removing from pan to a wire rack to cool completely. Dust with confectioners' sugar if desired.

YIELD: 12-16 servings.

PUMPKIN CREAM CHEESE PIE

DIANE SELICH, VASSAR, MICHIGAN
After spending an afternoon in the chilly October air at our town's pumpkin rolling contest, my family, including my grandchildren, head over to my house for a fun pumpkin-themed meal including this luscious dessert.

PREP: 10 min. **BAKE:** 70 min.

    1 package (8 ounces) cream cheese, softened
    3 tablespoons confectioners' sugar
  1/2 teaspoon vanilla extract
    1 unbaked pastry shell (9 inches)

FILLING:

1-2/3 cups heavy whipping cream
1-1/2 cups canned pumpkin
    2 eggs, lightly beaten
  3/4 cup sugar
1-3/4 teaspoons pumpkin pie spice

1 In a small bowl, beat the cream cheese, confectioners' sugar and vanilla until smooth. Spread into pastry shell. In another small bowl, whisk filling ingredients until smooth. Pour over cream cheese layer. Cover edges loosely with foil.

2 Bake at 350° for 70-80 minutes or until a knife inserted near the center comes out clean. Cool on a wire rack. Store in the refrigerator.

YIELD: 6-8 servings.

HOMEMADE PUMPKIN PIE SPICE

If you rarely use pumpkin pie spice in your cooking, you may want to make your own instead of buying it. Combine 4 teaspoons ground cinnamon, 2 teaspoons ground ginger, 1 teaspoon ground cloves and 1/2 teaspoon ground nutmeg. Store in an airtight container. Yield: 7-1/2 teaspoons.

APPLE HARVEST CAKE

E. BARTUSCHAT, ABINGTON, MASSACHUSETTS
Tender apple slices and subtle flavors make this old-fashioned cake one of our favorites.

PREP: 20 min. **BAKE:** 40 min. + cooling

2-1/4 cups sugar, divided
    1 cup canola oil
    4 eggs
  1/4 cup orange juice
2-1/2 teaspoons vanilla extract
    3 cups all-purpose flour
    3 teaspoons baking powder
  1/2 teaspoon salt
    4 medium tart apples, peeled and cubed
    2 teaspoons ground cinnamon
Whipped cream and additional cinnamon, optional

1 In a large bowl, beat 2 cups sugar, oil, eggs, orange juice and vanilla until well blended. Combine the flour, baking powder and salt; gradually beat into the sugar mixture until blended. Stir in the apples.

2 Spread half of the batter into a greased 13-in. x 9-in. baking dish. Combine cinnamon and remaining sugar; sprinkle over batter. Carefully spread remaining batter over the top.

3 Bake at 350° for 40-50 minutes or until a toothpick inserted near the center comes out clean. Cool on a wire rack. Garnish with whipped cream and additional cinnamon if desired.

YIELD: 12-15 servings.

GIANT UPSIDE-DOWN PECAN ROLLS

JANET MILLER, LAFAYETTE, INDIANA
I like to keep a baked batch of these extra-large sweet rolls in the freezer to surprise my family on weekends. To reheat, thaw in the refrigerator overnight, wrap in foil and bake at 350° for 20 to 30 minutes or until heated through.

PREP: 35 min. + rising BAKE: 35 min.
    2 packages (1/4 ounce each) active dry yeast
  1/2 cup warm water (110° to 115°)
1-3/4 cups sugar, divided
  2/3 cup warm milk (110° to 115°)
  3/4 cup butter, softened, divided
    1 teaspoon salt
    1 egg
    1 egg yolk
4-3/4 to 5-1/4 cups all-purpose flour
    1 tablespoon ground cinnamon
    1 cup chopped pecans

BROWN SUGAR-NUT SYRUP:
    1 cup packed dark brown sugar
  1/4 cup butter, cubed
    2 tablespoons water
    1 cup pecan halves

EGG WASH:
    1 egg white
    1 teaspoon water

1 In a large bowl, dissolve yeast in warm water. Add 3/4 cup sugar, milk, 1/2 cup softened butter, salt, egg, egg yolk and 3 cups flour. Beat on medium speed for 3 minutes. Stir in enough remaining flour to form a soft dough.

2 Turn onto a floured surface; knead until smooth and elastic, about 6-8 minutes. Place in a greased bowl, turning once to grease top. Cover and let rise in a warm place until doubled, about 1-1/2 hours.

3 Punch dough down. Turn onto lightly floured surface. Roll into a 24-in. x 18-in. rectangle. Melt remaining butter; brush over dough. Combine cinnamon and remaining sugar; sprinkle to within 1/2 in. of edges. Sprinkle with pecans. Roll up, jelly-roll style, starting with a short side; pinch seam to seal. Cut into six slices.

4 For syrup, combine brown sugar, butter and water in a saucepan. Bring to a boil; boil and stir for 1 minute. Pour into a greased 13-in. x 9-in. baking. Arrange pecan halves, flat side up, over syrup. Place rolls, cut side down, over pecans. Press down gently. Cover and let rise until doubled, about 1 hour.

5 Beat egg white and water; brush over rolls. Bake at 350° for 35-40 minutes or until golden brown. Immediately invert onto a serving platter.

YIELD: 6 rolls.

CHOCOLATE HAZELNUT PARFAITS

CHRISTY HINRICHS, PARKVILLE, MISSOURI
Hazelnut coffee creamer adds great flavor to the chocolate pudding in these special parfaits. Shortbread cookie crumbs and fresh strawberry slices complete the lovely layered desserts.

PREP: 10 min. + chilling
    3 cups cold milk
    1 cup refrigerated hazelnut nondairy creamer
    2 packages (3.9 ounces each) instant chocolate
       pudding mix
    1 cup crushed shortbread cookies
    2 cups sliced fresh strawberries
Whipped cream, optional

1 In a large bowl, whisk the milk, creamer and pudding mixes for 2 minutes. Let stand for 2 minutes or until soft-set.

2 Spoon 1/4 cup pudding into each of eight parfait glasses; sprinkle each with 1 tablespoon cookie crumbs. Top with the strawberries and remaining pudding and crumbs. Refrigerate for 1 hour before serving. Garnish with whipped cream if desired.

YIELD: 8 servings.

CRANBERRY SHORTBREAD BARS

TASTE OF HOME TEST KITCHEN

Look at the lovely confection our Test Kitchen came up with when it combined cranberries, coconut and white chocolate! Colorful and tasty, these bars and a glass of milk make the perfect treat after a dusty afternoon of raking leaves. You can wrap the bars in colored cellophane and ribbons for a pretty, homemade holiday gift.

PREP: 20 min. **BAKE:** 30 min. + cooling

     1   cup butter, softened
   1/2   cup confectioners' sugar
     1   egg
 1-1/2   cups all-purpose flour
   1/2   cup flaked coconut
   1/8   teaspoon salt
   1/2   cup sugar
   1/2   cup packed brown sugar
     3   tablespoons cornstarch
     1   package (12 ounces) fresh or frozen cranberries
     1   cup unsweetened apple juice
     1   cup chopped walnuts
     2   squares (1 ounce each) white baking chocolate, melted

1 In a large bowl, cream butter and confectioners' sugar until light and fluffy. Beat in egg. Combine the flour, coconut and salt; gradually add to creamed mixture and mix well. Set aside 1 cup for topping. Spread remaining mixture into a greased 13-in. x 9-in. baking dish. Bake at 425° for 10 minutes.

2 Meanwhile, in a small saucepan, combine the sugars and cornstarch. Stir in cranberries and apple juice. Bring to a boil. Reduce heat; cook and stir for 5 minutes or until thickened. Remove from the heat; stir in walnuts.

3 Spread over crust. Sprinkle with reserved crumb mixture. Bake for 20-25 minutes or until golden brown and bubbly. Cool on a wire rack. Drizzle with white chocolate. Cut into bars.

YIELD: 2 dozen.

APPLE STRUDEL

HELEN LESH, FORSYTH, MISSOURI

This is one of my favorite recipes during autumn. The aroma of this dessert baking on a cool, crisp day is absolutely wonderful.

PREP: 20 min. + chilling **BAKE:** 55 min. + cooling

     1   cup cold butter, cubed
     2   cups all-purpose flour
     1   cup (8 ounces) sour cream
   1/4   teaspoon salt

FILLING:

     2   cups dry bread crumbs
   1/4   cup butter, melted
     4   medium baking apples, peeled and chopped
     2   cups sugar
     1   cup golden raisins
   1/2   cup chopped pecans
     2   teaspoons ground cinnamon
Confectioners' sugar, optional

1 In a large bowl, cut butter into flour until mixture resembles coarse crumbs. Stir in sour cream and salt. Shape the dough into a ball; cover and refrigerate overnight.

2 For filling, combine bread crumbs and butter. Add the apples, sugar, raisins, pecans and cinnamon, set aside. Divide dough into thirds; turn onto a floured surface. Roll each into a 15-in. x 12-in. rectangle. Spoon filling evenly onto dough; spread to within 1 in. of edges. Roll up from one long side; pinch seams and ends to seal.

3 Carefully place each loaf seam side down on an ungreased baking sheet. Bake at 350° for 55-60 minutes or until light brown. Cool completely on wire racks. Dust with confectioners' sugar if desired.

YIELD: 3 strudels.

CRAN-APPLE COBBLER

JO ANN SHEEHAN, RUTHER GLEN, VIRGINIA

My cranberry-packed cobbler is the crowning glory of many of our late fall and winter meals. My family isn't big on pies, so this favorite is preferred at our Thanksgiving and Christmas celebrations. The aroma of cinnamon and fruit is irresistible.

PREP: 20 min. **BAKE:** 30 min.

2-1/2 cups sliced peeled apples
2-1/2 cups sliced peeled firm pears
    1 to 1-1/4 cups sugar
    1 cup fresh or frozen cranberries, thawed
    1 cup water
    3 tablespoons quick-cooking tapioca
    3 tablespoons red-hot candies
1/2 teaspoon ground cinnamon
    2 tablespoons butter

TOPPING:

3/4 cup all-purpose flour
    2 tablespoons sugar
    1 teaspoon baking powder
1/4 teaspoon salt
1/4 cup cold butter, cubed
    3 tablespoons milk
Vanilla ice cream

1 In a large saucepan, combine the first eight ingredients; let stand for 5 minutes. Cook and stir over medium heat until mixture comes to a full rolling boil, about 18 minutes. Transfer the cran-apple mixture to a greased 2-qt. baking dish; dot with the butter.

2 For topping, combine the flour, sugar, baking powder and salt in a bowl. Cut in butter until mixture resembles coarse crumbs. Stir in milk until a soft dough forms.

3 Drop topping by heaping tablespoonfuls onto hot fruit. Bake at 375° for 30-35 minutes or until golden brown. Serve warm with ice cream.

YIELD: 6-8 servings.

SPICE CUPCAKES

CARLA HODENFIELD, NEW TOWN, NORTH DAKOTA

These moist spicy cupcakes with creamy caramel frosting are a delicious treat. The recipe has been in my family for years. When I was growing up, it seemed these cupcakes were always in the freezer, just waiting to be snitched one at a time!

PREP: 40 min. **BAKE:** 20 min. + cooling

    2 cups water
    1 cup raisins
1/2 cup shortening
    1 cup sugar
    1 egg
1-3/4 cups all-purpose flour
    1 teaspoon baking soda
1/2 teaspoon salt
1/2 teaspoon each ground allspice, cloves, cinnamon and nutmeg
1/4 cup chopped walnuts

FROSTING:

    1 cup packed brown sugar
1/3 cup half-and-half cream
1/4 teaspoon salt
    3 tablespoons butter
    1 teaspoon vanilla extract
1-1/4 cups confectioners' sugar
Coarsely chopped walnuts, optional

1 In a large saucepan, bring water and raisins to a boil. Reduce heat; simmer for 10 minutes. Remove from heat and set aside (do not drain).

2 Meanwhile, in a large bowl, cream shortening and sugar until light and fluffy. Beat in egg. Stir in raisins. Combine dry ingredients; add to creamed mixture until well blended. Stir in walnuts.

3 Fill paper-lined muffin cups with 1/3 cup batter each. Bake at 350° for 20-25 minutes or until a toothpick comes out clean. Cool for 10 minutes; remove from pan to a wire rack.

4 For frosting, in a large saucepan, combine the brown sugar, cream and salt. Bring to a boil over medium-low heat; cook and stir until smooth. Stir in butter and vanilla. Remove from the heat; cool slightly. Stir in confectioners' sugar until smooth. Frost cupcakes; top with nuts if desired.

YIELD: 14 cupcakes.

AUTUMN SURPRISE PIE

KAREN GAUVREAU, CLEARWATER, FLORIDA

When the weather starts getting a little cooler and the leaves start falling, what better way to welcome in fall than with a homemade apple pie? This version calls for apples, pears and raisins flavored with rum extract. This pie is a sure way to a man's heart.

PREP: 30 min. **BAKE:** 45 min. + cooling

- 1-1/2 cups all-purpose flour
-   3 tablespoons sugar
- 1/4 teaspoon plus 1/8 teaspoon baking powder
- 1/4 teaspoon plus 1/8 teaspoon salt
-   6 tablespoons cold butter
- 1/4 cup fat-free milk
- 1-1/2 teaspoons cider vinegar

FILLING:

-   5 cups sliced peeled tart apples
-   2 cups sliced peeled ripe pears
- 1/3 cup raisins
- 1/2 cup plus 1 teaspoon sugar, divided
- 1/4 cup all-purpose flour
-   1 teaspoon ground cinnamon
- 1/4 teaspoon ground nutmeg
- 1/4 teaspoon ground cloves
- 3/4 teaspoon rum extract
-   1 egg white

1 In a large bowl, combine the flour, sugar, baking powder and salt; cut in butter until mixture resembles coarse crumbs. Combine milk and vinegar; gradually add to crumb mixture, tossing with a fork until dough forms a ball.

2 Divide dough into two balls, one slightly larger than the other. On a lightly floured surface, roll larger ball to fit a 9-in. pie plate. Coat pie plate with cooking spray; transfer pastry to plate.

3 In a large bowl, combine the apples, pears and raisins. Combine 1/2 cup sugar, flour, cinnamon, nutmeg and cloves; add to fruit mixture and toss. Sprinkle with extract; toss well. Spoon into crust.

4 Roll out remaining pastry; make a lattice crust. Trim, seal and flute edges. Brush lattice with egg white; sprinkle with remaining sugar.

5 Bake at 425° for 15 minutes. Reduce the heat to 350°; bake 30-35 minutes longer or until crust is golden and filling is bubbly. Cool on a wire rack.

YIELD: 8 servings.

MAPLE BUTTERSCOTCH BROWNIES

GRACE VONHOLD, ROCHESTER, NEW YORK

Generally, I'll make a double recipe of these brownies. They go so fast no matter where I take them! I've baked them for family dinners and church suppers, and never had any left over. They're very easy to make and freeze well.

PREP: 15 min. **BAKE:** 30 min. + cooling

- 1-1/4 cups packed brown sugar
- 1/2 cup butter, melted
- 1-1/2 teaspoons imitation maple flavoring
-   2 eggs
- 1-1/2 cups all-purpose flour
-   1 teaspoon baking powder
-   1 cup chopped walnuts

Confectioners' sugar, optional

1 In a large bowl, combine the brown sugar, butter and maple flavoring. Add the eggs, one at a time, beating well after each addition. Combine the flour and baking powder; add to egg mixture. Stir in nuts.

2 Pour into a greased 9-in. square baking pan. Bake at 350° for 27-32 minutes or until a toothpick inserted near the center comes out clean. Cool on a wire rack. Dust with confectioners' sugar if desired. Cut into bars.

YIELD: 16 brownies.

PERSIMMON NUT ROLL

NANCY WILSON, VAN NUYS, CALIFORNIA
For holiday gift-giving, I make a dozen or so of these rolls to share with friends and neighbors. They slice nicely straight from the freezer.

PREP: 25 min. **BAKE:** 15 min. + cooling

- 3 eggs
- 1 cup sugar
- 2/3 cup mashed ripe persimmon pulp
- 1 teaspoon lemon juice
- 1 cup self-rising flour
- 2 teaspoons ground cinnamon
- 1 teaspoon baking powder
- 1 teaspoon ground ginger
- 1/2 teaspoon salt
- 1/2 teaspoon ground nutmeg
- 1 cup chopped pecans

FILLING:

- 1 package (8 ounces) cream cheese, softened
- 1/4 cup butter, softened
- 1 cup confectioners' sugar
- 1 teaspoon vanilla extract

Additional confectioners' sugar

1 Line a 15-in. x 10-in. x 1-in. baking pan with waxed paper and grease the paper; set aside. In a large bowl, beat eggs for 5 minutes on medium speed or until lemon-colored. Gradually add the sugar, persimmon pulp and lemon juice; beat for 3 minutes. Combine the flour, cinnamon, baking powder, ginger, salt and nutmeg; add to egg mixture and beat well.

2 Spread batter evenly in prepared pan; sprinkle with pecans. Bake at 375° for 15 minutes or until lightly browned.

3 Cool in pan for 5 minutes. Turn cake onto a kitchen towel dusted with confectioners' sugar. Gently peel off waxed paper. Roll up cake in the towel jelly-roll style, starting with a short side. Cool completely on a wire rack.

4 For filling, in a small bowl, beat cream cheese and butter until smooth. Beat in the confectioners' sugar and vanilla until the mixture reaches spreading consistency.

5 Unroll cake and spread filling evenly over cake to within 1/2 in. of edges. Roll up again. Cover and refrigerate until serving. Dust with additional confectioners' sugar. Refrigerate or freeze leftovers.

YIELD: 10 servings.

EDITOR'S NOTE: As a substitute for 1 cup of self-rising flour, place 1-1/2 teaspoons baking powder and 1/2 teaspoon salt in a measuring cup. Add all-purpose flour to measure 1 cup.

GINGER PLUM TART

TASTE OF HOME TEST KITCHEN
Looking for a quick and easy dessert that's pretty as a picture? Try this mouth-watering tart from our Test Kitchen. For an extra-special effect, crown it with a scoop of low-fat ice cream, yogurt or a dollop of reduced-fat whipped topping.

PREP: 15 min. **BAKE:** 20 min. + cooling

Pastry for single-crust pie (9 inches)

- 3-1/2 cups sliced unpeeled fresh plums
- 3 tablespoons plus 1 teaspoon coarse sugar, divided
- 1 tablespoon cornstarch
- 2 teaspoons finely chopped crystallized ginger
- 1 egg white
- 1 tablespoon water

1 Roll pastry into a 12-in. circle. Transfer to a large baking sheet lined with parchment paper. In a large bowl, combine plums, 3 tablespoons sugar and cornstarch. Arrange plums in a pinwheel pattern over pastry to within 2 in. of edges; sprinkle with ginger. Fold edges of pastry over plums.

2 Beat egg white and water; brush over pastry. Sprinkle with remaining sugar. Bake at 400° for 20-25 minutes or until crust is lightly browned. Cool for 15 minutes before removing from pan to a serving platter.

YIELD: 8 servings.

238

233

239

237

SPECIAL OCCASIONS

237

APPLE PIE COOKIES

SHARON SMITH, NEOSHO, MISSOURI

To sweeten the school day, send along these soft sugar cookies with a homemade apple filling. The sandwich cutouts were taste-tested by my grandchildren, and they're certified kid-pleasers! To save time you can use purchased pie filling for the centers. Or instead of "painting" the tops with food coloring simply sprinkle them with a little cinnamon.

PREP: 30 min. + chilling **BAKE:** 10 min./batch

- 1/2 cup shortening
- 1 cup sugar
- 1 egg
- 1/2 cup milk
- 1 teaspoon vanilla extract
- 3-1/2 cups all-purpose flour
- 2 teaspoons cream of tartar
- 1 teaspoon baking soda
- 1 teaspoon salt

FILLING:

- 1/2 cup packed brown sugar
- 2 teaspoons all-purpose flour
- 1/2 teaspoon ground cinnamon
- 3 medium tart apples, peeled and grated (about 2 cups)
- 3/4 cup water

GLAZE:

- 4 tablespoons water
- Red and green liquid food coloring

1 In a large bowl, cream shortening and sugar until light and fluffy. Beat in the egg, milk and vanilla. Combine flour, cream of tartar, baking soda and salt; gradually add to creamed mixture. Divide dough in half. Refrigerate for 2-3 hours or until easy to handle (dough will be soft).

2 Meanwhile, in a small saucepan, combine filling ingredients. Cook over medium heat until apples are softened and mixture is thickened; cool.

3 On a lightly floured surface roll out each portion of dough to 1/8-in. thickness. Cut with a floured 2-1/2-in. apple cookie cutter. Place 2 in. apart on ungreased baking sheets. Spread with 2 teaspoons of filling to within 1/4 in. of edge. Top with another cutout; seal edges.

4 Bake at 375° for 10-12 minutes or until lightly browned. Remove to wire racks to cool completely. Meanwhile, in a small bowl, combine 3 tablespoons water and 18 drops red food coloring. In another small bowl, combine the remaining water and 6 drops green food coloring. Using a pastry brush, "paint" apples red with green leaves.

YIELD: 2 dozen.

RULER STROMBOLI

TASTE OF HOME TEST KITCHEN

If you're looking for a satisfying sandwich, this sensational stromboli is sure to measure up. Filled with deli turkey, Swiss cheese and sauteed peppers, refrigerated pizza dough makes it a snap to assemble.

PREP: 25 min. **BAKE:** 25 min. + standing

- 1/2 cup chopped green pepper
- 1/2 cup chopped sweet red pepper
- 1 tablespoon butter
- 1 tube (10.2 ounces) refrigerated pizza dough
- 6 slices Swiss cheese, divided
- 8 ounces sliced deli turkey
- 5 sweet red pepper strips (2 inch pieces)
- 12 green pepper strips (1-inch pieces)
- 2 ounces cream cheese, softened
- 1/2 teaspoon milk

1 In a large skillet, saute the chopped peppers in butter until tender. On an ungreased baking sheet, pat the dough into a 13-in. x 8-in. rectangle. Arrange four cheese slices lengthwise over half of the dough to within 1/2 in. of edge; top with turkey and

sauteed peppers. Fold dough over filling; pinch edges to seal. Bake at 400° for 20-25 minutes or until golden brown.

2 Cut remaining cheese slices in half lengthwise; place along one long edge of the sandwich. Bake 1-2 minutes longer or until cheese is melted. Immediately press red pepper strips into the cheese to create inch marks and add green pepper strips for fractions. Let stand for 10 minutes.

3 Beat cream cheese and milk until smooth. Spoon into a heavy-duty resealable plastic bag; cut a small hole in a corner of bag. Pipe numerals above red pepper strips. Slice; serve warm.

YIELD: 6-8 servings.

BACK-TO-SCHOOL COOKIES

FRANCES PIERCE, WADDINGTON, NEW YORK
These nutty treats are great for a classroom party or to share with friends. With a glass of cold milk, they're an irresistible snack.

PREP: 30 min. BAKE: 10 min./batch
    1 cup butter-flavored shortening
    1 cup creamy peanut butter
    2 cups packed brown sugar
    4 egg whites
    1 teaspoon vanilla extract
    2 cups all-purpose flour
    1 teaspoon baking soda
  1/2 teaspoon baking powder
    2 cups crisp rice cereal
1-1/2 cups chopped nuts
    1 cup flaked coconut
    1 cup quick-cooking oats

1 In a large bowl, cream shortening, peanut butter and brown sugar until light and fluffy. Beat in egg whites and vanilla. Combine the flour, baking soda and baking powder; gradually

add to creamed mixture and mix well. Stir in the cereal, nuts, coconut and oats.

2 Drop by rounded tablespoonfuls 2 in. apart onto ungreased baking sheets. Flatten with a fork, forming a crisscross pattern. Bake at 375° for 7-8 minutes. Remove to wire racks.

YIELD: 12 dozen.

EDITOR'S NOTE: Reduced-fat or generic brands of peanut butter are not recommended for this recipe.

SCHOOLHOUSE CHILI

MARY SELNER, GREEN BAY, WISCONSIN
When I was a school cook, the students loved my chili because they thought it didn't have beans in it. They didn't know I puree the beans, tomatoes, onions and green pepper to create a tasty, vitamin-packed chili!

PREP: 10 min. COOK: 65 min.
    1 can (14-1/2 ounces) diced tomatoes, undrained
    1 can (15-1/2 ounces) mild chili beans
  1/2 cup chopped onion
  1/4 cup chopped green pepper
    1 pound ground beef
1-1/2 teaspoons salt
    1 to 2 teaspoons chili powder
    1 teaspoon ground cumin
  1/2 teaspoon pepper
Hot cooked spaghetti, optional

1 In a blender, combine the tomatoes, beans, onion and green pepper; cover and puree until smooth.

2 In a large saucepan, cook beef over medium heat until no longer pink; drain. Add seasonings and pureed vegetables. Bring to a boil. Reduce heat; cover and simmer for 1 hour. Serve over spaghetti if desired.

YIELD: 6 servings.

CHOCOLATE SKELETON COOKIES

LISA RUPPLE, KEENESBURG, COLORADO
Put these cute treats out for your next ghost and goblin party and watch them disappear.

PREP: 45 min. **BAKE:** 10 min./batch + cooling

- 1 cup butter, softened
- 1 cup sugar
- 1/2 cup packed brown sugar
- 1 egg
- 1 teaspoon vanilla extract
- 2-3/4 cups all-purpose flour
- 1/2 cup baking cocoa
- 1 teaspoon baking soda
- 1-1/2 cups confectioners' sugar
- 2 tablespoons milk

1 In a large bowl, cream butter and sugars until light and fluffy. Beat in egg and vanilla. Combine the flour, cocoa and baking soda; gradually add to creamed mixture and mix well. Cover and refrigerate for 1-2 hours or until easy to handle.

2 On a lightly floured surface, roll dough to 1/8-in. thickness. Cut with a floured 3-in. gingerbread boy cookie cutter. Place on greased baking sheets.

3 Bake at 375° for 7-8 minutes or until set. Cool for 1 minute before removing from pans to wire racks to cool completely.

4 For icing, in a small bowl, combine confectioners' sugar and milk until smooth. Cut a small hole in the corner of a resealable plastic bag; fill with icing. Pipe skeleton bones on cookies.

YIELD: 3 dozen.

YUMMY MUMMY CALZONES

TASTE OF HOME TEST KITCHEN
Family favorite pizza toppings are the not-so-spooky surprise inside these clever calzones. If you serve these on wood "coffins" like we did, be sure to line the surface with plastic wrap or waxed paper.

PREP: 20 min. **BAKE:** 30 min.

- 2 loaves (1 pound each) frozen bread dough, thawed
- 1-1/2 cups (6 ounces) shredded part-skim mozzarella cheese
- 1/2 cup pizza sauce
- 50 slices pepperoni
- 1/2 cup chopped green pepper
- 1 egg, lightly beaten
- 1 pitted ripe olive, sliced and cut in half

1 Roll out each piece of dough into a rounded triangle shape, about 14-in. high x 11-in. wide at the base of the triangle. Place each on a parchment-lined baking sheet with the tip of the triangle toward you. Lightly score 4-in.-wide rectangle in the center of the triangle 2 in. from the top and bottom.

2 On each long side, cut 1-in.-wide strips at an angle up to the score line, leaving a triangle in the top center of the wide end for the head.

3 Inside the scored rectangle in the center, layer the cheese, pizza sauce, pepperoni and green pepper. Shape the top center triangle into a head. Starting at the head, fold alternating strips of dough at an angle across filling stopping at the last strip on each side. Fold the bottom dough tip up over the filling, then fold the remaining two strips over the top; press down firmly.

4 Brush dough with egg. Cover and let rise for 15 minutes. For eyes, press 1 olive slice into each head. Discard or save the remaining slices for another use.

5 Bake at 350° for 25-28 minutes or until golden brown. Let stand for 5 minutes before slicing.

YIELD: 8-10 servings.

CIDER CHEESE FONDUE

KIM MARIE VAN RHEENEN, MENDOTA, ILLINOIS
Cheese lovers are sure to enjoy dipping into this creamy, quick-to-fix fondue that has just a hint of apple. You can also serve this appetizer with apple or pear wedges.

PREP/TOTAL TIME: 15 min.

- 3/4 cup apple cider or apple juice
- 2 cups (8 ounces) shredded cheddar cheese
- 1 cup (4 ounces) shredded Swiss cheese
- 1 tablespoon cornstarch
- 1/8 teaspoon pepper
- 1 loaf (1 pound) French bread, cut into cubes

1 In a large saucepan, bring cider to a boil. Reduce the heat to medium-low. Toss cheeses with cornstarch and pepper; stir into cider. Cook and stir for 3-4 minutes or until cheese is melted.

2 Transfer to a small fondue pot or 1-1/2-qt. slow cooker; keep warm. Serve with bread cubes.

YIELD: 2-2/3 cups.

MAGIC POTION PUNCH

MICHELLE THOMAS, BANGOR, MAINE
At a Halloween party, the scarier the food, the better! I like to tuck gummy worms into an ice ring when I make this great green punch.

PREP/TOTAL TIME: 10 min.

- 2 packages (3 ounces each) lime gelatin
- 1/2 cup sugar
- 1 cup boiling water
- 3 cups cold water
- 1 quart non-carbonated lemon-lime drink, chilled
- 1-1/2 quarts lemon-lime soda, chilled

1 Dissolve gelatin and sugar in boiling water; add cold water. Transfer to a punch bowl. Stir in lemon-lime drink and soda.

YIELD: about 4 quarts.

MELTED WITCH PUDDLES

TASTE OF HOME TEST KITCHEN
In honor of the doomed wicked witch in "The Wizard of Oz," our home economists had fun fashioning these simply delicious snacks using a variety of convenience foods.

PREP: 1 hour + chilling

- 1 teaspoon water
- 4 drops yellow food coloring
- 1-1/2 cups flaked coconut
- 2 cups (12 ounces) semisweet chocolate chips
- 6 tablespoons shortening, divided
- 36 chocolate cream-filled chocolate sandwich cookies
- 36 Bugles
- 4 cups vanilla or white chips
- 36 pretzel sticks

1 In a large resealable plastic bag, combine the water and food coloring; add coconut. Seal bag and shake to tint coconut; set aside. In a microwave, melt chocolate chips and 2 tablespoons shortening; stir until smooth.

2 For witches' hats, place about 1/3 cup chocolate mixture in a resealable plastic bag; cut a small hole in a corner of bag. Pipe a small amount of the chocolate on a cookie. Dip a Bugle in some of the remaining chocolate; allow the excess to drip off. Position over chocolate on cookie, forming a witch's hat. Set on waxed paper to dry. Repeat with the remaining chocolate, Bugles and cookies.

3 For puddles, in a microwave, melt vanilla chips at 70% power for 1 minute; stir. Microwave at additional 10- to 20-second intervals, stirring until smooth. Place mixture in a large heavy-duty resealable plastic bag; cut a small hole in a corner of bag.

4 Pipe the mixture into the shape of a puddle onto waxed paper-lined baking sheets. Immediately place a witch's hat on the puddle. For the brooms, place a pretzel stick alongside the hat; sprinkle reserved tinted coconut at the end of the pretzel stick. Repeat with remaining puddles, hats and brooms. Chill for 15 minutes or until set. Store in an airtight container.

YIELD: 3 dozen.

GHOSTLY PIRATE CAKE

TASTE OF HOME TEST KITCHEN
Ahoy, mateys! Even land-lubbers will appreciate the sweet yet spooky details on this dessert that's perfect for a pirate-themed party. The moist white cake starts with a mix and the pirate's features are simple to create with storebought treats.

PREP: 45 min. **BAKE:** 25 min. + cooling

   1 package (18-1/4 ounces) white cake mix
  1/2 cup butter, softened
4-1/2 cups confectioners' sugar
   5 tablespoons milk
1-1/2 teaspoons vanilla extract
   3 red Fruit Roll-Ups, unrolled
Shredded coconut and black food coloring
Assorted candies of your choice (Fruit by the Foot fruit roll, M&M's, black licorice twists, caramels, plain chocolate bar, dark purple Gummi Life Saver, red-hot candy and gold candy coins)

1 Prepare and bake cake according to package directions, using two greased and floured 9-in. round baking pans. Cool for 10 minutes before removing from pans to cool completely.

2 Cut two pieces from the lower edges of each cake, forming a pirate's head (save small pieces for another use).

3 For frosting, in a large bowl, beat butter until fluffy. Gradually add the confectioners' sugar, milk and vanilla; beat until smooth.

4 Place one cake layer on a serving platter; top with 1/2 cup frosting; top with second cake layer. Frost top and sides with remaining frosting.

5 For pirate's bandanna, place Fruit Roll-Ups over top edge of cake. Tint coconut with black food coloring; sprinkle over chin for goatee. Decorate pirate's features with assorted candies.

YIELD: 10-12 servings.

JACK-O'-LANTERN BROWNIES

FLO BURTNETT, GAGE, OKLAHOMA
Hosting a Halloween party? Use a cookie cutter to easily cut these homemade chocolate brownies into pumpkin shapes, then give them personality with orange, black and green frosting. Our grandchildren think these are great.

PREP: 20 min. **BAKE:** 20 min. + cooling

  3/4 cup butter, melted
1-1/2 cups sugar
1-1/2 teaspoons vanilla extract
   3 eggs
  3/4 cup all-purpose flour
  1/2 cup baking cocoa
  1/2 teaspoon baking powder
  1/4 teaspoon salt
   1 can (16 ounces) vanilla frosting
Orange paste food coloring
Green and black decorating gel
Candy corn and milk chocolate M&M's, optional

1 In a large bowl, cream the butter, sugar and vanilla until light and fluffy. Beat in eggs. Combine flour, cocoa, baking powder and salt; gradually add to butter mixture and mix well.

2 Line a greased 13-in. x 9-in. baking pan with waxed paper; grease the paper. Spread batter evenly in pan. Bake at 350° for 18-22 minutes or until brownies begin to pull away from sides of pan. Cool on a wire rack.

3 Run a knife around edge of pan. Invert brownies onto a work surface and remove waxed paper. Cut brownies with a 3-in. pumpkin cookie cutter, leaving at least 1/8 in. between each shape. (Discard scraps or save for another use.)

4 Tint frosting with orange food coloring; frost brownies. Use green gel to create the pumpkin stems and black gel and candy corn and M&M's to decorate the faces if desired.

YIELD: about 1 dozen.

MONSTER CARAMEL APPLES

KAREN ANN BLAND, GOVE, KANSAS
This delicious recipe for caramel apples has added ingredients to make these Halloween treats extra special.

PREP: 40 min. **COOK:** 30 min. + cooling

  8 to 10 medium apples
  8 to 10 wooden sticks
  32 cream-filled chocolate sandwich cookies, coarsely chopped
  1 cup butter, cubed
  2 cups packed brown sugar
  1 can (14 ounces) sweetened condensed milk
  1 cup light corn syrup
  1 teaspoon vanilla extract
  8 squares (1 ounce each) white candy coating, coarsely chopped
  1/2 cup orange and brown sprinkles

1 Wash and thoroughly dry apples; insert a wooden stick into each. Place on a waxed paper-lined baking sheet; chill. Place cookie crumbs in a shallow dish; set aside.

2 In a heavy 3-qt. saucepan, combine the butter, brown sugar, milk and corn syrup; bring to a boil over medium-high heat. Cook and stir until mixture reaches 248° (firm-ball stage) on a candy thermometer, about 30-40 minutes. Remove from the heat; stir in vanilla.

3 Dip each apple into hot caramel mixture to completely coat, then dip the bottom in cookie crumbs, pressing lightly to adhere. Return to baking sheet to cool.

4 In a small microwave-safe bowl, heat white candy coating at 50% power for 1-2 minutes or until melted; stir until smooth. Transfer to a small plastic bag; cut a small hole in a corner of bag. Drizzle coating over apples. Decorate with sprinkles.

YIELD: 8-10 servings.

EDITOR'S NOTE: We recommend that you test your candy thermometer by bringing water to a boil; the thermometer should read 212°. Adjust your recipe temperature up or down based on your test.

PUMPKIN SNACK MIX

SHIRLEY ENGSTROM, GENOA, NEBRASKA
This yummy mix never lasts long. Feel free to use candy corn instead of the candy pumpkins—or a mix of both—if desired.

PREP: 25 min. **BAKE:** 1 hour + cooling

  3 quarts popped popcorn
  4 cups Cheerios
  4 cups Corn or Rice Chex
  2 cups salted peanuts
  1 cup packed brown sugar
  3/4 cup light corn syrup
  1/4 cup butter, cubed
  2 teaspoons vanilla extract
  1/2 teaspoon baking soda
  1 package (16 ounces) candy pumpkins

1 In a large greased roasting pan, combine the popcorn, cereal and peanuts. In a large saucepan, combine the brown sugar, corn syrup and butter; bring to a rolling boil. Boil for 6 minutes, stirring occasionally. Remove from heat; quickly stir in vanilla and baking soda until mixture is light and foamy.

2 Immediately pour over popcorn mixture; toss to coat. Bake, uncovered, at 250° for 1 hour, stirring every 15 minutes. Stir in candy pumpkins. Cool completely.

YIELD: about 5-1/2 quarts.

PERFECT POPCORN ON THE STOVE
One cup of unpopped kernels makes 8 cups of popcorn. Add 1/3 cup vegetable oil for every cup of kernels to a 3- or 4-quart pan with a loose-fitting lid (to allow steam to escape). Heat oil to between 400° and 460° (if the oil smokes, it's too hot). Drop in one kernel; when it pops, add enough kernels to create a single layer. Cover the pan and shake to spread the oil. When the popping begins to slow, remove the pan from the heat.

TURKEY WITH COUNTRY HAM STUFFING

BOBBIE LOVE, KAPAA, HAWAII
As delicious as this is right out of the oven, the bird and stuffing both taste great as leftovers, too. I am careful not to overcook the turkey.

PREP: 45 min. BAKE: 4-1/2 hours

    3 cups cubed day-old white bread, crust removed
    3 cups cubed day-old whole wheat bread, crust removed
1-1/2 cups cubed fully cooked ham
  1/2 cup butter, cubed
    3 cups chopped onion
    2 cups chopped celery
1-1/2 teaspoons rubbed sage
1-1/2 teaspoons dried thyme
  1/2 teaspoon pepper
    1 to 1-1/2 cups chicken broth
    1 turkey (12 to 14 pounds)

1 Place bread cubes in a single layer in a 13-in. x 9-in. baking pan. Bake at 325° for 20-25 minutes or until golden brown, stirring occasionally. Place in a large bowl; set aside.

2 In a large skillet, cook ham in butter for 5-10 minutes or until edges are crisp. Remove with a slotted spoon and place over bread cubes.

3 In the same skillet, saute the onion, celery, sage, thyme and pepper until vegetables are tender; toss with bread and ham. Stir in enough broth to moisten.

4 Just before baking, stuff the turkey. Skewer openings; tie drumsticks together. Place on a rack in a roasting pan. Bake at 325° for 4-1/2 to 5 hours or until the thermometer reads 185°.

5 When the turkey begins to brown, cover lightly with a tent of aluminum foil and baste if needed. Cover turkey and let stand for 20 minutes before removing stuffing and carving turkey.

YIELD: 10-12 servings.

BUTTERY CARROTS AND BRUSSELS SPROUTS

STACY DUFFY, CHICAGO, ILLINOIS
This is a wonderful side dish for the holidays. Fresh ginger and lemon add a delicious touch.

PREP/TOTAL TIME: 20 min.

    1 pound carrots, cut into 1/4-inch slices
  3/4 pound brussels sprouts, halved
  1/4 cup butter, cubed
    1 tablespoon minced fresh gingerroot
    1 tablespoon lemon juice
    2 teaspoons grated lemon peel
    1 teaspoon sugar
Salt and pepper to taste
Minced fresh parsley, optional

1 In a large saucepan over medium heat, cook sliced carrots and brussels sprouts in boiling water for 8-10 minutes or until tender; drain.

2 In a small saucepan, melt butter. Add the ginger; cook for 2 minutes. Add the lemon juice, peel, sugar, salt and pepper; pour over vegetables. Sprinkle with parsley if desired.

YIELD: 8 servings.

TWO-POTATO SWIRLS

RUTH PLAUSHIN, SWIFTWATER, PENNSYLVANIA
Here's a great way to serve yams (known as sweet potatoes) to those who think they don't like them. You can make this dish ahead and simply reheat it before serving.

PREP: 55 min. BAKE: 25 min.

    3 large russet potatoes, peeled and quartered
    3 medium sweet potatoes, peeled and quartered
    1 package (3 ounces) cream cheese, softened
    2 to 8 tablespoons milk
    2 tablespoons butter, divided
    2 tablespoons orange juice
    1 tablespoon honey

1 Place the russet potatoes in a large saucepan and cover with water. Bring to a boil. Reduce heat; cover and cook for 10-15 minutes or until tender. Place sweet potatoes in another saucepan and cover with water. Bring to a boil. Reduce heat; cover and cook for 10-15 minutes until tender.

2 Drain the russet potatoes and place in a large bowl; mash until smooth. Add the cream cheese, 2 tablespoons milk and 1 tablespoon butter; beat until light and fluffy, adding more milk as needed.

3 Drain sweet potatoes and place in another bowl; mash until smooth. Add the orange juice, honey and remaining butter.

4 Insert tip #409 into a pastry bag. Spoon the russet potato mixture into one side of the bag; spoon sweet potato mixture into the other side.

5 Pipe 3-in. swirls, forming large rosettes, onto a greased baking sheet. Bake at 350° for 25-30 minutes or until heated through and tops are lightly browned.

YIELD: 7-8 servings.

PUMPKIN CHEESECAKE WITH SOUR CREAM TOPPING

DOROTHY SMITH, EL DORADO, ARKANSAS
Why not surprise Thanksgiving guests with this luscious cheesecake instead of the traditional pie?

PREP: 15 min. + cooling **BAKE:** 55 min. + chilling
- 1-1/2 cups graham cracker crumbs
- 1/4 cup sugar
- 1/3 cup butter, melted

FILLING:
- 3 packages (8 ounces each) cream cheese, softened
- 1 cup packed brown sugar
- 1 can (15 ounces) solid-pack pumpkin
- 1 can (5 ounces) evaporated milk
- 2 tablespoons cornstarch
- 1-1/4 teaspoons ground cinnamon
- 1/2 teaspoon ground nutmeg
- 2 eggs, lightly beaten

TOPPING:
- 2 cups (16 ounces) sour cream
- 1/3 cup sugar
- 1 teaspoon vanilla extract
Additional ground cinnamon

1 In a small bowl, combine crumbs and sugar; stir in butter. Press onto the bottom and 1-1/2 in. up the sides of a greased 9-in. springform pan. Bake at 350° for 5-7 minutes or until set. Cool for 10 minutes.

2 For filling, in a large bowl, beat the cream cheese, brown sugar, pumpkin, milk, cornstarch, cinnamon and nutmeg until smooth. Add eggs; beat on low speed just until combined. Pour into crust.

3 Place pan on a baking sheet. Bake at 350° for 55-60 minutes or until center is almost set.

4 For topping, combine the sour cream, sugar and vanilla; spread over filling. Bake 5 minutes longer. Cool on a wire rack for 10 minutes. Carefully run a knife around edge of pan to loosen; cool 1 hour longer. Chill overnight.

5 Let stand at room temperature 30 minutes before slicing. Sprinkle with cinnamon. Refrigerate leftovers.

YIELD: 12-14 servings.

CRANBERRY CHUTNEY

JOYCE VIVIAN, MITCHELL, ONTARIO
While searching for something to enhance the taste of fowl years ago, I discovered this recipe. I revised it a little, and I've since served it at Thanksgiving and Christmas gatherings (it's a hit with either poultry or pork) and used it as a food-basket gift. It's been a popular item at church bazaars.

PREP: 15 min. + chilling **COOK:** 15 min.
- 3 cups fresh or frozen cranberries
- 1 cup chopped dried apricots
- 1/2 cup chopped dates
- 1/2 cup chopped onion
- 1/2 cup cider vinegar
- 1/2 cup light corn syrup
- 3/4 cup packed brown sugar
- 1 tablespoon grated orange peel
- 3/4 cup orange juice
- 1/2 teaspoon ground mustard
- 1/2 teaspoon salt
- 1/4 teaspoon ground ginger

1 In a large heavy saucepan, combine all ingredients. Bring to a boil. Reduce heat and simmer, uncovered, for 15-20 minutes or until thickened and cranberries have popped.

2 Chill. Serve as an accompaniment to turkey or pork.

YIELD: about 3-1/2 cups.

Winter weather, full of cold, blustery winds and snowfall, is the perfect time for cozying up to a fire with a mug of hot chocolate cradled between your hands. Casseroles, stews, hearty soups and slow-cooked meals are the kind of stick-to-your-ribs foods that satisfy cold-weather appetites. The meals in this section are as comforting as a warm woolen blanket draped around your shoulders at the end of a chilly jaunt outside. This section showcases the best in rustic wintertime recipes.

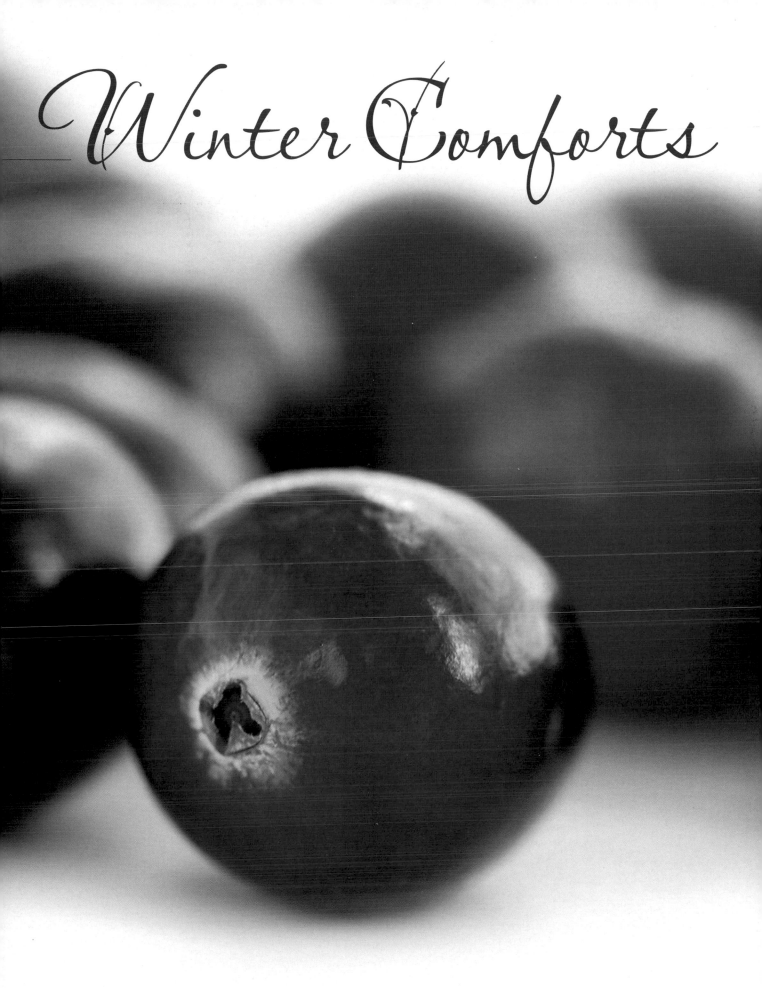

Winter Comforts

APPETIZERS & BEVERAGES

WINTER'S WARMTH HOT CHOCOLATE

JANINE JOHNSON, MINOOKA, ILLINOIS
I discovered this recipe as a newlywed when I was looking for something to warm us up during the season's first snowfall. We make it every year when we get our first snow—and on any other blustery days—that's why my husband gave it this name!

PREP/TOTAL TIME: 25 min.
-   4   squares (1 ounce each) semisweet chocolate, coarsely chopped
- 1/4   cup light corn syrup
- 1/2   teaspoon vanilla extract
- 1/4   teaspoon ground cinnamon
-   4   cups milk
-   1   cup heavy whipping cream

White chocolate curls, optional

1 In a small heavy saucepan, melt chocolate with corn syrup over low heat, stirring occasionally until smooth. Remove from the heat; stir in vanilla and cinnamon. Cover and set aside until cool. In a large saucepan, heat milk until small bubbles form around edge (do not boil).

2 Meanwhile, in a small bowl, beat the cream and cooled chocolate mixture on medium-low speed until soft peaks form. To serve, spoon chocolate cream into mugs; add hot milk and stir gently. Garnish with chocolate curls if desired.

YIELD: 4-6 servings.

SUGAR 'N' SPICE NUTS

LORI BROUWER, CUMBERLAND, BRITISH COLUMBIA
It just isn't Christmas at my house until these crunchy munchers are in the oven. The wonderful aroma of ginger, cinnamon and nuts fills the kitchen with festivity when I bake this snack.

PREP: 15 min. **BAKE:** 20 min. + cooling
-   3   egg whites
-   2   tablespoons water
-   3   cups walnut halves
-   2   cups pecan halves
-   1   cup whole unblanched almonds
-   2   cups sugar
-   2   tablespoons ground cinnamon
-   2   teaspoons ground ginger
-   2   teaspoons grated orange peel
-   1   teaspoon salt
-   1   teaspoon ground nutmeg
-   1   teaspoon ground allspice
- 1/2   teaspoon ground cloves

1 In a large bowl, beat egg whites and water until frothy. Add nuts; stir gently to coat. Combine the remaining ingredients. Add to nut mixture and stir gently to coat.

2 Spread nut mixture into two greased 15-in. x 10-in. x 1-in. baking pans. Bake, uncovered, at 300° for 20-25 minutes or until lightly browned, stirring every 10 minutes. Cool. Store in an airtight container.

YIELD: 8 cups.

STORING NUTS
To ensure nuts are readily available and to keep them from turning rancid, buy large bags of walnuts, pecans and other nuts from wholesale stores, pour them into freezer bags, label them and store them in the freezer. When fixing a recipe, just use the amount of nuts called for and put the rest back in the freezer.

POPPY SEED SQUARES

JO BADEN, INDEPENDENCE, KANSAS
When I came across these unusual yet tasty appetizers, I just knew I had to make them. Although I prepare these squares every Christmas, no one tires of them.

PREP: 35 min. **BAKE:** 25 min.

- 1 pound ground beef
- 1-1/2 cups finely chopped fresh mushrooms
- 1 medium onion, finely chopped
- 1 can (10-3/4 ounces) condensed cream of celery soup, or mushroom soup, undiluted
- 1 tablespoon prepared horseradish
- 1 teaspoon salt
- 1/2 teaspoon pepper

CRUST:
- 3 cups all-purpose flour
- 2 tablespoons poppy seeds
- 3/4 teaspoon baking powder
- 3/4 teaspoon salt
- 1 cup shortening
- 1/2 cup cold water

1 In a large skillet, cook the beef, mushrooms and onion over medium heat until the meat is no longer pink. Add the soup, horseradish, salt and pepper. Remove from the heat; set aside.

2 For crust, in a large bowl, combine the flour, poppy seeds, baking powder and salt. Cut in shortening until the mixture resembles coarse crumbs. Gradually add water, tossing with a fork until a ball forms. Divide dough in half. Roll out one portion into a 15-in. x 10-in. rectangle; transfer to an ungreased 15-in. x 10-in. x 1-in. baking pan.

3 Spoon meat mixture over dough. Roll out remaining dough into 15-in. x 10-in. rectangle; place over filling. Bake at 425° for 25 minutes or until golden brown. Cut into small squares.

YIELD: about 10 dozen.

GLAZED MEATBALLS

NANCY HORSBURGH, EVERETT, ONTARIO
Allspice adds a bit of a twist to typical barbecue meatballs in this recipe.

PREP: 30 min. **COOK:** 15 min.

- 2 eggs
- 2/3 cup milk
- 1-1/4 cups soft bread crumbs
- 1 tablespoon prepared horseradish
- 1-1/2 pounds ground beef
- 1 cup water
- 1/2 cup chili sauce
- 1/2 cup ketchup
- 1/4 cup maple syrup
- 1/4 cup soy sauce
- 1-1/2 teaspoons ground allspice
- 1/2 teaspoon ground mustard

1 In a large bowl, beat eggs and milk. Stir in bread crumbs and horseradish. Crumble beef over mixture and mix well. Shape into 1-1/2-in. balls.

2 Place the meatballs on a greased rack in a shallow baking pan. Bake at 375° for 15-20 minutes or until the meat is no longer pink; drain.

3 In a large saucepan, combine the remaining ingredients. Bring to a boil; add the meatballs. Reduce heat; cover and simmer for 15 minutes or until heated through, stirring occasionally.

YIELD: about 3-1/2 dozen.

PICANTE EGG ROLLS

MARILYN LONG, SPRING VALLEY, CALIFORNIA
Living near the Mexican border, we've developed a love of spicy cuisine. I came up with this recipe by mixing and matching different foods.

PREP: 20 min. **COOK:** 5 min./batch

- 2 pounds ground beef
- 2 cups (8 ounces) shredded cheddar cheese
- 1/2 cup picante sauce
- 1 envelope chili seasoning
- 1 teaspoon garlic powder
- 2 packages (16 ounces each) egg roll wrappers

Oil for deep-fat frying

SAUCE:

- 1 cup picante sauce
- 1/2 cup sour cream

1 In a large skillet, cook beef over medium heat until no longer pink; drain. Remove from the heat. Stir in the cheese, picante sauce, chili seasoning and garlic powder.

2 Place 1/4 cupful in the center of an egg roll wrapper. (Keep remaining wrappers covered with a damp paper towel until ready to use.) Fold bottom corner over filling. Fold sides toward center over filling. Moisten remaining corner with water; roll up tightly to seal. Repeat.

3 In an electric skillet, heat 1 in. of oil to 375°. Fry egg rolls, a few at a time, for 2-3 minutes on each side or until golden brown. Drain on paper towels. Combine sauce ingredients; serve with egg rolls.

YIELD: 2-1/2 dozen (1-1/2 cups sauce).

EDITOR'S NOTE: Fill egg roll wrappers one at a time, keeping the others covered until ready to use. Egg rolls may be reheated in a microwave for 2-1/2 to 3 minutes.

WARM CHRISTMAS PUNCH

JULIE STERCHI, HARRISBURG, ILLINOIS
Red-hot candies add rich color and spiciness to this festive punch, and the cranberry juice gives it a little tang. Our children always request it for our December 25th brunch.

PREP: 5 min. **COOK:** 2 hours

- 1 bottle (32 ounces) cranberry juice
- 1 can (32 ounces) pineapple juice
- 1/3 cup red-hot candies
- 1 cinnamon stick (3-1/2 inches)

Additional cinnamon sticks, optional

1 In a 3-qt. slow cooker, combine juices, candies and cinnamon stick. Cook on low for 2-5 hours. Discard cinnamon stick. Use additional cinnamon sticks as stirrers if desired.

YIELD: 2 quarts.

MARINATED CHICKEN WINGS

JANIE BOTTING, SULTAN, WASHINGTON
I've made these nicely flavored chicken wings many times for get-togethers. They're so moist and tender—I always get lots of compliments and many requests for the recipe.

PREP: 5 min. + marinating **COOK:** 3-1/2 hours

- 20 whole chicken wings (about 4 pounds)
- 2 cups soy sauce
- 1/2 cup white wine or chicken broth
- 1/2 cup canola oil
- 2 to 3 garlic cloves, minced
- 2 tablespoons sugar
- 2 teaspoons ground ginger

1 Cut chicken wings into three sections; discard wing tips. In a large bowl, combine remaining ingredients. Pour half the sauce into a large resealable plastic bag. Add wings, seal and toss to coat. Refrigerate overnight. Cover and refrigerate remaining marinade.

2 Drain and discard marinade from chicken. Place chicken in a 5-qt. slow cooker; top with reserved sauce. Cover and cook on low for 3-1/2 to 4 hours or until chicken juices run clear.

3 Transfer wings to a serving dish; discard cooking juices.

YIELD: 18-20 servings.

EDITOR'S NOTE: Uncooked chicken wing sections (wingettes) may be substituted for whole chicken wings.

APPETIZER TORTILLA PINWHEELS

PAT WAYMIRE, YELLOW SPRINGS, OHIO
A friend out in Arizona gave me this recipe, and whenever I serve these pretty and delicious appetizers, people ask me for the recipe!

PREP: 20 min. + chilling

- 1 cup (8 ounces) sour cream
- 1 package (8 ounces) cream cheese, softened
- 1 can (4-1/4 ounces) chopped ripe olives
- 1 can (4 ounces) chopped green chilies, well drained
- 1 cup (4 ounces) shredded cheddar cheese
- 1/2 cup chopped green onions
- Garlic powder to taste
- Seasoned salt to taste
- 5 flour tortillas (10 inches), room temperature
- Fresh parsley for garnish
- Salsa

1 In a large bowl, beat the first eight ingredients until blended. Spread over the tortillas; roll up tightly. Wrap each with plastic wrap, twisting ends; refrigerate for several hours.

2 Unwrap; cut into 1/2-in. to 3/4-in. slices. Discard the ends. Garnish with parsley. Serve with salsa if desired.

YIELD: about 4 dozen.

BLUE CHEESE WALNUT CHEESECAKE

RITA REIFENSTEIN, EVANS CITY, PENNSYLVANIA
This elegant party spread is smooth and creamy and has a mild blue cheese flavor. It's popular every time I serve it. Garnished with chopped walnuts, it looks like you fussed, but it's not that tricky to prepare.

PREP: 15 min. + chilling **BAKE:** 30 min. + cooling

- 2 packages (8 ounces each) cream cheese, softened
- 8 ounces crumbled blue cheese
- 2-1/4 cups sour cream, divided
- 3 eggs, lightly beaten
- 1/8 teaspoon pepper
- 1/2 cup chopped walnuts, toasted
- Red grapes, sliced star fruit and assorted fresh herbs, optional
- Assorted crackers

1 In a large bowl, beat cream cheese and blue cheese until fluffy. Add 1 cup of sour cream until blended. Add eggs; beat on low speed just until combined. Stir in pepper. Pour into a greased 9-in. springform pan. Place pan on a baking sheet.

2 Bake at 325° for 25-30 minutes or until center is almost set (top may crack). Let stand on a wire rack for 5 minutes; spread with remaining sour cream. Bake 5 minutes longer.

3 Cool on a wire rack for 10 minutes. Carefully run a knife around the edge of pan to loosen; cool 1 hour longer. Refrigerate overnight.

4 Sprinkle with walnuts. Garnish with grapes, star fruit and herbs if desired. Serve with crackers. Refrigerate leftovers.

YIELD: 26 servings.

CHEESECAKE BALANCING ACT
To remove a cheesecake from the bottom of a springform pan, make sure the cheesecake has chilled overnight. Remove the band from the pan; take a large knife and carefully run it under the bottom of the cheesecake to loosen it. Use two or three large pancake turners to carefully lift the cake over to the platter. Be sure the cake is equally supported by the turners so it won't crack.

HOT CHILI CHEESE DIP

JEANIE CARRIGAN, MADERA, CALIFORNIA
I simplify party preparation by using my slow cooker to create this thick cheesy dip. You won't believe how simple it is to make, and your guests won't believe how good it is.

PREP: 20 min. **COOK:** 4 hours

  1 medium onion, finely chopped
  2 garlic cloves, minced
  2 teaspoons canola oil
  2 cans (15 ounces each) chili without beans
  2 cups salsa
  2 packages (3 ounces each) cream cheese, cubed
  2 cans (2-1/4 ounces each) sliced ripe olives, drained
Tortilla chips

1 In a small skillet, saute onion and garlic in oil until tender. Transfer to a 3-qt. slow cooker. Stir in the chili, salsa, cream cheese and olives.

2 Cover and cook on low for 4 hours or until heated through, stirring occasionally. Stir before serving with tortilla chips.

YIELD: 6 cups.

ARTICHOKE DIP

MRS. WILLIAM GARNER, AUSTIN, TEXAS
It's easy to add a little color to this golden rich and delicious dip after it bakes by sprinkling the top with chopped fresh tomatoes and minced green onions.

PREP/TOTAL TIME: 30 min.

  1 can (14 ounces) water-packed artichoke hearts, rinsed, drained and chopped

  1 cup mayonnaise
  1/3 to 1/2 cup grated Parmesan cheese
  1 garlic clove, minced
Dash hot pepper sauce
Paprika, optional
Assorted crackers

1 In a large bowl, combine artichokes, mayonnaise, Parmesan, garlic and pepper sauce. Transfer to a greased 1-qt. baking dish. Sprinkle with paprika if desired.

2 Bake, uncovered, at 350° for 20-25 minutes or until top is lightly browned. Serve warm with crackers.

YIELD: 2 cups.

CRIMSON CRANBERRY PUNCH

JUDIE WHITE, FLORIEN, LOUISIANA
You can stir up this punch quickly because it calls for only a few ingredients. The pretty ice ring keeps it refreshing.

PREP: 20 min. + freezing

  1/2 cup frozen cranberries
  3-1/2 cups cold water
  1 bottle (48 ounces) white grape juice, chilled
  2 cans (12 ounces each) frozen cranberry juice concentrate, thawed
  4 cans (12 ounces each) diet lemon-lime soda, chilled
  3 orange slices
  3 lemon slices

1 Place the cranberries in a 4-1/2-cup ring mold coated with cooking spray. Slowly pour a small amount of cold water into the mold to barely cover berries; freeze until solid. Add remaining water; freeze until solid.

2 Before serving, combine grape juice and cranberry juice concentrate in a large punch bowl; stir in soda. Unmold ice ring; place fruit-side up in punch bowl. Add orange and lemon slices.

YIELD: 5 quarts.

PARMESAN FONDUE

GWYNNE FLEENER, COEUR D'ALENE, IDAHO
This recipe was given to me many years ago at a New Year's potluck. Since then, it has been a tradition to serve it at our holiday open house. The creamy mixture is always a hit.

PREP/TOTAL TIME: 15 min.
- 1-1/2 to 2 cups milk
- 2 packages (8 ounces each) cream cheese, cubed
- 1-1/2 cups grated Parmesan cheese
- 1/2 teaspoon garlic salt
- 1 loaf (1 pound) French bread, cubed

1 In a large saucepan, cook and stir the milk and cream cheese over low heat until cheese is melted. Stir in Parmesan cheese and garlic salt; cook and stir until heated through. Transfer to a fondue pot or 1-1/2-qt. slow cooker; keep warm. Serve with bread cubes.

YIELD: about 3-1/2 cups.

SPICED TEA

JANICE CONNELLEY, SPRING CREEK, NEVADA
Simply by simmering together spices, tea and fruit juices, I created a concoction that gives extra zip to festive party plans. It's easy to fix. For a nice touch, I put cinnamon stick "stirrers" in each of the cups before serving.

PREP/TOTAL TIME: 15 min.
- 3 quarts water, divided
- 4 tea bags
- 18 whole cloves
- 2 cinnamon sticks (3-1/2 inches)
- 1 can (12 ounces) frozen orange juice concentrate, thawed
- 1 can (12 ounces) frozen lemonade concentrate, thawed
- 1 cup sugar

1 In a large kettle or Dutch oven over medium heat, bring 1 qt. of water to a boil. Remove from the heat; add tea bags. Cover and steep for 5 minutes. Remove tea bags.

2 Place cloves and cinnamon sticks in a double thickness of cheesecloth; bring up corners of cloth and tie with a string (or, if desired, place loose spices in pan and strain tea before serving).

3 Place the cheesecloth bag in pan; add the concentrates, sugar, tea and remaining water; bring to a boil. Boil, uncovered, for 6 minutes. Serve hot.

YIELD: 3-1/2 quarts.

FRUIT AND CARAMEL BRIE

TRACY SCHUHMACHER, PENFIELD, NEW YORK
I'm a stay-at-home mother with two boys and I enjoy cooking—especially appetizers. It must run in the family because my mom served appetizers and desserts exclusively for several Christmas Eve celebrations. Brie is one of my favorite cheeses and this sweet-savory recipe is party-special but still fast to throw together.

PREP/TOTAL TIME: 15 min.
- 1 round (8 ounces) Brie cheese, rind removed
- 1/3 cup caramel ice cream topping
- 1/4 cup dried cranberries
- 1/4 cup chopped dried apples
- 1/4 cup chopped walnuts
- 1 loaf (1 pound) French bread baguette, sliced and toasted

1 Place Brie in a microwave-safe bowl. In a small bowl, combine caramel topping, cranberries, apples and walnuts. Spread over Brie. Microwave, uncovered, on high for 60-90 seconds or until cheese is heated through and slightly melted. Serve with toasted baguette slices.

YIELD: 8 servings.

ALL-DAY MEATBALLS

CATHY RYAN, RED WING, MINNESOTA
Folks who work outside the home can pop these meatballs into the slow cooker in the morning. By the time they get home, these are already prepared!

PREP: 15 min. **COOK:** 6 hours

- 1 cup milk
- 3/4 cup quick-cooking oats
- 3 tablespoons finely chopped onion
- 1-1/2 teaspoons salt
- 1-1/2 pounds ground beef
- 1 cup ketchup
- 1/2 cup water
- 3 tablespoons cider vinegar
- 2 tablespoons sugar

1 In a large bowl, combine the first four ingredients. Crumble beef over mixture and mix well. Shape into 1-in. balls. Place in a 5-qt. slow cooker.

2 In a small bowl, combine the ketchup, water, vinegar and sugar. Pour over meatballs. Cover and cook on low for 6-8 hours or until meat is no longer pink.

YIELD: 6 servings.

MAKING MEATBALLS OF EQUAL SIZE

Lightly pat meat mixture into a 1-in.-thick rectangle. Cut the rectangle into the same number of squares as meatballs in the recipe. Gently roll each square into a ball. Or if you have a 1-1/2- or 1-3/4-inch-diameter scoop, scoop the mixture into equally sized portions. Gently roll each into a ball.

MULLED WINE

TASTE OF HOME TEST KITCHEN
This mulled wine is soothing and satisfying with a delightful blend of spices warmed to perfection. Refrigerating the wine mixture overnight allows the flavors to blend, so don't omit this essential step.

PREP: 15 min. **COOK:** 30 min. + chilling

- 1 bottle (750 milliliters) fruity red wine
- 1 cup brandy
- 1 medium orange, sliced
- 1 medium lemon, sliced
- 1 cup sugar
- 1/8 teaspoon ground nutmeg
- 2 cinnamon sticks (3 inches)
- 1/2 teaspoon whole allspice
- 1/2 teaspoon aniseed
- 1/2 teaspoon whole peppercorns
- 3 whole cloves

GARNISH:
Cinnamon stick, star anise and orange twist

1 In a large saucepan, combine the wine, brandy, orange, lemon, sugar and nutmeg. Place remaining spices on a double thickness of cheesecloth; bring up corners of cloth and tie with string to form a bag. Add spice bag to wine mixture.

2 Bring to a boil, stirring occasionally. Reduce heat; cover and simmer gently for 20 minutes. Cool; cover and refrigerate overnight.

3 Strain; discard fruit and spice bag. Reheat wine; serve warm in mugs. Garnish as desired.

YIELD: 5 servings.

EDITOR'S NOTE: This recipe was tested with Rioja wine. Merlot would also work well.

CRAB AU GRATIN SPREAD

SUZANNE ZICK, LINCOLNTON, NORTH CAROLINA
For a warm and winning appetizer, serve this special cracker spread. It's rich tasting and easy to whip up with convenient canned crab.

PREP: 20 min. **BAKE:** 15 min.

    2 tablespoons plus 1 teaspoon butter, divided
    3 tablespoons all-purpose flour
1/2 teaspoon salt
1/8 teaspoon paprika
1/2 cup half-and-half cream
1/2 cup milk
1/4 cup white wine or chicken broth
    1 can (6 ounces) crabmeat, drained, flaked and cartilage removed or 2/3 cup chopped imitation crabmeat
    1 can (4 ounces) mushroom stems and pieces, drained and chopped
1-1/2 teaspoons minced chives
1/2 cup shredded cheddar cheese
    1 tablespoon dry bread crumbs
Assorted crackers

1 In a large saucepan, melt 2 tablespoons butter. Stir in the flour, salt and paprika until smooth. Gradually add the cream, milk and wine. Bring to a boil; cook and stir for 1-2 minutes or until thickened. Stir in the crab, mushrooms and chives; heat through. Stir in cheese just until melted.

2 Transfer to a greased shallow 1-qt. baking dish. Melt remaining butter; toss with bread crumbs. Sprinkle over crab mixture. Bake, uncovered, at 400° for 10-15 minutes or until bubbly. Let stand for 5 minutes. Serve with crackers.

YIELD: about 2 cups.

BROCCOLI CHEDDAR SPREAD

BETH PARKER, GRAYSVILLE, ALABAMA
I was able to lighten up the original recipe for this thick, warm spread without losing any of the flavor.

PREP: 15 min. **BAKE:** 20 min.

    4 cups chopped fresh broccoli
    1 tablespoon water
    2 cups (16 ounces) reduced-fat sour cream
1/2 cup plus 1 tablespoon shredded reduced-fat cheddar cheese, divided
    1 envelope vegetable soup mix
Pita chips or reduced-fat crackers

1 Place the broccoli and water in a 1-1/2-qt. microwave-safe dish. Cover and microwave on high for 3-4 minutes or until crisp-tender; drain. In a large bowl, combine the sour cream, 1/2 cup cheese and soup mix. Gently stir in broccoli.

2 Transfer to an ungreased shallow 1-qt. baking dish. Sprinkle with remaining cheese. Bake, uncovered, at 350° for 20-25 minutes or until heated through. Serve with pita chip or crackers.

YIELD: 3 cups.

RASPBERRY FONDUE DIP

EDNA HOFFMAN, HEBRON, INDIANA
My guests are delighted with this fun, non-traditional fondue. Creamy apple butter and cinnamon red hots add tangy flair!

PREP/TOTAL TIME: 25 min.

    1 package (10 ounces) frozen sweetened raspberries
    1 cup apple butter
    1 tablespoon red-hot candies
    2 teaspoons cornstarch
Assorted fresh fruit

1 Place raspberries in a small bowl; set aside to thaw. Strain the raspberries, reserving 1 tablespoon juice; discard seeds.

2 In a small saucepan, combine the strained berries, apple butter and red-hots; cook over medium heat until candies are dissolved, stirring occasionally.

3 In a small bowl, combine cornstarch and reserved juice until smooth; stir into berry mixture. Bring to a boil; cook and stir over medium heat for 1-2 minutes or until thickened.

4 Transfer to a serving dish, fondue pot or 1-1/2-qt. slow cooker. Serve warm or cold with fruit.

YIELD: 1 cup.

WINTER WARMER

SALLY SEIDEL, BANNER, WYOMING
I found this beverage recipe more than 15 years ago, when I was in high school. My husband and I also enjoy it after the children go to bed.

PREP/TOTAL TIME: 10 min.

- 2 envelopes (1 ounce each) instant hot cocoa mix or 1/2 cup instant hot cocoa mix
- 3 cups hot brewed coffee
- 1/4 cup half-and-half cream
- 3/4 teaspoon rum extract
- 1/4 cup whipped topping

Ground cinnamon, optional

1 In a small saucepan, whisk together the cocoa mix, coffee, cream and rum extract until heated through and cocoa is dissolved. Pour into mugs. Garnish with whipped topping; sprinkle with cinnamon if desired.

YIELD: 2 servings.

EDITOR'S NOTE: For grown-up Winter Warmers, omit the rum extract and pour 1 to 2 oz. dark rum into each mug before adding the coffee mixture.

TEA TODDY

TASTE OF HOME TEST KITCHEN
Soothing and comforting, this drink is a great way to wrap up an evening of entertaining. Although it contains alcohol, the taste is smooth. It's a great change-of-pace beverage.

PREP/TOTAL TIME: 5 min.

- 1 cup hot brewed Earl Grey tea
- 1-1/2 ounces Irish cream liqueur
- 1 teaspoon sugar
- 1 teaspoon Scotch or rye whiskey

1 In a tea cup, combine the tea, liqueur, sugar and Scotch. Serve immediately.

YIELD: 1 serving.

CHICKEN TURNOVERS

SANDRA LEE HERR, STEVENS, PENNSYLVANIA
This hot and filling appetizer is a wonderful way to use up leftover chicken. Sometimes, I serve it with fruit salad for a delicious, light meal for up to four people.

PREP/TOTAL TIME: 30 min.

- 1 cup diced cooked chicken breast
- 1 cup (4 ounces) shredded reduced-fat cheddar cheese
- 1/4 cup chopped celery
- 1 tablespoon finely chopped onion
- 1/4 teaspoon salt
- 1/4 teaspoon pepper
- 1 tube (8 ounces) refrigerated reduced-fat crescent rolls

1 In a small bowl, combine the chicken, cheese, celery, onion, salt and pepper. Separate crescent dough into eight triangles; top each with chicken mixture. Fold dough over and seal edges.

2 Place on an ungreased baking sheet. Bake at 375° for 13-17 minutes or until golden brown. Serve warm.

YIELD: 8 servings.

ONION BRIE APPETIZERS

CAROLE RESNICK, CLEVELAND, OHIO
Guests will think you spent hours preparing these cute appetizers, but they're really easy to assemble because they require convenient, purchased puff pastry. The tasty combination of Brie, caramelized onions and caraway is terrific.

PREP: 25 min. + chilling BAKE: 15 min.
       2 medium onions, thinly sliced
       3 tablespoons butter
       2 tablespoons brown sugar
    1/2 teaspoon white wine vinegar
       1 sheet frozen puff pastry, thawed
       4 ounces Brie or Camembert, rind removed, softened
       1 to 2 teaspoons caraway seeds
       1 egg
       2 teaspoons water

1 In a large skillet, cook the onions, butter, brown sugar and vinegar over medium-low heat until onions are golden brown, stirring frequently. Remove with a slotted spoon; cool to room temperature.

2 On a lightly floured surface, roll puff pastry into an 11-in. x 8-in. rectangle. Spread Brie over pastry. Cover with the onions; sprinkle with caraway seeds.

3 Roll up one long side to the middle of the dough; roll up the other side so the two rolls meet in the center. Using a serrated knife, cut into 1/2-in. slices. Place on parchment paper-lined baking sheets; flatten to 1/4-in. thickness. Refrigerate for 15 minutes.

4 In a small bowl, beat egg and water; brush over slices. Bake at 375° for 12-14 minutes or until puffed and golden brown. Serve warm.

YIELD: 1-1/2 dozen.

MARVELOUS MOCHA MIX

SHIRLEY BRAZEL, ROCKLIN, CALIFORNIA
A tin of this mix with serving instructions makes a ready-to-soothe Christmas gift. My husband and I take it to senior citizens we visit. It perks them right up! It's super easy to make, and it always makes people happy.

PREP/TOTAL TIME: 10 min.
       1 cup instant chocolate drink mix
       1 cup powdered nondairy creamer
    2/3 cup instant coffee granules
    1/2 cup sugar
    1/2 teaspoon ground cinnamon
    1/4 teaspoon ground nutmeg

1 In an airtight container, combine all ingredients. Store in a cool dry place for up to 6 months.

YIELD: 3 cups mix (24-36 servings).

2 To make one serving: Add 4-6 teaspoons mix to 3/4 cup boiling water; stir until dissolved.

YIELD: 1 serving.

ADDING FLAIR TO HOT COCOA AND COFFEE
A festive garnish or added flavorings can add pizzazz to any hot beverage. Along with a dollop of whipped cream topped with chocolate sprinkles or toasted coconut, accent with festive candy-cane swizzle sticks. You can also add flavorings, such as almond, orange or maple to spruce up your hot drink.

259 256 267 260

SOUPS, STEWS & SANDWICHES

265

MEATBALL SUB SANDWICHES

DEENA HUBLER, JASPER, INDIANA
Making these saucy meatballs in advance, then reheating, saves me precious time when I'm expecting company. These sandwiches are great casual fare for any get-together.

PREP/TOTAL TIME: 30 min.

   2 eggs, lightly beaten
   1 cup dry bread crumbs
   2 tablespoons grated Parmesan cheese
   2 tablespoons finely chopped onion
   1 teaspoon salt
1/2 teaspoon pepper
1/2 teaspoon garlic powder
1/4 teaspoon Italian seasoning
   2 pounds ground beef
   1 jar (28 ounces) spaghetti sauce
Additional Parmesan cheese, and sliced onion and green peppers, optional
12 sandwich rolls, split

1 In a large bowl, combine the first eight ingredients. Crumble beef over mixture and mix well. Shape into 1-in. balls. Place in a single layer in a 3-qt. microwave-safe dish.

2 Cover and microwave on high for 3-4 minutes. Turn meatballs; cook 3-4 minutes longer or until no longer pink. Drain. Add spaghetti sauce.

3 Cover and microwave on high for 2-4 minutes or until heated through. Top with Parmesan cheese, onion and green peppers if desired. Serve on rolls.

YIELD: 12 servings.

ROASTED CHICKEN NOODLE SOUP

JULEE WALLBERG, SALT LAKE CITY, UTAH
When the weather turns chilly and I need something to satisfy my hunger, I stock my soup pot with this warmer-upper. The creamy, nicely seasoned broth is chock-full of tender chicken, potatoes, carrots and celery. There's old-fashioned goodness in every spoonful of this thick, hearty soup!

PREP: 10 min. **COOK:** 30 min.

   1 cup chopped onion
   1 cup chopped carrots
   1 cup chopped celery
   1 garlic clove, minced
   2 teaspoons olive oil
1/4 cup all-purpose flour
1/2 teaspoon dried oregano
1/4 teaspoon dried thyme
1/4 teaspoon poultry seasoning
   6 cups reduced-sodium chicken broth
   4 cups cubed peeled potatoes
   1 teaspoon salt
   2 cups cubed cooked chicken breast
   2 cups uncooked yolk-free wide noodles
   1 cup fat-free evaporated milk

1 In a stockpot, saute onion, carrots, celery and garlic in oil for 5 minutes or until tender. Stir in the flour, oregano, thyme and poultry seasoning until blended; saute 1 minute longer.

2 Gradually add broth, potatoes and salt; bring to a boil. Reduce heat; cover and simmer for 15-20 minutes or until potatoes are tender.

3 Stir in the chicken and noodles; simmer for 10 minutes or until noodles are tender. Reduce heat. Stir in milk; heat through (do not boil).

YIELD: 8 servings.

PORK AND WINTER SQUASH STEW

EVELYN PLYLER, APPLE VALLEY, CALIFORNIA
Here in the high desert area of California, we do get snow. So this stew's especially popular in winter.

PREP: 25 min. **COOK:** 1-1/2 hours

- 2 pounds lean boneless pork, cut into 1-inch cubes
- 2 tablespoons canola oil, divided
- 2 cups chopped onion
- 2 garlic cloves, minced
- 3 cups sliced fresh mushrooms
- 2-1/2 cups diagonally sliced carrots
- 2 cans (14-1/2 ounces each) Italian stewed tomatoes
- 2 teaspoons dried thyme
- 1/2 teaspoon pepper
- 1-1/2 teaspoon salt, optional
- 4 cups cubed peeled butternut squash
Hot cooked noodles, optional

1 In a Dutch oven or saucepan, brown pork in 1 tablespoon of oil. Remove from pan; drain. Heat remaining oil in the same pan over medium heat. Saute onion and garlic for 3 minutes.

2 Return pork to pan. Add the mushrooms, carrots, tomatoes and seasonings; bring to a boil. Reduce heat; cover and simmer for 1 hour.

3 Add squash; simmer, uncovered for 30 minutes or until meat and vegetables are tender. Serve with noodles if desired.

YIELD: 8 servings.

SAUSAGE POTATO WRAPS

JULIA RATHBURN, BEGGS, OKLAHOMA
With our busy schedules, we're always on the lookout for quick recipes. My husband came up with these mouthwatering wraps we frequently rely on in a morning rush.

PREP/TOTAL TIME: 30 min.

- 1 pound bulk hot pork sausage
- 1 package (28 ounces) frozen O'Brien potatoes
- 4 eggs
- 1/2 cup milk
Salt and pepper to taste
- 12 flour tortillas (8 inches)
Sour cream and salsa, optional

1 In a large skillet, cook sausage over medium heat until no longer pink; drain. Add potatoes; cook until lightly browned, about 15 minutes.

2 In a large bowl, whisk the eggs, milk, salt and pepper; add to sausage mixture. Cook and stir over medium heat until eggs are completely set. Divide mixture between tortillas; roll up tightly.

3 Place in a greased 13-in. x 9-in. baking dish. Microwave, uncovered, on high for 2-4 minutes or until heated through, or microwave individually for 30 seconds. Serve with sour cream and salsa if desired.

YIELD: 6-8 servings.

HOT TURKEY SANDWICHES

MARGERY BRYAN, MOSES LAKE, WASHINGTON
I like to team these tasty sandwiches with a salad or green beans for a pretty meal that's really filling. They're also a great way to use up holiday leftovers. For a tasty twist, try substituting cranberry stuffing mix for the savory variety.

PREP/TOTAL TIME: 15 min.

- 1 package (6 ounces) chicken stuffing mix
- 4 slices white bread, toasted
- 1 pound thinly sliced deli turkey
- 1 cup turkey gravy

1 Prepare stuffing mix according to package directions. Place the toast on a large microwave-safe plate; top each with turkey, stuffing and gravy. Microwave, uncovered, on high for 30-40 seconds or until heated through.

YIELD: 4 servings.

HEARTWARMING CHILI

AUDREY BYRNE, LILLIAN, TEXAS

A touch of baking cocoa gives this chili a rich flavor without adding sweetness. When I was growing up in the North, we served chili over rice. But after I married a Texan, I began serving it with chopped onions, shredded cheese and, of course, corn bread!

PREP: 10 min. **COOK:** 20 min. + simmering

- 1 pound ground beef
- 1 large onion, chopped
- 2 cans (16 ounces each) kidney beans, rinsed and drained
- 2 cans (14-1/2 ounces each) diced tomatoes
- 1 can (8 ounces) tomato sauce
- 1 medium green pepper
- 3 tablespoons chili powder
- 1 tablespoon ground cumin
- 2 garlic cloves, minced
- 1 teaspoon baking cocoa
- 1 teaspoon dried oregano
- 1 teaspoon Worcestershire sauce, optional

Salt and pepper to taste

1 In a large saucepan, cook beef and onion over medium heat until the meat is no longer pink; drain. Add the remaining ingredients; bring to a boil. Reduce heat; cover and simmer for 3 hours, stirring occasionally.

YIELD: 4 servings.

ITALIAN SAUSAGE CALZONE

TERRI GALLAGHER, KING GEORGE, VIRGINIA

My teenage daughter and I have been experimenting in the kitchen to recreate some old-time family dishes. This calzone with spinach and sausage is definitely a favorite. Using a refrigerated pizza crust, it's a cinch to prepare just one or several for a crowd.

PREP: 20 min. **BAKE:** 30 min. + standing

- 1 tube (13.8 ounces) refrigerated pizza crust
- 1 can (8 ounces) pizza sauce
- 1 package (10 ounces) frozen chopped spinach, thawed and squeezed dry
- 1 pound bulk Italian sausage, cooked and drained
- 1 jar (4-1/2 ounces) sliced mushrooms, drained
- 2 cups (8 ounces) shredded part-skim mozzarella cheese

1 Unroll pizza dough onto an ungreased baking sheet; pat into a 14-in. x 11-in. rectangle. Spread pizza sauce over one long side of dough to within 1/2 in. of edges.

2 Layer the spinach, sausage, mushrooms and cheese over sauce. Fold dough over filling; pinch seams to seal.

3 Bake at 400° for 30-35 minutes or until golden brown. Let stand for 10-15 minutes before slicing.

YIELD: 6 servings.

SAY CHEESE!

When buying bulk cheese, 4 ounces equals 1 cup shredded. Store cheese in an airtight container, plastic bag or plastic wrap in the refrigerator (about 4 months for soft cheeses and 6 months for hard cheeses). Cheese can be frozen for longer storage time. Because the freezing process changes the cheese's texture slightly, it is best to use it in cooking or baking.

HOMEMADE TURKEY SOUP

JUNE SANGREY, MANHEIM, PENNSYLVANIA

You can make the most of even the smallest pieces of leftover meat from your holiday turkey. I simmer the bones to get the rich flavor, then easily remove any meat that remains. I add rice, vegetables and cream soup for a hearty soup that's tasty and economical.

PREP: 30 min. **COOK:** 2 hours 35 min.

- 1 leftover turkey carcass (from a 10- to 12-pound turkey)
- 2 quarts water
- 1 medium onion, halved
- 1/2 teaspoon salt
- 2 bay leaves
- 1 cup chopped carrots
- 1 cup uncooked long grain rice
- 1/3 cup chopped celery
- 1/4 cup chopped onion
- 1 can (10-3/4 ounces) condensed cream of chicken or cream of mushroom soup, undiluted

1 Place the turkey carcass in a stockpot; add the water, onion, salt and bay leaves. Slowly bring to a boil over low heat; cover and simmer for 2 hours.

2 Remove carcass; cool. Strain broth and skim off fat. Discard onion and bay leaves. Return broth to the pan. Add the carrots, rice, celery and chopped onion; cover and simmer until rice and vegetables are tender.

3 Remove turkey from the bones; cut into bite-size pieces. Add turkey and cream soup to broth; heat through.

YIELD: 8-10 servings (about 2 quarts).

OVEN BEEF STEW

DEBBIE PATTON, WESTCHESTER, ILLINOIS

A thick flavorful sauce makes this hearty dish one that will be requested time and again. I know your family will enjoy it.

PREP: 15 min. + standing **COOK:** 2 -1/2 hours

- 1 beef top round roast (2 pounds), cut into 1-1/2-inch cubes
- 2 medium potatoes, peeled and cut into 1/2-inch cubes
- 2 medium onions, cut into eighths
- 3 celery ribs, cut into 1-inch pieces
- 4 medium carrots, cut into 1-inch slices
- 1 can (11-1/2 ounces) tomato juice
- 1/3 cup dry sherry or water
- 1/3 cup quick-cooking tapioca
- 1 tablespoon sugar
- 1 teaspoon salt
- 1/2 teaspoon dried basil
- 1/4 teaspoon pepper
- 2 cups fresh green beans, cut into 1-inch pieces

1 In a Dutch oven, combine the beef, potatoes, onions, celery and carrots; set aside.

2 In a large bowl, combine the tomato juice, sherry or water, tapioca, sugar, salt, basil and pepper. Let stand for 15 minutes.

3 Pour over beef mixture. Cover and bake at 325° for 2 to 2-1/2 hours or until meat is almost tender.

4 Add the beans; cook 30 minutes longer or until beans and meat are tender.

YIELD: 8 servings.

SMOTHERED ONION PATTY MELTS

MARGIE JARVIS, DECATUR, TENNESSEE
Looking for a new twist on burgers? I created a patty melt loaded with onions and Swiss cheese on rye bread. This flavorful combination is a great way to use ground turkey as well.

PREP: 30 min. GRILL: 15 min.

- 2 medium onions, sliced
- 1 teaspoon canola oil
- 1/8 teaspoon plus 1/2 teaspoon salt, divided
- 1/4 teaspoon pepper, divided
- 2 teaspoons Dijon mustard
- 1 garlic clove, minced
- 1/4 teaspoon dried thyme
- 1/4 teaspoon dried oregano
- 1 pound ground beef or turkey
- 8 slices rye bread, toasted
- 4 slices Swiss cheese

1 In a large nonstick skillet, saute onions in oil for 3 minutes. Sprinkle with 1/8 teaspoon salt and 1/8 teaspoon pepper. Reduce heat; cover and simmer for 25-30 minutes or until onions are tender.

2 Meanwhile, in a large bowl, combine the mustard, garlic, thyme, oregano and remaining salt and pepper. Crumble beef over mixture and mix well. Shape into four patties.

3 Grill patties, covered, over medium-hot heat for 6-8 minutes on each side or until a meat thermometer reads 160° and juices run clear. Place each patty on a slice of toast; top with cheese, onions and remaining toast.

YIELD: 4 servings.

ITALIAN STEW

TASTE OF HOME TEST KITCHEN
Escarole is wonderful in soups and stews. Wash each leaf well, pat dry and trim off the white core.

PREP: 10 min. COOK: 30 min.

- 1 pound ground beef
- 1/2 pound bulk mild Italian sausage
- 1 cup chopped onion
- 1 can (15 ounces) cannellini or white kidney beans, rinsed and drained
- 2 cups cut fresh green beans
- 1 can (14-1/2 ounces) Italian stewed tomatoes
- 1 cup vegetable broth
- 1 can (6 ounces) tomato paste
- 2 teaspoons dried oregano
- 1 teaspoon salt
- 1/2 teaspoon pepper
- 1 bunch escarole, trimmed and torn
- 1/2 cup shredded Parmesan cheese

1 In a large skillet or Dutch oven, cook the beef, sausage and onion over medium heat until meat is no longer pink; drain. Add cannellini, green beans, tomatoes, broth, tomato paste, oregano, salt and pepper.

2 Bring to a boil. Reduce heat; cover and simmer for 15 minutes. Add the escarole; cover and simmer 5 minutes longer or until escarole is wilted. Sprinkle with Parmesan cheese.

YIELD: 6 servings.

ABOUT ESCAROLE
Escarole, a salad green in the endive family, has a slightly bitter taste (but not as bitter as curly or Belgian endive). With broad leaves that are slightly curled, escarole has bright green outer leaves that grow lighter toward the interior of the bunch. Escarole is available all year round with its peak season in winter and spring.

FLAVORFUL WHITE CHILI

WILDA BENSENHAVER, DELAND, FLORIDA

For a tasty twist on conventional chili, try this delicious version. It's packed with plenty of beans, tender grilled chicken and a zippy blend of spices.

PREP: 10 min. + standing **COOK:** 8 hours

- 1 pound dried great northern beans
- 4 cups chicken broth
- 2 cups chopped onions
- 3 garlic cloves, minced
- 2 teaspoons ground cumin
- 1-1/2 teaspoons dried oregano
- 1 teaspoon ground coriander
- 1/8 teaspoon ground cloves
- 1/8 teaspoon cayenne pepper
- 1 can (4 ounces) chopped green chilies
- 1/2 pound boneless skinless chicken breast, grilled and cubed
- 1 teaspoon salt
- 3/4 cup shredded reduced-fat Mexican cheese blend

1 Sort beans and rinse with cold water. Place beans in a soup kettle or Dutch oven; add water to cover by 2 in. Bring to a boil; boil for 2 minutes. Remove from the heat; cover and let stand for 1 hour. Drain and rinse beans, discarding liquid.

2 Place beans in a 3-qt. slow cooker. Add the broth, onions, garlic and seasonings. Cover and cook on low for 7-8 hours or until the beans are almost tender. Add the chilies, chicken and salt; cover and cook for 1 hour or until the beans are tender. Serve with shredded cheese.

YIELD: 6 servings.

SAVORY WINTER SOUP

DANA SIMMONS, LANCASTER, OHIO

Even my father, who doesn't particularly like soup, enjoys my full-flavored version of traditional vegetable soup. He asked me to share the recipe with Mom, and I gladly obliged!

PREP: 20 min. **COOK:** 8 hours

- 2 pounds ground beef
- 3 medium onions, chopped
- 1 garlic clove, minced
- 3 cans (10-1/2 ounces each) condensed beef broth, undiluted
- 1 can (28 ounces) diced tomatoes, undrained
- 3 cups water
- 1 cup each diced carrots and celery
- 1 cup fresh or frozen cut green beans
- 1 cup cubed peeled potatoes
- 2 tablespoons minced fresh parsley or 2 teaspoons dried parsley flakes
- 1 teaspoon dried basil
- 1/2 teaspoon dried thyme
Salt and pepper to taste

1 In a skillet, cook beef, onions and garlic over medium heat until the meat is no longer pink; drain. Transfer to a 5-qt. slow cooker. Stir in the remaining ingredients. Cover and cook on high for 8 hours or until heated through.

YIELD: 14 servings (3-1/2 quarts).

EDITOR'S NOTE: To save chopping time, use frozen sliced carrots and cubed hash brown potatoes in Savory Winter Soup.

SWEET POTATO KALE SOUP

TAMAR HOLMES, SAN DIEGO, CALIFORNIA

If you're looking for a healthier dish with a difference, try this recipe. White kidney beans, sweet potatoes, kale and plenty of garlic flavor this brothy blend. It's the perfect winter soup and has soothed me through many a cold. It's a cinch to make, too.

PREP: 15 min. **COOK:** 30 min.

- 1 large onion, chopped
- 3-1/2 teaspoons Italian seasoning
- 2 teaspoons olive oil
- 3 cans (14-1/2 ounces each) vegetable broth
- 2 cans (15 ounces each) white kidney or cannellini beans, rinsed and drained
- 1 pound sweet potatoes, peeled and cubed
- 5 cups chopped fresh kale
- 12 garlic cloves, minced
- 1/2 teaspoon salt
- 1/4 teaspoon pepper

1 In a large saucepan or Dutch oven, saute onion and Italian seasoning in oil until onion is tender.

2 Stir in the broth, beans, sweet potatoes and kale. Bring to a boil. Reduce heat; simmer, uncovered for 10 minutes. Stir in the garlic, salt and pepper. Simmer 10-15 minutes longer or until potatoes are tender.

YIELD: 8 servings (2 quarts).

PEPPER STEAK SANDWICHES

JULIE TULLOS, CLINTON, MISSISSIPPI

Piled high with steak and topped with sauteed vegetables, special sauce and gooey cheese, these sandwiches are a surefire hit.

PREP/TOTAL TIME: 25 min.

- 1 pound frozen beef sandwich steaks, thawed
- 4 teaspoons canola oil, divided
- 1 medium sweet onion, chopped
- 3/4 cup julienned green pepper
- 1/4 teaspoon salt
- 1/4 teaspoon pepper
- 1 cup chopped dill pickles
- 1/2 cup Italian salad dressing
- 1/2 cup chopped fresh tomato
- 1/4 cup chopped red onion
- 5 hard rolls, split
- 2 cups (8 ounces) shredded part-skim mozzarella cheese

1 In a large skillet, cook the steaks in 2 teaspoons oil in batches over medium heat for 3-4 minutes or until no longer pink. Meanwhile, in another skillet, saute the sweet onion and green pepper in remaining oil until tender; sprinkle with salt and pepper.

2 In a small bowl, combine the pickles, salad dressing, tomato and red onion; set aside.

3 Place the roll tops, cut side up, on a baking sheet. Sprinkle with cheese. Broil 4 in. from the heat for 2 minutes or until cheese is melted. Place a steak on each roll bottom; top with onion mixture and pickle mixture. Replace roll tops.

YIELD: 5 servings.

TOMATO-BACON RAREBIT

LINDA MAY, MOGADORE, OHIO

I've had an interest in cooking and baking since I was a young girl and love to experiment with recipes. With bacon and tomatoes, this is a tasty takeoff on a classic Welsh dish.

PREP/TOTAL TIME: 20 min.

- 1 tablespoon butter
- 1 tablespoon all-purpose flour
- 2/3 cup milk
- 1 teaspoon Worcestershire sauce
- 1/4 teaspoon ground mustard

1/4 teaspoon salt
1/8 teaspoon pepper
1/8 teaspoon paprika
2 cups (8 ounces) shredded sharp cheddar cheese
4 slices white bread, toasted
12 bacon strips, cooked and drained
2 medium tomatoes, sliced

1 In a large saucepan, melt butter over medium heat. Stir in the flour until smooth. Gradually stir in milk. Bring to a boil; cook and stir for 2 minutes or until thickened and bubbly. Reduce heat to low; add the Worcestershire sauce, mustard, salt, pepper, paprika and cheese. Cook and stir until cheese is melted.

2 Place toast on plates; top each piece with three bacon strips, two slices of tomato and cheese sauce.

YIELD: 4 servings.

MOZZARELLA TUNA MELTS

JO MAASBERG, FARSON, WYOMING
Our daughter's home economics teacher shared the recipe for these all-American treats. Using a mini food processor to chop the celery and onion for the filling helps shave preparation time. They're great with a hot bowl of soup.

PREP/TOTAL TIME: 30 min.
1 can (6 ounces) water-packed tuna, drained and flaked
1/4 cup finely chopped celery
1/4 cup finely chopped onion
1/4 cup mayonnaise
4 hamburger buns, split
4 slices part-skim mozzarella cheese
4 tomato slices
4 lettuce leaves

1 In a small bowl, combine tuna, celery, onion and mayonnaise. Spread on bottom of buns; set bun tops aside. Top tuna mixture with a slice of cheese and tomato.

2 Place on an ungreased baking sheet. Bake, uncovered, at 350° for 12-15 minutes or until heated through and cheese is melted. Top each with a lettuce leaf; replace bun tops.

YIELD: 4 servings.

KIELBASA CABBAGE SOUP

PATRICIA BOSSEE, DARIEN CENTER, NEW YORK
Cabbage is plentiful in upstate New York. During winter, I like to keep this hearty soup simmering on the stovetop all day.

PREP: 30 min. **COOK:** 1-1/4 hours
1 small head cabbage, coarsely chopped
1 medium onion, chopped
4 to 6 garlic cloves, minced
2 tablespoons olive oil
4 cups water
3 tablespoons cider vinegar
1 to 2 tablespoons brown sugar
1 pound smoked kielbasa or Polish sausage, halved, cut into 1/2-inch pieces
4 medium potatoes, peeled and cubed
3 large carrots, chopped
1 teaspoon caraway seeds
1/2 teaspoon pepper

1 In a Dutch oven or soup kettle, saute the cabbage, onion and garlic in oil for 5 minutes or until tender. Combine the water, vinegar and brown sugar; add to cabbage mixture.

2 Stir in the remaining ingredients. Bring to a boil. Reduce heat; cover and simmer for 60-70 minutes or until vegetables are tender.

YIELD: 8-10 servings.

A VARIETY OF VINEGARS
Distilled white vinegar is made from a grain alcohol mix. It has a strong sharp flavor and is most often used for pickling foods and as a cleaning agent. White wine vinegar is made from white wine and, although its flavor is pungent, it is milder than distilled white vinegar. For savory dishes, most people prefer white wine vinegar. Vinegar should be kept in a cool dark place. Unopened, it will keep indefinitely; once opened, it can be stored for up to 6 months.

ONION SOUP WITH SAUSAGE

SUNDRA HAUCK, BOGALUSA, LOUISIANA
With a yummy slice of mozzarella cheese bread on top, this hearty broth makes an impressive luncheon or light supper. It looks great and tastes wonderful.

PREP/TOTAL TIME: 20 min.

- 1/2 pound pork sausage links, cut into 1/2-inch pieces
- 1 pound sliced fresh mushrooms
- 1 cup sliced onion
- 2 cans (14-1/2 ounces each) beef broth
- 4 slices Italian bread
- 1/2 cup shredded part-skim mozzarella cheese

1 In a large saucepan, cook sausage over medium heat until no longer pink; drain. Add mushrooms and onion; cook for 4-6 minutes or until tender. Stir in the broth. Bring to a boil. Reduce heat; simmer, uncovered, for 4-6 minutes or until heated through.

2 Ladle into four 2-cup ovenproof bowls. Top each with a slice of bread; sprinkle with cheese. Broil until cheese is melted.

YIELD: 4 servings.

HOT SWISS CHICKEN SANDWICHES

EDITH TABOR, VANCOUVER, WASHINGTON
I've been making these open-faced sandwiches for years, and people always ask for the recipe. I sometimes serve the filling on slices of sourdough or tucked into pitas.

PREP/TOTAL TIME: 20 min.

- 1/4 cup reduced-fat mayonnaise
- 1/4 teaspoon salt
- 1/4 teaspoon lemon juice
- 1-1/2 cups diced cooked chicken breast
- 2/3 cup chopped celery
- 1/2 cup shredded reduced-fat Swiss cheese
- 4 teaspoons butter, softened
- 6 slices Italian bread (about 3/4 inch thick)
- 6 slices tomato
- 3/4 cup shredded lettuce

1 In a large bowl, combine the mayonnaise, salt and lemon juice. Stir in the chicken, celery and cheese. Spread butter on each slice of bread; top each with 1/3 cup chicken mixture.

2 Place in a 15-in. x 10-in. x 1-in. baking pan. Broil 4-6 in. from the heat for 3-4 minutes or until heated through. Top with tomato and lettuce.

YIELD: 6 servings.

SAUSAGE KALE SOUP

SUSAN PURSELL, FOUNTAIN VALLEY, CALIFORNIA
The hearty sausage slices, white kidney beans and colorful kale in this soup will keep your gang asking for seconds.

PREP: 10 min. **COOK:** 25 min.

- 3/4 cup chopped onion
- 2 garlic cloves, minced
- 1 tablespoon olive oil
- 4 cups reduced-sodium chicken broth
- 2 medium potatoes, peeled and cubed
- 1/4 teaspoon salt
- 1/4 teaspoon pepper
- 1 bunch kale, trimmed and chopped
- 1 can (15 ounces) white kidney or cannellini beans, rinsed and drained
- 1/2 pound reduced-fat fully cooked Polish sausage or turkey kielbasa, sliced

1 In a large saucepan or Dutch oven, saute onion and garlic in oil until tender. Add the broth, potatoes, salt and pepper. Bring to a boil. Reduce heat; cover and simmer for 10-15 minutes or until potatoes are tender.

2 Using a potato masher, mash potatoes slightly. Add the kale, beans and sausage; cook over medium-low heat until kale is tender.

YIELD: 7 servings.

FRENCH ONION-BEEF STRUDEL

SHERRY KEETHLER, LAKE ST. LOUIS, MISSOURI

I prepared this flavorful strudel for my craft club meeting, and everyone asked me for the recipe. It makes such a nice presentation, so it's great to serve at gatherings.

PREP: 45 min. + rising **BAKE:** 20 min.

- 1 loaf (1 pound) frozen bread dough, thawed
- 2 cups thinly sliced onion
- 1/4 cup butter, cubed
- 6 ounces beef tenderloin or sirloin steak (1 inch thick)
- 1 teaspoon all-purpose flour
- 1 teaspoon brown sugar
- 1/2 teaspoon ground cumin
- 1/4 teaspoon salt
- 1/4 teaspoon pepper
- 1/2 cup beef broth
- 3/4 cup shredded Monterey Jack cheese
- 6 tablespoons grated Parmesan cheese, divided
- 1 can (10 ounces) beef au jus gravy

1 Allow the dough to rise until nearly doubled. Meanwhile, in a skillet, saute the onion in butter for 15-20 minutes or until golden brown. With a slotted spoon, remove the onion from skillet; set aside.

2 Cut beef into 1/8-in. slices; add to skillet. Increase heat to medium; cook and stir for 3 minutes or until browned. Return onion to skillet. Stir in flour, brown sugar, cumin, salt and pepper. Add broth; cook and stir for 6-8 minutes or until liquid has evaporated. Remove from the heat.

3 Punch the dough down; roll on a floured surface to a 16-in. x 12-in. rectangle. Place on a greased baking sheet. Place beef mixture down center of the long side of the dough. Sprinkle with Monterey Jack cheese and 4 tablespoons Parmesan cheese.

4 With a sharp knife, cut dough on each side of beef filling into 1-3/4-in. wide strips. Fold strips alternately across filling. Sprinkle with remaining Parmesan cheese. Cover and let rise until nearly doubled, about 30 minutes.

5 Bake at 375° for 20-25 minutes or until golden brown. Heat gravy; serve as a dipping sauce.

YIELD: 6 servings.

SKIER'S STEW

TRACI GANGWER, DENVER, COLORADO

This recipe got its name because you put it in the slow cooker...and head for the slopes! I like to prepare it two or three times a month in the fall and winter. When I come home after a busy day and get in out of the cold, a good hot dinner is waiting for me.

PREP: 20 min. **COOK:** 4-1/2 hours

- 2 pounds beef stew meat, cut into 1-inch cubes
- 2 tablespoons canola oil
- 8 medium carrots, cut into 1-inch slices
- 6 large potatoes, peeled and cut into 1-inch cubes
- 1 to 1-1/2 cups water
- 1 can (15 ounces) tomato sauce
- 1 envelope onion soup mix

1 In a large skillet, brown meat in oil on all sides; drain. Transfer to a 5-qt. slow cooker. Top with vegetables. Combine the water, tomato sauce and soup mix; pour over meat and vegetables. Cover and cook on low for 4-1/2 to 5 hours or until meat and vegetables are tender.

YIELD: 8 servings.

GOULASH OR STEW?

Any dish where food is simmered in liquid for a long period of time in a covered pot can be considered stew. Stew most often refers to a main dish that contains meat, vegetables and a thick broth made from the stewing juices. Goulash is a kind of stew, usually Hungarian, made with meat, vegetables and paprika.

VENISON VEGETABLE STEW

JENNIFER WHITAKER, WINCHENDON, MASSACHUSETTS

This is a great way to use up venison stew meat. If you like, you can substitute beef stew meat for the venison.

PREP: 30 min. **COOK:** 2 hours

    3 bacon strips
    2 pounds venison stew meat, cut into 1-inch cubes
    2 large onions, chopped
3-1/2 cups water, divided
    1 can (8 ounces) tomato sauce
    1 envelope onion soup mix
    2 teaspoons salt
    1 bay leaf
    2 teaspoons Italian seasoning
    7 medium carrots, cut into 1-inch pieces
    5 medium potatoes, peeled and cut into 1-inch cubes
    4 celery ribs, sliced
    3 tablespoons all-purpose flour
Cooked noodles

1 In a 4-qt. Dutch oven, cook the bacon until crisp; drain on a paper towel and reserve drippings in pan. Crumble bacon and set aside. Cook venison and onions in drippings until meat is lightly browned. Add 3 cups water, tomato sauce, soup mix, salt, bay leaf and Italian seasoning; bring to a boil. Reduce heat; cover and simmer for 1-1/2 hours or until meat is almost tender.

2 Add carrots, potatoes and celery; return to a boil. Reduce heat; cover and simmer 30-45 minutes or until meat and vegetables are tender. Combine flour and remaining water until smooth; stir into stew. Cook and stir until boiling and slightly thickened; stir in bacon. Discard bay leaf. Serve over noodles.

YIELD: 8 servings.

REUBEN ROLL-UPS

PATTY KILE, PLYMOUTH MEETING, PENNSYLVANIA

This recipe turns the popular Reuben sandwich into an interesting and hearty snack. We love these roll-ups at our house.

PREP/TOTAL TIME: 30 min.

    1 tube (13.8 ounces) refrigerated pizza crust
    1 cup sauerkraut, well drained
    1 tablespoon Thousand Island salad dressing
    4 slices corned beef, halved
    4 slices Swiss cheese, halved

1 Roll dough into a 12-in. x 9-in. rectangle. Cut into eight 3-in. x 4-1/2-in. rectangles. Combine sauerkraut and dressing. Place a slice of beef on each rectangle. Top with about 2 tablespoons of sauerkraut mixture and a slice of cheese. Roll up.

2 Place with seam side down on a greased baking sheet. Bake at 425° for 12-14 minutes or until golden.

YIELD: 8 roll-ups.

CABBAGE ZUCCHINI BORSCHT

AGATHA WIEBE, WINKLER, MANITOBA

I know my family will get a hearty, healthy meal when I serve this soup. There are so many good vegetables to stir in!

PREP: 10 min. **COOK:** 3-1/2 hours

    1 meaty beef soup bones (beef shanks or short ribs)
    8 cups water
    4 cups shredded cabbage
    2 cups cubed peeled potatoes
    2 cups sliced carrots
    2 cups diced peeled tomatoes
    1 onion, chopped
1/2 cup chopped fresh parsley
    2 tablespoons dill weed
    1 tablespoon aniseed, tied in a cheesecloth bag
1-1/2 teaspoons salt
1/2 teaspoon pepper
    2 cups chopped cooked beets
    3 cups shredded zucchini

1 Place soup bone and water in a stockpock; bring to a boil. Reduce heat and simmer, uncovered, for 40-45 minutes.

2 Skim off fat. Add the cabbage, potatoes, carrots, tomatoes, onion, parsley, dill, aniseed, salt and pepper. Simmer, uncovered, 2-1/2 to 3 hours.

3 Remove meat from soup bone; discard bone and add meat to soup. Stir in beets and zucchini. Simmer 15-20 minutes longer or until zucchini is tender. Remove anise seed before serving.

YIELD: 12-14 servings (4 quarts).

EASY SEAFOOD BISQUE

CINDY ROGOWSKI, LANCASTER, NEW YORK
I've always enjoyed seafood bisque at restaurants and one day decided to try my hand at a homemade version. Everyone says this is one of the better recipes they've tasted.

PREP/TOTAL TIME: 30 min.

- 1/2 cup chopped onion
- 1 tablespoon butter
- 2-1/4 cups milk
- 1 can (10-3/4 ounces) condensed cream of celery soup, undiluted
- 1 can (10-3/4 ounces) condensed cream of shrimp soup, undiluted
- 1 package (8 ounces) imitation crabmeat, chopped
- 1 teaspoon chicken bouillon granules
- 1/2 teaspoon dried parsley flakes
- 1/4 teaspoon garlic powder
- 1/4 teaspoon dried marjoram
- 1/4 teaspoon pepper

1 In a 3-qt. saucepan, saute onion in butter until tender. Stir in remaining ingredients. Cover and cook over medium-low heat for 20 minutes or until heated through, stirring occasionally.

YIELD: 4-5 servings.

THREE-BEAN CASSOULET

CAROL BERIGAN, GOLDEN, COLORADO
Brimming with a trio of bean varieties, this recipe is as easy as one, two, three. You can serve it on the side or as a satisfying meatless main dish. The vegetables add an interesting mix of tastes, colors and textures.

PREP: 5 min. **BAKE:** 1 hour

- 2 cans (14-1/2 ounces each) stewed tomatoes
- 1 can (15 ounces) garbanzo beans or chickpeas, rinsed and drained
- 1 can (15-1/2 ounces) great northern beans, rinsed and drained
- 1 can (15 ounces) butter beans, rinsed and drained
- 1 cup finely chopped carrots
- 1 cup finely chopped onion
- 2 garlic cloves, minced
- 1 bay leaf
- 2 teaspoons dried parsley flakes
- 1 teaspoon dried basil
- 1/2 teaspoon salt
- 1/2 teaspoon dried thyme
- 1/8 teaspoon pepper

1 In an ungreased 3-qt. baking dish, combine all ingredients. Cover and bake at 350° for 60-70 minutes or until vegetables are tender, stirring occasionally. Discard bay leaf.

YIELD: 9 servings.

SIDES, SALADS & BREADS

BRAIDED EGG BREAD

MARLENE JEFFERY, HOLLAND, MANITOBA

Since I first made this bread a few years ago, it's become a much-requested recipe. I'm sure I'll pass it down to future generations.

PREP: 30 min. + rising **BAKE:** 25 min. + cooling

3-1/4 to 3-3/4 cups all-purpose flour
   1 tablespoon sugar
   1 package (1/4 ounce) active dry yeast
  3/4 teaspoon salt
  3/4 cup water
   3 tablespoons canola oil
   2 eggs

TOPPING:
   1 egg
   1 teaspoon water
  1/2 teaspoon poppy seeds

1 In a large bowl, combine 2-1/2 cups flour, sugar, yeast and salt. In a small saucepan, heat water and oil to 120°-130°. Add to dry ingredients along with eggs. Beat on medium speed for 3 minutes. Stir in enough remaining flour to form a soft dough.

2 Turn onto a lightly floured surface; knead until smooth and elastic, about 6-8 minutes. Place in a greased bowl, turning once to grease top. Cover and let rise in a warm place until doubled, about 1-1/2 hours.

3 Punch dough down. Turn onto a lightly floured surface. Set a third of the dough aside. Divide remaining dough into three pieces. Shape each into a 13-in. rope. Place ropes on a greased baking sheet and braid; pinch ends to seal and tuck under.

4 Divide reserved dough into three equal pieces; shape each into a 14-in. rope. Braid ropes. Center 14-in. braid on top of the shorter braid. Pinch ends to seal and tuck under. Cover and let rise until doubled, about 30 minutes.

5 In a small bowl, beat egg and water; brush over dough. Sprinkle with poppy seeds. Bake at 375° for 25-30 minutes or until golden brown. Cover with foil during the last 15 minutes of baking. Remove from pan to a wire rack to cool.

YIELD: 1 loaf (16 slices).

MARINATED CITRUS SALAD

KATRINA HEINRICH, UNDERHILL, VERMONT

This citrus salad evolved over the years by combining a little bit of what everyone in my family likes.

PREP: 15 min. + marinating

1-1/2 cups orange juice
  1/2 cup red wine vinegar
  1/4 cup orange marmalade
  1/4 cup sugar
  1/2 teaspoon pepper
  1/4 teaspoon salt
   3 medium grapefruit, peeled and sectioned
   3 medium navel oranges, peeled and sectioned
  32 fresh asparagus, trimmed
   1 medium cucumber, thinly sliced
   1 medium onion, sliced and separated into rings
   1 medium ripe avocado, peeled and cubed
   6 cups torn romaine
   6 cups torn red leaf lettuce
   1 teaspoon minced fresh mint

1 In a large bowl, combine orange juice, vinegar, marmalade, sugar, pepper and salt; stir until sugar is dissolved.

2 In another large bowl, combine the grapefruit, oranges, asparagus, cucumber, onion and avocado. Add the marinade and toss to coat. Cover and refrigerate for 2 hours.

3 Drain; reserve marinade. Arrange lettuce on plates; top with fruit mixture. Sprinkle with mint. Serve with reserved marinade.

YIELD: 12 servings.

GINGERED ORANGE BEETS

MARION TIPTON, PHOENIX, ARIZONA

The orange and ginger are a surprising complement, making this particular vegetable a wonderful addition to any holiday table.

PREP: 10 min. **BAKE:** 70 min.

1-1/2 pounds whole fresh beets (about 4 medium),
    trimmed and cleaned

6 tablespoons olive oil, divided
1/4 teaspoon salt
1/4 teaspoon white pepper
1 tablespoon rice vinegar
1 tablespoon orange juice concentrate
1-1/2 teaspoons grated orange peel, divided
1/2 teaspoon minced fresh gingerroot
1 medium navel orange, peeled, sectioned and chopped
1/3 cup pecan halves, toasted

1 Brush beets with 4 tablespoons oil; sprinkle with salt and pepper. Wrap loosely in foil; place on a baking sheet. Bake at 425° for 70-75 minutes or until fork-tender. Cool slightly.

2 In a small bowl, whisk the vinegar, orange juice concentrate, 1 teaspoon orange peel, ginger and remaining oil; set aside.

3 Peel beets and cut into wedges; place in a serving bowl. Add the orange sections and pecans. Drizzle with orange sauce and toss to coat. Sprinkle with remaining orange peel.

YIELD: 4 servings.

TANGERINE TOSSED SALAD

HELEN MUSENBROCK, O'FALLON, MISSOURI
I learned to cook from my mother when I was a young girl. I like the combination of sweet tangerines and crunchy caramelized almonds in this recipe.

PREP: 40 min.
1/2 cup sliced almonds
3 tablespoons sugar, divided
2 medium tangerines or navel orange
6 cups torn lettuce
3 green onions, chopped
2 tablespoons cider vinegar
2 tablespoons olive oil
1/4 teaspoon salt
1/4 teaspoon pepper

1 In a small skillet, cook and stir almonds and 2 tablespoons sugar over medium-low heat for 25-30 minutes or until the sugar is melted and the almonds are toasted. Remove from the heat. Peel and section the tangerines, reserving 1 tablespoon of the juice.

2 In a large bowl, combine the lettuce, onions, tangerines and almonds. In a small bowl, whisk the vinegar, oil, salt, pepper, reserved juice and remaining sugar. Drizzle over the salad and toss to coat.

YIELD: 6 servings.

SWEET POTATO SOUFFLE

LINDA HOFFMAN, FORT WAYNE, INDIANA
It's easy to see why this pretty orange side dish is a seasonal favorite for my family.

PREP: 20 min. **BAKE:** 40 min. + standing
3 large sweet potatoes (about 3 pounds)
2 tablespoons butter
1 egg, lightly beaten
2 egg whites, lightly beaten
1/4 cup packed brown sugar
1 teaspoon rum extract
1/2 teaspoon salt
1/4 teaspoon ground cinnamon

1 Arrange sweet potatoes in a microwave-safe dish; prick potatoes several times with a fork. Microwave, uncovered, on high for 13-15 minutes or until tender, turning once. Cool slightly.

2 Cut the potatoes in half lengthwise. Scoop out the pulp; discard shell. In a large bowl, mash pulp with butter. Stir in the remaining ingredients.

3 Spoon into a greased 1-1/2-qt. baking dish. Bake, uncovered, at 350° for 40-50 minutes or until heated through. Let stand 10 minutes before serving.

YIELD: 6 servings.

WINTER VEGETABLES

CHARLENE AUGUSTYN, GRAND RAPIDS, MICHIGAN
The flavor of thyme shines through in this recipe. The colorful array of vegetables is so appealing on the table. It's a great way to showcase often unused broccoli stalks.

PREP: 25 min. **COOK:** 20 min.

- 3 medium turnips, peeled and cut into 2-inch julienne strips
- 1 large rutabaga, peeled and cut into 2-inch julienne strips
- 4 medium carrots, cut into 2-inch julienne strips
- 3 fresh broccoli spears
- 1 tablespoon butter
- 1 tablespoon minced fresh parsley
- 1/2 teaspoon salt
- 1/2 teaspoon dried thyme
- Pepper to taste

1 Place the turnips, rutabaga and carrots in a large saucepan and cover with water. Bring to a boil. Reduce heat; cover and cook for 10 minutes.

2 Meanwhile, cut florets from broccoli and save for another use. Cut broccoli stalks into 2-in. julienne strips; add to saucepan. Cover and cook 5 minutes longer or until the vegetables are crisp-tender; drain well.

3 In a large skillet, saute vegetables in butter. Stir in the parsley, salt, thyme and pepper.

YIELD: 10-12 servings.

RUTABAGAS AND TURNIPS

When shopping for rutabagas and turnips, select those that are smooth-skinned, heavy, firm and not spongy. Look for rutabagas no larger than 4 inches in diameter and turnips no larger than 2 inches in diameter. Keep unwashed rutabagas and turnips in a plastic bag in your refrigerator's crisper drawer for up to 1 week.

EASY CRESCENT ROLLS

RUTH SANFORD, WASILLA, ALASKA
I learned to cook and bake under my mother's fantastic guidance. She always treated the family to home-baked bread, and I've learned to do the same.

PREP: 20 min. + rising **BAKE:** 10 min.

- 1 package (1/4 ounce) active dry yeast
- 1 cup warm water (110° to 115°)
- 3 eggs
- 4 to 4-1/2 cups all-purpose flour
- 1/2 cup sugar
- 1 teaspoon salt
- 1/2 cup shortening

1 In a small bowl, dissolve yeast in warm water. In a small bowl, beat eggs until light lemon-color. Add to yeast mixture; set aside. In a large bowl, combine 1 cup flour, sugar and salt. Cut in shortening until mixture resembles coarse crumbs. Stir in yeast mixture. Stir in enough remaining flour until dough leaves the side of the bowl and is soft (dough will be sticky). Do not knead. Cover and refrigerate overnight.

2 Punch dough down. Turn onto a well-floured surface; divide into thirds. Roll each into a 12-in. circle; cut each circle into 12 wedges. Roll up wedges from wide end and place with pointed end down 2 in. apart on greased baking sheets. Curve ends to form a crescent shape. Cover and let rise in a warm place until doubled, about 45 minutes.

3 Bake at 375° for 10-12 minutes or until light golden brown. Remove from pans to wire racks.

YIELD: 3 dozen.

RICE-STUFFED BUTTERNUT SQUASH

ELAINE SWEET, DALLAS, TEXAS

The combination of wild rice, mango chutney, cranberries and curry powder give this side dish an exotic flavor. It's delicious and beautiful, and tastes best when butternut squash is in season.

PREP: 40 min. **BAKE:** 15 min.

- 1 small butternut squash (1-1/2 pounds)
- 3/4 cup cooked long grain and wild rice
- 1/3 cup ricotta cheese
- 3 tablespoons dried cranberries
- 3 tablespoons mango chutney
- 1 green onion, chopped
- 3/4 teaspoon curry powder
- 1/4 teaspoon salt
- 1/4 teaspoon pepper
- 2 teaspoons butter

1 Cut squash in half lengthwise; discard seeds. Cut a thin slice from the bottom of each half so it sits flat. Place pulp side down in an 11-in. x 7-in. baking dish; add 1/2 in. of hot water. Bake, uncovered, at 350° for 30 minutes.

2 Drain water from pan; turn squash pulp side up. When cool enough to handle, scoop out pulp, leaving about a 1/4-in. shell.

3 In a large bowl, combine pulp, rice, ricotta cheese, cranberries, chutney, onion, curry powder, salt and pepper. Spoon into squash shells. Dot with butter. Bake for 15-20 minutes or until squash is tender.

YIELD: 2 servings.

HERBED TWICE-BAKED POTATOES

RUTH ANDREWSON, LEAVENWORTH, WASHINGTON

Cream cheese, garlic powder and butter make these classic potatoes irresistible. Replace the basil with parsley if you'd like, or mix in your favorite seasoning blend.

PREP: 1-1/4 hours **BAKE:** 15 min.

- 2 medium baking potatoes
- 1-1/2 ounces cream cheese, cubed
- 1 tablespoon minced chives
- 1/4 teaspoon salt
- 1/4 teaspoon dried basil
- Dash cayenne pepper
- 3 tablespoons milk
- 3 teaspoons butter, melted, divided
- Dash garlic powder
- Dash paprika

1 Scrub and pierce potatoes. Bake at 375° for 1 hour or until tender. Cool for 10 minutes. Cut potatoes in half. Scoop out pulp, leaving a thin shell.

2 In a large bowl, mash pulp with the cream cheese, chives, salt, basil and cayenne. Add milk and 1-1/2 teaspoons butter; mash. Spoon into potato shells. Drizzle with remaining butter; sprinkle with garlic powder and paprika.

3 Place on an ungreased baking sheet. Bake for 15-20 minutes or until heated through.

YIELD: 4 servings.

RUSSIAN KRENDL BREAD

ANN SODMAN, EVANS, COLORADO
While dining with a Russian immigrant family, I jumped at the chance to add this wonderful bread they served to my recipe collection. Of course, I never turn down hugs from my grandchildren after I've prepared something special...and this recipe always works.

PREP: 45 min. + rising **BAKE:** 45 min. + cooling

FILLING:
- 2 tablespoons butter
- 2 tablespoons sugar
- 1/3 cup chopped prunes
- 1/3 cup finely chopped dried apricots
- 1 large apple, peeled and chopped
- 1 cup apple juice
- 2/3 cup finely chopped dried apple

BREAD:
- 1 package (1/4 ounce) active dry yeast
- 5 tablespoons sugar, divided
- 3/4 cup warm half-and-half cream or milk (110° to 115°)
- 1/4 cup butter, softened
- 1-1/2 teaspoons vanilla extract
- 1/2 teaspoon salt
- 2 egg yolks
- 2-3/4 to 3-1/4 cups all-purpose flour
- Melted butter
- 1/2 teaspoon ground cinnamon
- Confectioners' sugar

1 In a large saucepan, combine the filling ingredients. Bring to a boil. Reduce the heat; simmer, for 30 minutes or until fruit is tender and mixture has jam-like consistency, stirring occasionally. Cool to room temperature.

2 For bread, in a large bowl, dissolve yeast and 3 tablespoons sugar in cream. Add butter, vanilla, salt, egg yolks and 1-1/2 cups of the flour; beat until smooth. Add enough remaining flour to form a soft dough.

3 Turn onto a floured surface; knead until smooth and elastic, about 6 to 8 minutes. Place in a greased bowl, turning once to grease top. Cover and let rise until doubled, about 1 hour.

4 Punch dough down. Roll into a 32-in. x 10-in. rectangle. Brush with melted butter. Combine cinnamon and remaining sugar; sprinkle over butter. Spread filling to within 1 in. of edges. Roll up from one of the long sides; pinch seams and ends to seal.

5 Place on a greased baking sheet; form into a pretzel shape. Cover and let rise until nearly doubled, about 30 minutes.

6 Bake at 350° for 45 minutes or until golden brown. Cool on a wire rack. Dust with confectioners' sugar.

YIELD: 24 servings.

HOT GERMAN POTATO SALAD

MARLENE MUCKENHIRN, DELANO, MINNESOTA
This zesty salad, with potatoes, celery and onion, is a terrific side dish when served warm with crumbled bacon and minced fresh parsley sprinkled on top.

PREP: 15 min. **COOK:** 4 hours
- 8 medium potatoes, peeled and cut into 1/4-inch slices
- 2 celery ribs, chopped
- 1 large onion, chopped
- 1 cup water
- 2/3 cup cider vinegar
- 1/3 cup sugar
- 2 tablespoons quick-cooking tapioca
- 1 teaspoon salt
- 3/4 teaspoon celery seed
- 1/4 teaspoon pepper
- 6 bacon strips, cooked and crumbled
- 1/4 cup minced fresh parsley

1 In a 3-qt. slow cooker, combine the potatoes, celery and onion. In a small bowl, combine water, vinegar, sugar, tapioca, salt, celery seed and pepper. Pour over potatoes; stir gently to coat.

2 Cover and cook on high for 4-5 hours or until potatoes are tender. Just before serving, sprinkle with bacon and parsley.

YIELD: 8-10 servings.

WINTER SQUASH BREAD

VIOLET RUNDELS, WAVERLY, OHIO
I modified my usual recipe when I couldn't find any zucchini at the grocery store. I used cooked squash from the freezer section instead, along with bananas. My family loves this bread.

PREP: 15 min. **BAKE:** 55 min. + cooling

- 3 cups all-purpose flour
- 2 cups sugar
- 2 teaspoons baking soda
- 2 teaspoons ground allspice
- 1-1/2 teaspoons baking powder
- 1 teaspoon salt
- 3 eggs
- 1 cup canola oil
- 2 teaspoons vanilla extract
- 1 cup frozen cooked winter squash, thawed
- 1 cup mashed ripe bananas (about 2 medium)
- 1 cup chopped walnuts

1 In a large bowl, combine the flour, sugar, baking soda, allspice, baking powder and salt. In another bowl, beat the eggs, oil and vanilla; add squash and bananas. Stir into dry ingredients just until moistened. Fold in walnuts.

2 Pour into two greased 8-in. x 4-in. loaf pans. Bake at 350° for 55-60 minutes or until a toothpick inserted near the center comes out clean. Cool for 10 minutes before removing from pans to wire racks.

YIELD: 2 loaves (16 slices each).

BACON-ONION GREEN BEANS

KAREN DARRELL, BETHALTO, ILLINOIS
These green beans are a snap to make, and the flavor is wonderful. It's a great side dish for weeknight dinners and special occasions alike.

PREP/TOTAL TIME: 25 min.

- 1-1/2 pounds fresh green beans, trimmed
- 6 bacon strips, diced
- 1 medium onion, chopped
- 2 tablespoons cider vinegar
- 1/4 teaspoon salt
- 1/8 teaspoon pepper
- 1 tablespoon sesame seeds, toasted

1 Place beans in a large saucepan and cover with water; bring to a boil. Cover and cook for 8-10 minutes or until crisp-tender; drain.

2 Meanwhile, in a large skillet, cook bacon over medium heat until crisp. Remove to paper towels; drain, reserving 1 tablespoon drippings. Saute onion in the drippings until tender. Stir in the vinegar, salt and pepper.

3 Drain beans; place in a large serving bowl. Stir in the onion mixture and bacon. Sprinkle with sesame seeds.

YIELD: 6-8 servings.

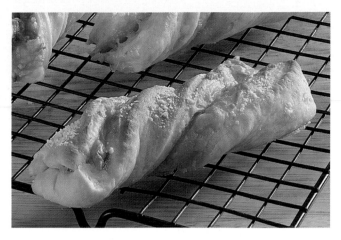

CHEDDAR-CHILI BREAD TWISTS

CAROL WHITFIELD, MENTMORE, NEW MEXICO
Green chilies are prolific here in New Mexico, so I'm always looking for ways to cook with them. These twists are often requested by my family.

PREP: 30 min. + rising **BAKE:** 15 min.

- 1-1/4 cups buttermilk
- 2 cups (8 ounces) shredded cheddar cheese
- 2 tablespoons sugar
- 1 package (1/4 ounce) active dry yeast
- 1/4 cup warm water (110° to 115°)
- 2 eggs
- 1/2 teaspoon salt
- 5-1/4 to 5-3/4 cups all-purpose flour

TOPPING:
- 1-1/2 cups (6 ounces) shredded cheddar cheese
- 1 can (4 ounces) chopped green chilies, drained
- Grated Parmesan cheese

1 In a large saucepan, heat the buttermilk and cheese over low heat, stirring until cheese is melted (mixture will appear curdled). Cool to 110° to 115°. In a large bowl, dissolve sugar and yeast in warm water. Add the buttermilk mixture, eggs, salt and 3 cups flour. Beat until smooth. Stir in enough remaining flour to form a soft dough.

2 Turn onto a floured surface; knead until smooth and elastic, about 6-8 minutes. Place in a greased bowl, turning once to grease top. Cover and let rise in a warm place until doubled, about 1 hour. Meanwhile, for topping, combine cheddar cheese and chilies; set aside.

3 Punch dough down; turn onto a lightly floured surface and divide in half. Roll each portion into an 18-in. x 12-in. rectangle. Spray one half with cooking spray. Top with cheese mixture and remaining dough.

4 Cut into twelve 1-1/2-in. strips. Cut each strip in half and twist. Place 1 in. apart on greased foil-lined baking sheets. Sprinkle with Parmesan cheese.

5 Bake at 375° for 15-20 minutes or until lightly browned. Remove to wire racks. Serve warm. Refrigerate any leftovers.

YIELD: 2 dozen.

SWISS CHARD WITH BEETS

TASTE OF HOME TEST KITCHEN
If you can't find Swiss chard, other types of leafy greens, such as kale or escarole, also work well in this recipe.

PREP: 25 min. **COOK:** 20 min.

- 2 bunches Swiss chard
- 1 small red onion, halved and sliced
- 2 garlic cloves, minced
- 1/2 teaspoon salt
- 1/4 teaspoon pepper
- 2 tablespoons olive oil
- 1 can (14-1/2 ounces) sliced beets, drained and julienned
- 3 tablespoons lemon juice
- 1 cup (4 ounces) crumbled feta cheese
- 1/4 cup coarsely chopped walnuts, toasted

1 Cut stems from chard; coarsely chop stems and leaves separately. Fill a Dutch oven with water; bring to a boil. Add chard leaves. Return to a boil; cook for 1-2 minutes or just until tender. Drain and rinse in cold water; set aside.

2 In a large skillet, saute the onion, garlic, salt, pepper and chard stems in oil for 10-15 minutes or until tender. Gently squeeze excess moisture from chard leaves. Add leaves and beets to skillet; saute for 1 minute. Add lemon juice; heat through. Just before serving, sprinkle with feta cheese and walnuts.

YIELD: 6 servings.

WINTER APPLE JELLY

MARIA WEBER, TOLEDO, OHIO
I give this spiced jelly away as Christmas presents. It's easy to prepare, and it makes a tasty and attractive gift.

PREP: 10 min. **PROCESS:** 5 min.

- 1 quart apple juice
- 1 package (1-3/4 ounces) powdered fruit pectin
- 2 tablespoons bottled lemon juice
- 3 to 6 drops red food coloring, optional
- 5-1/2 cups sugar
- 1 teaspoon ground cinnamon

1 In a Dutch oven, combine the apple juice, pectin, lemon juice and food coloring if desired. Bring to a full rolling boil, stirring constantly. Quickly stir in sugar; return to a full rolling boil. Boil for 2 minutes, stirring constantly.

2 Remove from the heat; skim off foam. Stir in cinnamon. Carefully ladle hot mixture into hot sterilized jars, leaving 1/4-in. headspace. Remove air bubbles; wipe rims and adjust lids. Process for 5 minutes in a boiling-water canner.

YIELD: 7 half-pints.

EDITOR'S NOTE: The processing time listed is for altitudes of 1,000 feet or less. Add 1 minute to the processing time for each 1,000 feet of additional altitude.

CLEAN CANNING

Canning can sometimes be messy. To save yourself the trouble of cleaning your stovetop, cover it with heavy-duty aluminum foil. Be sure to make holes for the burners. When you are done canning, simply remove the aluminum foil. This will prevent the need for a lot of stovetop scrubbing.

DINNER ROLLS

ANNA BAKER, BLAINE, WASHINGTON
A basic roll like this can be served with dinner or used for small appetizer sandwiches. Either way, it's a recipe you'll come to rely on.

PREP: 30 min. + rising **BAKE:** 20 min.

   2 packages (1/4 ounce each) active dry yeast
 1/2 cup warm water (110°-115°)
 1/3 cup plus 1 teaspoon sugar, divided
1-1/4 cups warm milk (110°-115°)
 1/2 cup butter, melted and cooled
1-1/2 teaspoons salt
   2 eggs, beaten
   6 to 6-1/2 cups all-purpose flour
Additional melted butter, optional

1 In a large bowl, dissolve yeast in warm water with 1 teaspoon sugar. Add milk, butter, salt, remaining sugar, eggs and 3 cups flour; beat until smooth. Stir in enough remaining flour to form a soft dough.

2 Turn out onto a floured surface; knead until smooth and elastic, about 6-8 minutes, adding additional flour as needed. Place in a greased bowl, turning once to grease top. Cover and let rise in a warm place until doubled, about 1 hour.

3 Punch dough down, then turn out onto a lightly floured surface. Divide the dough in half. Divide each half into 12 pieces. Shape each piece into a ball; place in two greased 13-in. x 9-in. baking pans. Cover and let rise until doubled, about 30 minutes.

4 Bake at 375° for 20-25 minutes or until golden brown. Lightly brush with melted butter if desired. Remove from pans to wire racks. Serve warm.

YIELD: 2 dozen.

IF COOKING FOR TWO: Freeze baked rolls in heavy-duty freezer bags, then thaw when ready to use.

NUTTY BARLEY BAKE

RENATE CRUMP, LOS ANGELES, CALIFORNIA
When I started bringing this distinctive dish to holiday dinners, a lot of people had never seen barley in anything but soup. They have since dubbed me "the barley lady," and now I wouldn't dare bring anything but this dish. Even if I double the recipe, I come home with an empty pan.

PREP: 15 min. **BAKE:** 1-1/4 hours

   1 medium onion, chopped
   1 cup medium pearl barley
 1/2 cup slivered almonds or pine nuts
 1/4 cup butter
 1/2 cup minced fresh parsley
 1/4 cup thinly sliced green onions
 1/4 teaspoon salt
 1/8 teaspoon pepper
   2 cans (14-1/2 ounces each) beef broth
Additional parsley, optional

1 In a large skillet, saute the onion, barley and nuts in butter until barley is lightly browned. Stir in the parsley, green onions, salt and pepper.

2 Transfer to a greased 2-qt. baking dish. Stir in broth. Bake, uncovered, at 350° for 1-1/4 hours or until the barley is tender and the liquid is absorbed. Sprinkle with parsley if desired.

YIELD: 6 servings.

GRANDMA'S ORANGE ROLLS

NORMA POOLE, AUBURNDALE, FLORIDA

Our two children and grandchildren love these fine-textured sweet rolls. We have our own orange, lime and grapefruit trees, and it's such a pleasure to go out and pick fruit right off the tree.

PREP: 20 min. + rising **BAKE:** 20 min.

   1 package (1/4 ounce) active dry yeast
1/4 cup warm water (110° to 115°)
   1 cup warm milk (110° to 115°)
1/4 cup shortening
1/4 cup sugar
   1 teaspoon salt
   1 egg, lightly beaten
3-1/2 to 3-3/4 cups all-purpose flour

FILLING:

   1 cup sugar
1/2 cup butter, softened
   2 tablespoons grated orange peel

GLAZE:

   1 cup confectioners' sugar
   4 teaspoons butter, softened
   4 to 5 teaspoons milk
1/2 teaspoon lemon extract

1 In a large bowl, dissolve the yeast in water. Add the milk, shortening, sugar, salt, egg and 3 cups flour. Beat until smooth. Stir in enough remaining flour to form a soft dough.

2 Knead on a lightly floured surface until smooth and elastic, about 6-8 minutes. Place in a greased bowl, turning once to grease top. Cover and let rise in a warm place until doubled, about 1 hour. Meanwhile, in a small bowl, combine filling ingredients; set aside.

3 Punch dough down; divide in half. Roll each half into a 15-in. x 10-in. rectangle. Spread half the reserved filling on each rectangle. Roll up, jelly-roll style, starting with a long end. Cut each into 15 rolls.

4 Place in two greased 11-in. x 7-in. baking pans. Cover and let rise until doubled, about 45 minutes.

5 Bake at 375° for 20-25 minutes or until lightly browned. In a small bowl, combine glaze ingredients until smooth; spread over warm rolls.

YIELD: 2-1/2 dozen.

WINTER CABBAGE SALAD

ELEANOR SHUKNECHT, ELBA, NEW YORK

My mother made this recipe for as long as I can remember. She'd serve it as a vegetable, salad or garnish at family meals, ladies' church luncheons and potluck parties.

PREP: 25 min. + chilling

   2 cups cider vinegar
   1 cup sugar
   2 tablespoons salt
   1 tablespoon mustard seed
3/4 teaspoon celery seed
1/2 teaspoon ground turmeric
 10 cups thinly sliced cabbage (about 2-1/4 pounds)
   3 medium onions, thinly sliced
   2 medium sweet red peppers, thinly sliced
   1 medium green pepper, thinly sliced

1 In a large saucepan, bring the first six ingredients to a boil. Reduce heat; simmer, uncovered, for 5 minutes. Remove from the heat and allow to cool.

2 In a large bowl, combine cabbage, onions and peppers. Pour vinegar mixture over vegetables; toss to coat. Cover and refrigerate overnight.

YIELD: 16-20 servings.

TURNIP CASSEROLE

DORIS HUBERT, EAST KILLINGLY, CONNECTICUT
Turnips are good alone or with other vegetables. Try chopping them to add texture and flavor to soups and stews.

PREP: 25 min. **BAKE:** 20 min.

    4 medium turnips, peeled and cubed
    1 cup water
    1 egg, lightly beaten
  1/3 cup sugar
    3 tablespoons butter
  1/2 teaspoon salt
  1/4 teaspoon ground cinnamon

1 Place turnips in a large saucepan and cover with water. Bring to a boil. Reduce heat; cover and cook for 15 minutes or until tender and drain. Transfer turnips to a bowl and mash. Add the egg, sugar, butter and salt.

2 Transfer to a greased 1-qt. baking dish; sprinkle with the cinnamon. Cover and bake at 350° for 20-25 minutes or until a thermometer reads 160°.

YIELD: 4 servings.

GOLDEN OLDIE VEGGIES

ALCY THORNE, LOS MOLINOS, CALIFORNIA
This delicious medley of root vegetables gets its pizzazz from rosemary and olive oil. These veggies are simple to prepare and have just the right amount of pep.

PREP: 15 min. **BAKE:** 25 min.

    3 medium parsnips, peeled and sliced
    5 medium carrots, cut into chunks
    2 medium turnips, peeled and cubed
   12 brussels sprouts, halved
    8 small red potatoes, quartered
    2 tablespoons minced fresh rosemary
  1/2 teaspoon salt
  1/4 teaspoon pepper
  1/4 cup olive oil

1 In a large bowl, combine the first eight ingredients. Drizzle with oil; toss to coat. Transfer to two greased 15-in. x 10-in. x 1-in. baking pans.

2 Bake, uncovered, at 400° for 25-35 minutes or until the vegetables are tender.

YIELD: 8 servings.

WILTED GREEN SALAD

LAVONNE HEGLAND, ST. MICHAEL, MINNESOTA
My husband refused to eat wilted lettuce until I read this recipe suggested by a friend. He likes this milder dressing with just a subtle hint of vinegar. Turkey bacon adds a satisfying crunch.

PREP/TOTAL TIME: 10 min.

   10 cups torn leaf lettuce
    6 cups torn fresh spinach
    2 green onions, sliced
  1/4 cup cider vinegar
    2 tablespoons water
    2 tablespoons canola oil
    2 teaspoons sugar
    4 turkey bacon strips, cooked and crumbled

1 In a large salad bowl, toss the lettuce, spinach and onions; set aside. In a small saucepan, bring the vinegar, water, oil and sugar to a boil. Pour over lettuce and toss; sprinkle with bacon. Serve immediately.

YIELD: 8 servings.

WINTER SQUASH CASSEROLE

GLENDORA HAUGER, SIREN, WISCONSIN
Years ago, our vegetable garden kept us well supplied all year long. Dad stored huge piles of potatoes and squash in the coldest part of the basement. In winter the squash was so hard, Mother sometimes used an ax to cut it into small pieces for cooking! Her hard work was worth it, because we really enjoyed this wonderful casserole!

PREP: 15 min. **BAKE:** 45 min.
- 6 cups mashed winter squash
- 1/2 cup butter, melted
- 6 eggs, lightly beaten
- 1 cup sugar
- 1/2 teaspoon salt

TOPPING:
- 1 cup packed brown sugar
- 1/2 cup butter, softened
- 1/4 cup all-purpose flour
- 1/2 cup slivered almonds

1 In a large bowl, combine the first five ingredients. Pour into an ungreased 13-in. x 9-in. baking dish.

2 Combine topping ingredients and crumble over the top. Bake, uncovered, at 350° for 45 minutes or until a thermometer reads 160°.

YIELD: 12 servings.

GRAPEFRUIT AVOCADO SALAD

MARY RELYEA, CANASTOTA, NEW YORK
Even in the dead of winter, it's easy to brighten up lettuce greens with the fresh and fruity tartness of pink grapefruit and orange juice. This sunny, elegant salad pairs well with most entrees. For extra color, I sometimes add sliced Kalamata or green olives.

PREP/TOTAL TIME: 20 min.
- 6 cups torn leaf lettuce
- 3 large pink grapefruit, peeled and sectioned

- 1 medium ripe avocado, peeled and sliced
- 1 small red onion, thinly sliced
- 1/4 cup orange juice
- 3 tablespoons olive oil
- 1 tablespoon lemon juice
- 3/4 teaspoon ground cumin
- 1 garlic clove, minced
- Dash hot pepper sauce
- 1/4 cup chopped pecans, toasted

1 Divide lettuce among eight salad plates. Arrange the grapefruit, avocado and onion over lettuce. In a small bowl, whisk the orange juice, oil, lemon juice, cumin, garlic and pepper sauce; drizzle over salads. Sprinkle with pecans.

YIELD: 8 servings.

CRANBERRY ORANGE SCONES

KAREN MCBRIDE, INDIANAPOLIS, INDIANA
Serve these cranberry-dotted goodies with the orange butter for an excellent breakfast with a smooth cup of coffee or tea.

PREP: 20 min. **BAKE:** 15 min.
- 2 cups all-purpose flour
- 10 teaspoons sugar, divided
- 1 tablespoon grated orange peel
- 2 teaspoons baking powder
- 1/2 teaspoon salt
- 1/4 teaspoon baking soda
- 1/3 cup cold butter
- 1 cup dried cranberries
- 1/4 cup orange juice
- 1/4 cup half-and-half cream
- 1 egg
- 1 tablespoon milk

GLAZE (optional):
- 1/2 cup confectioners' sugar
- 1 tablespoon orange juice

ORANGE BUTTER:
- 1/2 cup butter, softened
- 2 to 3 tablespoons orange marmalade

1 In a large bowl, combine the flour, 7 teaspoons sugar, orange peel, baking powder, salt and baking soda. Cut in butter until the mixture resembles coarse crumbs; set aside. In a small bowl, combine the cranberries, orange juice, cream and egg. Add to flour mixture and stir until a soft dough forms.

2 On a floured surface, gently knead 6-8 times. Pat dough into an 8-in. circle. Cut into 10 wedges. Separate wedges and place on an ungreased baking sheet. Brush with milk; sprinkle with remaining sugar.

3 Bake at 400° for 12-15 minutes or until lightly browned. Remove to a wire rack.

4 Combine glaze ingredients if desired; drizzle over scones. Combine orange butter ingredients; serve with warm scones.

YIELD: 10 scones.

LEMONY CAESAR SALAD

KATHY KOCHISS, HUNTINGTON, CONNECTICUT
I rely on this recipe, which I received from a friend, whenever I need a tasty tossed salad for dinner. To save time, I take advantage of convenient ready-to-serve romaine in a bag as well as garlic-seasoned croutons for extra flavor.

PREP/TOTAL TIME: 15 min.
   1/2 cup olive oil
     3 tablespoons lemon juice
     2 garlic cloves, minced
     1 teaspoon Dijon mustard
   1/2 teaspoon salt, optional
   1/8 teaspoon pepper
     9 cups torn romaine
   1/4 cup grated Parmesan cheese
     1 cup salad croutons, optional
Sliced red onion, optional

1 Combine oil, lemon juice, garlic, mustard, salt if desired and pepper. In a salad bowl, combine romaine and cheese. Drizzle with dressing; add croutons and onion if desired. Toss to coat.

YIELD: 6-8 servings.

APRICOT FRUITCAKE

CLARE BROOKS, JUNEAU, ALASKA
My husband didn't care for fruitcake, which I love, until he tasted this one. Apricots add a unique sweetness, while three kinds of nuts add a nice crunch.

PREP: 25 min. **BAKE:** 2-1/2 hours + cooling
     2 cups golden raisins
     2 cups each coarsely chopped dried apricots and dates
     1 cup each red and green candied cherries, halved
     2 cups each coarsely chopped pecans, walnuts and Brazil nuts
   1/2 cup honey
   1/4 cup water
     1 teaspoon lemon juice
     1 cup butter, softened
 1-1/4 cups packed brown sugar
     4 eggs
     2 cups all-purpose flour
     1 teaspoon ground cinnamon
   1/2 teaspoon each ground cloves, mace and nutmeg
   1/2 teaspoon salt
   1/4 teaspoon baking soda

1 In a large bowl, combine the fruits, nuts, honey, water and lemon juice; set aside.

2 In another large bowl, cream the butter and sugar until light and fluffy. Beat in the eggs. Fold into fruit mixture. Combine the dry ingredients; gradually fold into the fruit mixture until evenly coated. Pour into two greased and waxed paper-lined 9-in. x 5-in. loaf pans.

3 With a shallow pan of water in bottom of the oven, bake at 275° for 2-1/2 hours or until a toothpick inserted near the center comes out clean. Cover with foil during the last 30 minutes.

4 Cool 10 minutes; remove to wire rack to cool completely. Remove waxed paper and wrap each cake in foil. Place in plastic bags and store in a cool dry place.

YIELD: 2 loaves (18 slices each).

ENTREES

HEARTY NEW ENGLAND DINNER

CLAIRE MCCOMBS, SAN DIEGO, CALIFORNIA

This favorite slow-cooker recipe came from a friend. At first, my husband was a bit skeptical about a roast that wasn't fixed in the oven, but he loves the old-fashioned goodness of this version. The horseradish in the gravy adds zip.

PREP: 20 min. **COOK:** 7-1/2 hours

- 2 medium carrots, sliced
- 1 medium onion, sliced
- 1 celery rib, sliced
- 1 boneless beef chuck roast (about 3 pounds)
- 1 teaspoon salt, divided
- 1/4 teaspoon pepper
- 1 envelope onion soup mix
- 2 cups water
- 1 tablespoon white vinegar
- 1 bay leaf
- 1/2 small head cabbage, cut into wedges
- 3 tablespoons butter
- 2 tablespoons all-purpose flour
- 1 tablespoon dried minced onion
- 2 tablespoons prepared horseradish

1 Place the carrots, onion and celery in a 5-qt. slow cooker. Cut roast in half. Place roast over vegetables; sprinkle with 1/2 teaspoon salt and pepper. Add the soup mix, water, vinegar and bay leaf. Cover and cook on low for 7-9 hours or until beef is tender.

2 Remove beef and keep warm; discard bay leaf. Add cabbage. Cover and cook on high for 30-40 minutes or until the cabbage is tender.

3 Meanwhile, melt butter in a small saucepan; stir in flour and onion. Skim fat from cooking liquid in slow cooker. Add 1-1/2 cups cooking liquid to the saucepan. Stir in horseradish and remaining salt; bring to a boil. Cook and stir for 2 minutes or until thickened and bubbly. Serve with roast and vegetables.

YIELD: 6-8 servings.

ROAST BEEF WITH GRAVY

TRACY ASHBECK, WISCONSIN RAPIDS, WISCONSIN

Start this simple roast in the morning and you'll have savory slices of meat and gravy ready at suppertime. The tender beef is loaded with homemade taste and leaves plenty for main dishes later in the week.

PREP: 5 min. **COOK:** 6 hours

- 1 beef sirloin tip roast (4 pounds)
- 1/2 cup all-purpose flour, divided
- 1 envelope onion soup mix
- 1 envelope brown gravy mix
- 2 cups cold water

Hot mashed potatoes

1 Cut roast in half; rub with 1/4 cup flour. Place in 5-qt. slow cooker. In a bowl, combine the soup and gravy mixes and remaining flour; stir in water until blended. Pour over roast.

2 Cover and cook on low for 6-8 hours or until meat is tender. Slice roast; serve with mashed potatoes and gravy.

YIELD: 16 servings.

OLD-FASHIONED MACARONI AND CHEESE

JAMES BACKMAN, CENTRALIA, WASHINGTON

Sometimes classic comfort food is just what you need on a cold winter day. This recipe is a tried-and-true people pleaser.

PREP: 15 min. **BAKE:** 45 min.

- 3-1/2 cups uncooked elbow macaroni (about 12 ounces)
- 1/4 cup butter, cubed
- 1/4 cup all-purpose flour
- 1 teaspoon salt
- 3/4 teaspoon ground mustard
- 1/2 teaspoon pepper

Few dashes hot pepper sauce

- 3-1/2 cups milk
- 5 cups (20 ounces) shredded cheddar cheese, divided

1 Cook macaroni in boiling water until almost tender; drain.

2 Meanwhile, in a Dutch oven, melt butter. Stir in the flour, salt, mustard, pepper and pepper sauce until smooth. Cook for 1 minute or until bubbly. Stir in the macaroni, milk and 4 cups shredded cheese.

3 Transfer to an ungreased 13-in. x 9-in. baking dish. Cover and bake at 350° for 45-50 minutes or until bubbly. Uncover; sprinkle with the remaining cheese. Let stand for 5 minutes before serving.

YIELD: 12-16 servings.

WINTER PORK CHOP BAKE

VIRGINIA RICKS, ROY, UTAH
Pork has always been a family favorite, and this recipe is a surefire winner. All the work is done in the preparation, so there is very little cleanup after the meal.

PREP: 20 min. **BAKE:** 35 min.

- 1 medium tart apple, diced
- 1 small sweet red pepper, diced
- 1 small onion, chopped
- 1/4 cup golden raisins
- 1/4 cup chopped walnuts
- 1 tablespoon butter
- 3 slices rye bread, toasted and cubed
- 1/4 cup chicken broth
- 3 tablespoons apple juice
- 1/2 teaspoon rubbed sage
- 1/4 teaspoon dried basil
- 2 bone-in pork chops (1/2 inch thick)
- 1 tablespoon canola oil
- Salt and pepper to taste
- 1 medium sweet potato, peeled and cut into 1/2-inch pieces

1 In a large skillet, saute the first five ingredients in butter for 5 minutes or until red pepper and onion are tender. Remove from the heat; stir in the bread cubes, broth, juice, sage and basil.

2 Meanwhile, in another large skillet, brown chops in oil. Place stuffing in a greased 11-in. x 7-in. baking dish. Place chops on top; sprinkle with salt and pepper. Arrange sweet potato around edges of the dish.

3 Cover and bake at 350° for 35-40 minutes or until a meat thermometer reads 160°.

YIELD: 2 servings.

MELT-IN-YOUR-MOUTH MEAT LOAF

SUZANNE CODNER, STARBUCK, MINNESOTA
When my husband and I were first married, he refused to eat meat loaf because he said it was bland and dry. Then I prepared this version, and it became his favorite meal.

PREP: 15 min. **COOK:** 5-1/4 hours + standing

- 2 eggs
- 3/4 cup milk
- 2/3 cup seasoned bread crumbs
- 2 teaspoons dried minced onion
- 1 teaspoon salt
- 1/2 teaspoon rubbed sage
- 1-1/2 pounds ground beef
- 1/4 cup ketchup
- 2 tablespoons brown sugar
- 1 teaspoon ground mustard
- 1/2 teaspoon Worcestershire sauce

1 In a large bowl, combine the first six ingredients. Crumble beef over mixture and mix well (mixture will be moist). Shape into a round loaf; place in a 5-qt. slow cooker. Cover and cook on low for 5-6 hours or until a meat thermometer reads 160°.

2 In a small bowl, whisk the ketchup, brown sugar, mustard and Worcestershire sauce. Spoon over the meat loaf. Cook 15 minutes longer or until heated through. Let the meatloaf stand for 10-15 minutes before cutting.

YIELD: 6 servings.

INDIVIDUAL BEEF WELLINGTONS

TASTE OF HOME TEST KITCHEN

A savory mushroom-wine sauce is draped over the golden pastry in this recipe from our home economists. The elegant entree is perfect to present to guests on Christmas or New Year's Eve.

PREP: 30 min. **BAKE:** 25 min.

- 6 beef tenderloin steaks (1-1/2 to 2 inches thick and 8 ounces each)
- 4 tablespoons butter, divided
- 3 sheets frozen puff pastry, thawed
- 1 egg, lightly beaten
- 1/2 pound sliced fresh mushrooms
- 1/4 cup chopped shallots
- 2 tablespoons all-purpose flour
- 1 can (10-1/2 ounces) condensed beef consomme, undiluted
- 3 tablespoons port wine
- 2 teaspoons minced fresh thyme

1 In a large skillet, brown steaks in 2 tablespoons butter for 2-3 minutes on each side. Remove and keep warm.

2 On a lightly floured surface, roll each puff pastry sheet into a 14-in. x 9-1/2-in. rectangle. Cut into two 7-in. squares (discard scraps). Place a steak in the center of each square. Lightly brush pastry edges with water. Bring opposite corners of pastry over steak; pinch seams to seal tightly. Cut four small slits in top of the pastry.

3 Place in a greased 15-in. x 10-in. x 1-in. baking pan. Brush with egg. Bake at 400° for 25-30 minutes or until the pastry is golden brown and the meat reaches desired doneness (for medium-rare, a meat thermometer should read 145°; medium, 160°; well-done, 170°).

4 Meanwhile, in the same skillet, saute mushrooms and shallots in remaining butter for 3-5 minutes or until tender. Combine flour and consomme until smooth; stir into mushroom mixture. Bring to a boil; cook and stir for 2 minutes or until thickened. Stir in wine and thyme. Cook and stir 2 minutes longer. Serve with beef.

YIELD: 6 servings.

OVERNIGHT FRENCH TOAST

CATHERINE BUEHRE, WEEPING WATER, NEBRASKA

Youngsters who won't eat eggs cooked the traditional ways go crazy for this breakfast dish. I should know, because I have four children!

PREP: 10 min. + chilling **BAKE:** 45 min.

- 1 loaf (1 pound) unsliced cinnamon-raisin bread
- 5 eggs
- 2 egg yolks
- 1 cup half-and-half cream
- 3/4 cup packed brown sugar
- 2 teaspoons pumpkin pie spice
- 1 teaspoon maple flavoring
- 1 teaspoon vanilla extract
- 3 cups milk
- 1/4 cup butter, melted

Fresh strawberries or maple syrup, optional

1 Slice ends from bread and discard or save for another use. Slice remaining loaf into eight 1-in. slices and arrange in the bottom of two greased 8-in. square baking pans.

2 In a large bowl, beat the eggs, yolks, cream, brown sugar, pie spice and flavorings. Gradually add milk, beating until well blended; pour over bread. Cover and chill overnight.

3 Remove from the refrigerator 30 minutes before baking.

4 Drizzle with butter. Bake, uncovered, at 350° for 45-60 minutes or until a knife inserted near the center comes out clean. Serve warm; top with strawberries or syrup if desired.

YIELD: 6-8 servings.

EDITOR'S NOTE: If cinnamon-raisin bread is unavailable, substitute raisin bread and add 1/4 teaspoon ground cinnamon to the egg mixture.

"EGG"CELENT

According to the American Egg Board, fresh eggs can be stored in their carton in the refrigerator for 4 to 5 weeks beyond the pack date. Some manufacturers stamp their cartons with a date 30 days beyond the pack date. If you need to separate eggs, like for the recipe above, it's easier to separate eggs when they are cold.

SWISS WOODS SOUFFLE

WERNER AND DEBRAH MOSIMANN, LITITZ, PENNSYLVANIA
I developed this recipe to serve at breakfast to the guests at my bed and breakfast.

PREP: 15 min. **BAKE:** 45 min.

- 8 to 10 slices bread, torn in pieces
- 5 eggs
- 2 cups milk, divided
- 1/2 teaspoon ground mustard
- 1/4 teaspoon salt
- 1/4 teaspoon pepper
- 1 pound bulk pork sausage
- 1 can (10-3/4 ounces) condensed cream of mushroom soup, undiluted or 1 cup thick homemade white sauce with 1/2 cup sauteed mushrooms
- 1/2 cup shredded Gruyere cheese
- 1/2 cup shredded Emmenthaler Swiss cheese

1 Arrange bread in an ungreased 13-in. x 9-in. baking dish. Whisk together the eggs, 1-1/2 cups milk and seasonings; pour over bread and set aside.

2 Meanwhile, in a large skillet, cook sausage over medium heat until no longer pink; drain. Spoon over bread. Combine the soup, cheeses and remaining milk; spread over sausage.

3 Bake, uncovered, at 350° for 45-50 minutes or until the top is puffed and the center appears set. Let stand for 5 minutes before serving.

YIELD: 6-8 servings.

CREAMY LASAGNA CASSEROLE

SHELLY KORELL, EATON, COLORADO
Satisfy your gang with this casserole, which is a rich combination of cream cheese, sour cream and cheddar cheese layered with lasagna noodles and a beefy sauce.

PREP: 30 min. **BAKE:** 25 min. + standing

- 2 pounds ground beef
- 1 can (29 ounces) tomato sauce
- 1 teaspoon salt
- 1/2 teaspoon pepper
- 1/2 teaspoon garlic powder
- 2 packages (3 ounces each) cream cheese, softened
- 2 cups (16 ounces) sour cream
- 2 cups (8 ounces) shredded cheddar cheese, divided
- 4 green onions, chopped
- 12 to 14 lasagna noodles, cooked and drained

1 In a Dutch oven, cook beef over medium heat until no longer pink; drain. Add the tomato sauce, salt, pepper and garlic powder. Bring to a boil. Reduce heat; simmer, uncovered, for 15 minutes. In a bowl, beat cream cheese until smooth. Add sour cream, 1 cup cheddar cheese and onions; mix well.

2 Spread about 1/2 cup meat sauce into two greased 8-in. square baking dishes. Place two to three noodles in each dish, trimming to fit if necessary. Top each with about 1/2 cup cream cheese mixture and about 2/3 cup meat sauce. Repeat layers twice. Sprinkle 1/2 cup cheddar cheese over each.

3 Cover and freeze one casserole for up to 1 month. Bake remaining casserole, uncovered, at 350° for 25-30 minutes or until bubbly and heated through. Let stand for 15 minutes before cutting.

4 To use the frozen casserole: Thaw it in the refrigerator for 18 hours. Remove casserole from the refrigerator 30 minutes before baking. Bake, uncovered, at 350° for 40-50 minutes or until heated through.

YIELD: 2 casseroles (4-6 servings each).

EDITOR'S NOTE: Reduced-fat or fat-free cream cheese and sour cream are not recommended for this recipe.

NOSTALGIC CHICKEN AND DUMPLINGS

BRENDA EDWARDS, HERFORD, ARIZONA
Enjoy old-fashioned goodness without all the fuss when you fix this supper in your slow cooker. It features tender chicken, wonderfully light dumplings and a full-flavored sauce.

PREP: 20 min. **COOK:** 5 hours

- 6 bone-in chicken breast halves (10 ounces each), skin removed
- 2 whole cloves
- 1/2 cup frozen pearl onions, thawed
- 1 bay leaf
- 1 garlic clove, minced
- 1/2 teaspoon salt
- 1/2 teaspoon dried thyme
- 1/2 teaspoon dried marjoram
- 1/4 teaspoon pepper
- 1/2 cup reduced-sodium chicken broth
- 1/2 cup white wine or additional chicken broth
- 3 tablespoons cornstarch
- 1/4 cup cold water
- 1/2 teaspoon browning sauce, optional
- 1 cup reduced-fat biscuit/baking mix
- 6 tablespoons fat-free milk
- 1 tablespoon minced fresh parsley

1 Place the chicken in a 5-qt. slow cooker. Insert cloves into one onion; add to slow cooker. Add bay leaf and remaining onions. Sprinkle mixture with garlic, salt, thyme, marjoram and pepper. Add broth and wine or additional broth. Cover and cook on low for 4-1/2 to 5 hours or until a meat thermometer reads 170°.

2 Remove chicken to a serving platter and keep warm. Discard cloves and bay leaf. In a small bowl, combine the cornstarch, water and browning sauce if desired until smooth. Stir into slow cooker. Cover and cook on high until mixture reaches a simmer.

3 Meanwhile, combine the biscuit mix, milk and parsley. Drop by tablespoonfuls onto simmering liquid. Reduce heat to low; cover and cook for 20-25 minutes or until a toothpick inserted into the dumplings comes out clean (do not lift cover while simmering). Serve dumplings and sauce with chicken.

YIELD: 6 servings.

MEAL-IN-ONE CASSEROLE

DOROTHY PRITCHETT, WILLS POINT, TEXAS
Salsa gives zip to this hearty fix-and-forget-it meal. This recipe makes more than my husband and I can eat, so I freeze half of it. We think it tastes even better the second time.

PREP: 15 min. **COOK:** 4 hours

- 1 pound ground beef
- 1 medium onion, chopped
- 1 medium green pepper, chopped
- 1 can (15-1/4 ounces) whole kernel corn, drained
- 1 can (4 ounces) mushroom stems and pieces, drained
- 1 teaspoon salt
- 1/4 teaspoon pepper
- 1 jar (11 ounces) salsa
- 5 cups cooked medium egg noodles
- 1 can (28 ounces) diced tomatoes, undrained
- 1 cup water
- 1 cup (4 ounces) shredded cheddar cheese or blend of cheddar, Monterey Jack and American cheese

1 In a large skillet, cook the beef and onion over medium heat until meat is no longer pink; drain.

2 Transfer to a 5-qt. slow cooker. Top with the green pepper, corn and mushrooms. Sprinkle with salt and pepper. Pour salsa over mushrooms. Top with noodles. Pour tomatoes and water over all. Sprinkle with cheese.

3 Cover and cook on low for 4 hours or until heated through.

YIELD: 4-6 servings.

GARLIC BEEF STROGANOFF

ERIKA ANDERSON, WAUSAU, WISCONSIN
I'm a mom and work full-time, so I try to use my slow cooker whenever possible. This Stroganoff is perfect because I can get it ready in the morning before the kids get up.

PREP: 20 min. **COOK:** 7 hours

- 2 teaspoons beef bouillon granules
- 1 cup boiling water
- 1 can (10-3/4 ounces) condensed cream of mushroom soup, undiluted
- 2 jars (4-1/2 ounces each) sliced mushrooms, drained
- 1 large onion, chopped
- 3 garlic cloves, minced
- 1 tablespoon Worcestershire sauce
- 1-1/2 to 2 pounds boneless round steak, trimmed and cut into thin strips

2 tablespoons canola oil
1 package (8 ounces) cream cheese, cubed
Hot cooked noodles

1 In a 3-qt. slow cooker, dissolve bouillon in water. Add the soup, mushrooms, onion, garlic and Worcestershire sauce. In a skillet, brown beef in oil.

2 Transfer to the slow cooker. Cover and cook on low for 7-8 hours or until the meat is tender. Stir in cream cheese until smooth. Serve with noodles.

YIELD: 6-8 servings.

SLOW-COOKED SHORT RIBS

PAM HALFHILL, WAPAKONETA, OHIO
Smothered in a finger-licking barbecue sauce, these hearty, meaty ribs are a winner everywhere I take them. The recipe is great for a busy cook because once everything is combined, the slow cooker does all the work.

PREP: 25 min. **COOK:** 9 hours

2/3 cup all-purpose flour
2 teaspoons salt
1/2 teaspoon pepper
4 to 4-1/2 pounds boneless beef short ribs
1/4 to 1/3 cup butter
1 large onion, chopped
1-1/2 cups beef broth
3/4 cup red wine vinegar
3/4 cup packed brown sugar
1/2 cup chili sauce
1/3 cup ketchup
1/3 cup Worcestershire sauce
5 garlic cloves, minced
1-1/2 teaspoons chili powder

1 In a large resealable plastic bag, combine the flour, salt and pepper. Add ribs in batches and shake to coat. In a large skillet, brown ribs in butter.

2 Transfer to a 6-qt. slow cooker. In the same skillet, combine the remaining ingredients. Cook and stir until mixture comes to a boil; pour over ribs. Cover and cook on low for 9-10 hours or until meat is tender.

YIELD: 12 servings.

CHRISTMAS BREAKFAST CASSEROLE

MARYELLEN HAYS, WOLCOTTVILLE, INDIANA
After church services on Christmas morning, our family enjoys this easy, make-head casserole. I'd also recommend it for a special breakfast or brunch any time of the year.

PREP: 10 min. + chilling **BAKE:** 50 min. + standing

7 slices white bread, crusts removed and cubed
2 cups (8 ounces) shredded cheddar cheese
6 eggs
3 cups milk
1 teaspoon ground mustard
1/2 teaspoon salt
1/4 teaspoon pepper
6 bacon strips, cooked and crumbled

1 In a greased 11-in. x 7-in. baking dish, combine the bread cubes and cheese. In a large bowl, whisk the eggs, milk, mustard, salt and pepper; pour over bread and cheese. Top with bacon. Cover and refrigerate overnight.

2 Remove from the refrigerator 30 minutes before baking. Bake, uncovered, at 350° for 50-55 minutes or until a knife inserted near the center comes out clean. Let stand 10 minutes before serving.

YIELD: 6-8 servings.

TERIYAKI PORK ROAST

ROXANNE HULSEY, GAINESVILLE, GEORGIA

Since my husband works full-time and attends school, I do a great deal around the house, including getting our three children where they need to go. I'm always looking for no-fuss recipes, so I was thrilled to find this one. The moist teriyaki seasoned pork roast has become a family favorite.

PREP: 10 min. **COOK:** 7 hours + 10 min.

- 3/4 cup unsweetened apple juice
- 2 tablespoons sugar
- 2 tablespoons soy sauce
- 1 tablespoon white vinegar
- 1 teaspoon ground ginger
- 1/4 teaspoon garlic powder
- 1/8 teaspoon pepper
- 1 boneless pork loin roast (about 3 pounds), halved
- 7-1/2 teaspoons cornstarch
- 3 tablespoons cold water

1 In a greased 3-qt. slow cooker, combine the first seven ingredients. Add roast and turn to coat. Cover and cook on low for 7-8 hours or until a thermometer inserted into the roast reads 160°.

2 Remove roast and keep warm. In a small saucepan, combine cornstarch and cold water until smooth; stir into cooking juices. Bring to a boil; cook and stir for 2 minutes or until thickened. Serve with roast.

YIELD: 8 servings.

CHICKEN NOODLE CASSEROLE

CHERYL WATTS, NATURAL BRIDGE, VIRGINIA

This tasty dish gets even better after it's been refrigerated a day or two, so the leftovers are always great. We eat it hot in the winter and cold in the summer.

PREP: 20 min. **BAKE:** 35 min.

- 1 package (16 ounces) egg noodles
- 1 medium sweet red pepper, chopped
- 1 large onion, chopped
- 1 celery rib, chopped
- 2 garlic cloves, minced
- 1/4 cup butter, cubed
- 1-1/2 cups sliced fresh mushrooms
- 3 tablespoons all-purpose flour
- 3 cups chicken broth
- 3 cups half-and-half cream
- 2 packages (8 ounces each) cream cheese, cubed
- 12 cups cubed cooked chicken
- 1 to 1-1/2 teaspoons salt

TOPPING:

- 1 cup finely crushed cornflakes
- 2 tablespoons butter, melted
- 1 tablespoon canola oil
- 3 tablespoons minced fresh parsley
- 1/2 teaspoon paprika

1 Cook noodles according to package directions; drain. In a large skillet, saute the red pepper, onion, celery and garlic in butter until tender. Add mushrooms; cook 1-2 minutes longer or until tender. Remove vegetables with a slotted spoon; set aside.

2 Add flour to the skillet; stir until blended. Gradually add broth. Bring to a boil; cook and stir for 2 minutes or until thickened. Reduce heat. Gradually stir in cream. Add the cream cheese; cook and stir until cheese is melted. Remove from the heat.

3 In a large bowl, combine the chicken, salt, noodles, vegetables and cheese sauce. Transfer to two ungreased shallow 3-qt. baking dishes.

4 Combine topping ingredients. Sprinkle over top. Cover and bake at 350° for 20 minutes. Uncover; bake 15-20 minutes longer or until hot and bubbly.

YIELD: 2 casseroles (8-10 servings each).

MUSHROOM PEPPER STEAK

KATIE GOBLE, VALPARAISO, INDIANA
Round steak is slow-simmered until tender and smothered with a gravy that's packed with colorful peppers.

PREP: 15 min. **COOK:** 6-1/4 hours

- 2 pounds boneless beef top round steak
- 2 cups each sliced green, sweet red and yellow peppers (1/2-inch strips)
- 1 can (7 ounces) mushroom stems and pieces, drained
- 2 medium onions, quartered and sliced
- 1/2 cup water
- 1 teaspoon salt
- 1/2 teaspoon pepper
- 1 can (15 ounces) tomato sauce
- 1/4 cup cornstarch
- 1/4 cup cold water
- Hot mashed potatoes

1 Cut steak into serving-size pieces. Place in a 5-qt. slow cooker. Add the peppers, mushrooms, onions, water, salt and pepper. Pour tomato sauce over the top. Cover and cook on low for 6 to 6-1/2 hours or until meat is tender.

2 Using a slotted spoon, remove beef and vegetables; keep warm. Combine the cornstarch and cold water until smooth. Gradually stir into cooking juices; cover and cook on high for 15 minutes or until thickened. Serve with the beef, vegetables and mashed potatoes.

YIELD: 8 servings.

SWISS STEAK SUPPER

KATHLEEN ROMANIUK, CHOMEDEY, QUEBEC
To save a step while preparing the satisfying slow-cooked dinner, I keep seasoned salt to which I've already added ground pepper. It makes the preparation of the dish go faster.

PREP: 20 min. **COOK:** 5-1/2 hours

- 1-1/2 pounds boneless beef top round steak
- 1/2 teaspoon seasoned salt
- 1/4 teaspoon coarsely ground pepper
- 1 tablespoon canola oil
- 3 medium potatoes
- 1-1/2 cups fresh baby carrots
- 1 medium onion, sliced
- 1 can (14-1/2 ounces) Italian diced tomatoes
- 1 jar (12 ounces) home-style beef gravy
- 1 tablespoon minced fresh parsley

1 Cut the steak into six serving-size pieces; flatten to 1/4-in. thickness. Rub with seasoned salt and pepper. In a large skillet, brown beef in oil on both sides; drain.

2 Cut each potato into eight wedges. In a 5-qt. slow cooker, layer the potatoes, carrots, beef and onion. Combine the tomatoes and gravy; pour over top. Cover and cook on low for 5-1/2 to 6 hours or until meat and vegetables are tender. Sprinkle with parsley.

YIELD: 6 servings.

SLOW COOKER ADVANTAGE
One of the advantages of using a slow cooker is that it uses very little electricity because of its low wattage. We contacted our local utility company and found that it would cost just 21 cents to operate a slow cooker for a total of 10 hours.

SUNDAY CHICKEN SUPPER

RUTHANN MARTIN, LOUISVILLE, OHIO

I make this slow-cooked sensation with chicken, vegetables and seasonings. It's a hearty, homespun dish that satisfies even the biggest appetites.

PREP: 15 min. **COOK:** 6 hours

    4 medium carrots, cut into 2-inch pieces
    1 medium onion, chopped
    1 celery rib, cut into 2-inch pieces
    2 cups cut fresh green beans (2-inch pieces)
    5 small red potatoes, quartered
    1 broiler/fryer chicken (3 to 3-1/2 pounds), cut up
    4 bacon strips, cooked and crumbled
1-1/2 cups hot water
    2 teaspoons chicken bouillon granules
    1 teaspoon salt
  1/2 teaspoon dried thyme
  1/2 teaspoon dried basil
Pinch pepper

1 In a 5-qt. slow cooker, layer the first seven ingredients in order listed. In a small bowl, combine the water, bouillon, salt, thyme, basil and pepper; pour over the top. Do not stir.

2 Cover and cook on low for 6-8 hours or until vegetables are tender and chicken juices run clear. Remove chicken and vegetables. Thicken cooking juices for gravy if desired.

YIELD: 4 servings.

TUNA MUSHROOM CASSEROLE

JONE FURLONG, SANTA ROSA, CALIFORNIA

I love to serve this dressed-up version of a tuna casserole. The green beans add nice texture, color and flavor. The first time I made this dish, my uncle asked for seconds even though tuna casseroles are not usually his favorite.

PREP: 30 min. **BAKE:** 25 min.

  1/2 cup water
    1 teaspoon chicken bouillon granules
    1 package (9 ounces) frozen cut green beans
    1 cup chopped onion
    1 cup sliced fresh mushrooms
  1/4 cup chopped celery
    1 garlic clove, minced
  1/2 teaspoon dill weed
  1/2 teaspoon salt
  1/8 teaspoon pepper
    4 teaspoons cornstarch
1-1/2 cups cold milk
  1/2 cup shredded Swiss cheese
  1/4 cup mayonnaise
2-1/2 cups egg noodles, cooked and drained
    1 can (12-1/4 ounces) tuna, drained and flaked
  1/3 cup dry bread crumbs
    1 tablespoon butter

1 In a large saucepan, bring water and bouillon to a boil; stir until bouillon is dissolved. Add the next eight ingredients; bring to a boil. Reduce heat; cover and simmer for 5 minutes or until vegetables are tender.

2 Combine cornstarch and milk until smooth; gradually add to vegetable mixture. Bring to a boil; cook and stir for 2 minutes or until thickened. Remove from the heat; stir in cheese and mayonnaise until cheese is melted. Fold in noodles and tuna.

3 Pour into a greased 2-1/2-qt. baking dish. In a small skillet, brown bread crumbs in butter; sprinkle over casserole. Bake, uncovered, at 350° for 25-30 minutes or until heated through.

YIELD: 4-6 servings.

EDITOR'S NOTE: Reduced-fat or fat-free mayonnaise is not recommended for this recipe.

CHEDDAR CHICKEN POTPIE

SANDRA COTHRAN, RIDGELAND, SOUTH CAROLINA
I came up with this variation of potpie that both my husband and I enjoy. If I'm in a hurry and don't have the time this takes to bake, I'll leave off the crust, add extra milk and serve it as a chowder.

PREP: 30 min. **BAKE:** 40 min.

CRUST:
- 1 cup all-purpose flour
- 1/2 teaspoon salt
- 5 tablespoons cold butter, cubed
- 3 tablespoons cold water

FILLING:
- 1-1/2 cups chicken broth
- 2 cups peeled cubed potatoes
- 1 cup sliced carrots
- 1/2 cup sliced celery
- 1/2 cup chopped onion
- 1/4 cup all-purpose flour
- 1-1/2 cups milk
- 2 cups (8 ounces) shredded sharp cheddar cheese
- 4 cups cubed cooked chicken
- 1/4 teaspoon poultry seasoning

Salt and pepper to taste

1 For crust, in a small bowl, combine flour and salt. Cut butter in flour until mixture resembles coarse crumbs. Gradually add the water, mixing gently with a fork. Gather into a ball. Cover with plastic wrap and chill at least 30 minutes.

2 For filling, place broth in a Dutch oven; bring to a boil. Add vegetables. Reduce the heat; simmer 10-15 minutes or until the vegetables are tender.

3 Combine the flour and milk; stir into the broth mixture. Cook and stir over medium heat until slightly thickened and bubbly. Stir in the cheese, chicken, poultry seasoning, salt and pepper. Heat until cheese melts. Spoon into a 10-in. (2-1/2 to 3-qt.) casserole. Set aside.

4 On a lightly floured surface, roll crust to fit top of casserole, trimming edges as necessary. Place over filling; seal edges. Make several slits in center of crust for steam to escape.

5 Bake at 425° for 40 minutes or until golden brown.

YIELD: 6 servings.

BEEF IN MUSHROOM GRAVY

MARGERY BRYAN, MOSES LAKE, WASHINGTON
This is one of the best and easiest meals I've ever made. It has only four ingredients, and they all go into the pot at once. The meat is nicely seasoned and makes its own gravy—it tastes wonderful when you serve it over mashed potatoes.

PREP: 10 min. **COOK:** 7 hours
- 2 to 2-1/2 pounds boneless beef round steak
- 1 to 2 envelopes onion soup mix
- 1 can (10-3/4 ounces) condensed cream of mushroom soup, undiluted
- 1/2 cup water

Mashed potatoes, optional

1 Cut steak into six serving-size pieces; place in a 3-qt. slow cooker. Combine the soup mix, soup and water; pour over beef. Cover and cook on low for 7-8 hours or until meat is tender. Serve with mashed potatoes if desired.

YIELD: 6 servings.

CREAMY MASHED POTATOES RECIPE
Mashed potatoes are a classic accompaniment to any hearty beef dinner. Cook 3-1/2 to 4 pounds of peeled and quartered potatoes in boiling salted water until tender. Drain the potatoes and add 1/4 cup cubed butter, 1 ounce of softened cream cheese and 1/3 cup milk or cream. Mash with a potato masher, adding up to 1/3 cup of milk or cream as needed to make the potatoes light and fluffy. Season to taste with salt and pepper.

298 300 305 304

DESSERTS

302

FRENCH CREAM WITH SUGARED GRAPES

JUNE BRIDGES, FRANKLIN, INDIANA

Looking for a truly elegant finale for your holiday dinner? My dessert will do the trick. It looks so regal surrounded by pretty sugared fruit, and the flavor is divine. A friend gave me this recipe several years ago, and it's been in high demand at my house ever since.

PREP: 20 min. + chilling

- 1 cup (8 ounces) sour cream
- 1 cup heavy whipping cream
- 3/4 cup sugar
- 1 envelope unflavored gelatin
- 1/4 cup cold water
- 1 package (8 ounces) cream cheese, softened
- 1 teaspoon vanilla extract

Seedless green and red grapes

Additional sugar

1 In a large saucepan, combine sour cream and cream until well blended. Gradually stir in sugar. Cook and stir over medium heat just until mixture is warm and sugar is dissolved. Remove from the heat.

2 In a small microwave-safe bowl, sprinkle gelatin over cold water; let stand for 1 minute. Microwave, uncovered, on high for 40 seconds. Stir; let stand for 1 minute or until gelatin is completely dissolved. Stir into sour cream mixture.

3 In a small bowl, beat cream cheese until light and fluffy. Gradually add gelatin cream mixture and vanilla just until combined. Pour into a 4-cup mold coated with cooking spray. Chill for at least 4 hours or until set.

4 Dip grapes into water and shake off excess moisture; dip into sugar, turning to coat. Unmold dessert onto a serving platter; surround with sugared grapes.

YIELD: 6 servings.

EDITOR'S NOTE: Reduced-fat or fat-free sour cream and cream cheese are not recommended for this recipe.

CITRUS MERINGUE PIE

DONNA SCHWEIGHOFER, PICKERINGTON, OHIO

This pretty meringue pie stars grapefruit, orange and lemon juices. I made several changes to lighten up the original recipe. This pie has a very fresh citrus flavor, and the filling tastes nice and rich. It makes a refreshing finale to any meal.

PREP: 10 min. **BAKE:** 30 min. + chilling

MERINGUE:
- 3 egg whites
- 6 tablespoons sugar
- 1 tablespoon water
- 1/4 teaspoon plus 1/8 teaspoon cream of tartar
- 1-1/2 teaspoons cornstarch
- 2 tablespoons plus 1-1/2 teaspoons cold water
- 1/2 teaspoon vanilla extract
- 1/8 teaspoon salt

FILLING:
- 2/3 cup sugar
- 3 tablespoons cornstarch
- 1 cup grapefruit juice
- 1/2 cup water
- 1/4 cup orange juice
- 1 tablespoon lemon juice
- 1 egg
- 1 egg white
- 1 teaspoon grated grapefruit peel
- 7 drops yellow food coloring, optional
- 1 pastry shell (9 inches), baked

1 In a heavy saucepan, combine the egg whites, sugar, water and cream of tartar. Heat over low heat while beating with a portable mixer on low speed for 1 minute, scraping down sides of pan. Continue beating until mixture reaches 160°. Remove from the heat.

2 In a small saucepan, combine cornstarch and cold water until smooth. Bring to a boil; cook and stir for 1-2 minutes or until thickened. Remove from the heat; cool for 1 minute. Whisk into egg white mixture; add vanilla and salt. Beat on high until stiff peaks form. Set meringue aside.

3 For filling, in a large saucepan, combine sugar and cornstarch. Gradually add the grapefruit juice, water, orange juice and lemon juice until smooth. Bring to a boil over medium-high heat; cook and stir for 2 minutes or until thickened. Remove from the heat.

4 In a small bowl, whisk together egg and egg white; gradually stir 1/2 cup hot filling into egg mixture; return all to the pan, stirring constantly. Bring to a gentle boil; cook and stir for 2 minutes. Remove from the heat; stir in grapefruit peel and food coloring if desired. Pour hot filling into crust.

5 Spread meringue evenly over hot filling, sealing edges to crust. Broil for 30-60 seconds or until meringue is golden brown. Cool on a wire rack. Refrigerate for at least 3 hours before serving. Store leftovers in the refrigerator.

YIELD: 8 servings.

UPSIDE-DOWN APPLE PIE

SUSAN FRISCH, GERMANSVILLE, PENNSYLVANIA

This pie has won eight ribbons at area fairs. People say it looks and tastes like a giant apple-cinnamon bun. I take time off from work around the holidays to fill pie requests from family and friends. This recipe is everyone's favorite.

PREP: 30 min. + chilling **BAKE:** 50 min. + cooling

- 2 cups all-purpose flour
- 1/2 teaspoon salt
- 6 tablespoons shortening
- 2 tablespoons cold butter
- 5 to 7 tablespoons orange juice

FILLING:

- 6 tablespoons butter, melted, divided
- 1/2 cup packed brown sugar
- 1/2 cup chopped pecans
- 1 cup sugar
- 1/3 cup all-purpose flour
- 3/4 teaspoon ground cinnamon
- 1/4 teaspoon ground nutmeg
- 8 cups thinly sliced peeled Golden Delicious apples (about 1/8 inch thick)

GLAZE:

- 1/2 cup confectioners' sugar
- 2 to 3 teaspoons orange juice

1 In a large bowl, combine flour and salt; cut in shortening and butter until crumbly. Gradually add orange juice, tossing with a fork until dough forms a ball. Divide dough into two balls. Wrap in plastic wrap; refrigerate for at least 30 minutes.

2 Line a 9-in. deep-dish pie plate with heavy-duty foil, leaving 1-1/2 in. beyond edge; coat the foil with cooking spray.

3 For filling, combine 4 tablespoons butter, brown sugar and pecans; spoon into prepared pie plate. In a large bowl, combine the sugar, flour, cinnamon, nutmeg, apples and remaining butter; toss gently.

4 On waxed paper, roll out one ball of pastry to fit pie plate. Place pastry over nut mixture, pressing firmly against mixture and sides of plate; trim to 1 in. beyond plate edge. Fill with the apple mixture.

5 Roll out the remaining pastry to fit the top of pie; place over filling. Trim to 1/4 in. beyond plate edge. Fold bottom pastry over top pastry; seal and flute the edges. Cut four 1-in. slits in top pastry.

6 Bake at 375° for 20 minutes. Cover edges loosely with foil. Bake 30 minutes longer or until apples are tender and crust is golden brown.

7 Cool for 15 minutes on a wire rack. Invert onto a serving platter; carefully remove foil. Combine glaze ingredients; drizzle over pie.

YIELD: 6-8 servings.

OLD-FASHIONED RICE PUDDING

SANDRA MELNYCHENKO, GRANDVIEW, MANITOBA

This comforting dessert is a wonderful way to end any meal. As a girl, I always waited eagerly for the first heavenly bite. Today, my husband likes to top his serving with a scoop of ice cream. This recipe is comfort food at its best.

PREP: 10 min. **BAKE:** 1 hour

- 3-1/2 cups milk
- 1/2 cup uncooked long grain rice
- 1/3 cup sugar
- 1/2 teaspoon salt, optional
- 1/2 cup raisins
- 1 teaspoon vanilla extract

Ground cinnamon, optional

1 In a large saucepan, combine the milk, rice, sugar and salt if desired. Bring to a boil over medium heat, stirring constantly. Pour into a greased 1-1/2-qt. baking dish.

2 Cover and bake at 325° for 45 minutes, stirring every 15 minutes. Add raisins and vanilla; cover and bake for 15 minutes longer or until rice is tender. Sprinkle with cinnamon if desired. Serve warm or chilled. Store in the refrigerator.

YIELD: 6 servings.

MIXED NUT BRITTLE

NORMA FRANCEL, EDWARDSBURG, MICHIGAN
Nut fanciers have a lot to love about this irresistible brittle. The variety of nuts is what makes it so different.

PREP: 5 min. **COOK:** 30 min. + cooling
1-1/2 teaspoons plus 3 tablespoons butter, divided
1-1/2 cups sugar
   1 cup water
   1 cup light corn syrup
   1 can (10 ounces) mixed nuts without peanuts
   1 teaspoon vanilla extract
1-1/2 teaspoons baking soda

1 Butter a baking sheet with 1-1/2 teaspoons butter; set aside. In a large saucepan, combine the sugar, water and corn syrup. Cook over medium heat until a candy thermometer reads 270° (soft-crack stage), stirring occasionally.

2 Add the nuts; cook and stir until the mixture reaches 300° (hard-crack stage). Remove from the heat; stir in vanilla and remaining butter. Add baking soda and stir vigorously.

3 Quickly pour onto prepared baking sheet. Spread with a buttered metal spatula to 1/4-in. thickness. Cool before breaking into pieces. Store in an airtight container.

YIELD: about 1-3/4 pounds.

EDITOR'S NOTE: We recommend that you test your candy thermometer before each use by bringing water to a boil; the thermometer should read 212°. Adjust your recipe temperature up or down based on your test.

CANDY MAKING MADE EASY

It's actually quite easy to make candy from scratch if you keep in mind these pointers. Measure and assemble all ingredients for a recipe before beginning. Do not substitute or alter the basic ingredients. Use heavy-gauge saucepans that are deep enough to allow candy mixtures to boil freely without boiling over. For safe stirring, use wooden spoons with long handles.

CHOCOLATE HAZELNUT GATEAU

MICHELLE KRZMARZICK, REDONDO BEACH, CALIFORNIA
Gateau (pronounced ga-TOH) is the French word for any rich and fancy cake. I think you'll agree this dense chocolate dessert has just the right amount of sweetness.

PREP: 20 min. **BAKE:** 30 min. + cooling
2/3 cup butter, softened
3/4 cup sugar
   3 eggs, separated
   1 cup (6 ounces) semisweet chocolate chips, melted and cooled
   1 teaspoon vanilla extract
3/4 cup all-purpose flour
1/2 teaspoon salt
1/4 cup milk
2/3 cup ground hazelnuts, toasted
GLAZE:
   3 tablespoons butter
   2 tablespoons light corn syrup
   1 tablespoon water
   1 cup (6 ounces) semisweet chocolate chips
Toasted slivered almonds and fresh mint leaves

1 In a large bowl, cream butter and sugar until light and fluffy. Beat in egg yolks, melted chocolate and vanilla. Combine the flour and salt; gradually add to creamed mixture alternately with milk, beating well after each addition. Stir in the hazelnuts.

2 In a small bowl, beat the egg whites until stiff peaks form; carefully fold into batter. Spread into a greased 9-in. springform pan. Place pan on a baking sheet.

3 Bake at 350° for 30-35 minutes or until a toothpick inserted near the center comes out clean. Cool on wire rack for 10 minutes. Carefully run a knife around edge of pan to loosen; remove sides of pan. Cool completely.

4 For glaze, in a saucepan, bring the butter, corn syrup and water to a boil; stirring constantly. Remove from the heat. Add chocolate chips; stir until smooth. Cool to room temperature. Spread over top and sides of gateau. Garnish with the almonds and mint.

YIELD: 12 servings.

SUPER CHUNKY COOKIES

REBECCA JENDRY, SPRING BRANCH, TEXAS

Chocolate lovers will go crazy over these cookies that feature four kinds of chocolate! When friends ask me to make "those cookies," I know exactly what recipe they mean.

PREP: 15 min. **BAKE:** 10 min./batch

- 1/2 cup butter-flavored shortening
- 1/2 cup butter, softened
- 1 cup packed brown sugar
- 3/4 cup sugar
- 2 eggs
- 2 teaspoons vanilla extract
- 2-1/2 cups all-purpose flour
- 1 teaspoon baking soda
- 1/8 teaspoon salt
- 1 cup miniature semisweet chocolate chips
- 1 cup milk chocolate chips
- 1 cup vanilla or white chips
- 4 squares (1 ounces each) bittersweet chocolate, coarsely chopped
- 3/4 cup English toffee bits or almond brickle chips
- 1/2 cup chopped pecans

1 In a large bowl, cream shortening, butter and sugars until light and fluffy. Add eggs, one at a time, beating well after each addition. Beat in vanilla. Combine flour, baking soda and salt; gradually add to the creamed mixture and mix well. Stir in the remaining ingredients.

2 Drop by tablespoonfuls 3 in. apart on ungreased baking sheets. Bake at 350° for 10-12 minutes or until lightly browned. Cool for 2-3 minutes before removing to wire racks to cool completely.

YIELD: 8-1/2 dozen.

BUTTERSCOTCH GINGERBREAD COOKIES

KARA COOK, ELK RIDGE, UTAH

Every time I make these wonderful cookies, the spicy aroma takes me back to my childhood. I helped Mom make them and delivered them to neighbors.

PREP: 15 min. + chilling **BAKE:** 10 min. + cooling

- 1 cup butter, softened
- 1 cup packed brown sugar
- 2 eggs
- 3 cups all-purpose flour
- 2 packages (3-1/2 ounces each) cook-and-serve butterscotch pudding mix
- 3 teaspoons ground ginger
- 1 teaspoon baking powder
- 1 teaspoon ground cinnamon

1 In a large bowl, cream the butter and brown sugar until light and fluffy. Beat in the eggs. Combine the flour, pudding mixes, ginger, baking powder and cinnamon; gradually add to creamed mixture and mix well. Cover and refrigerate for 1 hour or until easy to handle.

2 On a lightly floured surface, roll out dough to 1/4-in. thickness. Cut with lightly floured cookie cutters. Place 1 in. apart on ungreased baking sheets.

3 Bake at 350° for 6-8 minutes or until firm. Remove to wire racks to cool. Decorate as desired.

YIELD: about 2 dozen.

LUSCIOUS LEMON CAKE ROLL

DARLENE BRENDEN, SALEM, OREGON
A co-worker shared the recipe for this elegant cake roll. It's perfect for rounding out a special meal.

PREP: 1 hour **BAKE:** 10 min. + chilling

- 4 eggs, separated
- 3/4 cup sugar, divided
- 1 tablespoon canola oil
- 1 teaspoon lemon extract
- 2/3 cup cake flour
- 1 teaspoon baking powder
- 1/4 teaspoon salt
- Confectioners' sugar

CREAMY LEMON FILLING:

- 1 can (14 ounces) sweetened condensed milk
- 1/3 cup lemon juice
- 2 teaspoons grated lemon peel
- 7 drops yellow liquid food coloring, divided
- 1-1/2 cups whipped topping
- 1/2 teaspoon water
- 1/2 cup flaked coconut

1 Line a greased 15-in. x 10-in. x 1-in. baking pan with waxed paper and grease the paper; set aside. In a large bowl, beat egg yolks until lemon-colored. Gradually beat in 1/4 cup sugar. Stir in oil and lemon extract; set aside.

2 In another large bowl, beat egg whites on medium speed until soft peaks form. Gradually add the remaining sugar, 2 tablespoons at a time, beating until stiff glossy peaks form and sugar is dissolved. Fold into egg yolk mixture. Combine the flour, baking powder and salt; fold into egg mixture.

3 Transfer to prepared pan. Bake at 375° for 10-12 minutes or until cake springs back when lightly touched. Cool for 5 minutes.

Turn cake onto a kitchen towel dusted with confectioners' sugar. Gently peel off waxed paper. Roll up cake in towel, starting with a short side. Cool completely on a wire rack.

4 For filling, in a small bowl, combine milk, lemon juice, lemon peel and 5 drops of food coloring. Fold in whipped topping. Unroll cake; spread half of the filling over cake to within 1 in. of edges. Roll up again. Place seam side down on a platter. Spread remaining filling over cake.

5 In a large resealable plastic bag, combine the water and remaining food coloring; add the coconut. Seal bag and shake to tint. Sprinkle the coconut over cake. Refrigerate for at least 2 hours before serving. Refrigerate leftovers.

YIELD: 10 servings.

DARK CHOCOLATE FONDUE

TASTE OF HOME TEST KITCHEN
The velvety, melt-in-your-mouth texture of this fudgy fondue is luscious. It's a delectable way to dress up chunks of pineapple, slices of banana or slices of cake.

PREP/TOTAL TIME: 20 min.

- 2 tablespoons all-purpose flour
- 1-1/2 cups milk
- 2 dark chocolate candy bars (1.55 ounces each), chopped
- 3 squares (1 ounce each) milk chocolate, chopped
- 2 tablespoons light corn syrup
- Cubed angel food cake and assorted fresh fruit

1 In a small saucepan, combine flour and milk until smooth. Bring to a boil over medium-high heat; cook and stir for 1 minute or until thickened. Reduce heat to low. Stir in chocolate and corn syrup. Cook and stir until melted.

2 Transfer to a small fondue pot and keep warm. Serve with cake cubes and fruit.

YIELD: 2 cups.

TOFFEE BROWNIE TRIFLE

WENDY BENNETT, SIOUX FALLS, SOUTH DAKOTA
This decadent combination of pantry items is a terrific way to dress up a brownie mix. Try it with other flavors of pudding.

PREP: 20 min. **BAKE:** 25 min. + cooling

    1 package fudge brownie mix (13-inch x 9-inch pan size)
2-1/2 cups cold milk
    1 package (3.4 ounces) instant cheesecake or vanilla pudding mix
    1 package (3.3 ounces) instant white chocolate pudding mix
    1 carton (8 ounces) frozen whipped topping, thawed
    2 to 3 Heath candy bars (1.4 ounces each), chopped

1 Prepare and bake brownies according to package directions for cake-like brownies, using a greased 13-in. x 9-in. baking pan. Cool completely on a wire rack.

2 In a large bowl, beat milk and pudding mixes on low speed for 2 minutes. Let stand for 2 minutes or until soft-set. Fold in whipped topping.

3 Cut the brownies into 1-in. cubes; place half in a 3-qt. glass trifle bowl or serving dish. Cover with half of the pudding. Repeat layers. Sprinkle with chopped candy bars. Refrigerate any leftovers.

YIELD: 16 servings.

ALMOND BREAD PUDDING

DEB MATHIE, SELLERSVILLE, PENNSYLVANIA
I played with a recipe from my mom, and the result has been popular with all of our customers at the Washington House in Sellersville.

PREP: 20 min. **BAKE:** 35 min.

    6 croissants
    8 eggs
    3 cups milk
    2 cups sugar
    2 teaspoons vanilla extract
    1 teaspoon almond extract
1/4 cup almond paste, cut into small cubes
1/2 cup chopped almonds
STRAWBERRY CARAMEL SAUCE:
    2 cups sugar
    2 cups heavy whipping cream
1/2 cup frozen sweetened sliced strawberries, thawed

1 Cut croissants into 1/2-in. pieces; place in a greased 13-in. x 9-in. baking dish. In a large bowl, combine the eggs, milk, sugar and extracts. Pour over croissants; let stand for 10 minutes. Dot with almond paste; sprinkle with almonds (dish will be full).

2 Bake at 350° for 35-40 minutes or until a knife inserted near the center comes out clean.

3 Meanwhile, for the sauce, in a heavy saucepan over medium heat, cook and stir sugar with a wooden spoon until sugar has melted and turned a deep amber color, about 20 minutes.

4 Add 1 cup cream (mixture will bubble). Stir in remaining cream; cook 10-15 minutes longer or until caramelized sugar is completely dissolved. Remove from the heat; stir in the strawberries. Serve with bread pudding.

YIELD: 12-15 servings.

CHOCOLATE TRUFFLES

DARLENE WEISE-APPLEBY, CRESTON, OHIO
You may be tempted to save this recipe for a special occasion since these smooth, creamy chocolates are divine. But with just a few ingredients, they're easy to make anytime.

PREP: 20 min. + chilling

    3 cups (18 ounces) semisweet chocolate chips
    1 can (14 ounces) sweetened condensed milk
    1 tablespoon vanilla extract
Chopped flaked coconut, chocolate sprinkles, colored sprinkles, baking cocoa and/or finely chopped nuts, optional

1 In a microwave-safe bowl, melt chocolate chips and milk; stir until smooth. Stir in vanilla. Chill for 2 hours or until mixture is easy to handle.

2 Shape into 1-in. balls. Roll in the coconut, sprinkles, cocoa or nuts if desired.

YIELD: about 4 dozen.

CHOCOLATE TRUFFLE TIPS
Before melting chocolate chips, be sure all equipment and utensils are completely dry. Any moisture may cause the chocolate to stiffen or "seize." You may need to use your hands to roll the chilled chocolate mixture into balls. Dusting cocoa powder onto the palm of your hands prevents the truffles from sticking. If the chocolate mixture becomes warm, cool it in the refrigerator again.

LEMON-BUTTER SPRITZ COOKIES

PAULA PELIS, ROCKY POINT, NEW YORK

Using a cookie press may be too difficult for children to master. Instead, have them help sprinkle the spritz cookies with colored sugar before baking.

PREP: 15 min. **BAKE:** 10 min./batch

- 2 cups butter, softened
- 1-1/4 cups sugar
- 2 eggs
- Grated peel of 1 lemon
- 2 teaspoons lemon juice
- 1 teaspoon vanilla extract
- 5-1/4 cups all-purpose flour
- 1/4 teaspoon salt
- Colored sugar

1 In a large bowl, cream butter and sugar until light and fluffy. Beat in the eggs, lemon peel, lemon juice and vanilla. Combine flour and salt; gradually add to creamed mixture and mix well.

2 Using a cookie press fitted with the disk of your choice, press dough 1 in. apart onto ungreased baking sheets. Sprinkle with colored sugar.

3 Bake at 400° for 8-10 minutes or until lightly brown around the edges.

YIELD: about 12 dozen.

TRIPLE CHOCOLATE DELIGHT

MRS. EDWIN HILL, SANTA BARBARA, CALIFORNIA

A fitting finale for any special occasion, this fudgy cake has three luscious layers for chocolate lovers to sink their forks into.

PREP: 50 min. + cooling **BAKE:** 30 min. + cooling

- 1 cup butter, softened, divided
- 2 cups sugar
- 4 eggs
- 5 Milky Way candy bars (2.15 ounces each)
- 1-1/4 cups buttermilk
- 2-1/2 cups all-purpose flour

- 1/2 teaspoon baking soda
- 1/4 teaspoon salt
- 1 cup chopped walnuts

FROSTING:

- 1/2 cup butter, divided
- 2-1/2 cups sugar
- 1 cup evaporated milk
- 1 jar (7 ounces) marshmallow creme
- 1 cup (6 ounces) semisweet chocolate chips
- Chopped walnuts, optional

1 In a large bowl, cream 1/2 cup butter and sugar until light and fluffy. Add eggs, one at a time, beating well after each addition.

2 In a heavy saucepan, stir candy bars and remaining butter over low heat until melted. Remove from the heat; stir in buttermilk.

3 Combine the flour, baking soda and salt; add to creamed mixture alternately with buttermilk mixture, beating well after each addition. Fold in nuts.

4 Pour into three greased and floured 9-in. round baking pans. Bake at 350° for 30-40 minutes or until a toothpick inserted near the center comes out clean. Cool for 10 minutes before removing from pans to wire racks to cool completely.

5 For frosting, lightly grease sides of a large saucepan with 1 tablespoon of butter; set remaining butter aside. Combine sugar and milk; cook over medium heat, stirring occasionally, until the mixture comes to a rolling boil. Boil until a candy thermometer reads 234° (soft-ball stage). Remove from the heat; stir in marshmallow creme, chips and remaining butter.

6 Transfer to a large bowl; cool to 110°. Beat on medium speed until smooth, about 5-7 minutes. Spread frosting between layers and over the top and sides of cake. Sprinkle with walnuts if desired.

YIELD: 12 servings.

COFFEE SHOP FUDGE

BETH OSBORNE SKINNER, BRISTOL, TENNESSEE

This recipe is one that my son, Jackson, and I worked on together. After several efforts, we decided this version was a winner. It is smooth, creamy and has an irresistible crunch from pecans. The coffee and cinnamon blend nicely to provide subtle flavor.

PREP: 15 min. + chilling

- 1 cup chopped pecans
- 3 cups (18 ounces) semisweet chocolate chips
- 1 can (14 ounces) sweetened condensed milk
- 2 tablespoons strong brewed coffee, room temperature
- 1 teaspoon ground cinnamon
- 1/8 teaspoon salt
- 1 teaspoon vanilla extract

1 Line an 8-in. square pan with foil and butter the foil; set aside. Place pecans in a microwave-safe pie plate. Microwave, uncovered, on high for 3 minutes, stirring after each minute; set aside.

2 In a 2-qt. microwave-safe bowl, combine the chocolate chips, milk, coffee, cinnamon and salt. Microwave, uncovered, on high for 1 minute. Stir until smooth. Stir in the vanilla and pecans. Immediately spread into the prepared pan.

3 Cover; refrigerate until firm, about 2 hours. Remove from pan; cut into 1-in. squares. Cover; store at room temperature.

YIELD: 2 pounds.

FUDGE FOILS

To prepare a foil-lined pan, line the pan with foil extending over the sides of the pan. Grease the foil with butter or coat with cooking spray. The foil allows the fudge to be lifted out of the pan in one piece. Cutting the fudge outside of the pan prevents the pan from being scratched by the knife and also allows for more evenly cut pieces.

CREME BRULEE

JOYLYN TRICKEL, GREENDALE, WISCONSIN

This is my favorite dessert, so I quickly learned to successfully make it on my own. Recently I was at a party where the guests finished off their own desserts by "broiling" the sugar on their portions with a small torch. What a great idea!

PREP: 30 min. **BAKE:** 45 min. + cooling

- 4 cups heavy whipping cream
- 9 egg yolks
- 3/4 cup sugar
- 1 teaspoon vanilla extract

Brown sugar

1 In a large saucepan, combine the cream, egg yolks and sugar. Cook and stir over medium heat until mixture reaches 160° or is thick enough to coat the back of a metal spoon. Stir in vanilla.

2 Transfer to eight 6-oz. ramekins or custard cups. Place cups in a baking pan; add 1 in. of boiling water to pan. Bake, uncovered, at 325° for 25-30 minutes or until centers are just set (mixture will jiggle). Remove ramekins from water bath; cool for 10 minutes. Cover and refrigerate for at least 4 hours.

3 One hour before serving, place custards on a baking sheet. Sprinkle each with 1-2 teaspoons brown sugar. Broil 8 in. from the heat for 4-7 minutes or until sugar is caramelized. Refrigerate any leftovers.

YIELD: 8 servings.

CHOCOLATE MOUSSE TORTE

TASTE OF HOME TEST KITCHEN

Although this mouse torte created by our home economists is very rich, people just can't seem to get enough of it. Decorate the cake with any variety of tasty chocolate candy.

PREP: 30 min. + freezing

- 1-1/4 cups chocolate wafer crumbs (about 25 wafers)
- 1/4 cup sugar
- 1/4 cup butter, melted

FILLINGS:

- 4 squares (1 ounce each) bittersweet chocolate
- 1/2 cup plus 2 tablespoons milk chocolate chips
- 4 squares (1 ounce each) white baking chocolate
- 1 tablespoon unflavored gelatin
- 1/4 cup water
- 5 egg yolks
- 1/4 cup sugar
- 1 cup half-and-half cream, warmed
- 1-3/4 cups heavy whipping cream
  Semisweet chocolate chips, melted

1 Combine the first three ingredients; press onto the bottom of a greased 9-in. springform pan. Bake at 375° for 8-10 minutes. Cool. Place each flavor of chocolate in a separate bowl; set aside. In another bowl, sprinkle gelatin over water; let stand for 1 minute or until softened.

2 In a small bowl, beat egg yolks on high speed for 3 minutes or until light and fluffy. Gradually add sugar, beating until thick and lemon-colored. Gradually whisk in half-and-half.

3 Transfer to a large saucepan; cook and stir over medium heat until a thermometer reads 160° and mixture has thickened, about 3 minutes.

4 Remove from heat; stir in gelatin until dissolved. Immediately pour a third of the egg mixture over each flavor of chocolate; quickly stir each until melted. Cool for 10 minutes.

5 In a large bowl, beat whipping cream until stiff peaks form. Fold a third of the whipped cream into each bowl. Pour the bittersweet chocolate mixture into prepared pan. Freeze until

firm, about 15 minutes. Repeat with milk chocolate mixture, then white chocolate mixture.

6 To serve, carefully run a sharp a knife around edge of pan to loosen. Remove sides of pan. Garnish if desired by drizzling with melted chocolate to create pine boughs.

YIELD: 16 servings.

EDITOR'S NOTE: Torte can be prepared 2 days in advance. Cover with plastic wrap and store in the refrigerator.

HAZELNUT SHORTBREAD

KAREN MORRELL, CANBY, OREGON

Traditional shortbread only contains flour, sugar and butter, resulting in a rich crumbly cookie. This version gets added flavor from chopped hazelnuts, some maple syrup and a touch of chocolate.

PREP: 15 min. + chilling **BAKE:** 15 min./batch + cooling

- 1 cup butter, softened
- 1/2 cup sugar
- 2 tablespoons maple syrup or honey
- 2 teaspoons vanilla extract
- 2 cups all-purpose flour
- 1-1/4 cups finely chopped hazelnuts
- 1/2 cup each white chocolate, dark chocolate, red, green and yellow candy coating disks

1 In a large bowl, cream butter and sugar until light and fluffy. Add syrup and vanilla. Beat in flour just until combined; fold in nuts. Shape into two 1-1/2-in. rolls; wrap tightly in waxed paper. Chill for 2 hours or until firm.

2 Cut into 1/4-in. slices and place 2 in. apart on ungreased baking sheets. Bake at 325° for 14-16 minutes or until edges begin to brown. Remove to wire racks to cool.

3 In separate microwave-safe bowls, melt candy coating disks; drizzle over cookies. Let stand until set.

YIELD: 6 dozen.

LEMONY WHITE CHOCOLATE CHEESECAKE

MARLENE SCHOLLENBERGER, BLOOMINGTON, ILLINOIS

Although it takes some time to prepare this eye-catching cheesecake, the combination of tangy lemon and rich white chocolate is hard to beat. It's an impressive (and scrumptious) way to end a meal. It's always a hit!

PREP: 30 min. **BAKE:** 65 min. + chilling

- 1-1/4 cups all-purpose flour
- 2 tablespoons confectioners' sugar
- 1 teaspoon grated lemon peel
- 1/2 cup cold butter, cubed

FILLING:

- 4 packages (8 ounces each) cream cheese, softened
- 1-1/4 cups sugar
- 2 tablespoons all-purpose flour
- 2 tablespoons lemon juice
- 2 tablespoons heavy whipping cream
- 2 teaspoons vanilla extract
- 4 eggs, lightly beaten
- 10 squares (1 ounce each) white baking chocolate, melted and cooled
- 2 teaspoons grated lemon peel

1 Place a 9-in. springform pan on a double thickness of heavy-duty foil (about 18 in. square). Securely wrap foil around pan; set aside.

2 In a small bowl, combine the flour, confectioners' sugar and peel; cut in butter until crumbly. Press onto the bottom and 1 in. up the sides of prepared pan. Place on a baking sheet. Bake at 325° for 25-30 minutes or until golden brown. Cool on a wire rack.

3 In a large bowl, beat the cream cheese, sugar, flour, lemon juice, cream and vanilla until well blended. Add eggs; beat on low speed just until combined. Stir in white chocolate and peel. Pour into crust.

4 Place pan in a large baking pan; add 1 in. of hot water to larger pan. Bake at 325° for 65-85 minutes or until center is just set and top appears dull.

5 Remove the pan from water bath. Cool on a wire rack for 10 minutes. Carefully run a knife around edge of pan to loosen; cool 1 hour longer. Refrigerate overnight. Remove the sides of pan before slicing.

YIELD: 12 servings.

TANGERINE CRANBERRY SORBET

PAMELA BROWN, INGERSOLL, ONTARIO

This is a very easy recipe to prepare and keep in the freezer before a party. It's a light and refreshing finish to a heavy holiday meal.

PREP: 15 min. + freezing

- 1-1/2 cups fresh or frozen cranberries
- 2 cups water
- 3 to 4 medium tangerines
- 2 tablespoons plus 1/2 cup sugar, divided
- 1 cup light corn syrup

1 In a large saucepan, bring cranberries and water to a boil. Reduce heat; simmer for 5 minutes. Meanwhile, using a sharp knife or zester, peel outer layer of one tangerine into strips for garnish. Toss the strips of peel with 2 tablespoons sugar; set aside. Squeeze tangerines to yield 1 cup of juice.

2 Place cranberries with liquid in a sieve over a large bowl. Press berries to remove juices. Discard pulp. Add the tangerine juice, corn syrup and remaining sugar to cranberry juice; stir until sugar is dissolved. Pour into a 9-in. square dish. Cover and freeze until firm, about 3 hours.

3 Remove from the freezer 30 minutes before serving. Spoon into dessert bowls. Garnish with reserved tangerine peel.

YIELD: 8 servings.

SPECIAL OCCASIONS

BERRY-FILLED DOUGHNUTS

GINNY WATSON, BROKEN ARROW, OKLAHOMA
Just four ingredients are all you need to prepare this sure-to-be-popular treat. Friends and family will never guess that refrigerated buttermilk biscuits are the base for these golden, jelly-filled doughnuts. They are yummy!

PREP/TOTAL TIME: 25 min.

  4 cups canola oil
  1 tube (7-1/2 ounces) refrigerated buttermilk biscuits, separated into 10 biscuits
  3/4 cup seedless strawberry jam
  1 cup confectioners' sugar

1 In an electric skillet or deep-fat fryer, heat oil to 375°. Fry biscuits, a few at a time, for 1-2 minutes on each side or until golden brown. Drain on paper towels.

2 Cut a small hole in the corner of a pastry or plastic bag; insert a very small tip. Fill bag with jam. Push the tip through the side of each doughnut to fill with jam. Dust with confectioners' sugar while warm. Serve immediately.

YIELD: 10 servings.

LATKES

RACHEL DELANO, TAPPAHANNOCK, VIRGINIA
I inherited my mother's love of cooking. I serve these crispy potato pancakes for Hanukkah and other celebrations.

PREP/TOTAL TIME: 30 min.

  2 cups shredded peeled potatoes (about 2 medium)
  1/2 cup finely chopped onion
  2 green onions, chopped
  1 egg, lightly beaten
Salt and pepper to taste
Oil for frying

1 Place potatoes in a clean linen towel; squeeze, reserving liquid in a measuring cup. Set aside until potato starch settles. Drain off top liquid; set potato starch aside.

2 In a large bowl, combine the potatoes, onions, egg, salt, pepper and reserved potato starch. Heat 2 tablespoons oil in a large skillet. Shape potato mixture by 2 tablespoonfuls into patties; place in hot oil, pressing lightly to flatten.

3 Fry until golden brown, about 1-1/2 minutes on each side. Drain on paper towels. Serve immediately or place in a warm oven until ready to serve.

YIELD: 1-1/2 dozen.

ONION KUGEL

TASTE OF HOME TEST KITCHEN
This traditional dish resembles a delicious classic souffle. Sliced eggplant, diced green pepper or shredded cabbage can be used in place of onions.

PREP: 15 min. **BAKE:** 35 min.

  6 eggs, separated
  2 cups finely chopped onions
  1/3 cup matzo meal
  1/3 cup canola oil
  3/4 teaspoon salt
  1/4 teaspoon pepper

1 In a large bowl, beat egg yolks on high speed for 2 minutes or until thick and lemon-colored. Add the onions, matzo meal, oil, salt and pepper; mix well.

2 In another bowl, beat egg whites on high until stiff peaks form; fold into onion mixture. Pour into an ungreased 2-qt. round baking dish.

3 Bake, uncovered, at 350° for 35-40 minutes or until a knife inserted near the center comes out clean. Serve immediately.

YIELD: 8 servings.

LAMB WITH APRICOTS

RACHEL DELANO, TAPPAHANNOCK, VIRGINIA

When I was a new bride, I decided to prepare a special Hanukkah for my husband, David, and me to share. The star was this lamb entree, which had been one of my favorites when I was growing up. Dried apricots add a touch of sweetness to the tender lamb, which is gently spiced.

PREP: 15 min. **BAKE:** 1-1/2 hours

- 1 large onion, chopped
- 2 tablespoons olive oil
- 1 boneless lamb shoulder roast (2-1/2 to 3 pounds), cubed
- 1 teaspoon each ground cumin, cinnamon and coriander

Salt and pepper to taste

- 1/2 cup dried apricots, halved
- 1/4 cup orange juice
- 1 tablespoon ground almonds
- 1/2 teaspoon grated orange peel
- 1-1/4 cups chicken broth
- 1 tablespoon sesame seeds, toasted

1 In a large skillet, saute onion in oil until tender. Add the lamb and seasonings. Cook and stir for 5 minutes or until meat is browned. Add apricots, orange juice, almonds and orange peel.

2 Transfer to a 2-1/2-qt. baking dish. Stir in broth. Cover and bake at 350° for 1-1/2 hours or until meat is tender. Sprinkle with sesame seeds.

YIELD: 8 servings.

CHEESY SOFT PRETZELS

RUTH ANN STELFOX, RAYMOND, ALBERTA

Fresh and warm from the oven, these chewy twists are a yummy snack even kids can make.

PREP: 20 min. **BAKE:** 15 min.

- 1-1/2 cups all-purpose flour
- 1/2 cup shredded cheddar cheese
- 2 teaspoons baking powder
- 1 teaspoon sugar
- 3/4 teaspoon salt
- 2 cups cold butter, cubed
- 2/3 cup milk
- 1 egg, lightly beaten

Coarse salt

1 In a large bowl, combine the flour, cheese, baking powder, sugar and salt. Cut in butter until crumbly. Stir in milk just until moistened.

2 Knead dough on a floured surface for 1 minute; divide in half. Roll each portion into a 12-in. x 8-in. rectangle; cut each into 8-in.-long strips. Fold strips in half, pinching the edges, and twist into pretzel shapes.

3 Place on greased baking sheets. Brush with egg and sprinkle with coarse salt. Bake at 400° for 12-15 minutes or until golden brown. Serve warm.

YIELD: 1-1/2 dozen.

SMOKED SALMON CHEESECAKE

BECKY APPLEBEE, CHINIAK, ALASKA

We live on Kodiak Island off the coast of Alaska, and salmon is one of our favorite foods. This elegant dish was the star attraction at the open house we hosted at my husband's business.

PREP: 20 min. + chilling **BAKE:** 35 min. + cooling

- 3 tablespoons dry bread crumbs
- 5 tablespoons grated Parmesan cheese, divided
- 1/2 cup chopped onion
- 1/2 cup chopped green pepper
- 3 tablespoons butter
- 4 packages (three 8 ounces, one 3 ounces) cream cheese, softened
- 1/2 cup heavy whipping cream
- 1/4 teaspoon pepper
- 4 eggs
- 5 ounces smoked salmon, diced
- 1/2 cup shredded Swiss cheese

Assorted crackers

1 Grease the bottom and sides of a 9-in. springform pan. Combine the bread crumbs and 2 tablespoons Parmesan cheese; sprinkle into pan, coating bottom and sides. Set aside.

2 In a skillet, saute onion and green pepper in butter until tender; set aside. In a bowl, beat cream cheese until fluffy. Beat in the cream, pepper and remaining Parmesan cheese. Add eggs; beat on low speed just until combined. Fold in the onion mixture, salmon and Swiss cheese.

3 Wrap a double thickness of heavy-duty foil around bottom of prepared pan. Pour salmon mixture into pan. Place in a large baking pan. Fill larger pan with hot water to a depth of 1-1/2 in. Bake at 325° for 35-40 minutes or until center is almost set. Cool on a wire rack for 1 hour. Refrigerate overnight.

4 Remove foil and sides of pan. Serve with crackers.

YIELD: 12-14 servings.

HOLIDAY APPETIZER PUFFS

KATHY FIELDER, DALLAS, TEXAS
These puffs are so versatile. Instead of the crab filling, you can also use your favorite chicken or tuna salad.

PREP: 20 min. **BAKE:** 25 min.
- 1 cup water
- 1/2 cup butter, cubed
- 1/2 teaspoon salt
- 1 cup all-purpose flour
- 4 eggs

FILLING:
- 1 package (8 ounces) cream cheese, softened
- 1/4 cup mayonnaise
- 1 can (6 ounces) crabmeat, drained and cartilage removed
- 1/2 cup shredded Swiss cheese
- 1 tablespoon minced chives
- 1 teaspoon garlic salt
- 1 teaspoon Worcestershire sauce
- 1/4 teaspoon pepper

1 In a small saucepan, bring the water, butter and salt to a boil. Add the flour all at once and stir until a smooth ball forms. Remove from the heat; let stand for 5 minutes. Add eggs, one at a time, beating well after each addition. Continue beating until mixture is smooth and shiny.

2 Drop by rounded teaspoonfuls 2 in. apart onto greased baking sheets. Bake at 400° for 25-30 minutes or until golden brown. Remove to wire racks. Immediately cut a slit in puffs to allow steam to escape. When cool, split puffs open; remove tops and set aside. Discard soft dough from inside.

3 For filling, in a small bowl, beat cream cheese and mayonnaise until smooth. Stir in the remaining filling ingredients. Just before serving, spoon filling into puffs; replace tops.

YIELD: 4 dozen.

EFFORTLESS EGGNOG

PAULA ZSIRAY, LOGAN, UTAH
This traditional beverage offers delicious flavor without any eggs!

PREP/TOTAL TIME: 5 min.
- 1/2 gallon cold milk, divided
- 1 package (3.4 ounces) instant French vanilla pudding mix
- 1/4 cup sugar
- 2 teaspoons vanilla extract
- 1/2 teaspoon ground cinnamon
- 1/2 teaspoon ground nutmeg

1 In a large bowl, whisk 3/4 cup milk and pudding mix until smooth. Whisk in the sugar, vanilla, cinnamon and nutmeg. Stir in the remaining milk. Refrigerate until serving.

YIELD: 16 servings (2 quarts).

CREAMED FRESH SPINACH

ROSEMARIE FORCUM, HEATHSVILLE, VIRGINIA
This flavorful no-frills side dish is a great way to incorporate the nutritious leafy greens into a meal.

PREP/TOTAL TIME: 20 min.
- 4 packages (9 ounces each) fresh baby spinach
- 1/4 cup butter, cubed
- 1/4 cup all-purpose flour
- 1 cup heavy whipping cream
- 1 cup milk
- 2 tablespoons finely chopped onion

Salt and white pepper to taste

1 Place the spinach in a Dutch oven over 1 in. of water. Bring to a boil; reduce heat. Cover and steam just until wilted, about 4 minutes. Drain; chop and set aside.

2 Melt butter in a large saucepan over medium heat. Whisk in the flour until smooth. Gradually add cream and milk. Bring to a boil; cook and stir for 2 minutes or until thickened. Stir in the onion, salt and pepper. Fold in spinach; heat through.

YIELD: 8 servings.

PRIME RIB WITH HORSERADISH SAUCE

PAULA ZSIRAY, LOGAN, UTAH
To ring in the holidays, we invite friends for dinner. A menu featuring tender prime rib is festive yet simple to prepare. A pepper rub and mild horseradish sauce complement the beef's great flavor.

PREP: 5 min. **BAKE:** 3 hours
- 1 bone-in beef rib roast (4 to 6 pounds)
- 1 tablespoon olive oil
- 1 to 2 teaspoons coarsely ground pepper

HORSERADISH SAUCE:

- 1 cup (8 ounces) sour cream
- 3 to 4 tablespoons prepared horseradish
- 1 teaspoon coarsely ground pepper
- 1/8 teaspoon Worcestershire sauce

1 Brush roast with oil; rub with pepper. Place roast, fat side up, on a rack in a shallow roasting pan. Bake, uncovered, at 450° for 15 minutes.

2 Reduce the heat to 325°. Bake for 2-3/4 hours or until the meat reaches desired doneness (for medium-rare, a meat thermometer should read 145°; medium, 160°; well-done, 170°), basting with pan drippings every 30 minutes.

3 Let stand for 10-15 minutes before slicing. Meanwhile, in a small bowl, combine the sauce ingredients. Serve with beef.

YIELD: 6-8 servings.

CRANBERRY-TOPPED CAKE

HELEN VAIL, GLENSIDE, PENNSYLVANIA

For me, part of the joy of Christmas is sharing tempting treats such as this special cake. I love trying new recipes, but I also rely on classics like this one.

PREP: 30 min. **BAKE:** 1-1/4 hours + cooling

- 1-1/3 cups sugar, divided
- 4 cups fresh or frozen cranberries, thawed

CAKE:

- 5 egg yolks
- 3/4 cup cold water
- 1/2 cup canola oil
- 2-1/2 teaspoons grated lemon peel
- 2-1/2 teaspoons vanilla extract
- 2 cups all-purpose flour
- 1-1/2 cups sugar
- 3 teaspoons baking powder
- 1 teaspoon salt
- 7 egg whites
- 1/2 teaspoon cream of tartar

FROSTING:

- 2 cups heavy whipping cream
- 2 tablespoons sugar
- 2 teaspoons vanilla extract

1 Grease two 8-in. square baking dishes; sprinkle each with 1 tablespoon sugar. Sprinkle 2 cups cranberries in each; sprinkle with remaining sugar. Cover and bake at 325° for 30 minutes. Uncover; cool for 1 hour.

2 For cake, in a small bowl, beat the egg yolks, water, oil, lemon peel and vanilla until well blended. In a large bowl, combine the flour, sugar, baking powder and salt; gradually add to egg mixture until blended.

3 In another large bowl, beat egg whites until foamy. Add cream of tartar; beat until stiff peaks form. Fold a fourth of the egg whites into batter. Fold in remaining whites. Spoon batter over cranberries.

4 Bake at 325° for 45-55 minutes or until cake springs back when lightly touched. Cool for 10 minutes before inverting on wire racks to cool completely.

5 For frosting, in a large bowl, beat cream until soft peaks form. Add the sugar and vanilla; beat until stiff peaks form. Place one cake on a serving plate; spread with some frosting. Top with remaining cake. Frost top and sides of cake. Cover and store in the refrigerator.

YIELD: 10-12 servings.

HOW TO FOLD IN INGREDIENTS

To fold a lighter mixture into a heavier one, use a rubber spatula to gently cut down through the middle of the ingredients. Move across the bottom of the bowl and bring up part of the heavier mixture. Repeat this circular motion just until mixture is combined.

NEW YEAR'S SURF 'N' TURF

TASTE OF HOME TEST KITCHEN
A mild mushroom sauce pulls together this pleasing pairing of tender steaks and firm shrimp.

PREP: 25 min. **COOK:** 10 min.

- 2 cups sliced fresh mushrooms
- 2 tablespoons finely chopped green onion
- 1-1/2 teaspoons minced garlic, divided
- 5 tablespoons olive oil, divided
- 5 tablespoons butter, divided
- 1/2 cup dry red wine or beef broth
- 2 tablespoons minced fresh parsley
- 2 tablespoons minced fresh basil
- 1/2 teaspoon browning sauce, optional
- 8 beef tenderloin steaks (1-1/2 to 2 inches and 8 ounces each)
- 24 uncooked medium shrimp, peeled and deveined

1 In a large skillet, saute mushrooms, onion and 1 teaspoon garlic in 2 tablespoons oil and 2 tablespoons butter until tender. Add wine; cook and stir for 1 minute. Stir in parsley, basil and browning sauce. Remove from skillet and keep warm.

2 In the same skillet, cook steaks in 2 tablespoons oil and 2 tablespoons butter over medium heat for 5-8 minutes on each side or until meat reaches desired doneness (for medium-rare, a meat thermometer should read 145°; medium, 160°; well-done, 170°). Return mushroom mixture to the pan; heat through.

3 Meanwhile, in another skillet, combine the remaining butter and oil. Add the shrimp and remaining garlic; cook and stir until shrimp turn pink. Serve with the steaks.

YIELD: 8 servings.

HOPPING JOHN

ANNE CREECH, KINSTON, NORTH CAROLINA
This is a quick and easy side dish that will become a favorite of your family. It's a classic New Year's Eve dish.

PREP: 10 min. **COOK:** 30 min.

- 1/2 pound sliced bacon, cut into 1-inch pieces
- 1/2 cup chopped green or sweet red pepper
- 2 celery ribs, chopped
- 6 green onions, sliced
- 1 cup uncooked long-grain rice
- 2 cups water
- Salt and pepper to taste
- 1 teaspoon ground red pepper
- 1/2 teaspoon dried basil
- 1/4 teaspoon dried thyme
- 1/4 teaspoon dried oregano
- 1 bay leaf
- 1 can (15 ounces) black-eyed peas, drained

1 In a large skillet, cook bacon over medium heat until crisp. Using a slotted spoon, remove to paper towels; drain, reserving 2 tablespoons drippings.

2 Saute the pepper, celery and onions in drippings until almost tender. Add the rice, water and seasonings. Cover and simmer for 10 minutes. Add the peas and bacon; cook for 10 minutes. Discard bay leaf.

YIELD: 4-6 servings.

MIDNIGHT MASHED POTATOES

TASTE OF HOME TEST KITCHEN
Garlic, onion salt and Parmesan cheese season these mashed potatoes that get a bit of richness from sour cream. For a fancy look, try using a pastry tip to pipe the potatoes into rosettes before baking.

PREP: 35 min. **BAKE:** 35 min.

- 6 medium russet potatoes, peeled and cubed
- 2 garlic cloves, minced
- 1 tablespoon butter
- 1/2 cup milk
- 1/2 cup sour cream
- 2 tablespoons grated Parmesan cheese
- 2 tablespoons minced chives
- 1 teaspoon salt
- 3/4 teaspoon onion salt
- 1/2 teaspoon garlic powder
- 1/4 teaspoon pepper

1 Place potatoes in a saucepan and cover with water. Bring to a boil. Reduce heat; cover and cook for 15-20 minutes or until tender. Meanwhile, in a small skillet, saute the garlic in butter.

2 Drain potatoes and place in a large bowl. Add garlic; beat until smooth. Add the remaining ingredients and mix well.

3 Transfer to a greased 2-qt. baking dish. Bake, uncovered, at 350° for 35-40 minutes or until heated through.

YIELD: 8 servings.

TUXEDO CREAM DESSERT

CAMILLA SAULSBURY, NACOGDOCHES, TEXAS

My adaptation of my grandmother's signature dessert always garners oohs and aahs. It's pretty and deliciously rich and creamy. Gran and I have both considered it a favorite for entertaining because it can be made up a day ahead.

PREP: 40 min. + chilling

1-3/4 teaspoons unflavored gelatin
    2 tablespoons cold water
1-1/2 cups heavy whipping cream, divided
    3/4 cup semisweet chocolate chips

VANILLA LAYER:

1-3/4 teaspoons unflavored gelatin
    2 tablespoons cold water
1-2/3 cups heavy whipping cream, divided
    1/4 cup sugar
    2 teaspoons vanilla extract

STRAWBERRY SAUCE:

    2 cups sliced fresh strawberries
    2 to 3 tablespoons sugar

1 In a small bowl, sprinkle gelatin over cold water; let stand for 1 minute. In a small saucepan, bring 1 cup cream to a simmer. Stir 1/2 cup into gelatin mixture until gelatin is completely dissolved. Stir chocolate chips into remaining warm cream until melted. Stir in gelatin mixture and remaining cream.

2 Transfer to an 8-in. x 4-in. loaf pan coated with cooking spray. Cover and refrigerate for 30 minutes or until firm.

3 For vanilla layer, in a small bowl, sprinkle gelatin over cold water; let stand for 1 minute. In a small saucepan, bring 1 cup cream and sugar to a simmer. Stir in the gelatin mixture until gelatin is completely dissolved. Stir in vanilla and remaining cream. Carefully spoon over the chocolate layer. Cover and refrigerate for at least 2 hours or until firm.

4 For sauce, in a blender, puree strawberries and sugar. Transfer to a bowl; cover and refrigerate until serving.

5 Just before serving, unmold dessert and cut into slices. Serve with strawberry sauce.

YIELD: 6-8 servings.

SIDECAR

TASTE OF HOME TEST KITCHEN

It always helps to have a steadfast recipe for a classic cocktail. You can't go wrong when serving this citrusy adult beverage when celebrating.

PREP/TOTAL TIME: 5 min.

Ice cubes
    1 ounce brandy
  2/3 ounce (4 teaspoons) triple sec
1-1/2 to 3 teaspoons lemon juice

GARNISH:

Lemon twist

1 Fill a shaker three-fourths full with ice. Add the brandy, triple sec and lemon juice. Cover and shake for 10-15 seconds or until condensation forms on outside of shaker. Strain into a chilled cocktail glass. Garnish with lemon twist.

YIELD: 1 serving.

RED VELVET CAKE

HOPE MEECE, AMBIA, INDIANA
I took a cherished family recipe, downsized it for a pair and came up with this cute rendition of a luscious old classic.

PREP: 25 min. **BAKE:** 15 min. + cooling

- 2 tablespoons butter, softened
- 6 tablespoons sugar
- 2 tablespoons sour cream
- 2 tablespoons beaten egg
- 1 tablespoon red liquid food coloring
- 3/4 teaspoon white vinegar
- 1/4 teaspoon vanilla extract
- 2/3 cup all-purpose flour
- 1 tablespoon baking cocoa
- 1/4 teaspoon baking soda
- 1/4 teaspoon salt
- 1/4 cup buttermilk

FROSTING:

- 2 tablespoons plus 1-1/2 teaspoons all-purpose flour
- 1/2 cup 2% milk
- 1/2 cup butter, softened
- 1/2 cup sugar
- 1/2 teaspoon vanilla extract

1 In a small bowl, cream butter and sugar until light and fluffy. Beat in the sour cream, egg, food coloring, vinegar and vanilla. Combine the flour, cocoa, baking soda and salt; add to creamed mixture alternately with buttermilk.

2 Pour into three 5-in. x 3-in. x 2-in. loaf pans coated with cooking spray. Bake at 350° for 14-18 minutes or until a toothpick inserted near the center comes out clean. Cool for 10 minutes before removing from pans to wire racks to cool completely.

3 For the frosting, in a small saucepan, whisk the flour and milk until smooth. Bring to a boil; cook and stir for 2 minutes or until thickened. Cover; cool to room temperature.

4 In a small bowl, cream butter and sugar. Beat in vanilla and milk mixture until fluffy. Spread frosting between layers and over top and sides of cake.

YIELD: 6 servings.

MOUSSE ROUNDS

LISA RENSHAW, KANSAS CITY, MISSOURI
Chocolate lovers will think they're in heaven when they taste these ambrosial treats. Creamy chocolate mousse is piped on a cocoa wafer and then topped with a pretty maraschino cherry. So cute!

PREP: 15 min. + chilling

- 1 package (3 ounces) cream cheese, softened
- 1/4 cup sugar
- 3 tablespoons baking cocoa
- 2 tablespoons 2% milk
- 1/4 teaspoon almond extract
- 6 chocolate wafers
- 6 maraschino cherries

1 In a small bowl, beat the cream cheese, sugar, cocoa, milk and almond extract. Place wafers flat side down on a plate; pipe or spoon chocolate mousse on top. Cover and refrigerate for at least 30 minutes. Just before serving, top each with a cherry.

YIELD: 6 pieces.

CHEESE-STUFFED POTATOES

JANET ENGLISH, PITTSBURGH, PENNSYLVANIA
Cottage cheese is the "secret" ingredient in this creamy side dish. I make two potatoes, one for dinner and one for lunch the next day.

PREP: 15 min. **BAKE:** 1 hour

- 2 medium baking potatoes
- 1 small onion, finely chopped
- 2 tablespoons water
- 1/2 cup 4% cottage cheese
- 1/4 cup buttermilk
- 3 tablespoons grated Parmesan cheese

Salt and pepper to taste

- 2 tablespoons thinly sliced green onions

1 Bake potatoes at 400° for 1 hour or until tender. Cut a thin slice off the top of each potato and discard. Scoop out pulp, leaving a thin shell. In a small bowl, mash pulp; set aside.

2 In a small skillet, cook and stir onion in water for 2-3 minutes or until tender. Add mashed potatoes, cottage cheese, buttermilk, Parmesan cheese, salt and pepper. Stir until blended and heated through. Spoon into potato shells. Sprinkle with green onions.

YIELD: 2 servings.

SWEETHEART STEAKS

DOLORES JENSEN, ARNOLD, MISSOURI
I created this recipe when I was planning a steak dinner and wanted a barbecue sauce to go with it. Try the sauce on pork and chicken.

PREP: 10 min. **COOK:** 50 min.

- 3 tablespoons Catalina salad dressing
- 3 tablespoons honey
- 3 tablespoons apricot preserves
- 3 tablespoons grape jelly
- 2 tablespoons minced chives
- 2 tablespoons balsamic vinegar
- 2 tablespoons olive oil
- 2 tablespoons ketchup
- 1 tablespoon soy sauce
- 3 garlic cloves, minced
- 1 teaspoon ground mustard
- 1 teaspoon Worcestershire sauce
- 1/2 teaspoon salt
- 1/2 teaspoon crushed red pepper flakes
- 1/4 teaspoon pepper
- 2 beef tenderloin steaks (1-1/2 to 2 inches thick and 8 ounces each)

1 In a small saucepan, combine the first 15 ingredients. Bring to a boil. Reduce heat; simmer, uncovered, for 30 minutes; stirring occasionally. Set aside 1/4 cup sauce for serving and keep warm.

2 Place the steaks on a broiler pan; top with some of the remaining sauce. Broil 4-6 in. from the heat for 10-16 minutes on each side or until meat reaches desired doneness (for medium-rare, a meat thermometer should read 145°; medium, 160°; well-done, 170°), basting occasionally with remaining sauce. Serve with reserved sauce.

YIELD: 2 servings.

CHOCOLATE VALENTINE CANDY HEARTS

TASTE OF HOME TEST KITCHEN
To prepare these cute confections, our home economists shaped melted candies with cookie cutters. Then they piped royal icing in all sorts of fun designs.

PREP: 25 min. + standing

- 3 to 3-1/2-inch heart-shaped metal cookie cutter
- 1 yard of 1/8-inch-wide satin ribbon in white or the color of your choice
- 1 package (7 ounces) watermelon-flavored hard candies

ROYAL ICING:

- 3/4 cup confectioners' sugar
- 4 teaspoons water
- 1-3/4 teaspoons meringue powder

1 Candy hearts: Place heart-shaped cookie cutters on a piece of foil, leaving space above the top of each cookie cutter for placing the ribbon hanger later. Coat the foil and cutters with cooking spray.

2 Cut the satin ribbon into six 6-in. lengths. Place the ends of one ribbon piece together to form a loop. Position the ribbon loop at the top of one cookie cutter so the ends are touching the foil and the loop drapes over the top of the cookie cutter. In the same way, position a ribbon loop on each remaining cookie cutter. Set aside.

3 Unwrap the hard candies and place in the large resealable heavy-duty plastic bag. Crush the candies using a mallet or rolling pin. Transfer the candies to the large heavy skillet. Cook over medium heat until melted, stirring occasionally.

4 Fill each prepared cookie cutter with the melted candy to a 1/4-in. thickness, covering the ends of each ribbon loop at the same time. Let stand for 1-2 minutes. Carefully remove the cutters. Let stand until set, about 1 hour.

5 Royal icing: In a small bowl, combine the confectioners' sugar, water and meringue powder. Beat on high speed for 6-8 minutes or until thickened. Insert the pastry tip in one corner of pastry or plastic bag and cut a hole in the bag. Place the icing in the bag. Pipe the desired designs or Valentine phrases on each heart.

YIELD: 6 candy hearts.

EDITOR'S NOTE: Meringue powder is available from Wilton Industries. Call 1-800/794-5866 or visit www.wilton.com.

GENERAL RECIPE INDEX

ALPHABETICAL RECIPE INDEX